The Remaking of Memory in the Age of the Internet and Social Media

The Remaking of Memory in the Age of the Internet and Social Media

Edited by

QI WANG AND ANDREW HOSKINS

OXFORD
UNIVERSITY PRESS

OXFORD
UNIVERSITY PRESS

Oxford University Press is a department of the University of Oxford. It furthers the University's objective of excellence in research, scholarship, and education by publishing worldwide. Oxford is a registered trade mark of Oxford University Press in the UK and certain other countries.

Published in the United States of America by Oxford University Press
198 Madison Avenue, New York, NY 10016, United States of America.

Library of Congress Cataloging-in-Publication Data
Names: Wang, Qi, 1968 April 21– editor. | Hoskins, Andrew, 1967– editor.
Title: The remaking of memory in the age of the internet and social media /
Qi Wang and Andrew Hoskins.
Description: New York, NY : Oxford University Press, [2024] |
Includes bibliographical references and index.
Identifiers: LCCN 2024030309 (print) | LCCN 2024030310 (ebook) |
ISBN 9780197661260 (hardback) | ISBN 9780197661284 (epub)
Subjects: LCSH: Memory. | Social media—Psychological aspects. |
Internet—Psychological aspects.
Classification: LCC BF371 .R379 2024 (print) | LCC BF371 (ebook) |
DDC 153.1/2—dc23/eng/20240710
LC record available at https://lccn.loc.gov/2024030309
LC ebook record available at https://lccn.loc.gov/2024030310

DOI: 10.1093/oso/9780197661260.001.0001

Printed by Marquis Book Printing, Canada

MIX
Paper | Supporting responsible forestry
FSC www.fsc.org
FSC® C103567

Contents

PART IV FAKE NEWS AND FALSE MEMORIES

PART V REMEMBERING THROUGH THE INDIVIDUAL AND THE NET

PART VI FROM THE PERSON TO THE COMMUNITY AND SOCIETY

Acknowledgments

We owe a big "Thank You" to our contributors whose work has inspired us to put together this volume and whose enthusiasm has been our impetus to get things done in a timely fashion. We are also grateful to the editorial team at OUP, especially Abby Gross who loved our book idea and encouraged us to pursue it further, and Emily Benitez who held our hands throughout the preparation and production process. We are in debt to our three endorsers, Daniel Schacter, James Wertsch, and José van Dijck, whose praises confirmed our conviction to the importance of this volume. Finally, we thank the brilliant Shona Illingworth who generously let us use the beautiful image for our book cover.

Qi Wang and Andrew Hoskins

Contributors

Amanda J. Barnier, Office of the Deputy Vice-Chancellor (Research) and Department of Psychological Sciences, Macquarie University, Sydney, Australia

Dana-Lis Bittner, University of California, Santa Cruz, USA

Shayla Dockery, John Jay College of Criminal Justice, USA

Ullrich K. H. Ecker, School of Psychological Science, University of Western Australia, Australia

Rebecca Egan, School of Applied Psychology, University College Cork, Ireland

Jennifer V. Evans, Carleton University, Canada

Tim Fawns, Monash University, Australia

Joanne Garde-Hansen, University of Leeds, United Kingdom

Ciara M. Greene, School of Psychology, University College Dublin, Ireland

Andrew Hoskins, University of Glasgow, United Kingdom

Emily Keightley, Loughborough University, United Kingdom

Megan O. Kelly, University of Waterloo, Canada

Heather M. Kleider-Offutt, Georgia State University, USA

Louis Klein, Department of Psychological Sciences, Macquarie University, Sydney, Australia

Xinyi Lu, University of Waterloo, Canada

Samuel Merrill, DIGSUM, Umeå University, Sweden

Gillian Murphy, School of Applied Psychology, University College Cork, Ireland

Katharina Niemeyer, Université du Québec à Montréal, Canada

April E. Pereira, University of Waterloo, Canada

Martin Pogačar, University of Nova Gorica, Slovenia

Suparna Rajaram, Stony Brook University, USA

Brandon Rigato, Carleton University, Canada

Evan F. Risko, University of Waterloo, Canada

Rik Smit, University of Groningen, Netherlands

Beth B. Stevens, Georgia State University, USA

Charles B. Stone, John Jay College of Criminal Justice and Graduate Center, City University of New York, USA

Benjamin C. Storm, University of California, Santa Cruz, USA

Li Qian Tay, School of Psychological Science, University of Western Australia, Australia

Noam Tirosh, Communication Studies, Ben-Gurion University of the Negev, Israel

Angelina N. Vasquez, John Jay College of Criminal Justice and The New School for Social Research, USA

Qi Wang, Cornell University, USA

Karen Worcman, Museu da Pessoa, Brazil

Jeremy K. Yamashiro, University of California, Santa Cruz, USA

PART 1
INTRODUCTION

1

The Internet Remaking of Memory

What Are the Important Questions?

Qi Wang and Andrew Hoskins

We offer an introduction to this ambitious volume by way of a dialogue between us, the two editors, from our different disciplinary traditions and perspectives (human (QW) and social sciences (AH)). We probe the key issues and effects of the remaking of memory in the Internet Age and the challenges for its interdisciplinary study and the unique visionary, theoretical, methodological, and empirical advances made by our contributors.

Our Motivations for Editing This Volume

QW: Not long ago I edited a special issue in the journal *Memory* that included a collection of empirical articles on the impact of social media and the Internet on memory (Wang, 2022a). I recognized in the process that in spite of the omnipresence of social media that has profoundly changed how we receive, retain, and share information, relevant empirical research is sparse and compartmented. What's more, the research done by cognitive researchers and psychologists like myself is largely disconnected from the burgeoning research in other fields, such as communication, sociology, cultural studies, media studies, history, and others, which has identified and investigated many important issues related to memory in the digital age. This separation between fields is not surprising given the differences in intellectual traditions and theoretical and methodological approaches which often make cross-disciplinary collaboration challenging. Yet, to fully understand the complex influences of social media and the Internet on memory, cross-disciplinary collaboration is the key. I then reached out to Andrew, who is the best person I know of doing interdisciplinary research on memory and media.

AH: I have long been curious as to how Qi so effortlessly combines cultural and cognitive approaches and questions to the study of memory, yet sitting within the context of the human sciences. So that was a key motivation for me when

Qi Wang and Andrew Hoskins, *The Internet Remaking of Memory* In: *The Remaking of Memory in the Age of the Internet and Social Media.* Edited by: Qi Wang and Andrew Hoskins, Oxford University Press. © Oxford University Press 2024.
DOI: 10.1093/oso/9780197661260.003.0001

Qi had the idea for this volume: to get an insight into her world! There isn't a work that has brought together a range of such interesting scholars with I think quite different views on their very starting point about what memory is, what memory does, and why that matters. This is even before we consider the ways in which social media and the Internet might—or might not—mark a radical change in this thing called "memory," for better and for worse, and how it is studied and (mis)understood.

Our Interests in Memory in the Context of Social Media and the Internet

QW: My foremost interest lies in the influence of culture on the process, organization, expression, and function of human memory. As much as memory is a product of the mind and brain and thus inherently private and personal, it operates as an open system saturated in cultural contexts and shaped by layers of dynamic cultural forces (Wang, 2021). As a key cultural force unique to our time of modern technology, the Internet and social media have brought about revolutionary transformations to how we receive, share, and remember information.

While working on my book, *The Autobiographical Self in Time and Culture* (Wang, 2013), I discussed how autobiographical memory, or memory for one's significant personal experiences, is influenced by cultural factors across historical times. Inevitably, I reflected on the mnemonic impact of the Internet as a technological and cultural tool and outlined various ways in which social media use - in the forms of blogging and microblogging - can shape our autobiographical memory and in turn our sense of self and identity (see an elaboration of the thesis in Wang, 2022b). A decade later, I'm excited to see the emerging field of research on this topic at the present time.

The Internet remaking of memory involves psychological, technological, social, and cultural processes. The externalization of our memories online, whether about our own personal experiences or factual knowledge of the world, is both enabled and constrained by the technological features, operational goals, and cultural norms of the social media platform as well as the platform's user community that posesses what I'd call "a transactive personality." There are then our personal characterics, beliefs, and motives that predetermine what memories and what aspects of the memories we share online. The consequence of the memory externalization for our "internal" memory thus rests on the dynamic interplay between a human actor and other human actors within a web of advancing technologies, cultural norms, and ideological diversities. These processes that remake our memory in the Internet age are all fascinating to me.

AH: My view, over 25 years studying the relationship between media and memory, is that each media environment—"ecology"—and each media age, shapes (extends as well as diminishes) individual human, as well as cultural and collective remembering, in different ways and with different effects (Hoskins, 2016). This era may be seen, with the benefit of hindsight, as exceptional, as a clear break from what went before. Yet, another view is that it was the mid to late twentieth century—the "broadcast era"—that was in fact the exception in the nature, function, and "effects" of media. The emergent digital era, of this century, is seen then as rather a "return to the one before last." This model is known as the "Gutenberg parenthesis" (see Sauerberg, 2008, and Pettitt, 2011, in Hoskins, 2018).

Nonetheless, the digital period is marked by a shift from reliance to dependency on apps, services, and platforms for everyday living and everyday remembering. In research with Kristina Cimova at Glasgow in 2021 and 2023, with memory app designers, we consider that the early 2010s represents a "tipping point" in this respect.

Furthermore, in the social media and Internet era, the principal challenge is in our individual human capacity, as well as at a societal level, to make humanly graspable the scale and complexity of digital and artificial intelligence (AI)-driven forces that shape what past elements may become findable, accessible, and usable and by who and to what ends.

Interdisciplinarity Research on Memory and the Internet in Our Disciplines

QW: The current cognitive and psychological research on memory and the Internet reflect three broad areas (Wang, 2022a): the Internet as storage for offloading memory, the externalization of autobiographical memory online, and fake news and false memory in the context of social media. There has been some great work to examine the complex and multifaceted influences of cyberspace on the processes, purposes, and consequences of remembering. Still, as I mentioned in the opening section, most of the research in psychology and cognitive sciences is self-contained and isolated from other disciplines. I believe it is crucial to carry out cross-disciplinary collaboration and interdisciplinary research where researchers can draw on and integrate diverse theories and methods and inform each other's work.

As a cognitive and developmental psychologist who also received training in anthropology, I often see interdisciplinary research as a given. This attitude of "taking things for granted" has also been "nurtured" through my 20 years of working in a top interdisciplinary department, the Department of Human Development at Cornell University, where people from diverse fields work together on interrelated topics. Interdisciplinary research is not a one-person job, however, and interdisciplinary collaboration is hard work. Like what Andrew mentioned when commenting on our motivations for editing this volume, people often don't even agree on the very definition of key concepts such as memory, morality, and culture or on disciplinary approaches, such as whether to make a priori predictions or let the data speak for itself. There is often a lack of shared language to understand each other's work. Being in an interdisciplinary environment makes the conversation and collaboration easier, where people appreciate intellectual diversity and are willing to hear out each other. We intend to have this volume serve as such an "environment" to facilitate intellectual dialogues across disciplines for the study of memory in the digital age.

AH: I don't find it easy to lay claim to my sitting clearly in a single discipline. I am a sociologist, but that doesn't define all of my identity and all of my work. Many years ago, I applied for a job in a sociology department, and the first question asked after my presentation was: "In what ways is your work sociological?" This reflects a suspicion, I think, in anyone who isn't seen to conform with the ideas and approaches and research seen as defining of a particular discipline, or that they do "other stuff" that isn't easily assimilable within a given disciplinary tradition.

There is a fault line in memory studies that runs between the human sciences and the social sciences, arts, and humanities. I have spent a lot of my career engaging in conversations across it. The cognitive psychologist Amanda Barnier and I spent several years finding a common language that we could use to talk about memory that enabled this bridging work and between what we call "memory in the head" and "memory in the wild" (Barnier & Hoskins, 2018).

To be clear, some researchers refer to a multidisciplinary project as an *adding together* of the advantages of different disciplinary approaches. But for me, interdisciplinary goes further, to engage in dialogue between different paradigms of thought and between their attached ideas, concepts, and methods.

I agree with Qi that interdisciplinarity isn't easy, and it is not always valued. Yet, it seems to me essential to grasp how digital media and AI not only shape remembering and forgetting, but also collide and collapse the very categories that are defining of the disciplinary study of memory (e.g. individual, social, collective, cultural.), as well as other ways of conceiving of and studying the past and its significance in the present.

Research on "memory" and the Internet in multiple disciplines is certainly thriving, albeit found more often in separate places and still with little cross-fertilization of ideas and approaches. Yet this volume, and journals such as *Memory, Mind & Media* (edited by Amanda Barnier and myself), are more self-conscious in addressing the value of interdisciplinarity and in finding a plain-speaking approach to appeal across disciplinary divides.

Burning Questions

QW: I'll comment on this in the context of this volume. The chapters in this volume address many of the burning questions: How would the Internet and social media enrich or deprive our personal memories (Wang, Chapter 2; Hoskins, Chapter 3; Stone et al., Chapter 4)? Would the Internet ease our burden of remembering or disrupt our memory processes and in turn related cognitive activities such as creativity and critical thinking (Risko et al., Chapter 5; Storm et al., Chapter 6; Fawns, Chapter 7)? Would the easy spread of and access to information online make our memories more vulnerable to errors and manipulation, and if yes, is there any hope to combat the impact of fake news (Murphy et al., Chapter 8; Tay & Ecker, Chapter 9; Kleider-Offutt & Stevens, Chapter 10; Evans & Rigato, Chapter 11)? What roles do social media users and social media platforms play in shaping the communication and memory representation of information (Rajaram, Chapter 12; Smit, Chapter 13; Niemeyer & Keightley, Chapter 14)? What are the ramifications of the remaking of memory in the digital age for our collective and cultural identity (Merrill, Chapter 15; Pogačar, Chapter 16; Tirosh, Chapter 17; Worcman & Garde-Hansen, Chapter 18)?

Additional burning questions emerged in the contributors' discussions and in the critical reflection by Louis Klein and Amanda Barnier (Chapter 19), which I leave the readers to explore.

AH: To add to what Qi noted above ("Our interests in memory" section) on the cognitive and cultural force of memory, the overriding question in this era of social media and the Internet is one also posed for earlier ecologies of media/memory: What is remembering and forgetting, who has agency or control over what endures and what disappears of the record of our lives and experiences, and why does this matter?

More specifically to this era: Does dependency (rather than reliance) on digital devices, platforms, and services for our being-in-world transform not only our human but also the societal capacity to both remember and forget, and to what ends? Furthermore, how does our growing inability to make visible and to grasp how digital technologies operate and how they might be controlled, to what extent, and by who to inhibit human agency over the uses and abuses to which memory may be put? This is particularly the case with the opacity of the workings and foundations of AI and algorithms that produce a past that never existed (see Hoskins, forthcoming, on AI and memory).

More on This Volume

QW: When Andrew and I conceived of this volume, we asked the questions: Would an active, willed, functional, deliberating human memory as fundamentally part of human identity, which functionally changes with time, be threatened by a shift from a healthy reliance to a dependency, an addiction, a placing of the past beyond our control? Or would it be afforded with greater power and agency given the infinite capacity of information storage, the explosion in information transmission, and the transformation of individuals from passive information consumers to active information creators?

These questions to some extent reflect our different views and approaches: I focus on the impact of social media on remembering and hold a more "optimistic" view, including the human agency in the active construction of a digital niche (Wang, 2019). Andrew focuses on the impact of social media on forgetting and holds a more "pessimistic" view. I see this intellectual "tension" also reflected throughout the chapters: Whereas some chapters articulate the negative and even detrimental effects of online platforms on memory and remembering, others delineate the beneficial outcomes brought to memory by social media. There are also chapters that take a more dialectic standpoint to analyze the pros and cons and the conditions that give rise to each. Together, the discussion in this collected volume reveals the dynamic, complex, multilayered interplay between the person, the net, and the social and technological ecologies of online platforms, as well as the cultural and political conditions in which the interplay situates in shaping and remaking human memory. To me that is the most important characteristic of this volume.

Another important characteristic of this volume is of course the interdisciplinary team of authors who bring diverse intellectual perspectives, methodological approaches, and investigative topics to the discussion of memory remaking in the digital age. To me, this is a ground-breaking integration of diverse research on the timely issues and will have ramifications down the road for theories and practices pertaining to the impact of the Internet and social media on remembering and forgetting.

There are so many other important and unique features to this volume. The one more that I'd like to pinpoint is that the conception of memory across the chapters is not dichotomized as either within the person or out in the wilderness of the social network, which can often be found in theories and empirical investigations. Instead, memory is construed as a multifaceted, dynamic construct and indeed an "ecology" that encompasses representations that can be in the person, by the person, about the person, as well as the community and society in which remembering takes place. This volume therefore accentuates the interconnectedness of personal memory, collective memory, and cultural memory that takes place in the context of social media and the Internet.

AH: What colleagues at least in the human sciences seem to agree about my take on these questions and debates is that I have quite a pessimistic view on the prospects for human agency in remembering and forgetting to overcome the challenges for memory in this era, as explored in this volume. My interview with Daniel Schacter probably reflects this position.[1]

What I can say is that algorithms and automation are only part of the story (see my Chapter 3, "The Forgetting Ecology," this volume). Apps, platforms, devices and services differ in features, design, and degrees of (platform) control. Individualization and personalization rub up against "digital nudging." Human agency over what comes to be posted, seen, shared, and stored, through our ongoing immersion in social media and the production of our digital lives, is uneven. See, for example, this volume, especially Smit on "Platformization" (Chapter 13), and also Stone et al. (Chapter 4); Tirosh (Chapter 17); Rajaram (Chapter 12); and Niemeyer and Keightley (Chapter 14).

My pessimism comes more from the growing uncertainty over not only how digital participation may shape what of the past may become accessible to us in the future and to what ends and at what cost, but also in our capacity to see and comprehend these transformations. This is part of what I have called the "new gray of memory," that a conscious, active, willed memory is obscured in the digital era (Hoskins & Halstead, 2021).

Making visible how digital and social media make human remembering fallible is a key concern in this volume, for example, when a historical reliance on human memory for justice is challenged when actors (police services, legal counsel, eyewitnesses, suspects, criminals) are all embedded in everyday digital media ecologies. Thus, Kleider-Offutt and Stevens (Chapter 10) show how social media infiltrates and impacts the integrity of multiple processes of the legal system, including contaminating eyewitness memory, leading to the misattribution of suspects.

Several of our contributors importantly illuminate the viral force of social media and the Internet as an "information disorder" (Tay & Ecker, Chapter 9), as fake news falsifying memories (Murphy et al.), and as fake and real historical media templates used to shape and legitimize interpretations of unfolding events (Evans & Rigato, Chapter 11).

Together, our contributors highlight how social media and the Internet offer the most astonishing communicative and archival resource for everyday, social, and historical remembering, unimaginable only 25 years ago. Yet they also reveal how we have arrived in the age of impossible provenance, in which uncertainties over the past are viral, and memory is increasingly suspect.

Our Expectation

This volume sets a milestone for the study of memory in the age of the Internet and social media. We expect it to provide guidance for future investigations. The theoretical frameworks, methodological recommendations, and first-hand empirical data are rich resources for researchers as well as practitioners and platform designers who are interested in how the social and technological features of social media platform influence people's engagement online and the consequences of social media use for personal and collective memories.

Note

1. Daniel Schacter interviewed by Andrew Hoskins for *Memory, Mind & Media,* June 9, 2021. https://vimeo.com/568738123

References

Barnier, A., & Hoskins, A. (2018). Is there memory in the head, in the wild? *Memory Studies, 11*(4), 386–390. https://doi.org/10.1177/1750698018806440

Hoskins, A. (2016). Memory ecologies. *Memory Studies, 9*(3), 348–357.

Hoskins, A. (2018). The restless past: An introduction to digital memory and media. In A. Hoskins (ed.), *Digital memory studies: Media pasts in transition* (pp. 1–24). Routledge.

Hoskins, A. (Forthcoming). AI & memory. *Memory, Mind & Media.*

Hoskins, A., & Halstead, H. (2021). The new grey of memory: Andrew Hoskins in conversation with Huw Halstead. *Memory Studies, 14*(3), 675–685. https://doi.org/10.1177/17506980211010936

Wang, Q. (2013). *The autobiographical self in time and culture.* Oxford University Press. doi:10.1093/acprof:oso/9780199737833.001.0001

Wang, Q. (2019). The individual mind in the active construction of its digital niche. *Journal of Applied Research in Memory and Cognition*, *8*, 25–28. https://doi.org/10.1016/j.jarmac.2018.12.005

Wang, Q. (2021). The cultural foundation of human memory. *Annual Review of Psychology*, *72*, 151–179. doi:10.1146/annurev-psych-070920-023638

Wang, Q. (2022a). Memory online: Remembering in the age of the Internet and social media. [Special issue]. *Memory*, *30*(4).

Wang, Q. (2022b). The triangular self in the social media era. *Memory, Mind & Media, 1*(E4), 1–12. https://doi.org/10.1017/mem.2021.6

PART II
THE DIGITAL SELF IN THE MAKING

2
The Online Extension of Autobiographical Memory
A Psycho-Cultural Perspective

Qi Wang

Remembering personal experiences, or autobiographical memory, is hardly a purely personal matter. We share memories with others on different occasions, for various reasons, such as to express a point of view, to entertain others, to reminisce about the good old days, and to seek or give advice. Social sharing is thus a key feature of autobiographical memory, reflecting the basic human needs of storytelling (Fivush, 2011; Pillemer, 1998). The process of memory sharing results in a social extension of autobiographical memory, which in turn shapes the organization and content of memory representations (Beike et al., 2017; Demiray et al., 2019; Kulkofsky et al., 2009). As a unique cultural tool of our time, the Internet and social media have drastically empowered memory sharing, so such so that we can share our experiences on the go, with anyone, at any place, at any time, and as frequently as we'd like (Wang, 2013, 2021a; this volume also see Stone et al., Chapter 4, and Smit, Chapter 13). This new way of remembering and sharing personal experiences is unprecedented in human history. It has essentially revolutionized memory expression and communication, creating a tangible online extension of autobiographical memory with infinite possibilities.

What I delineate in this chapter is that the online extension of autobiographical memory is a result of the interaction between the social media user and the cyber community, a process situated in the larger context of culture. Autobiographical memory is a product of co-construction between individuals and their sociocultural environments. From the initial perception and encoding to later retention and recall, the processes of autobiographical remembering are not only influenced by the rememberer's goals and characteristics but also conditioned by many cultural factors (Wang, 2013, 2021a). In the context of social media, the co-constructive nature of autobiographical memory is brought to the forefront, where individual users interact with the cyber community to co-construct their life stories via technological tools afforded on social media platforms, in line with their personal goals and cultural beliefs. I discuss the co-construction of the

Qi Wang, *The Online Extension of Autobiographical Memory* In: *The Remaking of Memory in the Age of the Internet and Social Media.* Edited by: Qi Wang and Andrew Hoskins, Oxford University Press. © Oxford University Press 2024.
DOI: 10.1093/oso/9780197661260.003.0002

online extension of autobiographical memory from the framework of the triangular theory of self in the social media era (Wang, 2022), examining the psychological and cultural characteristics of memory representations in the person, on the social media platform, and in the cyber community. In delineating the online extension of autobiographical memory from a psycho-cultural perspective, I also discuss the implications of autobiographical memory in the social media era for individuals' sense of self and well-being.

The Triangular Self in the Social Media Era

The triangular theory of self is proposed to characterize the sense of selfhood that is unique in the age of the Internet and social media (Wang, 2022). The theory conceptualizes the self in the social media era as comprising three interactive components: private representations in the mind of the social media user, public representations on social media platforms, and transactive representations constructed by the virtual community (see Figure 2.1). Specifically, the social media user plays an active role in perceiving, encoding,

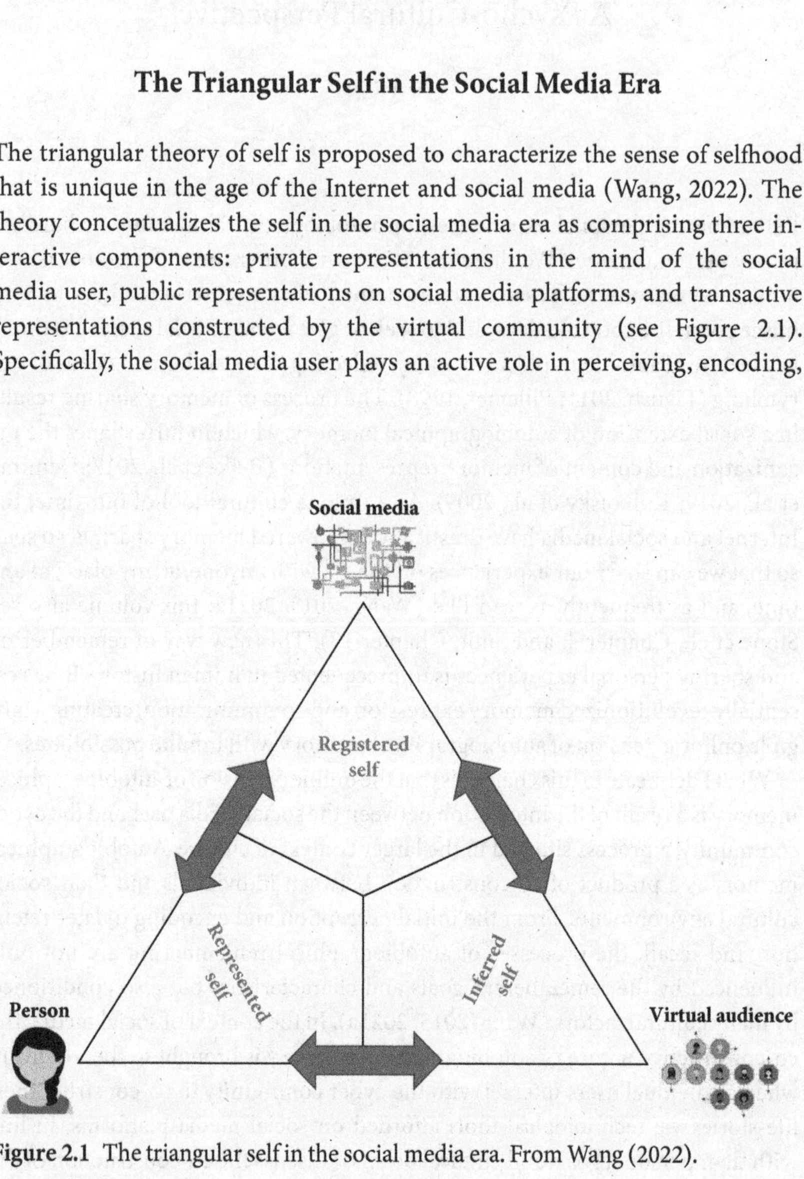

Figure 2.1 The triangular self in the social media era. From Wang (2022).

and representing their own attributes, roles, and experiences, which constitutes the "represented self." Social media platforms supply easy access to diverse technological tools that enable the social media user to record and share their opinions and experiences with a wide range of audiences, which creates the "registered self." The virtual audience makes sense of the social media user's online posts and forms views about who they are, which gives rise to the "inferred self." The represented self, while in line with the traditional notion of selfhood (James, 1890; Neisser, 1988; Truong & Todd, 2017), is externalized online to the registered self as its *digital extension* and to the inferred self as its *transactive extension* (Wang, 2022).

Autobiographical memory is one form of self-representation and a critical ingredient of the self-memory system (Conway & Pleydell-Pearce, 2000), dubbed as the "autobiographical self" (Wang, 2013). The triangular theory of self can thus be applied to understanding the unique characteristics of autobiographical memory in the social media era. Importantly, the three components of the triangular self and their interactions are subject to the influence of psychological (e.g., self-esteem) and cultural factors (e.g., independent vs. interdependent values). Extensive research on autobiographical memory has shown marked individual and cultural variations in how people remember their personal experiences (for reviews, see Wang, 2013, 2021a). When the private representations of autobiographical memory are externalized online, the process and product of the externalization—in both digital and transactive forms—are likely to be influenced by psychological and cultural factors as well, resulting in individual and cultural variations in the online extension of autobiographical memory. Here I extend the triangular theory of self to analyze the characteristics of autobiographical memory in the social media era from a psycho-cultural perspective.

The Person-Culture Co-Construction of Autobiographical Memory

To understand the psycho-cultural characteristics of the online extension of autobiographical memory, it is necessarily to first consider the psycho-cultural characteristics of autobiographical memory as represented in the private mind of the rememberer. The construction of autobiographical memory, or memory for event information related to the self, takes place in the self-memory system and is therefore subject to the influences of self-goals, motives, and personal attributes (Conway & Pleydell-Pearce, 2000; Greenwald, 1980). The construction is further situated in the cultural context, being subject to the influences of cultural values, norms, and practices (Wang, 2013, 2021a). Here I focus on self-esteem and agentic versus communal self-motives as examples to demonstrate how psychological factors interact with cultural beliefs in influencing the valence and content of autobiographical memory. I show further in later sections that these factors operate in a similar fashion in affecting the online extension of autographical memory.

Individuals' self-esteem, or how individuals evaluate and feel about themselves, affects the valence characteristics of their autobiographical memories. For instance, compared with those with low self-esteem, individuals with high self-esteem are more likely to remember their past performance as worse than their current performance, which helps to create an illusion of improvement and thus enhance their current selves (Ross & Wilson, 2000). Also, individuals with high self-esteem feel psychologically closer to positive past events (Demiray & Janssen, 2015) and to events in which they achieved their goals (Demiray & Freund, 2017), compared with those with low self-esteem. Individuals with high self-esteem also recall their daily life events more positively than those with low self-esteem (Christensen et al., 2003). Individuals with low self-esteem, on the other hand, tend to recall less memory detail due to engaging in rumination and avoidance coping (Roberts et al., 2021).

Culture further plays a role in the relation between self-esteem and autobiographical memory. Western cultures value high self-esteem and encourage individuals to feel good about themselves, whereas East Asian cultures emphasize accurate and even diagnostic self-evaluations based on which individuals can achieve future improvement (Hamamura, 2017; Jeon et al., 2020). These different cultural values have mnemonic consequences. When asked to recall as many situations as they can in which their self-esteem either increased or decreased, Americans recall more situations in which their self-esteem increased, whereas Japanese show even-handed recall of the two kinds of situations (Kitayama et al., 1997). Similarly, when recalling incidences of success and failure in their lives, Americans recall more success stories than failure stories, whereas Japanese recall more failure stories than success stories (Endo & Meijer, 2004). Whereas Canadians find it easier to recall events that made them feel proud than events that made them feel embarrassed, Japanese find no difference in the ease of recalling proud and embarrassing events (Ross et al., 2005). Furthermore, recalling success relative to failure memories is associated with positive self-views among European Ameircans, but not among Asians (Wang et al., 2024).

Another example of psycho-cultural influences on the construction of autobiographical memory concerns agentic (self-focused) and communal (other-focused) orientations in relation to memory content. It has been shown that individuals who exhibit agentic, self-oriented traits (e.g., self-reliance, ambition) tend to recall autobiographical memories focusing on their own roles (e.g., self-mastery, achievement). In contrast, individuals who exhibit communal, socially oriented traits (e.g., warmth, compassion) tend to recall memories that involve significant others and relationships (e.g., enjoyable social interactions; Costabile & Austin, 2020; Gebauer et al., 2013). Furthermore, when people are primed with agentic motives, they show better recall and recognition of event information related to differentiation (i.e., making distinctions between oneself and others via comparisons, contrasts, or restrictions). In contrast, when people are primed with communal motives, they show better recall and recognition of event information related to integration (i.e., making connections with others via dynamic relationships, similarities, and overarching themes) (Woike et al., 2001).

These self-motives and goals further operate in the cultural context in shaping autobiographical memory. Western cultures prioritize agentic self-goals and encourage individuals to be distinct and to exercise control and free choice. In contrast, many non-Western cultures such as those in East Asia prioritize communal self-goals and encourage individuals to attend to the needs of significant others and social groups (Shweder et al., 1998; Wang, 2013). Accordingly, when recalling autobiographical events, Western adults and children retrieve more idiosyncratic details and more frequently refer to their own roles, predilections, and unique experiences than do Asians, who focus more on the roles of others and group activities (e.g., Peterson et al., 2009; Wang, 2016; Wang et al., 2018). Paralleling cultural differences in memory content have been observed in memory conversations between mothers and their young children about shared past experiences, which indicates the influence of early narrative interactions on children's autobiographical memory development in line with specific cultural expectations (Wang, 2013, 2021b).

Thus, individuals' psychological characteristics such as self-esteem and agentic versus communal traits and motives influence information processing and organization in long-term memory. They function as a "filter" to privilege the encoding of event information consistent with the individuals' level of esteem, self-goals, and motives. Such information is subsequently well-integrated into the self-memory system and remains highly accessible at recall. Nonconfirmatory information, on the other hand, tends to be inhibited or distorted at encoding, retention, or retrieval and therefore may be never encoded, hardly accessible, or altered to be in line with the individuals' self-esteem and goals and motives (Conway & Pleydell-Pearce, 2000; Greenwald, 1980). These cognitive processes further take places in the cultural context that ascribes culture-specific meanings to the psychological characteristics and, in turn, shapes autobiographical remembering (Wang, 2013, 2021a).

Psychological Impact on the Online Extension of Autobiographical Memory

Beyond memory representations private to the mind or brain of the rememberer, autobiographical memory is externalized through personal storytelling and memory sharing (Fivush, 2011; Pillemer, 1998). In the age of the Internet and social media, memory externalization takes a digital form to be registered online, where individuals encode and record moment-to-moment personal events as life unfolds; share intimate details of experiences publicly with friends, family, and strangers; and create permanent online archives of events and life stories that can be revisited, revised, and even revoked. The memory externalization online further takes a transactive form in which the cyber community forms opinions about the social media user's persona through interpreting and responding to their online posts and via communicative interaction and information exchange among the community members (Wang, 2013, 2022). The process and product of the online memory extension are subject to the influence of many psychological factors.

The online digital extension of autobiographical memory is characterized by a combination of social disclosure and diary-keeping and sustained by diverse technological tools. The remembering process thus follows general memory mechanisms on the one hand and is shaped by the social media context on the other. Just like memories offline, memories for personal events that have previously been posted online succumb to cognitive mechanisms such as recent events are better remembered than distant ones and images are more effective cues than text to facilitate memory accessibility (Talarico, 2022). Also, people's memories about how they learned about a shocking news event (i.e., flashbulb memory) fade over time whether they received the news via social media or from traditional media (e.g., TV; Talarico et al., 2019). However, initial memory reports from those who learned from social media are less vivid and of a lower sense of recollection than those who learned from traditional media, possibly due to information overload online (Jiang et al., 2016; also see Hoskins, Chapter 3, this volume). In addition, social media posts that involve important experiences and people and contain specific contextual details are more likely to trigger future recall (Cosley et al., 2012), similar to everyday memories.

Furthermore, social media serves as an important context to facilitate autobiographical remembering. Personal events posted on social media platforms (e.g., Facebook, Snapchat) are better remembered and less forgotten than those not posted, independent of the characteristics of the events (Johnson & Morley, 2021; Wang et al., 2017). This may be because sharing memories online allows individuals to rehearse and make sense of what happened, thus facilitating long-term memory retention (Stone & Wang, 2019). Online feedback such as comments and likes as well as technological features such as digital nudges, algorithms, and periodic reminders can further serve as memory cues for the posted event details and, as a result, event details shared on social media are likely stabilized and remembered over time, whereas those not shared may become inaccessible or forgotten (Hou et al., 2022; Stone et al., Chapter 4, this volume). Importantly, individuals play an active role in selectively posting their experiences online and thus determine what experiences and what aspects of the experiences will likely be remembered or forgotten (Wang, 2019).

Personality factors further influence why individuals post their personal experiences online. For instance, individuals who score high on communal or interdependent traits more frequently share autobiographical memories online to make social connections and provide advice to others, whereas individuals who have low self-esteem and those who are high on loneliness share memories online more for therapeutic reasons (Stone et al., 2022; also see Stone et al., Chapter 4, this volume). Extraverts and individuals who exhibit traits to disclose information are more eager than their counterparts to post personal experiences on social media to express themselves, interact with others, and give and receive advice (Hollenbaugh, 2011; Stone et al., 2022). Furthermore, Facebook users who score high on extraversion and openness frequently post status updates about their personal experiences for self, social, and directive purposes, whereas those high on neuroticism post status updates for self and directive purposes and those high on conscientiousness post for directive purposes (Caci et al., 2019). In addition, individuals with high trait emotional intelligence frequently use social media to present a more popular self (Süral et al., 2019). On the other hand, individuals with low self-worth often share their negative experiences on social media to seek emotional support and validation from others (e.g., Zhao et al., 2021).

Different motives for sharing autobiographical experiences online can, in turn, influence the ways individuals use social media for personal documentation. For instance, Facebook users who endorse self and directive functions of autobiographical memory frequently post status updates and disclose personal information about their life events on both positive and negative topics (Caci et al., 2020). Men and women tend to present themselves on social media in line with traditional gender roles, with men exaggerating their personal achievement and women exaggerating their physical attractiveness (Kolesnyk et al., 2021). People with more salient impression management goals spend more time crafting their messages and thus make more sophisticated posts on social media sites (Oh & LaRose, 2016). Furthermore, many social media users consider making social connections to be the primary motive for them to share personal experiences online (Caci et al., 2020; Stone et al., 2022). To engage the virtual audience and capitalize on memory sharing, they often utilize a variety of tactics to make their posts stand out and to highlight their unique personas, such as to provide captivating details of their experiences, to portrait themselves in a positive light, and to adopt a wide array of multimedia strategies (Wang, 2013, 2022). Interestingly, the virtual audience tends not to appreciate social media posts with excessive self-presentations, but favor those with self-disclosure of personal information that serves as social cues for interaction (Hong et al., 2020; Walsh et al., 2020). Motivated by the need to maintain or enhance social ties, social media users often disclose their thoughts and feelings and the intimate details of their experiences, which may in turn have positive impacts on their social networking and well-being (H.-T. Chen & Li, 2017; Ko & Pu, 2010; Wang, 2022).

Self-esteem has been shown to play a particularly important role in shaping online sharing patterns and audience views. For instance, compared with high self-esteem individuals, low self-esteem individuals find it safer to express themselves on Facebook, view Facebook as a more helpful venue to connect with others, and feel more comfortable to disclose their thoughts and feelings on Facebook than in person (Forest & Wood, 2012). However, low self-esteem individuals post overall less positive and more negative status updates, and they express more negative emotions such as sadness, anger, frustration, anxiety, fear, and irritability and fewer positive emotions such as happiness, excitement, and gratitude in their posts when compared with their higher self-esteem peers. As a result, low self-esteem individuals are liked less by their virtual audience, including both strangers and their Facebook friends (Forest & Wood, 2012). In a similar vein, Facebook users with higher psychological distress and self-presentational concerns more frequently use depression language in their status updates, and they are also less satisfied with audiences' responses and their overall interaction with audiences (Bazarova et al., 2017). Furthermore, upward social comparisons on social media are detrimental to self-esteem particularly for low self-esteem individuals, who are inclined to make more frequent and more extreme upward comparisons when browsing on social media (Midgley et al., 2021). In turn, self-esteem mediates the negative effect of excessive use of social media on cognitive performance and mental health (Hou et al., 2019). In addition, after sharing autobiographical memories with an audience who holds a negative attitude toward the memory topic, individuals experience lower self-perceived authenticity and self-esteem when compared with when the audience holds a positive attitude (Boytos et al., 2023).

Thus, psychological and personality factors influence individuals' motives to share their personal experiences on social media and further shape the form and content of the digital extension of autobiographical memory. The psychological characteristics of social media users further interact and the psychological characteristics of the cyber community in influencing the transactive extension of autobiographical memory, which is reflected in the audience's views, attitudes, and reactions to the users' online posts. The audience's feedback or the lack of it, in turn, can influence how and how frequently social media users make future posts about their experiences. For example, social media users post more frequently and more openly after receiving likes and comments from their audience, but they change the content of their future posts when there is a lack of audience response (Stsiampkouskaya et al., 2021; Walsh et al., 2020). The digital and transactive extensions of autobiographical memory on social media thus interact and influence each other through psychological processes.

Cultural Impact on the Online Extension of Autobiographical Memory

In the public sphere of cyberspace, gaining social capital is an important motive for individuals to share autobiographical experiences online. This can manifest through different purposes of posting on social media, such as to expand one's social networks or for entertainment among social media users in the United States (Krasnova et al., 2012; Steinfield et al., 2008) and to seek information and social support among Asian users (Kim et al., 2011). As a result, the role of cultural values and norms in shaping what and how personal information is shared becomes particularly salient in the online context (Wang, 2013).

Indeed, there seem to be culture-specific ways of social interaction on social media platforms. It is my observation that whereas East Asians often form social media groups based on relationships—in line with their cultural emphasis on interconnectedness and communal orientation; Westerners often form social media groups based on interests—in line with their cultural emphasis on individuality and agentic orientation (Shweder et al., 1998; Wang, 2013). As someone of Chinese origin, I am a member of many relationship-based groups (e.g., family groups, school alumni groups, hometown fellow groups, parent groups, close friend groups, and so on) on WeChat, a popular Chinese social media site with functionalities similar to Facebook. Even for family relations alone, for example, there are groups of the nuclear family, the extended family of my father's side, the extended family of my mother's side, networks of cousins and second cousins, and more intimate groups with selected family members. In contrast, as someone living and working in the United States, I am a member of many interest-based groups on Facebook, such as autobiographical memory research group, cognitive development group, and midcentury modern architecture group. This personal observation is in line with research showing that compared with Asian social media users whose networks primarily consist of close friends and family members, US users have broader networks of yet weaker and less intimate social ties (Kim et al., 2011; Yoo et al., 2012). It appears that Asians tend to use social media as an effective venue to strengthen their existing relationship networks, whereas Westerners often use social media to forge connections that fulfill their professional and personal interests and needs. In turn, the function and form of sharing personal experiences online can be dictated by the prominent type of social media groups in specific cultural contexts.

In general, although posting personal experiences online is an act of the individual social media user, it is constrained by cultural expectations pertaining to specific self-goals and the characteristics of interpersonal relations (Wang, 2013). This process is illustrated in a study that compared the top 200 most popular blogs in Taiwan and the United States (Y.-N. K. Chen, 2010). It was found that popular American blogs had a higher degree of self-revelation in which bloggers were more open about sensitive personal details, such as gender, age, and contact information than Taiwanese blogs. This inclination for self-disclosure among American bloggers was in line with their cultural emphasis on self-expression and individuality. It also reflects the bloggers' intentional effort to forge and maintain relationships, which is necessary in the Western cultural context, where relationships tend to be voluntary and require active maintenance (Schug et al., 2010). In contrast, popular Taiwanese blogs tended to focus on existing social networks: Approximately 50% of the Taiwanese blogs were about relationships with family, friends, and coworkers, compared with fewer than 15% of American blogs. Also, Taiwanese bloggers showed more agreement, compliments, warmth, and understanding than did their American counterparts, presenting themselves as more likable, in line with the Chinese cultural expectation for smooth interaction and social harmony. In addition, consistent with their cultural emphasis on intellectual attainment, Taiwanese bloggers more frequently showcased their competence and intellectuality than did American bloggers.

Research has further shown that Westerners tend to recall more idiosyncratic details of their unique personal experiences than Asians, which is in line with their agentic self-goals and in turn linked to positive psychological well-being. In contrast, Asian individuals tend not to dwell on the details of their personal experiences so as to avoid an excessive focus on oneself that is incongruent with Asian cultural norms (Peterson et al., 2009; Wang et al., 2018). Similar cultural differences were found in a study that compared ways of storytelling in Western and Asian literature (Wang & Yang, 2023). Content analysis on Amazon.com and *New York Times* best-selling fictions and memoirs by Western and Asian authors revealed that Western authors depicted events episodes in greater detail than Asian authors in both fiction and memoirs. Thus, different cultural ways of personal storytelling are evident in both private recall and public sharing, and they are likely to be present in social media posts as well. In a related vein, as noted above, Westerners are more comfortable than Asians to disclose personal details online for the purposes of self-expression and social connection (Y.-N.

K. Chen, 2010; Schug et al., 2010). In contrast, Asians are more concerned than Westerners about unauthorized third-party access to self-disclosures on social media (Thomson et al., 2015).

Cultural affective values have also been found to influence information-sharing behavior on social media (Hsu et al., 2021). The ideal affect, namely the affective states that people ideally would like to feel, differs across cultural contexts, whereby Western cultures value more high-arousal positive emotions (e.g., joy, excitement) and East Asian cultures value more low-arousal positive emotions (e.g., calm, peacefulness). Accordingly, Facebook users from Hong Kong, Singapore, and Taiwan show lower intensity in facial expressions in their profile pictures than their American counterparts (Huang & Park, 2013). Furthermore, Hsu and colleagues (2021) found that US Twitter (now called X) users produced primarily positive (relative to negative) content, whereas Japanese Twitter users produced primarily low-arousal (relative to high-arousal) content. Interestingly, while Twitter users tended to produce content in line with their cultural affective values, they were more likely to be influenced by content that violated their values and subsequently produced similar affective content after the exposure: US Twitter users were influenced more by others' high-arousal negative (e.g., angry) tweets, whereas Japanese were influenced more by others' high-arousal positive (e.g., excited) tweets. In other words, although most social media posts observe their respective cultural values, those that violate the cultural values seem particularly "contagious" to the virtual audience, and, as a result, their affective content tends to spread on social media. Accordingly, one may expect that information conveyed in such posts is more likely to stick in memory over time.

Thus, in addition to shaping the digital extension of autobiographical memory online, cultural values and norms also shape the transactive extension of autobiographical memory by influencing how the virtual audience perceives and interacts with the social media user. This process is further highlighted in a study on how the cyber audience made sense of Facebook users' status updates (Wang et al., 2023). In this study, Facebook users answered questions about their personal characteristics and provided their twenty most recent status updates. Independent viewers, who were blind to the demographic information of the Facebook users, then answered questions about the Facebook users' personal characteristics based on the status updates. It was found that viewers perceived Western Facebook users as more extroverted than Asians, even when Western and Asian Facebook users did not differ in their self-reported extroversion. Furthermore, viewers perceived higher self-esteem in Western than Asian Facebook users, differences that also appeared in Facebook users' self-reports. These findings are consistent with the notion that Western cultures place a greater value on extraversion and positive self-regard as preferred personality traits than East Asian cultures (Hamamura, 2017; Jeon et al., 2020; Song & Kwon, 2012). They further suggest that Facebook users present themselves in status updates within their respective cultural frameworks, and that the audience is able to discern the users' cultured persona through meaning making of the status updates. Cultural influences may take place both on the characteristics of the social media posts (i.e., the digital extension of autobiographical memory) and the meaning-making process of the cyber community (i.e., the transactive extension of autobiographical memory).

Taken together, extant research has demonstrated that the impact of cultural norms and values on autobiographical remembering extends from the offline world to the online world and may in fact be magnified in the public sphere of social media platforms. Online social interactions tend to take different forms in service of different motives and goals in specific cultural contexts. Social media users post their personal experiences online in ways consistent with their cultural values and expectations. Under some circumstances, however, those who violate cultural values may receive greater attention from their audience. Furthermore, the virtual audience plays an active role in making sense of the social media user's posts and discerning the user's persona in line with their cultural values and expectations. Cultural factors thus condition the digital and transactive extensions of autobiographical memory and their dynamic interactions.

Concluding Remarks

The Internet and social media have permeated into our everyday life and profoundly changed how we remember and share our personal experiences. More than ever, autobiographical memory is extended, externalized, and transactive. I have applied the triangular theory of self (Wang, 2022) to analyzing the characteristics of autobiographical memory and its online extension—in digital and transactive forms—in the social media era. Taking a psycho-cultural perspective, the analysis reveals important pathways via which psychological and cultural factors shape memory representations in the person, on the social media platform, and in the cyber community. It illustrates that the online extension of autobiographical memory entails a dynamic, interactive process that is shaped by the psychological characteristics of the social media user and the cyber community and further constrained by cultural norms and values to which the user and the cyber community adhere. Autobiographical memory online is thus the product of a co-construction between the individual social media user and the cyber community in specific cultural contexts. It in turn serves important functions for individuals' sense of self and well-being in our digitally mediated society.

Despite the encompassing impact of the Internet and social media as a cultural tool specific to our time on memory representation, expression, and socialization (Wang, 2013, 2021a), empirical research is still limited. Much research is needed to examine the purposes, processes, and consequences of autobiographical remembering on social media. The research should include diverse populations, examining the online extension of autobiographical memory within and across cultures. Research should also examine technological tools such as "total recall" apps, digital nudges, and algorithms in shaping autobiographical remembering and forgetting online (Hoskins, Chapter 3, this volume). Furthermore, research should consider societal factors that may influence why and how individuals share memories online. For example, ethnic minority individuals in the United States are more likely than White Americans to post personal experiences online for therapeutic reasons, possibly because they experience greater psychological distress and have less access to mental health services (Stone et al., 2022). It is thus critical to identify individual, technological, cultural, and societal factors that affect the online extension of autobiographical memory and further leverage memory sharing on social media to facilitate well-being. In addition, effective strategies need to be developed to overcome methodological challenges in studying autobiographical memory on social media, such as sampling issues, lack of experimental control, and social desirability concerns, as well as ethical issues such as privacy risk. A combination of lab research that utilizes realistic social media simulations (e.g., Bilgin & Wang, 2024; Hou et al., 2022; Masur et al., 2021) and field research that ensures ecological validity (Talarico, 2022; Stone et al., Chapter 4, this volume) will be the most productive way moving forward to uncover the dynamic interaction between the person and the net in the remaking of autobiographical memory in the Internet age.

References

Bazarova, N. N., Choi, Y. H., Whitlock, J., Cosley, D., & Sosik, V. (2017). Psychological distress and emotional expression on Facebook. *Cyberpsychology, Behavior, and Social Networking, 20*(3), 157–163. https://doi.org/10.1089/cyber.2016.0335

Beike, D. R., Cole, H. E., & Merrick, C. R. (2017). Sharing specific "we" autobiographical memories in close relationships: The role of contact frequency. *Memory, 25*(10), 1425–1434.

Bilgin, E., & Wang, Q. (2024). The mnemonic effect of central and peripheral misinformation on social media. *Memory, 32*(3), 369–382. https://doi.org/10.1080/09658211.2024.2323935

Boytos, A. S., Costabile, K. A., & Logan, T. R. (2023). Describing autobiographical memories: Effects of shared reality and audience attitude valence on perceived authenticity and self-esteem. *Self and Identity, 22*, 77–101. https://doi.org/10.1080/15298868.2022.2029553

Caci, B., Cardaci, M., & Miceli, S. (2019). Autobiographical memory, personality, and Facebook mementos. *Europe's Journal of Psychology, 15*(3), 614–636. https://doi.org/10.5964/ejop.v15i3.1713

Caci, B., Scrima, F., Cardaci, M., & Miceli, S. (2020). The Italian version of the Thinking About Life Experiences Questionnaire and its relationship with gender, age, and life events on Facebook. *Applied Cognitive Psychology, 34*(2), 472–488. https://doi.org/10.1002/acp.3635

Chen, H.-T., & Li, X. (2017). The contribution of mobile social media to social capital and psychological well-being: Examining the role of communicative use, friending and self-disclosure. *Computers in Human Behavior, 75*, 958–965. https://doi.org/10.1016/j.chb.2017.06.011

Chen, Y.-N. K. (2010). Examining the presentation of self in popular blogs: A cultural perspective. *Chinese Journal of Communication, 3*(1), 28–41.

Christensen, T. C., Wood, J. V., & Barrett, L. F. (2003). Remembering everyday experience through the prism of self-esteem. *Personality and Social Psychology Bulletin, 29*(1), 51–62. https://doi.org/10.1177/0146167202238371

Conway, M. A., & Pleydell-Pearce, C. W. (2000). The construction of autobiographical memories in the self-memory system. *Psychological Review, 107*(2), 261–288. https://doi.org/10.1037/0033-295X.107.2.261

Cosley, D., Sosik, V. S., Schultz, J., Peesapati, S. T., & Lee, S. (2012). Experiences with designing tools for everyday reminiscing. *Human Computer Interaction, 27*, 175–198. https://doi.org/10.1080/07370024.2012.656047

Costabile, K. A., & Austin, A. B. (2020). Memories of me, memories of we: Trait self-knowledge, prototypical norms, and autobiographical memories. *Self and Identity, 19*(8), 925–947. https://doi.org/10.1080/15298868.2019.1706629

Demiray, B., & Freund, A. M. (2017). The psychological distance of memories: Examining causal relations with mood and self-esteem in young, middle-aged, and older adults. *Consciousness and Cognition, 49*, 117–131. https://doi.org/10.1016/j.concog.2017.01.004

Demiray, B., & Janssen, S. M. J. (2015). The self-enhancement function of autobiographical memory. *Applied Cognitive Psychology, 29*(1), 49–60. https://doi.org/10.1002/acp.3074

Demiray, B., Mischler, M., & Martin, M. (2019). Reminiscence in everyday conversations: A naturalistic observation study of older adults. *Journals of Gerontology: Series B, 74*(5), 745–755.

Endo, Y., & Meijer, Z. (2004). Autobiographical memory of success and failure experiences. In Y. Kashima, Y. Endo, E. S. Kashima, C. Leung, & J. McClure (Eds.), *Progress in Asian social psychology* (Vol. 4, pp. 67–84). Kyoyook-Kwahak-Sa Publishing Company.

Fivush, R. (2011). The development of autobiographical memory. *Annual Review of Psychology, 62*, 559–582. https:doi.org/10.1146/annurev.psych.121208.131702

Forest, A. L., & Wood, J. V. (2012). When social networking is not working: Individuals with low self-esteem recognize but do not reap the benefits of self-disclosure on Facebook. *Psychological Science, 23*, 295–302. https://doi.org/10.1177/0956797611429709

Gebauer, J. E., Haddock, G., Broemer, P., & von Hecker, U. (2013). The role of semantic self-perceptions in temporal distance perceptions toward autobiographical events: The semantic congruence model. *Journal of Personality and Social Psychology, 105*(5), 852–872.

Greenwald, A. G. (1980). The totalitarian ego: Fabrication and revision of personal history. *American Psychologist, 35*(7), 603–618. https://doi.org/10.1037/0003-066X.35.7.603

Hamamura, T. (2017). Cultural differences in self-esteem. In V. Zeigler-Hill & T. Shackelford (Eds.), *Encyclopedia of personality and individual differences* (pp. 1–3). Springer. https://doi.org/10.1007/978-3-319-28099-8_1126-1

Hollenbaugh, E. E. (2011). Motives for maintaining personal journal blogs. *CyberPsychology, Behavior & Social Networking, 14*(1/2), 13–20.

Hong, S., Jahng, M. R., Lee, N., & Wise, K. (2020). Do you filter who you are? Excessive self-presentation, social cues, and user evaluations of Instagram selfies. *Computer in Human Behavior, 104*, 106159. https://doi.org/10.1016/j.chb.2019.106159

Hou, Y., Pan, X., Cao, X., & Wang, Q. (2022). Remembering online and offline: The effects of retrieval contexts, cues, and intervals on autobiographical memory. *Memory, 30*(4), 441–449. https://doi.org/10.1080/09658211.2021.1953078

Hou, Y., Xiong, D., Jiang, T., Song, L., & Wang, Q. (2019). Social media addiction: Its impact, mediation, and intervention. *Cyberpsychology, 13*(1), 4. https://doi.org/10.5817/CP2019-1-4

Hsu, T. W., Niiya, Y., Thelwall, M., Ko, M., Knutson, B., & Tsai, J. L. (2021). Social media users produce more affect that supports cultural values, but are more influenced by affect that violates cultural values [Supplemental material]. *Journal of Personality and Social Psychology, 121*(5), 969–983. https://doi.org/10.1037/pspa0000282.supp

Huang, C.-M., & Park, D. (2013). Cultural influences on Facebook photographs. *International Journal of Psychology, 48*, 334–343. http://dx.doi.org/ 10.1080/00207594.2011.649285

James, W. (1890). *The principles of psychology*. H. Holt and Company.

Jeon, H. J., Wang, Q., Burrow, A. L., & Ratner, K (2020). Perspectives of future health in self and others: The moderating role of culture. *Journal of Health Psychology, 25*(5), 703–712. https://doi.org/10.1177/1359105317730897

Jiang, T.-L., Hou, Y., & Wang, Q. (2016). Does micro-blogging make us "shallow"? Sharing information online interferes with information comprehension. *Computers in Human Behavior, 59*, 210–214. https://doi.org/10.1016/j.chb.2016.02.008

Johnson, A. J., & Morley, E. G. (2021). Sharing personal memories on ephemeral social media facilitates autobiographical memory. *Cyberpsychology, Behavior, and Social Networking, 24*(11), 745–749. https://doi.org/10.1089/cyber.2020.0511

Kim, Y., Sohn, D., & Choi, S. M. (2011). Cultural difference in motivations for using social network sites: A comparative study of American and Korean college students. *Computers in Human Behavior, 27*(1), 365–372. https://doi.org/10.1016/j.chb.2010.08.015

Kitayama, S., Markus, H., Matsumoto, H., & Norasakkunkit, V. (1997). Individual and collective processes in the construction of the self: Self-enhancement in the United States and self-criticism in Japan. *Journal of Personality and Social Psychology, 72*(6), 1245–1267.

Ko, H.-C., & Pu, H.-J. (2010). Can blogging enhance resilience through self-disclosure? A positive net perspective. *Review of Business Research, 10*(2), 28–36.

Kolesnyk, D., de Jong, M. G., & Pieters, R. (2021). Gender gaps in deceptive self-presentation on social-media platforms vary with gender equality: A multinational investigation. *Psychological Science, 32*(12), 1952–1964. https://doi.org/10.1177/09567976211016395

Krasnova, H., Veltri, N. F., & Günther, O. (2012). Self-disclosure and privacy calculus on social networking sites: The role of culture: Intercultural dynamics of privacy calculus. *Business & Information Systems Engineering, 4*(3), 127–135. https://doi.org/10.1007/s12599-012-0216-6

Kulkofsky, S., Wang, Q., & Koh, J. B. K. (2009). Functions of memory sharing and mother-child reminiscing behaviors: Individual and cultural variations. *Journal of Cognition and Development, 10*, 92–114. https://doi.org/10.1080/15248370903041231

Masur, P., DiFranzo, D., & Bazarova, N. (2021). Behavioral contagion on social media: Effects of social norms, design interventions, and critical media literacy on self-disclosure. *PloS One, 16*(7), e0254670. https://doi.org/10.1371/journal.pone.0254670

Midgley, C., Thai, S., Lockwood, P., Kovacheff, C., & Page-Gould, E. (2021). When every day is a high school reunion: Social media comparisons and self-esteem [Supplemental material for]. *Journal of Personality and Social Psychology, 121*(2), 285–307. https://doi.org/10.1037/pspi0000336.supp

Neisser, U. (1988). Five kinds of self-knowledge. *Philosophical Psychology, 1*, 35–59.

Oh, H. J., & LaRose, R. (2016). Impression management concerns and support-seeking behavior on social network sites. *Computers in Human Behavior, 57*, 38–47. https://doi.org/10.1016/j.chb.2015.12.005

Peterson, C., Wang, Q., & Hou, Y. (2009). "When I was little": Childhood recollections in Chinese and European Canadian grade school children. *Child Development, 80*(2), 506–518. https://doi.org/10.1111/j.1467-8624.2009.01275.x

Pillemer, D. B. (1998). *Momentous events, vivid memories*. Harvard University Press.

Roberts, J. E., Kyung, Y., Koscinski, B., Rosenfeld, E., & Lee, H.-J. (2021). Response styles to sad mood and self-esteem as predictors of autobiographical memory: Distinctions between memory specificity and detail. *Personality and Individual Differences, 21,* 110142. https://doi.org/10.1016/j.paid.2020.110142

Ross, M., Heine, S. J., Wilson, A. E., & Sugimori, S. (2005). Cross-cultural discrepancies in self-appraisals. *Personality and Social Psychology Bulletin, 31,* 1175–1188.

Ross, M., & Wilson, A. E. (2000). Constructing and appraising past selves. In D. L. Schacter & E. Scarry (Eds.), *Memory, brain, and belief* (pp. 231–259). Harvard University Press.

Schug, J., Yuki, M., & Maddux, W. (2010). Relational mobility explains between- and within-culture differences in self-disclosure to close friends. *Psychological Science, 21*(10), 1471–1478.

Shweder, R. A., Goodnow, J., Hatano, G., LeVine, R. A., Markus, H., & Miller, P. (1998). The cultural psychology of development: One mind, many mentalities. In W. Damon (Series Ed.), & R. M. Lerner (Vol. Ed.), *Handbook of child psychology, Vol. 1. Theoretical models of human development* (5th ed., pp. 865–937). Wiley & Sons.

Song, H., & Kwon, N. (2012). The relationship between personality traits and information competency in Korean and American students. *Social Behavior and Personality, 40,* 1153–1162. http://dx.doi.org/10.2224/sbp.2012.40.7.1153

Steinfield, C., Ellison, N. B., & Lampe, C. (2008). Social capital, self-esteem, and use of online social network sites: A longitudinal analysis. *Journal of Applied Developmental Psychology, 29*(6), 434–445. https://doi.org/10.1016/j.appdev.2008.07.002

Stone, C. B., Guan, L., LaBarbera, G., Ceren, M., Garcia, B., Huie, K., Stump, C., & Wang, Q. (2022). Why do people share memories online? An examination of the motives and characteristics of social media users. *Memory, 30*(4), 450–464. https://doi.org/10.1080/09658211.2022.2040534

Stone, C. B., & Wang, Q. (2019). From conversations to digital communication: The mnemonic consequences of consuming and sharing information via social media. *Topics in Cognitive Science, 11*(4), 774–793. https://doi.org/10.1111/tops.12369

Stsiampkouskaya, K., Joinson, A., Piwek, L., & Ahlbom, C. (2021). Emotional responses to likes and comments regulate posting frequency and content change behaviour on social media: An experimental study and mediation model. *Computers in Human Behavior, 124,* 106940. https://doi.org/10.1016/j.chb.2021.106940

Süral, I., Griffiths, M. D., Kircaburun, K., & Emirtekin, E. (2019). Trait emotional intelligence and problematic social media use among adults: The mediating role of social media use motives. *International Journal of Mental Health and Addiction, 17*(2), 336–345. https://doi.org/10.1007/s11469-018-0022-6

Talarico, J. M. (2022). Replicating autobiographical memory research using social media: A case study. *Memory, 30*(4), 429–440. https://doi.org/10.1080/09658211.2021.1903040

Talarico, J. M., Kraha, A., Self, H., & Boals, A. (2019). How did you hear the news? The role of traditional media, social media, and personal communication in flashbulb memory. *Memory Studies, 12,* 359–376.

Thomson, R., Yuki, M., & Ito, N. (2015). A socio-ecological approach to national differences in online privacy concern: The role of relational mobility and trust. *Computers in Human Behavior, 51,* 285–292. https://doi.org/10.1016/j.chb.2015.04.068

Truong, G., & Todd, R. M. (2017). SOAP opera: Self as object and agent in prioritizing attention. *Journal of Cognitive Neuroscience, 29,* 937–952. https://doi.org/10.1162/jocn_a_01083

Walsh, R. M., Forest, A. L., & Orehek, E. (2020). Self-disclosure on social media: The role of perceived network responsiveness. *Computer in Human Behavior, 104,* 106162. https://doi.org/10.1016/j.chb.2019.106162

Wang, Q. (2013). *The autobiographical self in time and culture.* Oxford University Press. https://doi.org/10.1093/acprof:oso/9780199737833.001.0001

Wang, Q. (2016). Remembering the self in cultural contexts: A cultural dynamic theory of autobiographical memory. Special issue: Memory and Connection: Remembering the Past and Imagining the Future in Individuals, Groups, and Cultures. *Memory Studies*, *9*(3), 295–304. https://doi.org/10.1177/1750698016645238

Wang, Q. (2019). The individual mind in the active construction of its digital niche. *Journal of Applied Research in Memory and Cognition*, *8*, 25–28. https://doi.org/10.1016/j.jarmac.2018.12.005

Wang, Q. (2021a). The cultural foundation of human memory. *Annual Review of Psychology*, *72*, 151–179. https://doi.org/10.1146/annurev-psych-070920-023638

Wang, Q. (2021b). Cultural pathways and outcomes of autobiographical memory development. *Child Development Perspectives*, *15*(3), 196–202. https://doi.org/10.1111/cdep.12423

Wang, Q. (2022). The triangular self in the social media era. *Memory, Mind & Media*, 1(E4), 1–12. https://doi.org/10.1017/mem.2021.6

Wang, Q., Hou, Y., Koh, J. B. K., Song, Q., & Yang, Y. (2018). Culturally motivated remembering: The moderating role of culture for the relation of episodic memory to well-being. *Clinical Psychological Science*, *6*(6), 860–871. https://doi.org/10.1177/2167702618784012

Wang, Q., Khuu, A., & Jivotovski, M. (2023). The self online: When meaning-making is outsourced to the cyber audience. *PLoS One*, *18*(12): e0294990. https://doi.org/10.1371/journal.pone.0294990

Wang, Q., Lee, D., & Hou, Y. (2017). Externalising the autobiographical self: Sharing personal memories online facilitated memory retention. *Memory*, *25*(6), 772–776. https://doi.org/10.1080/09658211.2016.1221115

Wang, Q., Mert, N., & Tian, Y. (2024). Remembering the good and bad and the self and others in a culturally modulated self-memory system. *Memory*. https://doi.org/10.1080/09658211.2024.2372373

Wang, Q., & Yang, J. C.-I. (2023). Culture and storytelling in literature. *Narrative Inquiry*, *33*(1), 112–122. https://doi.org/10.1075/ni.21093.wan

Woike, B., Lavezzary, E., & Barsky, J. (2001). The influence of implicit motives on memory processes. *Journal of Personality and Social Psychology*, *81*(5), 935–945. https://doi.org/10.1037/0022-3514.81.5.935

Yoo, J. J., Kim, D., & Moon, J. (2012). Exploring cross-cultural differences in self-presentation and self-disclosure in social networking sites: A comparison of Korean and American SNS users. *Journal of Advertising and Promotion Research*, *1*(2), 77–118. https://doi.org/10.2139/ssrn.2422292

Zhao, P., Lapierre, M. A., Rains, S. A., & Segrin, C. (2021). When and why we disclose distress on SNSs: Perceived affordances, disclosure goals, and anticipated negative evaluations. *Computers in Human Behavior*, *125*, 106964. https://doi.org/10.1016/j.chb.2021.106964

3
The Forgetting Ecology
Losing the Past through Digital Media and AI

Andrew Hoskins

The past is everywhere! Contemporary experiences don't feel real unless captured and shared, as we devote an ever-expanding set of devices, platforms, apps, and services to recording the details and minutiae of our lives, experiences, movements, and thoughts in a "self-paparazzization" for our friends, family and subscribed publics (Merrin, 2021). This is accumulating a new kind of past. This is not only a past made from the mass smartphone accumulation of recording of experience and events around the self, but also that the very acts of *production* through messaging, editing, posting, sharing, linking, liking, mixing, and remediating of digital content entangles humans and machines in hugely uncertain futures. Who or what ultimately will determine the outcome of these entanglements and their uses as a form of new memory?

The Reversal of Media Making Memory

The inexorable interplay of humans and digital tech over the recent two decades, including the smartphone-induced overproduction of experience, has driven a seemingly contradictory desire for what to do with a past in need of new kinds of control.

The first is to tame the past, premised on a vision of "total memory": that we can record, collect, sort, and mine *everything* via digital management systems and memory apps. This is premised on the impulse not to be forgotten. This is not a new idea (see Hoskins, 2015a) but one that is increasingly realized by artificial intelligence (AI). For example, the service called Hereafter AI[1] offers an app to help you create what appears as an immortal you. By uploading images and recording messages and stories, Hereafter AI claims to "securely save and organize everything for loved ones to hear, right away or years in the future."[2] More widely, the apps and services devoted to collecting and managing your personal (Personal AI[3]) or business (Rewind AI[4]) pasts are proliferating, especially

Andrew Hoskins, *The Forgetting Ecology* In: *The Remaking of Memory in the Age of the Internet and Social Media.* Edited by: Qi Wang and Andrew Hoskins, Oxford University Press. © Oxford University Press 2024.
DOI: 10.1093/oso/9780197661260.003.0003

since the 2022 popularization of "foundation models"—large pretrained models trained on large amounts of data.[5] These underpin the conversational chat agent ChatGPT and can be adapted for a wide range of applications.

The second impulse in response to the growing interplay of humans and digital tech and the overproduction of experience is to try to be forgotten. This is reflected in the European 2012 legislation on the Right to Be Forgotten (RtbF). This right (later enshrined in Article 17 of the EU General Data Protection Regulation) gives an individual the right to have their personal data deleted in certain circumstances.[6] But as Ghezzi et al. (2014) observe: "This proposal raises dilemmas, unreasonable expectations and controversies of a societal, legal, economical and ethical, as well as a practical nature." There is a lot of attention afforded to the RtbF legislation and its uses and effectiveness in recent years (Brock, 2016; Jones, 2016; Lambert, 2019).

Yet less attention—at least as a matter of memory—has been afforded to how growing human and digital entanglements threaten privacy and anonymity (see Hoskins, 2024). This is the past as surveillance: the multiple ways in which memory is employed as a form of identification of you. Just as proliferating forms and scale of individual and social remembering require new means of management, so new ways in which you are being seen, known, and remembered through data points and the digital spreadability of information have led to the development of services claiming to help you to become less knowable, to be forgotten. The selective remembering of the human mind enables us to forget. This can be seen as a kind of trade-off, especially around emotionally arousing versus background experience (Waring & Kensinger, 2011). We wouldn't want to or need to remember everything in this view. Yet the personal control offered by imaginaries and services of the digital capture of all of our past—a total memory—also foreground the importance of being able to forget and increasingly of being able to be forgotten.

New forms of being remembered in the world require new forms of forgetting. Eliminalia, for example, is just one such company that offers to "erase your past."[7] However, even in the emerging market for "deleting unwanted and erroneous information"[8] about you, what was once delineated as the "remembered self" (Singer & Salovey, 1993) is massively expanded today as one that is known, scattered, sampled, recorded, monitored, tracked, and surveilled.

In this chapter, I consider this new environment of digital participation and entanglement as a *forgetting ecology*. I have long argued for the value of seeing memory as an "ecology" (Brown & Hoskins, 2010; Hoskins, 2016, 2017, 2018). This is how the memory of the day can be understood like organic life forms, existing in a complex set of relationships within a balanced environment. Technological shifts change these interrelationships, impacting the entire "ecology," transforming the "balance of creation, adaptation, and circulation" of memory (Winter, 2006, p. 26).

To understand the processes and impact of remembering and forgetting in and on individuals and societies, we need to grasp the messiness of the multiple connectivities of brains and bodies, individuals and groups, as we collide and interact with others and events over time. Yet we must also recognize that the ecology in which all this occurs is increasingly saturated by data that mixes the human and the nonhuman (Hoskins & Halstead, 2021). Here, then, there are growing uncertainties and perils for how individuals and societies may come not only to remember, but also in our human capacity to recognize and comprehend these shifts and harness or resist them.

We have passed a "tipping point" in the human capacity to know about these shifts precisely at the same time as the digital and AI-shaped transformations of the ecology herald a new era of the past that has slipped beyond our grasp. This is the forgetting ecology.

My work on ecologies draws on an established tradition in media studies of "media ecologies." Elements of this work can be found in the work of Mumford (2010), Ellul (1973), Innis (1986), and Postman (1970). However, it is in Marshall McLuhan's (1964) work that we find the constellation of ideas that form the basis for a theory of media ecology. These include an emphasis on technological form; a discussion of media as both natural, organic extensions and evolving life forms; an interest in their specific properties and creation of sensory balances; and a discussion of the dominant media's creation of an invisible, surrounding "environment."

But the past of today, which is being scraped anew, is nothing like the past of before because a change in a key component in the ecology upsets the interconnected whole. As Merrin (2021)[9] argues:

> Ecological theory includes the concept of the "trophic cascade," understood as the knock-on effect of changes in the food-web of one trophic level. So, for example, the loss of wolves might allow a deer population to grow, impacting on the plants they eat and hence also on species dependent on those plants. With each ecological system being carefully-balanced and formed through a complex web of interconnections and dependencies, then any change to key species can potentially cause an "extinction cascade"—a series of secondary or subsidiary extinctions impacting the whole network. Media ecosystems are similarly vulnerable.

There is a trophic cascade in the tsunami of digital data and most recently in developments in AI—which transforms the entire memory ecology—to one of forgetting. This revolutionizes how the mixing of the human and the machine and how the past is representable, seen or not seen, mined, fabricated, and erased. For example, generative AI is a trophic cascade in its impact in upsetting the balance in the relationships between its remembering and forgetting actors and communicational forms, the modes of representation and archiving—making it difficult for individuals to catch a glimpse of themselves, to be confident in their agency in shaping what the past is, and their capacity to determine its provenance and authenticity. AI increasingly renders a black box memory.

One of the ways that the trophic cascade of AI poses a danger to what will be accessible of the past through the kind of publicly available AI developed in recent years "is based on this wholesale appropriation of existing culture, the scope of which we can barely comprehend" (Bridle, 2023). Furthermore, AI training models will eventually have been fed all human-made digital material (Shumailov et al., 2023). This includes all of that produced through the forms of individual digital participation I have outlined. In other words, AI training models require being fed with a feedback loop of synthetic data (memory), infecting the production of future data (memory). This seems like a description of the workings of a trophic cascade. This also correlates to work in the cognitive sciences on the "human remembering imagining system," which links memories of the recent past with images and expectations of the near future (Conway et al., 2016, p. 257).

Instead of seeing that digital technologies and media have only upset the balance in remembering and forgetting, rather it is that today's digital infrastructure of experience that has thrown the relationship between media and memory into *reverse*—from visioning, vitalizing, and strengthening to hiding, dissipating, and weakening the past. Our dependency on apps, platforms, networks, and all the vagaries of the Internet shape a systemized and inescapable ecology of forgetting. And a key characteristic of all the stuff that has been recorded, stored, messaged, and uploaded in the digital age is that there has accumulated a kind of junk past. The junk past is characterized by overproduction, distraction and attention deficit, excess, the 'enshittification' (Doctorow, 2022) of social media, and ultimately blockage.

In these circumstances, it becomes impossible to generalize about automated, algorithmic, or social media–shaped remembering. Rather, digital feeds shard highly individualized and personalized worlds, yet on a planetary scale. However, this concerns not only algorithms and "automated" remembering, but also individualization and personalization, which are features of digital platforms, with very little overarching moderation or regulation. This is certainly the case with the hybrid messaging social media platform Telegram (see Hoskins & Shchelin, 2023, for an overview).

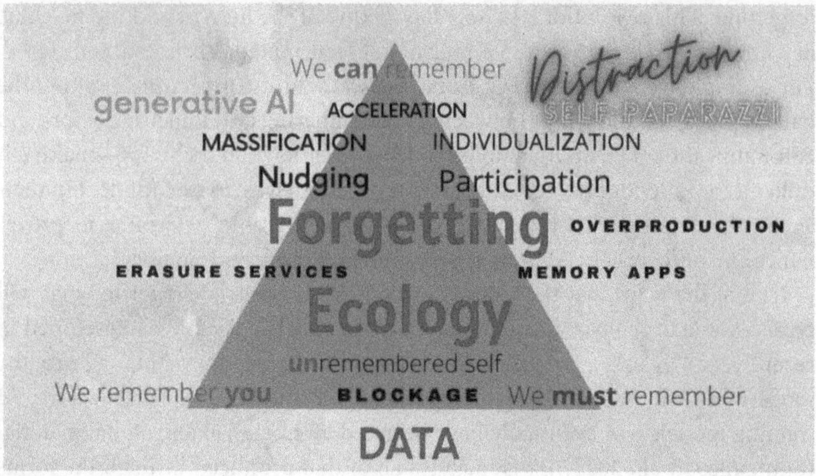

Figure 3.1 The forgetting ecology.

In summary, the key forces of the forgetting ecology are set out in the diagram in Figure 3.1. These are:

1. Participation in and overproduction of the past (massively expanded remembering self).
2. Individualization yet massification (design and algorithmic nudging, AI scraping of Internet content).
3. Key forces 1 and 2 make hugely uncertain what content (images, messages, videos, personal data) about the self might endure to haunt one's future or disappear without trace; this is a matter of forms of "accessibility" (vs. "availability") of the past.

In what follows, I develop these key forces of the forgetting ecology. First, I consider the challenges with even considering the idea and concept of forgetting, especially when compared with remembering.

The Problem with Forgetting

Remembering and forgetting I take as a subset of "memory" and as always in dynamic interplay with one another. Viet Thanh Nguyen (2016, p. 281), for instance, writes: "Remembering and forgetting are in a seesaw relationship, never perhaps, to achieve equilibrium." This idea of balance between remembering and forgetting is also useful in the notion of ecology I explore in the discussion that follows in terms of shifts in the media ecology of the day putting this out of sorts.

Instead, what would our relationship to the past look like if we took forgetting as the defining mode of our relationship with it, rather than as remembering's more often silent partner? Furthermore, in the digital era, smartphones, social media apps, and digital platforms and services utterly transform what it means, and individuals' and societies' capacity, to forget. At the same time, these very same technologies and media render the nature and influences on forgetting less visible. My approach treats forgetting—its worth and possibility—as a conundrum. Forgetting must be avoided, yet it is easy; it is essential yet impossible.

One explanation is that the excess of the past made present—societies have become increasingly swamped in connectivities and cultures of remembrance and haunted by all the digital traces of self—makes forgetting vital. The past seems bloated, yet the workings of our algorithmic present seem beyond our ready grasp and impossible to capture and preserve for use in the future.

I take at the heart of this conundrum digital infrastructures and cultures of participation in fostering new and unpredictable entanglements between humans and machines ushering in challenges of both forgetting and not being forgotten. There is an individual and collective past that is suddenly made available and newly revived through a combination of technological exposure and connectivity and digitization. A key mode of forgetting is paradoxically a consequence of the heightened cultural and political force of the digitally fostered values of openness: unbridled commentary, open access, freedom of information, the "right to know," the immediacy of instant search, confessional culture, and the recording of everything. In other words, digital cultures and technologies help incite a desire for total memory, yet this very demand can push unanticipated loss and forgetting. This applies to individuals and to societies. For example, as my research into military operational records shows, changes in legislation to require an earlier review of UK government department records (from 30 years to 20 years) has fed a perfect storm of blockage and stasis in the face of a digital tsunami rather than in any greater public availability of records (Hoskins, 2015b, forthcoming).

Also pivotal here is *how* this technological impetus heightens and colludes with a contemporary desire to turn over and turn on that past. But all of this—and there is so much!—acts as the principal mechanism of forgetting of our time through post-trust informational and connective overload: distraction, blockage.

Work on forgetting has long been enshrined in the scientific (cognitive and psychological) study of memory, a legacy of the work of Ebbinghaus's (1885/1964) pioneering experiments (Erdelyi, 1996, p. 179), including the ideas of "decay" and "interference" (Dewer et al., 2007). In the social sciences and humanities, although there are clear milestones in the understanding of the nature and significance of forgetting (Connerton, 2008; Ricoeur, 2004; Rieff, 2016), it is memory that is most often foregrounded in how we come to understand, use, and abuse the past. One explanation for this divergence is that the fragility of human memory has long been revealed by attempts to bring it external aid and the attention afforded to technologies, media, archives, and so on has been a matter of the study of memory in the social sciences and humanities (Moss & Thomas, 2018).

Memory "in the head" (Barnier & Hoskins, 2018) has long been seen to have been supported and strengthened by the storage, representational, reproductive, and connective capacities of technologies and media of the day, all external to the self. It is media that afford memory its substance, strength, and vitality. Successive transformations in writing, print, and the electronic media have transformed human cognition and the capacity, control, and power to remember (Hoskins, 2017). And in this era in which social media platforms and apps manage our everyday lives, pasts, and futures, these metaphors and ideas have proliferated. Memory is said to be networked (Hoskins, 2009), connective (Hoskins, 2011a and b), and algorithmic (Sluis, 2010).

Meanwhile, in the last decade in the human sciences, there has been increasing attention afforded to the effects of external stimuli in the form of digital tech in messing with the cognitive system. There has been a significant acceleration in psychological work testing the influence of media forms, technologies, and practices, including Internet usage, on the capacity and reliability of human memory (Marsh & Rajaram, 2019). Experimental work in psychology by Henkel (2013, for instance, shows that the act of photographing objects in a museum adversely affected the individual memory of the objects.

Daniel Schacter (2022) provides an excellent review of psychological work on the impact of media and technology on four of his "sins" of memory, developing from his highly influential "seven sins of memory," notably seven categories of error or distortion of individual human remembering (transience [forgetting over time], absent-mindedness [lapses in attention that produce forgetting], misattribution [attributing a memory to the wrong source], and suggestibility [implanted memories]).

Schacter (2022), in his review, is cautious in making claims about the impact of digital technologies and media in a wider ("domain-general") context beyond "task-specific" and "domain-specific" effects. In an interview on these issues for the journal of *Memory, Mind &* Media, I asked Professor Schacter more about domain-general effects, he replied: "By engaging with and frequently experiencing social media and the run of images. . . you eventually fundamentally alter the underlying experience of memory in multiple domains."[10] He summarized: "It is not inconceivable that that effect, the domain general effect, could eventually happen but I don't know of any evidence that it has yet happened."[11]

One possible response to the challenge set by Schacter here is to see his memory domains as inextricably related through the digital technologies of the day, through the related individualization and massification processes here, as part of a connected ecology. To this end, with Kristina Čimová since 2021 we have been talking with key designers and developers of memory apps and services to illuminate their vision and work as central actors in forging the ways in which the past is being made and remade, individually and yet globally. Thus, the digital nudging of memory occurs at the scale of the number of smartphone and app users, namely, billions. Jacob Appel, one of our expert interviewees (an algorithmic auditor for tech companies) makes this point [on push notifications]:

> Certainly, that's where a lot of the action is happening. That's where a lot of the feedback loops, the behavioural feedback loops that you think about where you get a little hit of satisfaction. . . . If you looked at examples of commercial applications, I'm sure you would find zillions of cases where it's the font that we used or the colour that was the background for this splash bubble made a difference. . . .You could think the same thing about if a push notification, on average, increased the time of engagement with an app by just two seconds per user, but that app has a billion users, then many person hours of time get moved by that little push notification. I believe strongly that those subtle design features are really an important frontier where this is happening.[12]

Surely this is a new frontier of memory at which billions of nudges shape the clicking, liking, downloading, sharing, and erasing of the messages, images, videos, texts, and so on from which the remembering and forgetting of this era will be determined. This involves the mass production of dopamine-induced memories, both through what of today's pasts are being clicked on or ignored and equally what will be accessible or not tomorrow.

The digital dopamine hit is released not only through the actual revealed content (reward) of the message, snap, image, video, email, and so on, but also to an even greater extent through the anticipation of that content generated through its delivery and potential for delivery. Thus, Greenfield (2021, p. 38) describes this as: "The maybe factor—the expectation of a possible reward: Who's texting me? Who tagged me on social media? What is in this email?" And the smartphone is central to what will become of the past as it is the supreme vehicle for continuously creating such expectations and relatedly it is the primary means of the individual and personal connection to the forgetting ecology. In short, digital nudges nudge the past.

Involuntary Memory

The forging, processing, and prompting of memories is thus part of a system that rewards an ever-greater immersion in and dependency on algorithmically informed nudges. Yet, this is not universally applicable; not all (media and forgetting) ecologies are the same. However, the spread, support, and survival of individual human memories, in other words their collective or social existence, in the wild have long been seen to be dependent on their validation or direction through the consensus of (or manipulation) by others, groups, and institutions. As the founding influencer of the modern study of collective memory Maurice Halbwachs (1980, p. 23) asks: "Don't we believe that we relive the past more fully because we no longer represent it alone, because we see it now as we saw it then, but through the eyes of another as well?"

It is digital nudging that then supremely combines the effects of the two elements to Halbwachs's formulation here of what is needed to forge trust or belief in memory. Even putting aside the forms of digital validation of an experience or event through its posting or sharing online, the visual memory nudge on your smartphone has this quality of "we see it now as we saw it then." But memory apps and services such as Timehop transform the contemporary experience of remembering of a very particular kind, namely, of "involuntary" memory.

Voluntary memory is the idea of actively working on one's own memories to consciously remember something good or to suppress more difficult experiences. In contrast, "involuntary" memory is that which intervenes suddenly and unexpectedly in our consciousness, a kind of disruption of the present. This is often associated with some kind of reminder of a past experience brought back through a sensation such as a taste or smell. It is an idea famously associated with the work of Marcel Proust. Proust (1912/1950, p. 189) writes:

> When an odour, a taste, rediscovered under entirely different circumstances evoke for us, in spite of ourselves, the past, we sense how different is this past from the one we thought we remembered and which our voluntary memory was painting like a bad painter using false colours. . . . [He] will suddenly rediscover forgotten years, gardens, people in the taste of a sip of tea in which he found a piece of *madeleine* . . . because they are involuntary, because they take shape of their own accord, inspired by the resemblance to an identical minute, they alone have a stamp of authenticity . . . as they make us savour the same situation under wholly different circumstances, they free from all context, they give us the extra-temporal essence.

And today, it is memory apps such as Timehop that afford precisely this "extra-temporal essence," not though through an instant evocation of an experience *in real life*, but rather through the flash of an image or video on our smartphone. Timehop, founded by Jonathan Wegener and Benny Wong in 2011, was a key driver of digital nostalgia and the memory app market. The company was recently acquired by the Sincere collection of brands.[13] Timehop prompts users with an image or video you previously posted to social media to remind you of what happened on that day a year or a few years ago. The "today in your history" became a standard feature of an array of platforms and photo management services, including Facebook, Google, and Apple.

Spontaneity and authenticity have become nudges that are paradoxically produced by the machine and through all our former interactions with the machine. Proust (see preceding quotation) suggests the process of involuntary memory is also special given its capacity to revisit a past that has also been forgotten. Timehop inspired memory apps not only restructure the capacity of the individual to remember in this particularly vivid way—through the shock of the old—but also at the same time inhibit that which would ultimately have been forgotten.

However, users of memory apps such as Timehop are not necessarily confronted with a shock of a past image or video suddenly reintroduced as though a genuinely involuntary memory had been presented or promoted. Rather, there is a growing organizing or curating of experiences being recorded, precisely to shape what will be remembered. For example, Kristina Čimová and I spoke with Matt Raoul, "vice president (VP) of memories" at Sincere, who explains: "People are now generating memories with the context of knowing that you're going to relive this in a year. . . . People understood that 'Oh, I'm going to see this in a year. I'm going to check into more places because now I know that there's future value in this.' We're at the point where everyone understands the future value and what they're currently doing and how has that changed behavior.[14]" Part of this trend is toward a greater personalization of digital content so that photos and videos used on apps such as Timehop or 1 Second Everyday are not posted to the more open platforms of Facebook or Instagram. Rather, this is the kind of content that exists primarily on each user's smartphone.

To return to the question of different "domains" and claims about the generalizability of remembering and forgetting on different levels or scales (Schacter, earlier quotation), another way to consider the nature and impact of digital content more holistically across the forgetting ecology is in making a distinction between availability and accessibility. We can begin to imagine the existence of the huge proliferation of billions of messages, images, videos, and so on that have accumulated especially over the past decade (including on smartphones) as something that is available to memory, but very little of it is actually humanly accessible (also see Stone et al., Chapter 4, and Wang, Chapter 2, this volume, on selective remembering and forgetting). In other words, this is a kind of blockage, a principal form of forgetting of this era.

Accessibility versus Availability

I have suggested that our relationship to the past is often characterized as an abundance of memory. Yet instead, the contemporary features of digital society of connectivity, abundance, too much information (TMI), and oversharing, rather than heralding a new golden era of archives and of future memory, are instead part of an ecology of forgetting. This is not just that digital existence weakens what was once an active memory, a human memory that had to work hard to sustain a continuity of past—of identity, of place, of relationships—with the shift from reliance to dependency on the search devices of our machines. Rather, TMI, overload, and distraction affect forgetting not only as erasure, or a loss or absence, but also as *blockage*. Forgetting seen in these terms then enables a grasp on the conundrum of the apparent digital excess and availability of information and data versus its accessibility.

If we see remembering as dynamic, as a product of interconnections (instead of static and stable) with the potential to be cued, then forgetting can be conceived as a kind of blockage of or interference with that connectivity, of that memory's coming into being, of it being accessible. To help with this view of forgetting, it is useful to look at the innovative interdisciplinary work of neuropsychologists such as the late Martin Conway and the artist Shona Illingworth. Here is an extract of Conway in conversation with Illingworth, around "Connectome" (which is a map of neural connections in the brain)[15]:

> MEMORY
> Is distributed through different networks
> In the brain
> When you remember
> The activation
> INTERLOCKS across these networks
> And a memory is
> CONSTRUCTED
> It doesn't really
> EXIST
> until it becomes interconnected in a
> DYNAMIC
> Act of remembering

Conway, Illingworth, and Catherine Loveday have been working with Claire, a patient, for several years.[16] Following a trauma to her brain at the age of 44, Claire can no longer remember much of her past, create new memories, or recognize anyone—not even herself. Claire suffers from retrograde amnesia, anterograde amnesia, and prosopagnosia. I vividly remember meeting Claire, although it is highly unlikely that she will remember me. And to focus on forgetting at this everyday level highlights how fundamental memory is to our sense of self and our whole social existence. Claire suffers from a lesion—a kind of petrified scar tissue—that prevents many of the neurons beyond this area of damage from firing: They simply "do not get the signals they used to from other neurons or neural networks and so they too will be changed."[17]

And Conway, Loveday, and Illingworth have worked with Claire using sensecam, a small sensor-equipped camera worn around the neck that takes point-of-view images every time the camera moves or every 30 seconds. When Claire reviews these images, an image on occasion will cue access to a sudden flood of intense recollection of an event she would otherwise be unable to remember anything about.

This important work highlights remembering as both a dynamic process and one vulnerable to being damaged or hidden or isolated through interference and blockage. In relation to the new forgetting ecology, then, we can learn from this view of forgetting in the mind to explore interference and blockage of the past in the wild. Again, if we take remembering as dynamic, as a product of interconnections with the potential to be cued, then the digital era utterly transforms what is possible in remembering the past through the astonishing connectivity between individuals, groups, organizations, and so on.

To this end, I have previously identified "connective memory" (Hoskins, 2011a, 2011b) to highlight the moment of connection as the moment of memory. The past is made and remade then, not because of individual or collective remembrances, but rather as generated through the flux of contacts between people, technologies, and media. In the digital age, these connections spiral out of individual human control. This ramps up the prospects of the future *emergence* of aspects of a growingly complex, partly hidden, and hugely forgotten past. These shifts also constitute a new relationship between privacy and memory.

Participation occurs in the glare of social media, seemingly visible to all, affording the sense that users are empowered in producing, curating, sharing, and remembering through the individual management of their digital devices and active immersion in their feeds.

Yet, this agency is attained at the cost of the harvesting and the exploiting of personal data. We have all become information accidents waiting to happen. This is the increased potential of digital trails being open to emerge, awaiting (re)discovery, (re)connection, and (re)mediation in unpredictable future times. And what do all your personal data, all those messages, images, and videos from you or depicting you, scattered across the ether add up to? The answer is that you don't know. In this way, the self is not really known, recognized, or "remembered" in a traditional sense, but rather unknown, unrecognized, and unremembered, mirror defying, at least by the self and your loved ones.

Data points (pieces of digital information about you) or personal data are a whole new category of remembrance of the self. Surely this opens complex and transformative terrain for memory studies in comprehending how individuals are being and could be remembered and forgotten? I call this individual the "unremembered self" (Hoskins, forthcoming) in that we are knowable and rememberable through data and information in ways that are difficult to grasp, as with the work of algorithms, recommender engines, data brokers, and so on.

Conclusion: The Unremembered Self

One way to explore the unremembered self is through the accessibility/availability paradigm. For example, drawing on Tulving and Pearlstone (1966), Hirst and Yamashiro (2017, p. 81) argue:

> We think it fair to state that unavailability only holds when a memory is "totally erased." If it were simply difficult to find, it would be classified as inaccessible.
>
> Tulving (1985) considered both unavailability and inaccessibility as instances of forgetting, but by and large, as far as we can assess, a memory is usually forgotten because of inaccessiblity, not unavailablity.
>
> Although he puts together the labels of inaccessibility and unavailability, Ricoeur makes a similar distinction, when he states: "Many memories . . . have not been definitively erased but simply rendered inaccessible, unavailable, which makes us say that one forgets less than one thinks or fears (Ricoeur, 2004, p. 416)."

The condition of the unremembered self is one that is not easily accessible or remembered by the individual whose personal data is scattered, sampled, recorded, monitored, tracked, and surveilled, but it certainly *is* accessible to all those doing the collecting, storing, hacking, and stealing of that personal data.

By way of a trend in the forgetting ecology (see Figure 3.1), as drivers of remembering (that lead to forgetting) we can start with the bottom right of the diagram—we must remember. The idea that we must remember foregrounds the value and moral weight of remembering over forgetting is a story long told in memory studies on the value of the (particularly traumatic) pasts seen in the context of learning lessons, preventing repetition, honoring victims, assuaging trauma, and pursuing the sometimes-incompatible ideas of reconciliation, justice, and reparation.

Several critics have observed that some acts of remembrance are not about memory, but more a matter of creating emotional or accountable distance from past events. The "spectacular promotion of a phenomenon" (Baudrillard, 1994, p. 23) or, as Runia (2014, p. 9) puts it: "The more we commemorate what we did, the more we transform ourselves into people who did not do it." In this commemoration, blockage is an effective strategy of forgetting through either overwhelming the present so that other past and ongoing wars are smothered and pushed to the periphery of the public gaze, or rendering the past so intimately and pervasively present that it is pixelated to a blur.

To move to the top of the diagram, these forms of remembering as forgetting have become more widespread in the digital era in the ease through which we apparently *can* remember. Here this is again the sudden availability, if not accessibility, through all the new ways in which the past can be captured, mined, and represented through participation, digital technologies, and AI. Yet, as I have argued, participation also gives us the bottom left of the diagram—we remember *you*, which is the myriad invisible and humanly knowable ways in which the unremembered self becomes a key part of all our pasts.

Overall, in this chapter, I have set out some of the emergent aspects of a new forgetting ecology. This is to help illuminate how datafied individuals and societies, overwhelmed by the overproduction of experiences and events, are reversing the relationship between media and memory—from a once (and sometimes assumed) extending, vitalizing, and strengthening to a past, that is instead weakened by the complexity and scale of digital content that increasingly escapes individual human control.

The unremembered self is that perpetually open to disruption and discovery, enmeshed in the data we have scattered and which may come back to haunt us yes, but as I have argued it is also forged by a past made from us that we cannot recognize, a past that never existed, a kind of alienation of memory.

The forgetting ecology then is already infected, leaching out what remains of the once more human experience in the ever-changing relationship between media, technologies, and memory.

Acknowledgements

This work is developed from my chapter published in German as 'Das vergessene Vergessen' (The forgetting conundrum) in the open access collection *The Future of Memory/Media Studies*. De Gruyter, pp.561–580. https://www.degruyter.com/document/doi/10.1515/978311

0629743-027/html?lang=de. Thank you to the editors Christine Lohmeier and Christian Pentzold for all their advice and help.

I am also very grateful for help and advice on this chapter by Qi Wang, William Merrin and Danny Pilkington. Thank you also to Jake Appel and to Matt Raoul for being so generous with their time and for sharing their great insights.

I am also grateful for feedback from the keynote I gave at the Indian Network for Memory Studies (IIT Madras) international conference on Memory, Ecology, and Sustainability, on the 20 September 2023, that helped shape this work, and thanks to Avishek Paruí for organising this event and for inviting me.

Notes

1. https://www.hereafter.ai/
2. Ibid.
3. https://www.personal.ai/
4. https://www.rewind.ai/
5. https://www.gov.uk/government/news/cma-launches-initial-review-of-artificial-intelligence-models
6. https://gdpr.eu/article-17-right-to-be-forgotten/
7. https://eliminalia.com/en/
8. Ibid.
9. Section from unpublished part of Merrin (2021).
10. Hoskins interview with Daniel Schacter for *Memory, Mind & Media.* https://vimeo.com/568738123
11. Ibid.
12. Jacob Appel, company external algorithmic auditor, interviewed by Andrew Hoskins and Kristina Čimová (via Zoom), June 4, 2021.
13. https://techcrunch.com/2023/06/13/party-planning-platform-punchbowl-is-acquiring-timehop/
14. Matt Raoul, VP of memories, Sincere, interviewed by Andrew Hoskins and Kristina Čimová (via Zoom), August 31, 2023.
15. Shona Illingworth "The Amnesia Museum" exhibition part of "Lesions in the Landscape," Foundation for Art and Creative Technology (FACT), September 18 to November 22, 2015.
16. https://thepsychologist.bps.org.uk/volume-28/july-2015/lesions-landscape
17. Shona Illingworth, "The Amnesia Museum" exhibition.

References

Barnier, A. J., & Hoskins, A. (2018). Is there memory in the head, in the wild? *Memory Studies, 11*(4), 386–390. https://doi.org/10.1177/1750698018806440

Baudrillard, J. (1994). *The illusion of the end.* Polity Press.

Bridle, J. (2023). The stupidity of AI. *The Guardian.* 16 March. https://www.theguardian.com/technology/2023/mar/16/the-stupidity-of-ai-artificial-intelligence-dall-e-chatgpt.

Brock, G. (2016). *The right to be forgotten: Privacy and the media in the digital age.* I. B. Tauris.

Brown, S. D., & Hoskins, A. (2010). Terrorism in the new memory ecology: Mediating and remembering the 2005 London bombings. *Behavioural Sciences of Terrorism and Political Aggression, 2*(2), 87–107. https://doi.org/10.1080/19434471003597399

Connerton, P. (2008). Seven types of forgetting. *Memory Studies, 1*(1), 59–70.

Conway, M. A., Loveday, C., & Cole, S. N. (2016). The remembering-imagining system. *Memory Studies, 9*(3), 256–265. https://doi.org/10.1177/1750698016645231

Dewer, M. T., Cowan, N., & Della Sala, S. (2007). Forgetting due to retroactive interference: A fusion of Müller and Pilzecker's (1900) early insights into everyday forgetting and recent research on anterograde amnesia. *Cortex, 43*(5), 616–634. https://doi.org/10.1016/S0010-9452(08)70492-1

Doctorow, C. (2022). Pluralistic: How monopoly enshittified Amazon. https://pluralistic.net/2022/11/28/enshittification/#relentless-payola, 28 November.

Ebbinghaus, H. (1885/1964). *Memory: A contribution to experimental psychology*, trans. H. A. Ruger & C. E. Bussenius. Dover.

Ellul, J. (1973). *The technological society*. Random House.

Erdelyi, M. H. (1996). *The recovery of unconscious memories: Hypermnesia and reminiscence*. University of Chicago Press.

Ghezzi, A., Guimarães Pereira, A., & Vesnić-Alujević, L. (Eds.). (2014). *The ethics of memory in a digital age: Interrogating the right to be forgotten*. Palgrave Macmillan.

Greenfield, D. N. (2021). Digital distraction: What makes the Internet and smartphone so addictive? In S. M. Lane & P. Atchley (Eds.), *Human capacity in the attention economy* (pp. 27–47). American Psychological Association. https://doi.org/10.1037/0000208-003

Halbwachs, M. (1980). *The collective memory* (F. J. Ditter Jr. and V. Y. Ditter, Trans.; Introduction by Mary Douglas). Harper & Row.

Henkel, L. A. (2013). Point-and-shoot memories: The influence of taking photos on memory for a museum tour. *Psychological Science, 25*(2), 396–402. https://doi.org/10.1177/0956797613504438

Hirst, W., & Yamashiro, J. K. (2017). Social aspects of forgetting. In M. Meade, Harris, C.B., Van Bergen, P., Sutton, J. & Barnier, A.J. (Eds.), *Collaborative remembering: Theories, research, and applications* (pp.76–99). Oxford University Press. https://doi.org/10.1093/oso/9780198737865.003.0005

Hoskins, A. (2009). Digital network memory. In A. Erll & A. Rigney (Eds.), *Mediation, remediation, and the dynamics of cultural memory* (pp. 91–106). Mouton de Gruyter.

Hoskins, A. (2011a). Media, memory, metaphor: Remembering and the connective turn. *Parallax, 17*(4), 19–31.

Hoskins, A. (2011b). 7/7 and connective memory: Interactional trajectories of remembering in post-scarcity culture. *Memory Studies, 4*(3), 269–280. https://doi.org/10.1177/1750698011402570

Hoskins, A. (2015a). Archive me! Media, memory, uncertainty. In A. Hajek, C. Lohmeier & C. Pentzold (Eds.), *Memory in a mediated world: Remembrance and reconstruction* (pp. 13–35). Palgrave Macmillan.

Hoskins, A. (2015b). Are we losing the history of warfare? https://archivesofwar.gla.ac.uk/are-we-losing-the-history-of-warfare-by-andrew-hoskins-37/

Hoskins, A. (2016). Memory ecologies. *Memory Studies, 9*(3), 348–357. https://doi.org/10.1177/1750698016645274

Hoskins, A. (2017). Digital media and the precarity of memory. In M. Meade, C.B. Harris, P. Van Bergen, J. Sutton & A.J. Barnier (Eds.), *Collaborative remembering: Theories, research, and applications* (pp. 371–385). Oxford University Press. https://doi.org/10.1093/oso/9780198737865.003.0021

Hoskins, A. (2018). Memory of the multitude: The end of collective memory. In A. Hoskins (Ed.), *Digital memory studies: Media pasts in transition* (pp. 85–109). Routledge.

Hoskins, A. (2024). AI & memory. *Memory, Mind & Media.*

Hoskins, A. (Forthcoming). *Breaking the past.* Oxford University Press.

Hoskins, A., & Halstead, H. (2021). The new grey of memory: Andrew Hoskins in conversation with Huw Halstead. *Memory Studies, 14*(3), 675–685. https://doi.org/10.1177/17506980211010936

Hoskins, A., & Shchelin, P. (2023). The war feed: Digital war in plain sight. *American Behavioral Scientist, 67*(3), 449–463. https://doi.org/10.1177/00027642221144848

Innis, H. (1986). *Empire and communications.* Beach Holme Publications.

Jones, M. L. (2016). *Ctrl + Z: The right to be forgotten.* New York University Press.
Lambert, P. (2019). *The right to be forgotten: Interpretation and practice.* Bloomsbury Professional.
Marsh, E. J., & Rajaram, S. (2019). The digital expansion of the mind: Implications of Internet usage for memory and cognition. *Journal of Applied Research in Memory and Cognition, 8*(1), 1–14. https://doi.org/10.1016/j.jarmac.2018.11.001
McLuhan, M. (1964). *Understanding media: The extensions of man.* Routledge and Kegan Paul.
Merrin, W. (2021). Hyporeality: The society of the selfie and identification politics. *MAST: The Journal of Media Art Study and Theory, 2*(1), 16–39. https://doi.org/10.59547/26911566.2.1.02
Moss, M., & Thomas, D. (2018). The accidental archive. In C. Brown (Ed.), *Archival futures* (pp. 117–136). Facet Publishing.
Mumford, L. (2010). *Technics and civilisation.* Chicago University Press.
Nguyen, V. T. (2016). *Nothing ever dies: Vietnam and the memory of war.* Harvard University Press.
Postman, N. (1970). The reformed English curriculum. In A. C. Eurich (Ed.), *The shape of the future in American secondary education* (pp. 160–168). Pitman Publishing.
Proust, M. (1950). Letter to Antoine Bibesco. In M. Curtiss (Ed. and Trans.) (1950) *Letters of Marcel Proust* (p. 189). Chatto & Windus. (Original work published 1912)
Ricoeur, P. (2004). *Memory, history, forgetting* (K. Blamey & D. Pellauer, Trans.). University of Chicago Press.
Rieff, D. (2016). *In praise of forgetting.* Yale University Press.
Runia, E. (2014). *Moved by the past: Discontinuity and historical mutation.* Columbia University Press.
Schacter, D. L. (2022). Media, technology, and the sins of memory. *Memory, Mind & Media, 1*, e1. https://doi.org/10.1017/mem.2021.3
Shumailov, I., Shumaylov, Z., Zhao, Y., Gal, Y., Papernot, N., & Anderson, R. (2023). The curse of recursion: Training on generated data makes models forget. *arXiv.* https://doi.org/10.48550/arXiv.2305.17493
Singer, J. A. & Salovey, P. (1993). *The remembered self: Emotion and memory in personality.* Free Press.
Sluis, K. (2010). Algorithmic memory? Machinic vision and database culture. In A. Mousoutzanis & D. Riha (Eds.), *New media and the politics of online communities* (pp. 227–236). Inter-Disciplinary Press.
Tulving, E. (1985). *Elements of episodic memory.* Oxford University Press.
Tulving, E., & Pearlstone, Z. (1966). Availability versus accessibility of information in memory for word. *Journal of Verbal Learning and Verbal Behavior, 5*(4), 381–391. https://doi.org/10.1016/S0022-5371(66)80048-8.
Waring, J. D., & Kensinger E. A. (2011). How emotion leads to selective memory: neuroimaging evidence. *Neuropsychologia, 49*(7), 1831–1842. https://doi.org/10.1016/j.neuropsychologia.2011.03.007
Winter, J. (2006). *Remembering war: The great war between memory and history in the twentieth century.* Yale University Press.

4
Sharing Personal Memories on Social Media

Motives and Mnemonic Consequences

*Charles B. Stone, Shayla Dockery, and Angelina N. Vasquez**

As the erudite contributions in this book make clear, the Internet, specifically social media, is a powerful means through which individuals and groups can share and remember their personal and collective pasts, respectively (cf., in this volume Fawns, Chapter 7; Niemeyer & Keightley, Chapter 14; Storm et al., Chapter 6). This is particularly pertinent given that, for example, 69% of American adults say they use *Facebook* (Auxier & Anderson, 2021). Despite this ever-growing reliance, dependence, and addiction to social media (e.g., Hou et al., 2019), psychologists are only beginning to understand and appreciate the motives and mnemonic consequences associated with producing or sharing personal memories on social media (see Stone & Wang, 2019). Thus, the aim of the present chapter is threefold: review the state-of-the-art research examining the psychological motives and mnemonic consequences associated with producing or sharing content on social media; present the latest research from our lab and colleagues extending these lines of research; and discuss the methodological difficulties associated with conducting social media research (e.g., managing/controlling for attrition rates) and present avenues for future research.

Motives for Social Media Use

Understanding the motives why individuals produce and/or consume content on social media is paramount for anyone interested in the mnemonic

* Author Note: The last two authors made equal contributions to the chapter and are listed alphabetically by last name.

Charles B. Stone, Shayla Dockery, and Angelina N. Vasquez, *Sharing Personal Memories on Social Media* In: *The Remaking of Memory in the Age of the Internet and Social Media.* Edited by: Qi Wang and Andrew Hoskins, Oxford University Press. © Oxford University Press 2024. DOI: 10.1093/oso/9780197661260.003.0004 consequences associated with social media use. Research examining social influences (e.g., conversations) on memory has made it clear that an individual's motive (e.g., to develop a shared reality) during a social interaction has important implications for how such social interactions shape the speaker's memory (e.g., Echterhoff, 2010; see also Rajaram, Chapter 12, this volume). Not surprisingly, then, researchers have begun to examine the motives why individuals use social media more generally.

However, the multifaceted ways in which social media researchers have examined motives associated with social media use have elicited various types of motives. For example, a study by Luchman et al. (2014) asked participants questions that included: "How often do you use [social media site] to find places to eat or services to use?" Through the administration of their scale, Luchman et al. found that there were two primary motives for using social media: fun related (e.g., giving updates) and content related (e.g., learning something new). Alternatively, Whiting and Williams's (2013) uses and gratification approach found that the motives guiding social media use included social interaction, information seeking, passing time, entertainment, relaxation, communicatory utility, convenience utility, expression of opinion, information sharing, and surveillance or knowledge about others (see also Oh & Syn, 2015, for a similar list of motives). And further, Nadkarni and Hofmann (2012) found that individuals use social media (i.e., Facebook) to "belong" and for "self-presentation" (see also Ellison et al., 2007; Seidman, 2013). Others have argued that the motives driving social media use are surveillance, network expansion, and intrapersonal and relationship maintenance (Lee & Kim, 2014; Schivinski et al., 2020). Similarly, Kircaburun et al. (2018; see also Horzum, 2016, for the original scale for Facebook usage) found that individuals used social media to (1) maintain existing relationships; (2) meet new people and socialize; (3) make, express, or present a more popular oneself; (4) pass time; (5) as a task management tool; (6) for entertainment; and (7) for informational and educational purposes.

What becomes clear is the field is full of various ways to measure, conceptualize, and interpret the motives individuals may have for why they use social media. However, an underappreciated factor is how a social media user's motives may differ depending on whether the user is producing (sharing) versus consuming (viewing/interacting; see Stone & Wang, 2019) social media content. Furthermore, individuals may use different and specific motives for different social media platforms (e.g., Twitter vs. Facebook, Davenport et al., 2014; see also Tandoc et al., 2019). Here, however, we focus on general motives to produce or share personal memories via social media (see Stone, Guan, et al., 2022; Wang, 2020).

Motives for Sharing Personal Memories Online

Sharing personal experiences with others is a uniquely human endeavor (Hirst & Stone, 2015). For decades, psychologists have examined the motives driving individuals to share these personal experiences with others and have largely agreed that humans share personal experiences with others for self (e.g., identity); social (e.g., relationship maintenance); therapeutic (e.g., psychological well-being; Pillemer, 1998; Wang, 2013); and directive (e.g., guiding future decisions/behaviors) reasons (see Alea & Bluck, 2003; Conway & Pleydell-Pearce, 2000; Del Vicario et al., 2016). Building on this research, Wang (2020) hypothesized that the motives guiding the functions of personal memories offline (i.e., conversations) mirror those for sharing memories online. Indeed, there are reasons to believe this is the case. For example, in earlier work, Wang (2013) observed that the reasons why individuals share personal information on social media appeared to fall within three motives guiding why individuals share personal memories offline: self, social, and directive functions. Thus, to further examine this possibility, Wang (2020) developed the Purposes of Online Memory Sharing Scale (POMSS). The scale consists of twenty items and asks participants, for example, why they post personal experience online. In her analysis, Wang found that the four motives for sharing personal experiences offline also guide when individuals will share personal experiences online, that is, self (five items, e.g., to get attention); social (six items, e.g., to entertain people); therapeutic (five items, e.g., to ease my distress); and directive (four items, e.g., to help others).

Recently, in two studies, Stone, Guan, et al. (2022) further tested the POMSS and examined whether the motives for sharing personal experiences on social media were associated with psychological characteristics (e.g., extraversion) and amount of social media usage. For Study 1, student participants completed the POMSS as well as scales measuring, for example, extraversion, disclosure, self-esteem (Rosenberg, 1965), and self-construal (Singelis, 1994). For Study 2, participants were recruited from the public to ensure a larger and more diverse (e.g., age) sample. The survey for Study 2 was identical to Study 1 except for the inclusion of questions measuring social media usage (e.g., how often they used social media) and general loneliness.

Overall, across two studies, Stone, Guan, et al.'s (2022) results provided additional support for Wang's (2020) results. Furthermore, Stone, Guan, et al. found that individuals shared personal experiences on social media primarily for social reasons. While this may not seem surprising given that social is in the name of social media, it also supports more general memory research showing that individuals primarily report a social function for why they disclose personal memories to others (e.g., through conversation)—lending further support to the inherently social nature of humans (e.g., Hirst & Stone, 2015). Interestingly, across the two studies, another pattern emerged: Individuals are least likely to share personal experiences on social media for therapeutic reasons. However, Stone, Guan, et al. (2022) did find that the therapeutic motive was associated with ethnicity, such that people of color were more likely to share personal experiences on social media for therapeutic reason than White individuals as well as those with lower self-esteem and more lonely.

The former result may speak to the distress caused by living in a White (supremacist) culture and using social media as a coping mechanism. It could also be because of a fear of mental health stigma (e.g., Gary, 2005). For example, African Americans underutilize mental health services more than any other race and/or ethnicity (e.g., Cummings & Druss, 2011). As such, social media may fill in as a coping mechanism rather than seeking professional help (Croiter & Yanos, 2022) and/or provide the necessary space for marginalized individuals and groups to voice their experiences and help build solidarity and collective action.

The latter results suggest that those who may be "suffering" (in this case, low self-esteem and loneliness) may use social media as an outlet to either commiserate and/or alleviate their feelings of low self-esteem and loneliness. Indeed, recent research found that actively using social media during the COVID-19 pandemic was associated with greater well-being (e.g., Masciantonio et al., 2021; see Hamilton et al., 2022, for a review).

In terms of the directive motive, a positive association was found between extraversion, disclosure, interdependence, and directive motives. That is, such individuals are more likely to share personal experiences on social media to provide advice to other individuals, which is perhaps not surprising, especially in terms of interdependence: The more connected one feels with others or a group, the more likely one may wish to pass along helpful information to them (e.g., "friends," followers, etc.). Similarly, those who are more likely to engage and communicate with other individuals may use those opportunities to help provide advice and helpful information.

Overall, the research by Wang, Stone, and colleagues suggests that sharing personal experiences on social media serves similar functions as sharing personal memories more generally, and that individual differences influence when and how individuals will share their experiences. By better understanding the motives for sharing personal experiences online, researchers, in turn, will better understand the mnemonic consequences associated with such sharing (cf., see, e.g., Ekelund, 2022; Niemeyer & Keightley, 2020).

The Mnemonic Effects of Online Sharing

Social media is a ubiquitous means by which individuals can disseminate and share both public and personal information with their friends and/or followers, which Stone and Wang (2019) refer to as "producers." Here, and in line with the above discussion, we focus on producing personal information. For example, individuals may share intimate photos or narratives about the birth of a child or successfully defending their own doctoral dissertation. In what follows, we briefly discuss the mnemonic consequences associated with sharing personal information and how our lab and colleagues have attempted to extend this line of research through efforts of increasing both internal and ecological validity (see Rajaram, Chapter 12, this volume, for an overview of general social influences on memory).

The extant research suggests there are mnemonic benefits to sharing personal information on social media. For example, Wang et al. (2017) had participants record personal experiences in a diary, and these events were then coded as to whether they were shared via social media or not. Overall, Wang et al. found that participants recalled more of the personal experiences shared on social media than those that were not shared on social media. Furthermore, participants rated 98% of those experiences shared on social media as more important and emotional than those not shared on social media. There was no difference in terms of pleasantness between those experiences shared and not shared. Thus, the act of sharing information on social media may enhance the memorability of the information. However, it is possible that the information they chose to share on social media was already more memorable (and important/emotional), which, in turn, led individuals to share those personal experiences on social media. Additionally, Tamir et al. (2018) found, across three studies, that when individuals believe that their documented personal experiences will be later shared with others, they exhibited poorer recall of the experienced event and/or object. While the results of Tamir et al. (2018) did not actually examine the consequences of sharing information on social media, their results, combined with the self-selective nature of Wang et al.'s (2017) study, do raise questions surrounding the mnemonic consequences associated with sharing personal information on social media. Furthermore, it remains unclear whether the aforementioned mnemonic consequences of sharing personal memories on social media extend to instances when they are shared via photographs. Indeed, the motives and affordances of different types of social media and their respective content may prove critical in understanding how they shape the way individuals remember the past (Davenport et al., 2014; see also Tandoc et al., 2019). To provide some answers to these questions, our lab and colleagues conducted a couple of studies to examine the mnemonic consequences associated with selectively sharing personal information on social media by using and adapting the retrieval-induced forgetting (RIF) paradigm (Anderson et al., 1994).

Retrieval-Induced Forgetting

In the original RIF study, Anderson et al. (1994) had participants study a list of paired associates such that they were categories and exemplars of the categories. For example, participants would study *Fruit-Strawberry, Fruit-Banana, Professions-Engineer, Professions-Accountant,* and the like. In the next phase of the experiment, participants would receive selective retrieval practice such that they retrieved half of the items from half of the categories. For example, they may receive extra practice with Strawberry (e.g., Fruit-St_____), but none of the other fruits and none of the Profession items. In doing so, this created three types of items: Rp+ (retrieved item from a retrieved category; Fruit-Strawberry), Rp– (nonretrieved item from a retrieved category, e.g., Fruit-Banana), and Nrp (nonretrieved items from a nonretrieved category, e.g., all the professions). After a distractor task, the experimenter provided participants with the category names and instructed them to recall all the exemplar items from all the categories. Not surprisingly, they found that participants recalled the Rp+ items the best, given that the participants received extra retrieval practice on these items. Counterintuitively, however, they found that individuals recalled the Nrp items better than the Rp– items. That is, selectively retrieving certain items (e.g., Strawberry) impaired the retrieval of related, but not retrieved, items (e.g., Banana), whereas no such impairment was found for the nonretrieved items from the nonretrieved category (e.g., Professions). This is what is known as the RIF effect.

Critically, this line of research has been extended to more ecologically valid materials and contexts. For example, in terms of the former, Barnier et al. (2004; see also Stone, Barnier, et al., 2013; Stone, Luminet, et al., 2013) adapted the RIF paradigm to emotional and unemotional autobiographical memories and, importantly, Ford et al. (2004) adapted the paradigm using photographs.

In terms of the latter, RIF has also been extended to social interactions (Cuc et al., 2007) with more meaningful materials (e.g., autobiographical memories, Stone, Barnier, et al., 2013; justifications of war atrocities, A. Coman et al., 2014); politically sensitive topics (A. Coman & Hirst, 2012); and in the context of listening to a real public speech (Stone, Luminet, et al., 2022). Most relevant, Bilgin and Wang (2022) recently extended and demonstrated RIF in the context of social media using a modified Twitter interface (Bilgin & Wang, 2022).

Selectively Sharing Personal Photographs via Social Media

Building on Bilgin and Wang's work with Twitter, our lab and colleagues over the years have begun examining the mnemonic consequences associated with selectively sharing personal experiences in the form of photographs on social media (see also, Fawns, Chapter 7, this volume). To this end, Wong and Stone (2017) developed a novel procedure to adapt the RIF paradigm to social media and photographs. Participants maintained a diary over the course of a week whereby they provided two sentences summarizing sixteen different events they personally experienced across the following four categories: happy, funny, exciting, and entertaining, with four events per category. Notably, they also had to take a photograph associated with each event. After the diary week concluded, the experimenter reached out to each participant and instructed them to share half of the photographs from half of the categories via Instagram. Participants then returned to the lab, where they completed a recall and recognition test for all the summaries and photographs, respectively. While there were no significant differences in terms of recognizing their own photographs (relative to lures or in terms of RIF) or any association between social endorsements (i.e., likes and comments), they did find the standard RIF effect when recalling the descriptions of each event. That is, participants recalled the descriptions of the photographs shared on Instagram the best. However, they recalled the related but not shared descriptions of photographs worse than those descriptions of photographs unrelated and not shared on Instagram.

While promising and suggestive, the Wong and Stone (2017) study suffered from several limitations. First and foremost, the study was significantly underpowered due to dropout rates and failures to follow the experimental protocol: Sixty-seven participants were recruited; however, of those, forty dropped out before completing the study, and a further twelve violated the experimental protocol, thereby excluding them from the final analysis. This left a paltry fifteen participants for the final analysis. And second, there is some concern surrounding the similarities across categories (i.e., the Rp+/Rp– and Nrp photographs all consisted of positive emotion categories). More distinct categories would be needed to better mirror and extrapolate the RIF paradigm to social media. Last, while erring on the side of ecological validity, the "noise" associated with this more applied study makes it difficult to ascertain what might be driving their results.

Thus, to address these issues, our lab and colleagues developed two new studies (Vasquez et al., 2022). The first study attempted to minimize the amount of noise associated with the Wong and Stone (2017) study. To do so, in Study 1, Vasquez and colleagues found and created several photographs and associated summaries, respectively, for participants to study/learn and then selectively share on social media. Study 2 attempted to increase ecological validity by having participants, again, like Wong and Stone, record their own events and selectively share associated photographs on social media. Each of these studies are described and discussed in turn.

Study 1 consisted of three phases over the course of three days: (1) study phase; (2) selective sharing phase; and (3) final recognition and recall phase. On Day 1 of the study phase, participants received an email with a link to a Qualtrics slideshow. They were instructed to carefully study and remember twenty-four experimenter-contrived photographs and descriptions in the slideshow. There were six categories (i.e., food, college, work, family, friends, and weather) in which four photographs and descriptions were associated with each category (food and weather always acted as controls for primacy and recency effects and thus were not analyzed). Day 2 was the selective sharing phase, whereby participants received an email instructing them to share four photographs and descriptions from the slideshow on Instagram, two each from two different categories (e.g., college and work, but not family and friends). On Day 3, participants completed the final recognition and recall phase.

Overall, the results did *not* reveal a RIF effect: Participants recalled more correct details for those photographs and descriptions shared on social media (i.e., Rp+). There was no difference between the number of correct details for the related but not shared (Rp–) and unrelated and not shared photographs and descriptions (Nrp). However, the inverse was also true: Participants recalled fewer incorrect details for the Rp+ photographs and descriptions and more incorrect details for the Rp– and Nrp photographs and descriptions (see Figure 4.1). However, due to the depersonalized nature of the material, it is possible that these results may not extend to more meaningful and personal material.

To address this concern, Study 2 semireplicated Wong and Stone's (2017) study using the social media platform Facebook (Vasquez et al., 2022). This study spanned fourteen days and included daily diaries. Participants were instructed to take a photograph that pertained to a particular category (i.e., food, weather, college, work, personal relationships, and professional relationships) each day for six days and answer detailed questions about the surrounding information of each photograph (i.e., What was the approximate temperature at the time of this photograph? What color was the bottom half of your clothing? And there are others). Day 1 was dedicated to explaining the procedures of the study. Between Days 2 and 7, participants were sent a daily diary whereby they uploaded one photograph per category (six photographs per day) and answered fifteen to eighteen detailed questions per photograph. On Day 8 they were instructed to share half of the photographs from half of the categories to their personal

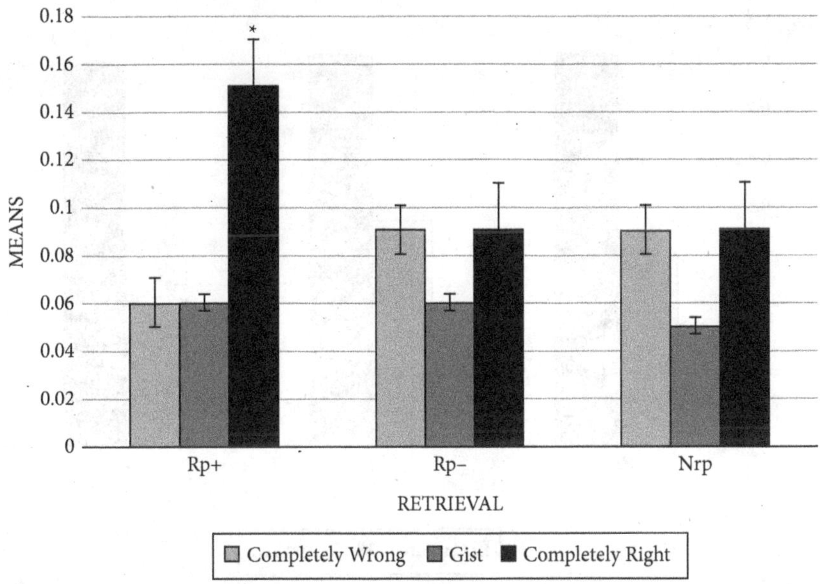

Figure 4.1 Details reported by retrieval and accuracy (Study 1).

Facebook page (e.g., the first three photographs uploaded in the college category and the last three photographs uploaded in the personal relationship category). Their final recall, like Study 1, did not show the traditional RIF effect (i.e., details of the photographs shared on social media did not induce forgetting of the details of the related but not shared photographs). However, there was an interaction between retrieval type and detail type, such that participants remembered the captured details (i.e., the details captured in the photograph vs. those details not captured in the photograph) associated with the shared photographs (Rp+) more than captured details in the related but not shared photographs (Rp–) and the unrelated and not shared photographs (Nrp; see Figure 4.2).

Overall, the "picture" emerging supports the results of Wang et al. (2017): Sharing photographs on social media similarly enhances memorability of the captured details of the shared photograph relative to the uncaptured details of the shared photograph and the photographs not shared on social media (Barasch et al., 2017; in this volume, see also Fawns, Chapter 7; Johnson & Morley, 2021; Risko et al., Chapter 5; Standing et al., 1970; Storm et al., Chapter 6; but see Henkel, 2014; Henkel et al., 2021). Despite these results and their support for prior research, there were some methodological issues in both studies that are worth highlighting to improve and facilitate future research in this domain.

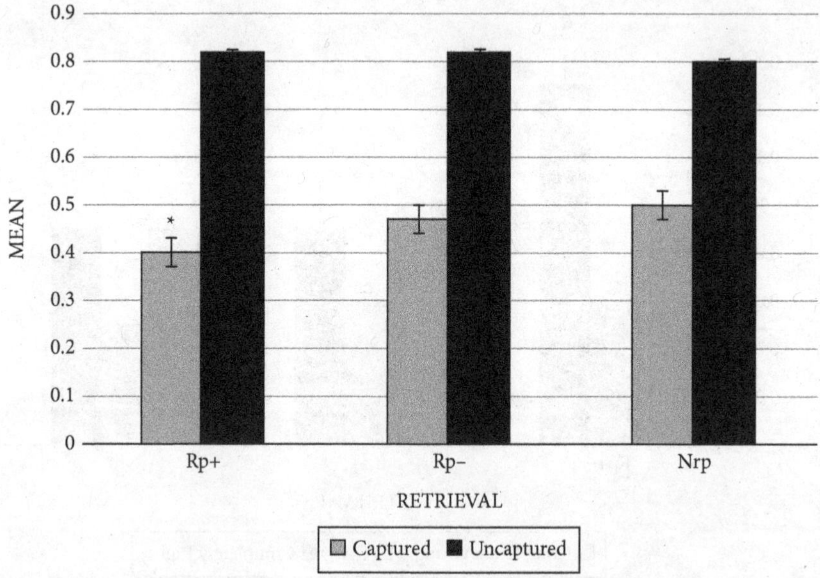

Figure 4.2 Accuracy scores by retrieval and captured versus uncaptured details (Study 2).

Methodological Issues Associated with Social Media Research

Any attempts to examine how individuals and groups remember "in the wild" (see, e.g., Hoskins, Chapter 3, this volume; Wagoner et al., 2020) is strewed with pitfalls and difficulties, ranging from attempts to maintain some form of internal validity to difficulties in discerning and analyzing complex and rich data. But as other researchers have noted (e.g., Marsh & Rajaram, 2019; Storm & Soares, in press), the Internet and social media are particularly arduous domains to conduct psychological research, as my own lab can attest. In what follows, we highlight some of the trials and tribulations (i.e., attrition rates, ecological validity, and the evolving nature of social media) my colleagues and I encountered as we conducted this line of research in the hopes of pooling our mishaps such that we can learn from each other and help streamline and troubleshoot potentially problematic methodological issues in the future before they arise. In doing so, we hope to expedite the conduction and completion of sound, rigorous research examining the motives and mnemonic consequences associated with social media usage (in this volume, see also Merrill, Chapter 15, for a discussion of methodological considerations). Note, however, while we discuss them separately, they are all intimately intertwined (a further issue to address!).

Attrition Rates

Conducting social media research is labor intensive, in terms of both coordinating the study and coding the data. However, it is also labor intensive and intrusive for the participants. Assuming one is pushing for ecological validity, researchers are asking participants to share information on their personal social media sites, which may raise concerns on the part of the participant as well as questions from their friends, family, and/or followers. As our first foray into social media research made clear (i.e., Wong & Stone, 2017), participants are prone to withdraw and/or fail to complete the experimental protocol. The reasons why would be speculative. Regardless, this is something researchers are going to have to grapple with to avoid staggering attrition rates through either the ingenuity of a "faux" and, in turn, closed social media site (for more control) or more traditional, yet high, compensation rates. Indeed, the principal concern surrounding attrition rates is a self-selection bias whereby external and internal validity are compromised. Under these circumstances it then becomes unclear what characteristics of the sample are driving their willingness and/or motives to complete the experiment (see, e.g., Zhou & Fishbach, 2016) and, in turn, biasing the results.

Ecological Validity

Anyone interested in social media research should be interested in ecological validity. The variety and immensity of social media platforms cannot completely be captured in a lab or more internally valid setting. This is not to say that more lab-based research cannot inform social media research; indeed, that is precisely the guiding principle of our lab (e.g., Vasquez et al., 2022; see also Bilgin & Wang, 2022). However, the goal should be to build up to individuals sharing their personal and public information via real social media platforms and allow users to interact with their shared content as naturally as possible (e.g., revisiting their shared content when receiving a like or comment). Only through such research will a more accurate and holistic understanding surrounding the motives and mnemonic consequences associated with social media usage emerge. As has been noted elsewhere (e.g., Eliseev & Marsh, 2021; Marsh & Rajaram, 2019; Sherman et al., 2016; Stone & Wang, 2019; Storm & Soares, in press), a multitude of factors (e.g., "likes," comments, its semipermanence, manipulation of photos/narratives, etc.) may facilitate or impair how individuals engage with social media and influence their memory. Perhaps the crux of the problem is not each factor individually, as they can be isolated and examined "in the lab" to a certain degree. Rather, the critical question is how they may interact and lead to varying degrees of mnemonic consequences. For example, if one of the authors shares a photograph of their trip to Morocco on social media, how they come to subsequently remember this trip will likely depend, in part, on whether they received five likes and twenty comments (and the content of the comments!) or twenty likes and five comments (but see, e.g., Zubiaga & Ji, 2014). Whether such a supposition is correct or not is an empirical question, including the multitude of other combinations.

The Evolving Nature of Social Media

As with all technologies, they evolve. They become more efficient or change to better suit the needs of their customers and/or the current culture and milieu. Thus, to state that social media "evolves" is not a grand statement. However, there are two ways worth highlighting that make social media and, more generally, the Internet, qualitatively different from prior forms of technology (e.g., pen and paper). The first, less astonishing way is the additions and subtractions to any social media site (e.g., when Facebook introduced "likes" to the platform in 2009). Obviously, as additions and subtractions are made to various social media sites, researchers will have to appreciate these and incorporate them into their corpus of research to understand how said evolutions similarly change and shape the way people interact and remember the past (see also Storm & Soares, in press).

The second, and arguably more nefarious, way in which social media evolves is through its use of artificial intelligence (AI) algorithms. These algorithms fundamentally shape how each user interacts with social media. The dynamic nature of the AI algorithms is such that they can change from top-down and bottom-up. In terms of the former, the chief executive officer or an engineer of a social media platform can alter the algorithm to change the content that is deemed relevant (a concern that has, e.g., spiked on Twitter with Elon Musk taking over Twitter in October 2022 and subsequent rebranding as X). In terms of the latter, the AI algorithms change the content it deems relevant based on user demographics, choices, clicks, time elapsed, purchases, and more (Mitchell & Bagrow, 2020). Thus, on the one hand, "the powers that be" choose how the algorithms are designed and thus must be appreciated to understand how they influence the design and layout of social media. On the other hand, because of the designed algorithm, users' choices shape the content they are provided on social media. In a very real sense, not all users have the same experience when interacting with social media. Thus, researchers must appreciate the design of social media AI algorithms and how they cater and shape everyone's own experiences with their shared personal content as well as the content shared by others.

Future Research

On top of addressing the methodological issues raised above, there are numerous interesting and important avenues of future research that should be address moving forward. Here we provide a select few.

First, research is needed to bridge the gap between the motives for sharing personal (and otherwise) information on social media and how said sharing shapes how individuals remember their personal (and otherwise) past. It is likely the case that the motives individuals have for sharing any piece of information on social media will likely facilitate or impair various mnemonic consequences. Furthermore, a clinical population may reveal a different pattern of motives, such that they are more likely to share personal experiences on social media for therapeutic reasons (Croiter & Yanos, 2022; see also Lu, 2017, and Sheldon et al., 2003). Further research is needed to examine these possibilities.

Second, the present research has focused on the "producer" and personal information (see Stone & Wang, 2019). It is less clear what the mnemonic consequences are when "consuming" personal information (i.e., seeing your friend share a photograph of the two of you on your last trip to Disney World) and whether the present results extend to more public information for both the producers and consumers (e.g., sharing/viewing a *New York Times* article on Facebook). Examining both the role of the user (i.e., producer vs. consumer) and type of content (public vs. personal) will provide a more holistic understanding, of how social media use shapes the way not only individuals remember the past, but also groups (e.g., collective memories; see, e.g., Stone & Jay, 2019; Stone & Wang, 2019; Storm & Soares, in press; see Rajaram, Chapter 12, this volume).

Third, one of the criticisms and strengths of Wang et al.'s (2017) study was that they allowed participants to choose what they shared on social media. While this has the advantage of being more ecologically valid, it makes it difficult to ascertain the mechanism driving their results: Was it the actual sharing of personal experiences on social media, or were the experiences already memorable and, consequently, shared on social media? Unlike Wang et al., Vasquez et al. (2022), across both studies, controlled which photographs participants shared. Thus, to increase ecological validity, future research should replicate the methodological design of Vasquez et al. (2022) but allow individuals to choose for themselves which photographs to share on social media to examine whether their results extend to conditions that better match how individuals naturally use social media.

Last, it is worth noting that the absence of RIF in Vasquez et al.'s (2022) studies is not evidence that sharing information on social media will not lead to induced forgetting under all circumstances. Indeed, Bilgin and Wang (2022) have already provided some evidence that social media use may lead to induced forgetting. But, as prior research has shown, the RIF effect does have certain boundary conditions (e.g., when information is integrated, RIF is eliminated; see Anderson & McCulloch, 1999). Additionally, retrieval (or at least attempting to retrieve; Storm et al., 2006) is key to eliciting induced forgetting (Anderson et al., 1994; see also Karpicke & Roediger, 2007, for the importance of retrieval). It is possible that the adapted paradigms used by Vasquez et al. (2022) may have prevented retrieving and/or it may not have even been necessary to retrieve their memories of the event when simply sharing personal photographs on social media. The possibilities are plentiful. Thus, further research is needed to better understand the cognitive/mnemonic processes undertaken when sharing personal photographs on social media and the conditions under which sharing photographs via social media may, if at all, lead to induced forgetting of the details associated with related, but not shared photographs.

Conclusion

Social media is an important means by which individuals share personal and public information with their friends, family, and the world more generally. As such, for those interested in how individuals and groups remember in the "real world," it is critically important to better understand how social media shapes the way humans think, behave, and remember. Here we have focused on the nascent research examining the motives and mnemonic consequences associated with sharing personal information on social media. We have shown how others and our lab have begun to demonstrate the varied and nuanced motives individuals have for sharing personal information on social media and how such sharing results in how individuals remember their personal past. We have also attempted to provide a nonexhaustive list of methodological issues and future research to better facilitate and expedite the development and implementation of social media research. In doing so, we hope the field will gain a fuller and more holistic understanding of how social media use shapes the way individuals and groups remember their personal and collective pasts.

References

Alea, N., & Bluck, S. (2003). Why are you telling me that? A conceptual model of the social function of autobiographical memory. *Memory, 11*, 165–178. https://doi.org/10.1080/741938207

Anderson, M. C., Bjork, R. A., & Bjork, E. L. (1994). Remembering can cause forgetting: Retrieval dynamics in long-term memory. *Journal of Experimental Psychology: Learning, Memory, and Cognition, 20*(5), 1063–1087. https://doi.org/10.1037/0278-7393.20.5.1063

Anderson, M. C., & McCulloch, K. C. (1999). Integration as a general boundary condition on retrieval-induced forgetting. *Journal of Experimental Psychology: Learning, Memory, and Cognition, 25*(3), 608–629. https://doi.org/10.1037/0278-7393.25.3.608

Auxier, B., & Anderson, M. (2021, April). Social media use in 2021. Pew Research Center. https://www.pewresearch.org/internet/wp-content/uploads/sites/9/2021/04/PI_2021.04.07_Social-Media-Use_FINAL.pdf

Barasch, A., Diehl, K., Silverman, J., & Zauberman, G. (2017). Photographic memory: The effects of volitional photo taking on memory for visual and auditory aspects of an experience. *Psychological Science, 28*(8), 1056–1066. https://doi.org/10.1177/0956797617694868

Barnier, A., Hung, L., & Conway, M. (2004). Retrieval-induced forgetting of emotional and unemotional autobiographical memories. *Cognition and Emotion, 18*(4), 457–477. https://doi.org/10.1080/0269993034000392

Bilgin, E., & Wang, Q. (2022). Remembering and forgetting information about the COVID-19 vaccine on Twitter. *Memory, 31*(2), 247–258. https://doi.org/10.1080/09658211.2022.2144892

Coman, A., & Hirst, W. (2012). Cognition through a social network: The propagation of induced forgetting and practice effects. *Journal of Experimental Psychology: General, 141*(2), 321–336. https://doi.org/10.1037/a0025247

Coman, A., Stone, C. B., Castano, E., & Hirst, W. (2014). Justifying atrocities: The effect of moral-disengagement strategies on socially shared retrieval-induced forgetting. *Psychological Science, 25*(6), 1281–1285. https://doi.org/10.1177/0956797614531024

Conway, M. A., & Pleydell-Pearce, C. W. (2000). The construction of autobiographical memories in the self-memory system. *Psychological Review, 107*(2), 261–288. https://doi.org/10.1037/0033-295X.107.2.261

Croiter, A., & Yanos, P. (2022). *Motivation for social media use among people with mental illness.* Unpublished manuscript. John Jay College of Criminal Justice, City University of New York.

Cuc, A., Koppel, J., & Hirst, W. (2007). Silence is not golden: A case for socially shared retrieval-induced forgetting. *Psychological Science, 18*(8), 727–733. https://doi.org/10.1111/j.1467-9280.2007.01967.x

Cummings, J. R., & Druss, B. G. (2011). Racial/ethnic differences in mental health service use among adolescents with major depression. *Journal of the American Academy of Child & Adolescent Psychiatry, 50*(2), 160–170. https://doi.org/10.1016/j.jaac.2010.11.004

Davenport, S. W., Bergman, S. M., Bergman, J. Z., & Fearrington, M. E. (2014). Twitter versus Facebook: Exploring the role of narcissism in the motives and usage of different social media platforms. *Computers in Human Behavior, 32*, 212–220. https://doi.org/10.1016/j.chb.2013.12.011

Del Vicario, M., Bessi, A., Zollo, F., Petroni, F., Scala, A., Caldarelli, G., & Quattrociocchi, W. (2016). The spreading of misinformation online. *Proceedings of the National Academy of Sciences of the United States of America, 113*(3), 554–559. http://doi.org/10.1073/pnas.1517441113

Echterhoff, G. (2010). Shared reality: Antecedents, processes, and consequences. *Social Cognition, 28*(3), 273–276. https://doi.org/10.1521/soco.2010.28.3.273

Ekelund, R. (2022). Fascination, nostalgia, and knowledge desire in digital memory culture: Emotions and mood work in retrospective Facebook groups. *Memory Studies, 15*(5), 1248–1262. https://doi.org/10.1177/17506980221094517

Eliseev, E. D., & Marsh, E. J. (2021). Externalizing autobiographical memories in the digital age. *Trends in Cognitive Sciences, 25*, 1072–1081. https://doi.org/10.1016/j.tics.2021.08.005

Ellison, N. B., Steinfield, C., & Lampe, C. (2007). The benefits of Facebook "friends": Social capital and college students' use of online social network sites. *Journal of Computer-Mediated Communication, 12*(4), 1143–1168. https://doi.org/10.1111/j.1083-6101.2007.00367.x

Ford, R. M., Keating, S., & Patel, R. (2004). Retrieval-induced forgetting: A developmental study. *British Journal of Developmental Psychology, 22*(4), 585–603. https://doi.org/10.1348/0261510042378272

Gallion, A. J. (n.d.). *Applying the uses and gratifications theory to social networking sites*. Indiana University. http://bit.ly/1c73Knc

Gary, F. A. (2005). Stigma: Barrier to mental health care among ethnic minorities. *Issues in Mental Health Nursing, 26*(10), 979–999. https://doi.org/10.1080/01612840500280638

Hamilton, J. L., Nesi, J., & Choukas-Bradley, S. (2022). Reexamining social media and socioemotional well-being among adolescents through the lens of the COVID-19 pandemic: A theoretical review and directions for future research. *Perspectives on Psychological Science, 17*(3), 662–679. https://doi.org/10.1177/17456916211014189

Henkel, L. A. (2014). Point-and-shoot memories: The influence of taking photos on memory for a museum tour. *Psychological Science, 25*, 396–402. https://doi.org/10.1177/0956797613504438

Henkel, L. A., Nash, R. A., & Paton, J. A. (2021). "Say cheese!": How taking and viewing photos can shape memory and cognition. In S. M. Lane & P. Atchley (Eds.), *Human capacity in the attention economy* (pp. 103–133). American Psychological Association. https://doi.org/10.1037/0000208-006

Hirst, W., & Stone, C. (2015). A unified approach to collective memory: Sociology, psychology, and the extended mind. In S. Kattago (Ed.), *The Ashgate research companion to memory studies* (pp. 103–16). Ashgate.

Horzum, M. B. (2016). Examining the relationship to gender and personality on the purpose of Facebook usage of Turkish university students. *Computers in Human Behavior, 64*, 319–328. https://doi.org/10.1016/j.chb.2016.06.010

Hou, Y., Xiong, D., Jiang, T., Song, L., & Wang, Q. (2019). Social media addiction: Its impact, mediation, and intervention. *Cyberpsychology: Journal of Psychosocial Research on Cyberspace, 13*(1), article 4. http://dx.doi.org/10.5817/CP2019-1-4

Johnson, A. J., & Morley, E. G. (2021). Sharing personal memories on ephemeral social media facilitates autobiographical memory. *Cyberpsychology, Behavior, and Social Networking, 24*(11), 745–749. https://doi.org/10.1089/cyber.2020.0511

Karpicke, J. D., & Roediger, H. L. (2007). Repeated retrieval during learning is the key to long-term retention. *Journal of Memory and Language, 57*(2), 151–162. https://doi.org/10.1016/j.jml.2006.09.004

Kircaburun, K., Jonason, P. K., & Griffiths, M. D. (2018). The Dark Tetrad traits and problematic social media use: The mediating role of cyberbullying and cyberstalking. *Personality and Individual Differences, 135*, 264–269. https://doi.org/10.1016/j.paid.2018.07.034

Lee, E. J., & Kim, Y. W. (2014). How social is Twitter use? Affiliative tendency and communication competence as predictors. *Computers in Human Behavior, 39*, 296–305. https://doi.org/10.1016/j.chb.2014.07.034

Lu, Y., Wu, Y., Liu, J., Li, J., & Zhang, P. (2017). Understanding health care social media use from different stakeholder perspectives: A content analysis of an online health community. *Journal of Medical Internet Research, 19*(4), e109. https://doi.org/ 10.2196/jmir.7087

Luchman, J. N., Bergstrom, J., & Krulikowski, C. (2014). A motives framework of social media website use: A survey of young Americans. *Computers in Human Behavior, 38*, 136–141. https://doi.org/10.1016/j.chb.2014.05.016

Marsh, E. J., & Rajaram, S. (2019). The digital expansion of the mind: Implications of Internet usage for memory and cognition. *Journal of Applied Research in Memory and Cognition, 8*(1), 1–14. https://doi.org/10.1016/j.jarmac.2018.11.001

Masciantonio, A., Bourguignon, D., Bouchat, P., Balty, M., & Rimé, B. (2021). Don't put all social network sites in one basket: Facebook, Instagram, Twitter, TikTok, and their relations with well-being during the COVID-19 pandemic. *PloS One, 16*(3), e0248384. https://doi.org/10.1371/journal.pone.0248384

Mitchell, L., & Bagrow, J. (2020, October 11). Do social media algorithms erode our ability to make decisions freely? The jury is out. *The Conversation*. https://theconversation.com/do-social-media-algorithms-erode-our-ability-to-make-decisions-freely-the-jury-is-out-140729

Nadkarni, A., & Hofmann, S. G. (2012). Why do people use Facebook? *Personality and Individual Differences, 52*(3), 243–249. https://doi.org/10.1016/j.paid.2011.11.007

Niemeyer, K., & Keightley, E. (2020). The commodification of time and memory: Online communities and the dynamics of commercially produced nostalgia. *New Media & Society, 22*(9), 1639–1662. https://doi.org/10.1177/1461444820914869

Oh, S., & Syn, S. Y. (2015). Motivations for sharing information and social support in social media: A comparative analysis of Facebook, Twitter, Delicious, You Tube, and Flickr. *Journal of the Association for Information Science and Technology, 66*(10), 2045–2060. https://doi.org/10.1002/asi.23320

Pillemer, D. B. (1998). *Momentous events, vivid memories*. Harvard University Press.

Rosenberg, M. (1965). *Society and the adolescent self-image*. Princeton University Press.

Schivinski, B., Brzozowska-Wos, M. M., Stansbury, E., Satel, J., Montag, C., & Pontes, H. M. (2020). Exploring the role of social media use motives, psychological well-being, self-esteem, and affect in problematic social media use. *Frontiers in Psychology, 11*, 3576. https://doi.org/10.3389/fpsyg.2020.617140

Seidman, G. (2013). Self-presentation and belonging on Facebook: How personality influences social media use and motivations. *Personality and Individual Differences, 54*(3), 402–407. https://doi.org/10.1016/j.paid.2012.10.009

Sheldon, K., Williams, G., & Joiner, T. (2003). *Self-determination theory in the clinic: Motivating physical and mental health*. Yale University Press.

Sherman, L. E., Payton, A. A., Hernandez, L. M., Greenfield, P. M., & Dapretto, M. (2016). The power of the like in adolescence effects of peer influence on neural and behavioral responses to social media. *Psychological Science, 27*(7), 1027–1035. https://doi.org/10.1177/0956797616645673

Singelis, T. M. (1994). The measurement of independent and interdependent self-construals. *Personality and Social Psychology Bulletin, 20*(5), 580–591. https://doi.org/10.1177%2F0146167294205014

Standing, L., Conezio, J., & Haber, R. N. (1970). Perception and memory for pictures: Single-trial learning of 2500 visual stimuli. *Psychonomic Science, 19*(2), 73–74. https://doi.org/10.3758/BF03337426

Stone, C. B., Barnier, A., Sutton, J., & Hirst, W. (2013). Forgetting our personal past: Socially shared retrieval-induced forgetting of autobiographical memories. *Journal of Experimental Psychology: General, 142*(4), 1084–1099. https://doi.org/10.1037/a0030739

Stone, C. B., Guan, L., LeBarbera, G., Ceren, M., Garcia, B., Huie, K., Stump, C., & Wang, Q. (2022). Why do people share memories online? An examination of the motives and characteristics of social media users. *Memory, 30*(4), 450–464.

Stone, C. B., & Jay, A. C. V. (2019). From the individual to the collective: The emergence of a psychological approach to collective memory. *Applied Cognitive Psychology, 33*, 504–515. https://doi.org/10.1002/acp.3564

Stone, C. B., Luminet, O., & Hirst, W. (2013). Induced forgetting and reduced confidence in our personal past? The consequences of selectively retrieving emotional autobiographical memories. *Acta Psychologica, 144*(2), 250–257. https://doi.org/10.1016/j.actpsy.2013.06.019

Stone, C. B., Luminet, O., Jay, A. C., Klein, O., Licata, L., & Hirst, W. (2022). Do public speeches induce "collective" forgetting? The Belgian king's 2012 summer speech as a case study. *Memory Studies, 15*(4), 713–730. https://doi.org/10.1177/1750698019900949

Stone, C. B., & Wang, Q. (2019). From conversations to digital communication: The mnemonic consequences of consuming and producing information via social media. *Topics in Cognitive Science, 11*(4), 774–793. https://doi.org/10.1111/tops.12369

Storm, B. C., Bjork, E. L., Bjork, R. A., & Nestojko, J. F. (2006). Is retrieval success a necessary condition for retrieval-induced forgetting? *Psychonomic Bulletin and Review, 13*(6), 1023–1027. https://doi.org/10.3758/BF03213919

Storm, B. C., & Soares, J. S. (in press). Memory in the digital age. In M. J. Kahana & A. D. Wagner (Eds.), *Handbook of human memory: Foundations and applications*. Oxford University Press.

Tamir, D., Templeton, E., Ward, A., & Zaki, J. (2018). Media usage diminishes memory for experiences. *Journal of Experimental Social Psychology*, *76*, 161–168. https://doi.org/10.1016/j.jesp.2018.01.006

Tandoc, E. C., Jr., Lou, C., & Min, V. L. H. (2019). Platform-swinging in a poly-social-media context: How and why users navigate multiple social media platforms. *Journal of Computer-Mediated Communication*, *24*(1), 21–35. https://doi.org/10.1093/jcmc/zmy022

Vasquez, A. N., Dockery, S., Karanian, J., Wang, Q., & Stone, C. B. (2022). Sharing personal memories on social media and its mnemonic consequences. *Mind, Media & Memory*, *1*, e12.

Wagoner, B., de Luna, I. B., & Zadeh, S. (Eds.). (2020). *Memory in the wild*. IAP.

Wang, Q. (2013). *The autobiographical self in time and culture*. Oxford University Press.

Wang, Q. (2020). Creation of the purposes of online memory sharing scale. *International Journal of Applied Psychology*, *10*(3), 65–70. https://doi.org/10.31234/osf.io/jh5sx

Wang, Q., Lee, D., & Hou, Y. (2017). Externalising the autobiographical self: sharing personal memories online facilitated memory retention. *Memory*, *25*(6), 772–776. https://doi.org/10.1080/09658211.2016.1221115

Whiting, A., & Williams, D. (2013). Why people use social media: a uses and gratifications approach. *Qualitative Market Research: An International Journal*, *16*(4), 362–369. https://doi.org/10.1108/QMR-06-2013-0041

Wong, C. L., & Stone, C. B. (2017). *Retrieval-induced forgetting via social media: The mnemonic consequences of posting photographs on* Instagram. Unpublished manuscript. John Jay College of Criminal Justice, City University of New York.

Zhou, H., & Fishbach, A. (2016). The pitfall of experimenting on the web: How unattended selective attrition leads to surprising (yet false) research conclusions. *Journal of Personality and Social Psychology*, *111*(4), 493–504. https://doi.org/10.1037/pspa0000056

Zubiaga, A., & Ji, H. (2014). Tweet, but verify: Epistemic study of information verification on twitter. *Social Network Analysis and Mining*, *4*(1), 163. https://doi.org/10.1007/s13278-014-0163-y

PART III

THE "GOOGLE EFFECT"?

5

Varieties of Offloading Memory

A Framework*

Evan F. Risko, Megan O. Kelly, Xinyi Lu, and April E. Pereira

The Internet Age has ushered in a renewed interest in how we use technology in the service of cognition (e.g., Carr, 2008; Clark, 2010; Ferguson et al., 2015; Marsh & Rajaram, 2019; Risko, 2019; Risko & Gilbert, 2016; Sparrow et al., 2011; Storm et al., 2017; Wang, 2019). One domain that has attracted much attention is the use of technology to offload memory. For example, the Internet affords a near-limitless capacity to store information that might instead, at some time in the past, have been stored in our internal, biological memory (hereon simply *internal memory*). Offloading information we would like to remember to external locations is, of course, not new. That said, when understood as an external memory store, the Internet can be argued to represent a sizable leap forward, for example, in sheer capacity, ease of access, and other potentially important features (e.g., its shareability with and availability to others). Motivated, at least in part, by these and related issues, recent research has aimed to better understand the integration of external memory stores in our day-to-day memory activities (e.g., Eskritt & Ma, 2014; Gilbert, 2015a, 2015b; Grinschgl et al., 2021; Kelly & Risko, 2019a, 2019b, 2022a, 2022b; Lu et al., 2020, 2021; Meyerhoff et al., 2021; Park et al., 2022; Pereira et al., 2022; Risko & Dunn, 2015; Risko et al., 2019; Redshaw et al., 2018; Runge et al., 2019; Sparrow et al., 2011; Schooler & Storm, 2021; Storm & Stone, 2015).

In this chapter, our goal is to develop a framework for situating the different uses of an external memory store with the aims of both organizing existing research and guiding future research on offloading memory. We begin by describing two dimensions that can be used to characterize how an external memory store is being used. We then consider the consequences of external memory store use for cognition and performance within this framework and

* This work was supported by a Discovery Grant (#04091) from the Natural Sciences and Engineering Research Council of Canada (NSERC), an Early Researcher Award from the Province of Ontario (#ER14-10-258), funding from the Canada Foundation for Innovation and Ontario Research Fund (#37872) from the Canada Research Chairs (#950-232147) program to EFR, and Alexander Graham Bell Canada Graduate Scholarships from NSERC to MOK, XL, and AEP.

Evan F. Risko, Megan O. Kelly, Xinyi Lu, and April E. Pereira, *Varieties of Offloading Memory* In: *The Remaking of Memory in the Age of the Internet and Social Media.* Edited by: Qi Wang and Andrew Hoskins, Oxford University Press.
 DOI: 10.1093/oso/9780197661260.003.0005

situate existing research within it. Finally, we consider briefly how this framework could help guide the design of external memory stores and particular challenges raised by the Internet as a form of external memory store.

The Framework

The framework developed here consists of two dimensions—the substitutive-duplicative dimension and the redistribution dimension. Consider, first, the substitutive-duplicative dimension. This dimension captures the extent to which people, when storing to-be-remembered information in an external store, also attempt to store the same information internally. At one end of the continuum, the external store is used in place of any attempts to store information internally; we refer to this use of an external store as *substitutive*. At the other end of the continuum, the external store is used *in addition* to internal storage attempts, an approach that we refer to as *duplicative*. Here, "attempts to store" is meant to denote the controlled, intentional, or active steps that a person can take to store information in their internal memory (e.g., rehearsal, imagery). Furthermore, store here is used, in both the internal and external memory case, to denote activities taken to make available some information at a future date (e.g., I try to store the items I need to purchase so that I can select the correct items when out shopping). We would expect "attempts" to store information in our internal memory to be experienced as cognitively effortful, consistent with Inzlicht and coworkers' (2018) definition of effort as

> The subjective intensification of mental and/or physical activity in the service of meeting some goal. . . . Effort is a volitional, intentional process, something that organisms apply, and as such, it corresponds to what organisms are actively doing and not to what is passively happening to them.

As such, we refer to such attempts to store as *effortful mnemonic activities*, which can be distinguished from the more automatic, unintentional, or passive processes that can also lead to information being stored in one's internal memory.

To illustrate, imagine that a person has generated a list of items they need to pick up at the supermarket on the way home from work. In the absence of an external memory store, they might engage in mental rehearsal (i.e., some kind of effortful mnemonic activity) with the aim of storing their shopping list in their internal memory (see Figure 5.1, Panel A). Imagine, now, that the person has access to an external memory store, for example, a cloud-based note-taking application that lets them store information online and access it via an appropriate

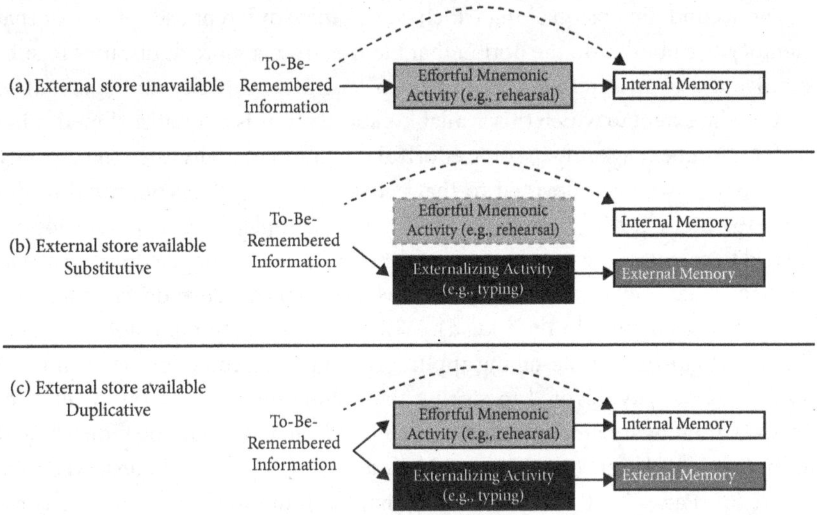

Figure 5.1 Storing to-be-remembered information (A) when an external memory store is unavailable, (B) when an external memory store is available and used in a substitutive manner, and (C) when an external memory store is available and used in a duplicative manner. The dotted lines represent noncontrolled processes leading to storage in one's internal memory. See text for more details.

Internet-connected device like a smartphone. In the latter case, they could use that application to forgo the mental rehearsal (see Figure 5.1, Panel B). That is, the person could access the note-taking application and type the items they need to pick up at the supermarket into it (i.e., an externalizing activity) *instead of* engaging in the mental rehearsal (i.e., effortful mnemonic activity). This would represent the substitutive use of the external memory store.

Alternatively, one could use the external memory store in more of a duplicative manner (see Figure 5.1, Panel C). In this case, the person would engage in some kind of effortful mnemonic activity (e.g., rehearsal) with the aim of storing the to-be-remembered information internally *in addition to* engaging in the externalizing activity required to store the information externally. In this duplicative case, the internal and external contributions are doing functionally equivalent work (i.e., acting as stores for the same to-be-remembered information), although, of course, not in the same manner. This redundant storage might be thought of as a kind of insurance to minimize the likelihood of losing the information. Returning to the shopping list example, in the duplicative case, the individual would engage in mental rehearsal with the aim of storing the list in their internal memory as well as access the cloud-based note-taking application via the Internet and type the list into it.

The second dimension along which we organize different uses of an external memory store builds on the notion that moving from a more duplicative to substitutive use of an external store "frees up" cognitive capacity and is meant to capture the extent to which this available capacity is or is not redistributed. That is, if one forgoes engaging in some effortful mnemonic activity, then the capacity that would have been devoted to that activity can be either conserved or devoted to other effortful cognitive activities. For example, imagine if our shopper wished to calculate the cost per unit of different cereals (imagine for the sake of argument that they want to make the most economical cereal decision and are doing this calculation in their head). With an external memory store available (i.e., the cloud-based note-taking application), a person could forgo the effortful mnemonic activity devoted to storing their shopping list (i.e., the mental rehearsal), thereby freeing up capacity. This freed capacity could be redistributed to mental calculation (see Figure 5.2, Panel B) or it could be conserved (see Figure 5.2, Panel C). It is worth noting that the framework takes as a basic assumption that humans have a limited capacity for information processing. The capacity referred to herein might best be equated with one's working memory capacity (Cowan, 2010). Furthermore, we also assume that the extent to which this capacity is deployed will be related to the experience of cognitive effort (see Kurzban et al., 2013).

In summary, we suggest that external memory use can be described along at least two dimensions: (1) the *substitutive-duplicative* dimension, which represents what people attempt to store in their internal memory when using an external memory store, and (2) the *redistribution* dimension, which represents what people do with any processing capacity "freed" by using that external store. Next, we consider the consequences of external memory store use for cognition and performance.

Consequences for Cognition and Performance

The Internet Age represents a significant change to our technological environments. As such, researchers have explored how such changes might impact cognition. In the case of external stores, we can use the framework developed above to generate predictions about that impact. In this discussion, we focus mainly on the impact on cognitive effort and memory performance (i.e., accurate retrieval of the to-be-remembered information).

Moving along the substitutive-duplicative dimension and the redistribution dimension leads to different predictions for cognitive effort. First, if we assume for simplicity that people tend to conserve any freed capacity (i.e., do not redistribute it to other processing), moving from a more substitutive to a more

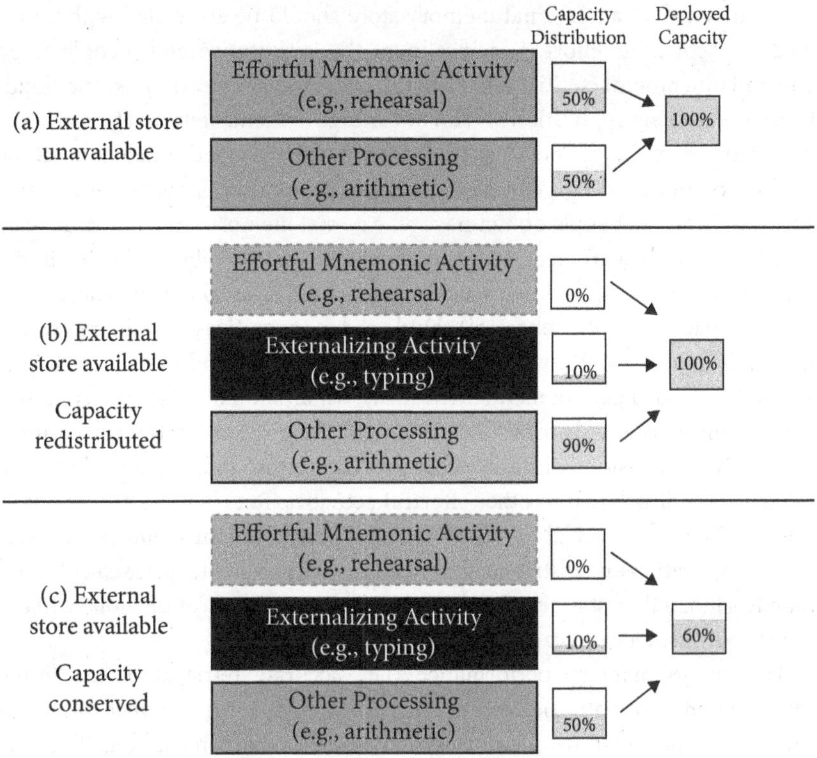

Figure 5.2 Redistribution of available capacity across different scenarios. In (A) individuals do not have an external store available and decide to distribute 50% of their available capacity to each process (for example). Thus, they have deployed 100% of their capacity. In (B) individuals have an external store available and use it to offload the effortful mnemonic activity and redistribute the freed capacity to other processing. Thus, no capacity is deployed to effortful mnemonic activity, some capacity (in this case 10%) is devoted to processes required to use the external store, and the remainder is deployed to other processing. All capacity has been deployed. In (C) individuals have an external store available and use it to offload the effortful mnemonic activity but do not redistribute the freed capacity to other processing (i.e., the capacity is conserved). Thus, no capacity is deployed to effortful mnemonic activity, some capacity (in this case 10%) is devoted to processes required to use the external store and to other processing (in this case 50%), and the remainder is conserved. As such, all capacity is not deployed. The figure is meant for illustrative purposes only.

duplicative use of an external memory store should be associated with an increase in cognitive effort. Specifically, at the substitutive end, people forgo effortful mnemonic activities related to memory storage (e.g., they use the cloud-based note-taking application and do not engage in mental rehearsal), and at the duplicative end, they do not (e.g., they not only use the cloud-based note-taking application but also engage in mental rehearsal). In a similar vein, relative to a situation in which people do not have an external memory store available (e.g., they have to engage in mental rehearsal), having one available and using it in a substitutive manner (e.g., they use the cloud-based note-taking application and do not engage in mental rehearsal) should reduce cognitive effort, in contrast to using it in a more duplicative manner (e.g., they use the cloud-based note-taking application and engage in mental rehearsal), which should not reduce cognitive effort. Considering redistribution, if we hold the position on the substitutive-duplicative dimension constant, effort should increase to the extent that freed capacity is redistributed to other effortful activities. Returning to our example, it would be more effortful to offload the shopping list to the cloud-based note-taking application and distribute that freed capacity to mental price calculations than to offload the list to the cloud-based note-taking application alone *without* redistributing that freed capacity.

Turning to memory performance (i.e., accurate retrieval of the to-be-remembered information), we consider two situations: performance of the entire internal-plus-external memory system (e.g., the human user together with the cloud-based note-taking application) and performance when the external store becomes (unexpectedly) unavailable (e.g., the user of the cloud-based note-taking application loses access to the Internet). The latter allows us to capture those instances in which we have used an external memory store but are deprived of its services at retrieval. When considering memory performance, the effectiveness of the particular external memory store in question becomes an important consideration. For simplicity, we will assume that the external memory store in question (when it operates as it should) provides a perfect record or copy of the information stored in it (e.g., that the cloud-based note-taking application stores the notes accurately or reliably; e.g., Pereira et al., 2022; Risko et al., 2019; Schooler & Storm, 2021; Storm & Stone, 2015). This covers a large swath of the types of external memory stores people use in their day-to-day lives, but of course, not all. For example, in many cases, external memory stores provide only partial cues to the to-be-remembered information (e.g., the string around the finger used to remind you to take your medication). For the most part, the predictions derived will be qualitatively similar, but there are likely important differences as well. For example, an external store that contains only partial cues would be unlikely to produce the same level of performance as one that contains an exact copy of the to-be-remembered information. For this reason, the comparison of different types of external stores and the consideration of their fidelity represents important future research directions.

Starting again with the assumption that people conserve any freed capacity, moving from a more substitutive to a more duplicative use of an external memory store should have little effect on the memory performance of the entire internal-plus-external memory system. For example, in our shopping example, memory performance (i.e., selecting the correct items from the supermarket) should be similar in the case where individuals store the list in the cloud-based note-taking application and do not engage in mental rehearsal (i.e., substitutive) and where individuals store the list in the cloud-based note-taking application *and* engage in mental rehearsal (i.e., duplicative). This is because in the case of the internal-plus-external memory system, the cloud-based note-taking application (i.e., the external store) provides a perfect record and is available in both cases. Given the assumed accuracy of the external store and fallibility of our internal memory, this also leads to the expectation that the memory performance of the entire internal-plus-external memory system will necessarily be superior to instances when a person does not have an external memory store available (although this might not be the case when the outcome is not memory performance). This would only be expected to be incorrect under limited circumstances (e.g., a small amount of information to be remembered for a short time); in those circumstances, memory performance would be expected to be equivalent across situations regardless of whether the external store was present. This general improvement in memory performance when the entire internal-plus-external memory system is available likely represents the central reason to use an external memory store.

More interesting predictions emerge when we consider what should happen when the external store becomes unexpectedly unavailable at the time of retrieval. In this case, if the external store was used in a more substitutive manner, then performance impairments should emerge in tests designed to index the engagement of the forgone process(es). Specifically, if engaging in effortful mnemonic activities increases the likelihood of future retrieval from our internal memory store, then forgoing those activities should lead to impairments when people are tested on their unaided ability to retrieve externally stored information. Returning to our shopping example, if the individual uses the cloud-based note-taking application to store the shopping list, forgoes mental rehearsal (i.e., substitutive), and then loses Internet access (and consequently the stored shopping list), then their ability to select the correct items from the supermarket will suffer. This impairment should emerge relative to situations wherein the external store was used in a more duplicative manner (e.g., they used the cloud-based note-taking application *and* engaged in mental rehearsal) because in that case, individuals have engaged in the effortful mnemonic activities that support internal memory. This impairment should also emerge relative to situations wherein people *do not* use an external memory store to store the to-be-remembered information (e.g., they have to engage in mental rehearsal), again because one does not forgo engaging in effortful mnemonic activities that support memory.

When one loses access to an external memory store, the duplicative use of an external store (i.e., engaging in an externalizing activity to store information externally and engaging in mnemonic effort to store it internally) and not having an external store available (i.e., where engaging in mnemonic effort to store it internally is the only option) might yield comparable memory performance. However, it depends on how demanding it is to use the external store. To the extent that the externalizing behavior is demanding, unaided performance should suffer in the duplicative case relative to when one does not have access to an external memory store. This is because using an external store in a duplicative manner creates a form of dual tasking (i.e., one is engaging in attempts to store information both internally and externally). Returning to our shopping example, trying to store the list internally (e.g., via mental rehearsal) and externally (e.g., in the cloud-based note-taking application) would lead to a performance impairment (relative to just trying to store the list internally), if engaging in the externalizing activity (e.g., typing items into the note-taking application) interferes with trying to store the list internally (assuming loss of the external store at retrieval).

Considering the performance consequences of moving along the redistribution dimension requires consideration of other aspects of performance (e.g., whatever else one might redistribute capacity to). Consider, again, the shopping and mental calculation scenario. Beginning at the substitutive end of the continuum (where there would be capacity to be redistributed), the extent to which the individual redistributes freed capacity to the calculation (i.e., the other processes) should increase performance on the calculation task (i.e., tasks supported by those processes). In the substitutive case, as long as the external memory store remains available, overall performance (on the shopping list memorization and unit price calculation tasks) should be superior to cases wherein one uses the external store in a more duplicative manner. This is because in this case capacity is devoted to storing the shopping list; thus, less is available to devote to the price calculation. In a similar vein, overall performance should be superior to cases wherein individuals do not have an external memory store available because there will be less capacity overall.

Taken together, the performance implications of using an external memory store rely heavily on how one situates themselves on the substitutive-duplicative and redistribution dimensions. In the following section, we review recent research on external memory store use and situate it within our framework.

Empirical Investigations

The substitutive use of an external memory store (with seemingly little in the way of redistribution) provides a reasonable description of several studies that we have conducted investigating the influence of external memory store availability in the context of a traditional word list memory paradigm (Kelly & Risko 2019a, 2019b, 2022a, 2022b; Lu et al., 2020, 2021; Park et al., 2022). The basic procedure consists of a series of trials, each with its own study and test phases. On each of these trials, participants are presented lists of words that they are instructed to remember (the study phase) for an upcoming memory test (the test phase). During study, participants are instructed to type (or to write down) the to-be-remembered items into a list. They are told that their list—their external memory store—will be made available to them at testing. After a brief period of having this external memory store out of view, they then perform a recall test. On the first three trials (the *trust* trials), their external memory store is, indeed, available. But on the *critical* final trials, participants do *not* have access to their external stores at the time of the recall test. The key manipulation on the critical trials is that participants are either told *before* the study phase that their external store will not be available or they are only told this *after* the study phase, on testing.

Across a number of studies, results on trust trials are typically close to ceiling and far above performance on trials wherein people do not have access to an external memory store (i.e., trials where people would be relying completely on their internal memory stores). Not surprisingly, performance is superior when people can use an external memory store compared to when they cannot. This pattern has been documented across a variety of paradigms, including cases in which the external stores do not provide a perfect record of the to-be-remembered information (e.g., Gilbert, 2015a, 2015b; Grinschgl et al., 2021; Risko & Dunn, 2015). Having the Internet function as an external memory store will serve to (arguably vastly) improve our day-to-day "memory" performance if we consider the performance of the internal-plus-external system, which most of us do.

Another consistent result to emerge from this work is that memory performance on critical trials (wherein one does not have access to an external store during recall) is significantly worse when participants expect access to their external memory stores relative to when they know they cannot expect such memory support (Kelly & Risko, 2019a, 2019b, 2022a, 2022b; Lu et al., 2020,2021; Park et al., 2022). This impairment when their external memory store is not available is consistent with the idea that participants use the external store in a more substitutive manner than in a duplicative manner. This cost has been suggested to reflect, at least in part, the intentional withdrawal of cognitive effort

(Kelly & Risko, 2022b). This draws support from demonstrations that memory phenomena more dependent on such effort are more strongly influenced by the availability of an external store than are memory phenomena less dependent on such effort (Kelly & Risko, 2019a, 2019b, 2022a, 2022b).

Consider, for example, the long-established finding that the primacy portion of the serial position curve is more influenced by rehearsal than is the recency portion (e.g., Rundus, 1971). Kelly and Risko (2019b, 2022a) demonstrated that memory for early list items tended to be more negatively affected by the unanticipated unavailability of an external memory store than did memory for later list items. Another line of research examined memory phenomena putatively dependent on associative processes, long held to occur in a more obligatory way (e.g., Roediger et al., 2001). Lu and colleagues (2020, 2021) demonstrated that the recall of critical (unpresented) lures (e.g., SLEEP) when participants are presented with lists of semantically associated items (e.g., BED, REST, AWAKE, TIRED), increased when an external store was available. Additionally, Lu and colleagues (2021) found no detriment of external store availability on the finding that recall is better from a single category word list (e.g., fruit) than a multicategory word list (e.g., fruit, furniture, animals, instruments). Indeed, in a number of experiments, this memory benefit actually increased. Taken together, this body of research provides a detailed picture of the substitutive form of using an external memory store.

In the research just outlined, it is ambiguous whether the capacity freed by forgoing effortful mnemonic processes was redistributed to other functions. One domain in which researchers have often discussed the substitutive form of offloading, under conditions where the freed capacity is redistributed to other task-related functions, is high-level problem-solving (e.g., Scaife & Rogers, 1996; Vallée-Tourangeau et al., 2016; Zhang & Norman, 1994). For example, people might use an external representation of a problem (e.g., a diagram) instead of representing that information internally, thus freeing resources for problem-solving. Consistent with this idea, Vallée-Tourangeau and colleagues (2016) compared performance in calculating sums across a low-interactivity condition, wherein no external resource was available, to a high-interactivity condition, wherein participants could physically move wooden tokens to aid in their calculations. The researchers also crossed this manipulation with an articulatory suppression manipulation designed to tax working memory during performance. Critically, Vallée-Tourangeau and colleagues (2016) found that having the external resource available improved performance most in the condition with articulatory suppression, suggesting that the participants with the wooden tokens available could better deal with the added load. One interpretation of this result is that the participants used the tokens as a kind of external memory store for parts of the problem, forgoing storing that information in working memory (i.e., a substitutive use of the store) and thus freeing capacity to better deal with the secondary task (i.e., redistributing the freed capacity), thus improving performance relative to a situation in which that external store was not available.

Evidence for what might be considered a more duplicative use of an external store comes from studies examining the influence of external store reliability (Pereira et al., 2022; Risko et al., 2019; Runge et al., 2019; Schooler & Storm, 2021; Storm & Stone, 2015). Pereira and colleagues (2022) examined the influence of external store reliability on the likelihood that people endorse the information in their external memory stores. This work built on a demonstration by Risko and colleagues (2019) that participants often endorse information as having been studied despite that information having been surreptitiously inserted into their external memory stores after study. Briefly, Risko and colleagues (2019) presented participants with lists of unrelated words and had them store those words in a file for a later memory test. During a distractor task, a novel word (not studied) was inserted into the external memory stores of participants when their store was out of their view. Critically, at retrieval, participants rarely noticed the insertion, choosing to report the inserted word as having actually been presented at study (i.e., implying that they had externally stored it themselves). Risko and colleagues (2019) proposed that this susceptibility to external store manipulation might have resulted from participants forgoing the storage or maintenance of the items in internal memory and hence not having the internal memory fidelity necessary to reject the inserted items as having been presented at study. To use the terminology introduced in this chapter, Risko and colleagues (2019) suggested that the participants used the external store in a more substitutive manner, thereby leaving themselves vulnerable to external memory manipulation.

Returning to the evidence of duplicative use, Pereira and colleagues (2022) reasoned that people should be less likely to use the external store in a substitutive manner if they doubt the store's reliability. As a result, people should be less likely to endorse the inserted item. Consistent with this prediction, Pereira and colleagues demonstrated that an explicit notification—a warning—of a previous manipulation of the external store that they had been using led to participants displaying decreased susceptibility to a subsequent manipulation of that store at test (i.e., less endorsement of the inserted item). Thus, participants appeared to be shifting from a more substitutive to a more duplicative use of the external store as a function of their beliefs about its reliability (also see Runge et al., 2019; Storm & Stone, 2015).

Taken together, it seems clear that the framework described here provides a means of bringing together a diverse set of findings under the same proverbial roof. That said, much work remains to be done in understanding the varieties of offloading memory, as well as the broader memorial consequences of our relationship with technologies such as the Internet (e.g., Storm et al., Chapter 6 this volume). While our general approach has focused on deriving theoretical implications from controlled experiments, work exploring these sorts of questions in more natural settings will also continue to be important in bettering this understanding (e.g., Fawns, Chapter 7 this volume).

Design Considerations: Toward Better Offloading Tools

The framework offered here captures both a number of different uses of an external memory store and the cognitive and performance consequences that we would expect from enacting them. As such, this framework could help to inform the design of the external memory stores that we employ in our day-to-day lives. One interesting area to consider is how to mitigate the costs of using an external memory store in a substitutive manner, with such costs most evident when we unexpectedly lose access to that store. Ideally, we could mitigate these costs without (completely) losing the benefits (in terms of effort savings and accuracy) when the store is available. One option might be to design a low-effort task that one could perform in conjunction with the externalization activity. This would then improve the likelihood of recall from one's internal memory store (in a manner similar to engaging in an effortful mnemonic activity) should the external store be unavailable. For example, after someone types an important date into one's calendar (i.e., an externalizing activity), a prompt that asks the user, "Have we got the information right?" might result in a retrieval that would benefit later memory. Further, one could customize the frequency of these prompts. This would be consistent with the well-established testing effect (e.g., Roediger & Karpicke, 2006), wherein testing memory can later lead to better performance than a further study opportunity. Other possibilities could be for the tool to suggest a stock picture or an AI generated image of the event for the user to include or asking for a quick doodle by the user to represent the event, thereby leveraging our superior memories for images compared to plain text (Paivio, 1991; Wammes et al., 2016). The design of such aids would allow users to better reap the benefits of external memory stores while minimizing the associated costs. In Chapter 7 of this book, Fawns discusses further the implications of the Internet for the use and design of supports meant to aid future remembering.

Offloading in the Internet Age

As noted in our Introduction, the Internet represents a recent form of external memory store. While the ability to store information online shares many characteristics with other external memory stores, storing information online has features that make it unlike the external stores that came before. One feature worth considering is that when we store our memories online, those memories are often accessible by others, whether by design (e.g., sharing one's calendar) or not (e.g., hackers). As further discussed in following chapters (e.g., see Worcman and Garde-Hansen's Chapter 18 in this volume), this feature likely represents an important and interesting connection between individual and community, allowing for more developed collective and cultural memory keeping (although not free from hidden agendas; see this volume's Chapter 13 by Smit). This accessibility also introduces the potential for a novel form of "memory" manipulation. If we trust a particular store to be reliable, then manipulations of its contents are, in an important sense, functionally equivalent to manipulations of our internal memory. For example, if a bad actor were to gain access to and change a shopping list we stored online, then this could lead to errors in selecting items for purchase. As noted in the Empirical Investigations section above, Risko and colleagues (2019) as well as Pereira and colleagues (2022) demonstrated individuals' susceptibility to this exact type of manipulation. When individuals had their external memory stores manipulated, they often did not notice and endorsed the information in the external store as their own. While the consequences in our shopping example might be rather mundane, it is easy to imagine cases where such manipulation might carry more serious consequences (e.g., doctor's appointments, medication schedules, emergency phone numbers). More broadly, when our external memories are accessible to others, as in the case of the Internet, we face a novel kind of endorsement problem (Arango-Muñoz, 2013). That is, how do we decide that the information in our external memory stores is veridical? Future research examining this question and others that emerge from the use of the Internet as an external memory store promise further insights into how we think together with technology and how we might intercede to optimize those interactions. The importance of continuing to address these types of questions is highlighted by the numerous findings that suggest technologies like the Internet represent a potential to both amplify memorial capabilities in some respects and diminish them in others (see Chapter 6 this volume).

Conclusion

Understanding the intersection between cognition and technology represents a fundamental challenge for cognitive scientists. How do we think about thinking when thinking becomes so deeply intertwined with a technology like the Internet (Carr, 2008; Risko et al., 2016; Sparrow et al., 2011)? We have focused on one form that such an interaction can take, namely, the Internet as a means of storing to-be-remembered information—an external memory. We have presented a framework to capture the different ways that people can integrate external memory stores into their cognitive activities, the varieties of offloading memory, and the resulting consequences for cognition and performance. This framework represents one attempt to capture the complexity of this situation, and we hope that it will contribute to the accumulating empirical and theoretical work on offloading memory in particular and distributed cognition more generally. The use of the Internet as an external memory store, of course, represents only one form that such interactions can take. How the Internet comes to influence our thinking rests in the many possible forms that it can take, many of which are discussed in other chapters in this volume.

References

Arango-Muñoz, S. (2013). Scaffolded memory and metacognitive feelings. *Review of Philosophy and Psychology, 4*, 135–152.

Carr, N. (2008). Is Google making us stupid? *Yearbook of the National Society for the Study of Education, 107*(2), 89–94.

Clark, A. (2010). Memento's revenge: The extended mind, extended. In R. Menary (Ed.), *The extended mind* (pp. 43–66). MIT Press.

Cowan, N. (2010). The magical mystery four: How is working memory capacity limited, and why? *Current Directions in Psychological Science, 19*(1), 51–57.

Eskritt, M., & Ma, S. (2014). Intentional forgetting: Note-taking as a naturalistic example. *Memory & Cognition, 42*(2), 237–246.

Ferguson, A. M., McLean, D., & Risko, E. F. (2015). Answers at your fingertips: Access to the Internet influences willingness to answer questions. *Consciousness and Cognition, 37*, 91–102.

Gilbert, S. J. (2015a). Strategic offloading of delayed intentions into the external environment. *Quarterly Journal of Experimental Psychology, 68*(5), 971–992.

Gilbert, S. J. (2015b). Strategic use of reminders: Influence of both domain-general and task-specific metacognitive confidence, independent of object memory ability. *Consciousness and Cognition, 33*, 245–260.

Grinschgl, S., Papenmeier, F., & Meyerhoff, H. S. (2021). Consequences of cognitive offloading: Boosting performance but diminishing memory. *Quarterly Journal of Experimental Psychology, 74*(9), 1477–1496.

Inzlicht, M., Shenhav, A., & Olivola, C. Y. (2018). The effort paradox: Effort is both costly and valued. *Trends in Cognitive Sciences, 22*(4), 337–349.

Kelly, M. O., & Risko, E. F. (2019a). The isolation effect when offloading memory. *Journal of Applied Research in Memory and Cognition, 8*(4), 471–480.

Kelly, M. O., & Risko, E. F. (2019b). Offloading memory: Serial position effects. *Psychonomic Bulletin and Review, 26*(4), 1347–1353.

Kelly, M. O., & Risko, E. F. (2022a). Revisiting the influence of offloading memory on free recall. *Memory & Cognition, 50*(4), 710–721.

Kelly, M. O., & Risko, E. F. (2022b). Study effort and the memory cost of external store availability. *Cognition, 228*, 105228.

Kurzban, R., Duckworth, A., Kable, J. W., & Myers, J. (2013). An opportunity cost model of subjective effort and task performance. *Behavioral and Brain Sciences*, *36*(6), 661–679.

Lu, X., Kelly, M. O., & Risko, E. F. (2020). Offloading information to an external store increases false recall. *Cognition*, *205*, 104428.

Lu, X., Kelly, M. O., & Risko, E. F. (2021). The gist of it: Offloading memory does not reduce the benefit of list categorization. *Memory*, *30*(4), 396–411.

Marsh, E. J., & Rajaram, S. (2019). The digital expansion of the mind: Implications of internet usage for memory and cognition. *Journal of Applied Research in Memory and Cognition*, *8*(1), 1–14.

Meyerhoff, H. S., Grinschgl, S., Papenmeier, F., & Gilbert, S. J. (2021). Individual differences in cognitive offloading: a comparison of intention offloading, pattern copy, and short-term memory capacity. *Cognitive Research: Principles and Implications*, *6*(1), 34.

Paivio, A. (1991). Dual coding theory: Retrospect and current status. *Canadian Journal of Psychology/Revue canadienne de psychologie*, *45*(3), 255–287.

Park, J. S., Kelly, M. O., Hargis, M. B., & Risko, E. F. (2022). The effect of external store reliance on actual and predicted value-directed remembering. *Psychonomic Bulletin & Review*, *29*(4), 1367–1376.

Pereira, A. E., Kelly, M. O., Lu, X., & Risko, E. F. (2022). On our susceptibility to external memory store manipulation: Examining the influence of perceived reliability and expected access to an external store. *Memory*, *30*(4), 412–428.

Redshaw, J., Vandersee, J., Bulley, A., & Gilbert, S. J. (2018). Development of children's use of external reminders for hard-to-remember intentions. *Child Development*, *89*(6), 2099–2108.

Risko, E. F. (2019). Examining the implications of Internet usage for memory and cognition: Prospects and promise. *Journal of Applied Research in Memory and Cognition*, *8*(1), 36–39.

Risko, E. F., & Dunn, T. L. (2015). Storing information in-the-world: Metacognition and cognitive offloading in a short-term memory task. *Consciousness and Cognition*, *36*, 61–74.

Risko, E. F., Ferguson, A. M., & McLean, D. (2016). On retrieving information from external knowledge stores: Feeling-of-findability, feeling-of-knowing and Internet search. *Computers in Human Behavior*, *65*, 534–543.

Risko, E. F., & Gilbert, S. J. (2016). Cognitive offloading. *Trends in Cognitive Sciences*, *20*(9), 676–688.

Risko, E. F., Kelly, M. O., Patel, P., & Gaspar, C. (2019). Offloading memory leaves us vulnerable to memory manipulation. *Cognition*, *191*, 103954.

Roediger, H. L., & Karpicke, J. D. (2006). Test-enhanced learning: Taking memory tests improves long-term retention. *Psychological Science*, *17*(3), 249–255.

Roediger, H. L., Watson, J. M., McDermott, K. B., & Gallo, D. A. (2001). Factors that determine false recall: A multiple regression analysis. *Psychonomic Bulletin & Review*, *8*(3), 385–407.

Rundus, D. (1971). Analysis of rehearsal processes in free recall. *Journal of Experimental Psychology*, *89*(1), 63–77.

Runge, Y., Frings, C., & Tempel, T. (2019). Saving-enhanced performance: Saving items after study boosts performance in subsequent cognitively demanding tasks. *Memory*, *27*(10), 1462–1467.

Scaife, M., & Rogers, Y. (1996). External cognition: How do graphical representations work? *International Journal of Human-Computer Studies*, *45*(2), 185–213.

Schooler, J. N., & Storm, B. C. (2021). Saved information is remembered less well than deleted information, if the saving process is perceived as reliable. *Memory*, *29*(9), 1101–1110.

Sparrow, B., Liu, J., & Wegner, D. M. (2011). Google effects on memory: Cognitive consequences of having information at our fingertips. *Science*, *333*, 776–778.

Storm, B. C., & Stone, S. M. (2015). Saving-enhanced memory: The benefits of saving on the learning and remembering of new information. *Psychological Science*, *26*(2), 182–188.

Storm, B. C., Stone, S. M., & Benjamin, A. S. (2017). Using the Internet to access information inflates future use of the Internet to access other information. *Memory*, *25*(6), 717–723.

Vallée-Tourangeau, F., Sirota, M., & Vallée-Tourangeau, G. (2016). Interactivity mitigates the impact of working memory depletion on mental arithmetic performance. *Cognitive Research: Principles and Implications*, *1*(1), 26.

Wammes, J. D., Meade, M. E., & Fernandes, M. A. (2016). The drawing effect: Evidence for reliable and robust memory benefits in free recall. *Quarterly Journal of Experimental Psychology*, *69*(9), 1752–1776.

Wang, Q. (2019). The individual mind in the active construction of its digital niche. *Journal of Applied Research in Memory and Cognition*, *8*(1), 25–28.

Zhang, J., & Norman, D. A. (1994). Representations in distributed cognitive tasks. *Cognitive Science*, *18*(1), 87–122.

6

The Changing Dynamics and Consequences of Memory Retrieval in the Age of the Internet

Benjamin C. Storm, Dana-Lis Bittner, and Jeremy K. Yamashiro

Memory provides the ability to learn and recall information. It is also constructive, susceptible to bias and distortion, and limited by how information is learned and the cues that happen to be available at a given time (Roediger & Guynn, 1996; Schacter, 1999). Retrieval plays a pivotal role in the functioning of memory, serving to update it in meaningful ways by making certain information and experiences more and less accessible than it would have been otherwise (Anderson et al., 1994; Karpicke & Roediger, 2006). In the current chapter, we consider how access to the Internet has altered—and will continue to alter—the nature, roles, and consequences of retrieval, focusing on how the Internet is changing the way information and experiences are remembered. In pursuit of this goal, we discuss evidence that people are increasingly relying on the Internet as part of an integrated transactive memory system, how the act of looking for information online can replace and/or affect internal retrieval processes, and how these dynamics have influenced the metacognitive judgments people make about what they know. In some ways, the Internet has the potential to expand the power of memory, providing access to more information than would otherwise be possible. In other ways, it may disrupt memory, preventing the types of flexible and constructive processes that are critical for the adaptive use and updating of memory. We discuss these and other potential consequences, focusing on what is known now, and on the questions and methodological challenges that remain to be investigated.

Transactive Memory and Digital Amnesia

People have long relied on external resources to expand the functions and abilities of memory. Such reliance has included everything from the use of fingers to count, abacuses to calculate, and quipus to keep records of financial obligations

Benjamin C. Storm, Dana-Lis Bittner, and Jeremy K. Yamashiro, *The Changing Dynamics and Consequences of Memory Retrieval in the Age of the Internet* In: *The Remaking of Memory in the Age of the Internet and Social Media.* Edited by: Qi Wang and Andrew Hoskins, Oxford University Press. © Oxford University Press 2024.
DOI: 10.1093/oso/9780197661260.003.0006

(Nestojko et al., 2013). For centuries, people have stored and communicated information using the written word, often organized in books, and made accessible to some through collections and libraries. Today, the external storage of information has become largely digitized, with information available online and accessible via search engines like Google. Digital assistants have become common, with Siri and Alexa able to set reminders and answer questions via spoken command. People are now able to store and maintain access to more information than previously possible, and, as technology continues to advance, this capacity is likely to expand. Indeed, online platforms may increasingly harness artificial intelligence in a way that allows them to predict (based on some combination of behavioral and contextual probabilities) the information that a person might want to retrieve before the person even realizes the need to retrieve it, such as by supporting prospective memory, providing interpersonal reminders about friends and family, or drawing attention to new insights or perspectives related to ongoing projects at work.

The partnership formed between internal and external memory can be thought of as a type of transactive memory system (Wegner, 1995; Wegner et al., 1985, 1991). Transactive memory systems have been studied traditionally in the context of pairs or groups of individuals dividing responsibility for learning and remembering. Individuals can remember together in a way that is more efficient than remembering alone, relying on each other when needed, and in a way that draws on each other's expertise. These more traditional memory partnerships, however, have been increasingly supplanted by the Internet (Ward, 2013). Whereas people may have relied on their friends and colleagues to access information in the past, they can now access the same information via search engines. In this way, the Internet can be thought of as a new type of transactive memory partner—one that is almost always available, updated continuously, and effectively unlimited in capacity. Indeed, owing to these attributes, the Internet could be considered the most powerful transactive memory partner that ever existed.

Relying on the Internet as a transactive memory partner is likely to have consequences for the everyday use and functioning of human memory (Firth et al., 2019; Marsh & Rajaram, 2019; Storm & Soares, 2023). Schacter (2022) argues for the need to distinguish between task-specific effects, domain-specific effects, and domain-general effects. Task-specific effects refer to direct consequences on a specific task being performed (e.g., using GPS to navigate to a destination might impair later memory for that specific route). Domain-specific effects refer to more general consequences for performance within a given domain (e.g., that habitually using GPS impairs memory for routes more generally). Domain-general effects refer to consequences that extend beyond the limits of a given domain (e.g., if habitual GPS use impairs memory for other, non-route-related information).

To date, most research has examined task-specific effects. Sparrow et al. (2011), for example, found that people remember information less well when they believe it is saved on a computer than when they do not. In one experiment, participants read trivia statements and typed them into a computer. Some participants were told that the statements would be saved, and that they would later have access to them (save condition). Other participants were told that the statements would be deleted, and that they would not have access to them (delete condition). When tested, participants in the delete condition recalled more statements than participants in the save condition. This memory impairment in the save condition can be thought of as a kind of digital amnesia effect (it has also been referred to as a Google effect), suggesting that when people assume that information is saved or accessible online, their efforts and abilities to remember that information internally are diminished. Importantly, and consistent with the transactive memory framework, although people may forget the details of saved information, they do not forget where to find that information.

The research reported by Sparrow et al. (2011) has been highly impactful, focusing attention on the general question of how interaction with the Internet and other digital technologies impacts memory. However, despite this scholarly impact, the actual empirical effect has been relatively controversial, with several labs reporting failures to replicate (e.g., Marsh & Rajaram, 2018). One boundary condition for the digital amnesia effect may be whether participants perceive the saving process as reliable. To function effectively, a transactive memory system needs to be trusted (Lewis, 2003; Wegner, 1987). If participants do not trust the saving process (or the delete process), then memory performance should not differ between the two conditions. Consistent with this explanation, Schooler and Storm (2021) found a large and robust digital amnesia effect when participants were given a practice phase to personally experience the reliability of the save/delete manipulation. In contrast, when the practice phase gave participants reason to doubt the reliability of the save/delete manipulation, no evidence of a digital amnesia effect was observed. Given that many participants may go into psychology experiments skeptical of the instructions, it is not surprising that the effect sometimes fails to be observed.

Digital amnesia and other task-specific consequences of relying on the Internet are often attributed to cognitive offloading, namely, the use of external resources to reduce the cognitive demands of a given task (Risko & Gilbert, 2016). When information is saved and made available online, it becomes retrievable in a way that relies less on internal memory. There is less need to process information in a way that is going to make it accessible internally when it is expected to be accessible externally. An important consequence of cognitive offloading is that it allows cognitive resources to be reallocated. Storm and Stone (2015), for example, had participants study lists of words contained in PDF files on a flash drive. By saving an initial file, participants became significantly better at remembering a subsequent file, a phenomenon referred to as the saving-enhanced memory effect (also see Runge et al., 2019; Runge, Frings, & Tempel, 2021; Runge, Frings, Tempel, & Pastötter, 2021; Tsai et al., 2023).

Compared to task-specific consequences of using the Internet as a transactive memory partner, domain-specific and domain-general consequences remain relatively unknown. It is unclear, for example, just how far the consequences of cognitive offloading extend. Clearly, offloaded information can become less accessible because of having been offloaded. Even if the resulting impairment is restricted to that specific information, however, at a certain point, as more information within a domain is offloaded, the consequences could extend to affect expertise for the entire domain. When information is stored within internal memory, it is integrated with other information in a way that potentiates new learning (Bjork & Bjork, 1992), and that allows people to make connections, generate new ideas, and engage in analogical reasoning (Gick & Holyoak, 1983). The more someone knows about a topic, the easier it becomes to learn and remember new information about that topic and to make connections between disparate contexts and ideas. Collections of information saved entirely online would seem unlikely to provide these kinds of cognitive benefits, thus preventing the development of the kind of expertise afforded when information is stored internally. Of course, information is unlikely to be stored entirely online or in memory. Rather, it may be more useful to think of transactive memory as reflecting a blended memory system (Fawns, 2019) characterized by collaboration between internal and external processes. Indeed, one could expect internal memory processes to adapt to the benefits afforded by access to the Internet in a way that expands (rather than constrains) the expertise and capabilities of human memory.

This last point bears on theoretical and methodological quandaries that arise while researchers try to study how Internet use changes the nature of memory retrieval—whether in task-specific, domain-specific, or domain-general ways. It requires us to reconsider an assumption (often implicit) that the unaided individual mind, perhaps even the unaided individual brain, is the proper object of psychological study. For example, in the Sparrow et al. experiment showing evidence of digital amnesia, although the manipulation involves interaction with a digital "partner," in the final recall, the experimenter tests the unaided individual's retrieval. Such methodological individualism has historically been an extremely generative frame for cognitive research. However, it could be a major impediment to advancing knowledge on cognition-technology interactions.

Researchers may need to take the integrated human-technology system, across time, as the unit of analysis, rather than focusing exclusively on the human end of the coupling (Latour, 1996). This approach has variously been termed an "extended" or "distributed" approach to memory and cognition (Clark & Chalmers, 1998; Hutchins, 1995; Michaelian & Sutton, 2013; see Fawns, Chapter 7, this volume). Such an approach might, for instance, examine remembering not as an isolated individual's act of retrieval at a given moment, but as the coordination of brain-based and technological resources, integrated into cognitive assemblages, with a given memory being a product of these hybrid interactions (Menary, 2007; Sutton, 2010). Rather than deciding a priori what counts as cognition (in this case, the isolated individual's recall during an unaided test), researchers would consider the full set of factors—internal and external—making relevant causal contributions to the activity of remembering. This is quite a different project than examining how presumably self-contained, internal mental faculties like memory are "impacted" by outside forces like technology. Characterizing and detecting domain-general effects also would likely require a longitudinal approach, with fine-grained attention paid to how cognition is reorganized holistically over time in response to a relatively persistent technological ecology (Menary, 2007, 2013).

Characterizing these cognitive assemblages for remembering becomes a central task in the study of memory and technology—how are they assembled and for what ends? What are the affordances and constraints immanent in specific ad hoc assemblages, and how does this shape what is remembered? What are the assemblage's longitudinal characteristics (how do they persist over time, supported by what environmental and institutional contexts, etc.)? How do internal and external processes adapt to one another? Many other questions could be asked. Sustained focus on cognitive assemblages *as* assemblages is very difficult to maintain if our experimental methods attend only to decontextualized, individual minds, making these questions important for future researchers to consider.

Online Search and Memory Retrieval

Information can usually be accessed through multiple pathways. On the one hand, information can be accessed internally via the type of retrieval processes studied by memory researchers for the past 100+ years (Rajaram & Barber, 2008; Roediger & Guynn, 1996; Tulving, 2002). On the other hand, information can be accessed externally, such as by referring to books, other people, or the Internet. When conducting experiments, memory researchers are often careful to ensure that external resources are unavailable, thus also ensuring that the participant's performance is a consequence of internal processes acting independently. In the everyday use of memory, however, external resources are almost always available. It is often an option to call a friend or ask a partner or to conduct a Google Search or refer to Wikipedia. What factors determine when a person chooses to rely on internal memory? What factors determine how a person searches for information? In the use of memory, retrieval is messy, and as technology advances, it may get messier, involving both explicit and implicit decision-making processes that are affected by the metacognitive appraisals people make about what they know internally and what they think they can access externally.

The probability of using—or thinking about using—the Internet as a transactive memory partner has likely increased over recent decades. Looking back, people may wonder why they did not think to use Google in past predicaments, even though the benefit of doing so may seem obvious today. In some general sense, the inclination to rely on Google may be becoming increasingly habitual. Indeed, as demonstrated by Storm et al. (2017), the inclination can be exacerbated within the context of a half-hour experiment. In their study, participants were presented with two blocks of trivia questions. In the first block, the questions were relatively difficult, and participants were required to answer the questions either from memory (memory condition) or by conducting a Google Search (Internet condition). In the second block, the questions were relatively easy, and all participants were given the option to either answer the questions from memory or conduct a Google Search. The critical dependent variable was the proportion of the questions in the second block of trials for which participants chose to use Google Search. Demonstrating what the authors termed an Internet fixation effect, participants in the Internet condition were significantly more likely to choose to use Google Search than participants in the memory condition.

The Internet fixation effect can be considered a type of *Einstellung* (Luchins, 1942). People become fixated on methods of doing things, and they will continue to use existing methods even when simpler or more effective methods become available. Once people become accustomed to using Google, they will continue to do so even when it is no longer necessary. Indeed, the Internet fixation effect was observed by Storm et al. (2017) even when using Google was made inconvenient, such as by requiring participants to walk across the room and use a less user-friendly device. Moreover, participants in the Internet condition reported being less interested in challenging themselves cognitively, and they were quicker to commence a Google search than participants in the memory condition, suggesting that participants in the Internet condition were less likely than participants in the memory condition to query internal memory before choosing to rely on the Internet (also see Barr et al., 2015; Wang et al., 2017).

Evidence that the availability of the Internet can disrupt internal memory processes was also observed by Ferguson et al. (2015). In their study, participants responded to general knowledge questions. In one condition, they responded by indicating whether they knew the answer and then, if they did, to provide the answer. In the other condition, they were given the same instruction except that if they indicated not knowing the answer, they would need to look it up on the Internet. Interestingly, participants were less likely to volunteer answers in the latter condition than in the former, a finding that may be attributed to participants with access to the Internet either becoming less confident in their internal memory or raising the threshold for how confident they need to be to provide an answer.

Potential Consequences of Replacing Internal Retrieval Processes

The research by Ferguson et al. (2015) and Storm et al. (2017) suggests that people are less likely to rely on internal memory when they have access to the Internet or when they become primed to use the Internet. Although such effects might seem maladaptive, they can be beneficial. In the study by Ferguson et al. (2015), participants with access to the Internet answered relatively fewer questions from memory, but when they did, they were more likely to be correct. Furthermore, in the study by Storm et al. (2017), participants in the Internet condition may have become more reliant on Google than participants in the memory condition but given the information they accessed online they also answered more questions correctly. These observations suggest something important—that relying on the Internet as a transactive memory partner is likely to provide advantages in problem-solving, especially in terms of ensuring that information is accurate.

Offsetting these immediate benefits, however, relying on the Internet could disrupt the kind of internal processes that are critical for the adaptive long-term functioning of memory. In many ways, retrieval acts as a memory modifier (Bjork, 1975). When information is retrieved, both it and other information can be fundamentally altered. Research has shown, for example, that retrieval can make retrieved information more likely to be retrieved in the future than it would have been otherwise (retrieval-practice effects; Roediger & Karpicke, 2006), and other, nonretrieved information less likely to be retrieved in the future than it would have been otherwise (retrieval-induced forgetting; Anderson, 2003). Moreover, retrieval does not involve the replaying of memories in the same way they were encoded; it involves the construction of something new, a process that may facilitate the updating of memory through reconsolidation (Hupbach et al., 2013). Reactivating memories via retrieval renders information susceptible to disruption, and alteration is likely to be fundamental to the updating of memory over time. If the Internet disrupts the use of internal retrieval processes, it may also disrupt how memory is updated, which could have important implications for everything from learning to autobiographical memory. In autobiographical memory, for example, there is a bias to remember the past in ways that coheres with one's self-concept (Conway, 2005). If past experiences are retained externally, and in a way that does not involve mechanisms to help memories evolve over time to maintain coherence, then it could disrupt the functioning of autobiographical memory.

A potential starting point for exploring the limitations or side effects of using the Internet as a transactive memory system is in the context of retrieval-practice effects. As mentioned, retrieval can promote long-term learning by making retrieved information more likely to be retrieved in the future. Such effects are often demonstrated in experiments comparing the effects of retrieval and restudy. Information that is retrieved tends to become more recallable—especially after a long delay—than information that is restudied. Retrieval-practice effects are likely observed for many reasons. From a transfer-appropriate processing perspective (Morris et al., 1977), for example, the type of processing required for subsequent retrieval tends to also be involved in earlier retrieval attempts, thereby making retrieval an excellent form of practice for subsequent retrieval. Retrieval may also benefit memory by creating new retrieval pathways, expanding the set of cues capable of activating learned information (McDaniel & Masson, 1985), or by updating contextual representations in a way that enhances a person's ability to retrieve that information (Karpicke et al., 2014). By accessing information externally, such as through the Internet, people may prevent themselves from experiencing the kind of retrieval-based learning opportunities afforded by attempting to retrieve information internally.

Storm et al. (2022) examined this idea in the context of the pretesting effect (Kornell & Vaughn, 2016). Retrieval attempts do not need to be successful to benefit memory. Even failed retrieval attempts can enhance learning, presumably in part by activating long-term memory structures in a way that allows to-be-learned information to be encoded more effectively than it would be otherwise. In the study by Storm et al. (2022), participants answered difficult trivia questions either using their memory or by searching Google. Either way, participants were subsequently provided the correct answers and then tested again on a follow-up test without Google. As compared to control items that were studied intact, both groups of participants demonstrated robust pretesting effects. Specifically, participants benefited from the attempt to retrieve the answers (before being given the answers) regardless of whether they did so internally or by conducting a Google search. One interpretation of this finding is that people may engage in internal retrieval processes even when they are given the opportunity to search for answers online. Of course, it is also possible that searching the Internet benefits memory via mechanisms distinct from those that facilitate memory owing to internal retrieval attempts. Future research will need to examine the underlying mechanisms more directly. It also remains to be seen whether similar results would be observed in other contexts and with other populations. From a point of parsimony, it may be better to assume that internal memory processes co-occur with external memory processes until evidence is found to suggest otherwise.

It is also important to consider how other effects of retrieval—specifically, on unretrieved information—might be affected by reliance on a transactive memory partner. Research on *retrieval-induced forgetting* has shown that the retrieval of a subset of information can cause the forgetting of other, nonretrieved information (Anderson et al., 1994; Storm et al., 2015). This effect is often demonstrated using a retrieval-practice paradigm in which participants study a list of categorized items and then selectively retrieve some items from some of the categories. Not surprisingly, when participants are given a subsequent final test, items that received retrieval practice are recalled best. More importantly for observing evidence of retrieval-induced forgetting, nonpracticed items from practiced categories are recalled less well than nonpracticed items from the nonpracticed categories. Retrieval processes are thought to be at the core of producing retrieval-induced forgetting, and there is evidence that retrieval can cause forgetting in ways that other forms of practice may not (e.g., Murayama et al., 2014; Storm & Levy, 2012). Moreover, whereas some mechanisms that cause forgetting are likely to be observed regardless of whether information is found online versus retrieved internally (e.g., part-set cueing, Barber & Rajaram, 2011; cue overload, Watkins & Watkins, 1975), there are reasons to think that retrieval-induced forgetting might be less likely to be observed when information is found online than when retrieved internally.

Retrieval-induced forgetting is thought to be the consequence—at least in part—of an inhibitory process that occurs during retrieval practice (Anderson, 2003). Specifically, the retrieval cues activate not only the target items but also other competing items; successfully retrieving the target items is facilitated by the inhibition of those competing items. This inhibition results in the competing items becoming less recallable when they are cued at the time of the final test. Inhibitory dynamics may play a critical role in the use of internal memory, but they may be less involved in the use of external memory. When retrieving information externally, it is often unnecessary to inhibit potentially competing information. That said, if people tend to retrieve concurrently with an Internet search or while attending a transactive memory partner's rehearsal, then retrieval-induced forgetting should be observed, a pattern that has been well documented in the case of socially shared retrieval-induced forgetting (Coman & Hirst, 2015; Cuc et al., 2007). In the case of human partners, listeners' motivations in attending to a speaker (e.g., relational, epistemic, or social identity protection motives) moderate whether socially shared, retrieval-induced forgetting occurs (Stone et al., 2012). Such a nuanced picture is likely to hold true as well for technological partners that are not obviously human (for recent work on the memory consequences of exposure to online information in the context of social media, see, e.g., Bilgin & Wang, 2023; Stone & Wang, 2019).

Finally, using the Internet to retrieve information may result in a different kind of retrieval-induced forgetting, one that involves selection processes that reshape the contents of memory both internally and externally. Although the contents of the Internet are vast, the actual output provided to users tends to be limited. When conducting a Google search, only a small fraction of the potentially relevant information is provided, and depending on the algorithms at play, it is likely to do so in a way that is biased by factors independent of the mnemonic needs of the person conducting the search. Moreover, many search platforms adapt to the behavior of users, leading to a kind of self-reinforcing cycle of providing access to the same information while ignoring other, potentially relevant, information. In this way, external retrieval may cause external forgetting, a type of retrieval-induced forgetting that might determine the set of information a person encodes internally and can access externally.

Retrieving with the Internet and Metacognition

In this final section, we consider the metacognitive dynamics surrounding interactions with the Internet. A person's subjective assessment of how and what they know can, after all, influence and guide their behavior (Schwartz et al., 1997). Applying a metacognitive lens can therefore provide insight into how retrieving information from the Internet is comparable to retrieving information from internal memory or from other external transactive memory partners. Recent research has focused on not only the metacognitive considerations that precede querying the Internet, but also how metacognitive judgments of one's actions and knowledge are affected by access to the Internet, as well as by even the knowledge that one has access to the Internet.

People seem to have a good heuristic understanding of the information available to them online, often making relatively accurate metacognitive judgments about how long it will take, and how difficult it will be, to find information. Risko et al. (2016), for example, compared judgments of the relative availability of internally stored information (*feeling-of-knowing* about information "in your head") to the relative availability of information stored online (*feeling-of-findability* about information on the Internet). Similar to how feeling-of-knowing judgments are correlated with how long it takes to recall information from memory (Koriat, 1993), Risko et al. (2016) found that feeling-of-findability ratings are correlated with how long it takes to retrieve information online. Specifically, participants took longer to search for information they initially judged as having a relatively lower level of findability.

Online searching itself can also skew metacognitive judgments. For example, Stone and Storm (2021) found that search fluency, or how easily and quickly information is found online, can predict the extent to which people think they will be able to access that same information internally. Participants predicted that they would be better able to recall the information they accessed quickly from the Internet than the information they accessed more slowly, even though the opposite was the case. This finding is in line with what Benjamin et al. (1998) found about retrieval fluency, with participants being more confident in the ability to recall information retrieved more quickly from internal memory than information retrieved more slowly, even though the opposite was the case. People may use analogous heuristics while retrieving information from memory and the Internet to infer how well they will remember that information, suggesting that the metacognitive dynamics involved in the use of internal and external memory processes may be similar.

Researchers have also explored how the Internet affects metacognitive judgments. Search fluency, and the ease with which information can be accessed online more generally, may blur the boundaries between what people think is in memory versus accessible online. Fisher et al. (2015), for example, found that participants who searched the answers to explanatory questions online expressed higher confidence that they could explain completely unrelated topics than participants who did not search the Internet. This inflated metacognitive confidence pertaining to internal knowledge has also been observed in the context of learning new information. Fisher et al. (2022) found that, despite performing worse on a test after searching for to-be-learned information online, participants reported feeling just as confident, if not more confident, in having mastered the material, than participants who were provided the same to-be-learned information without querying the Internet. The mechanisms underlying these effects remain unclear, but one possibility is that viewing not only the to-be-learned information while searching the Internet, but also information related to the topic gives people the illusion of a broader or more contextualized understanding of the to-be-learned information.

Marsh and Rajaram (2019) refer to the tendency to inflate one's metacognitive judgments of internal knowledge after using an Internet search as a type of *information appropriation*. There are conditions, however, that can mitigate the blurring of internal and external knowledge. Fisher and Oppenheimer (2021) found that when outside assistance is delayed or actively chosen, people make more accurate metacognitive assessments of their reliance on outside help. This suggests that trying to retrieve information from memory first, or even just waiting before initiating an online search, could potentially reduce the impact of online search on metacognitive judgments.

A major challenge will be to explore and define the boundary conditions of the impact that retrieving information from the Internet has on metacognitive judgments. At this point, researchers are starting to investigate the tension between behavioral and metacognitive findings. Future research should explore, for example, which metacognitive mechanisms coincide with increased dependency on the Internet (Storm et al., 2017; Wang et al., 2017) and why this dependency occurs in the first place (Fisher et al., 2015). Research should also investigate how different types of knowledge (e.g., explanatory, factual) differ in their metacognitive impact, whether the effects of an online search on metacognition vary depending on the motivation behind querying the Internet (e.g., to look up something; to learn new information; to jog memory). People use the Internet differently, both interindividually and intraindividually over time and across contexts, and how they do so is likely to be important for determining the mnemonic and metacognitive consequences.

Conclusion

Although the empirical study of cognition in digital contexts is in its infancy, researchers have already demonstrated a variety of ways in which cognition may be transformed by sustained interaction with the Internet. These studies have tended to focus on two points of the human-technology interface: cognitive offloading onto external storage and Internet search. Of course, there are many other potential points of interface, and the field promises to be a ripe one for future development. Here we reviewed the extant literature suggesting that people often treat the Internet as a reliable cognitive partner in an extended transactive memory system, recruiting it to complement "onboard" capacities to carry out cognitive tasks. Importantly, such sustained collaboration with the Internet and other digital contexts can impact both the quantity and form of retrieval, as well as metacognitive judgments concerning one's own knowledge. In both cases, the open-ended nature of human cognition seems to be adapting itself, as has historically always been the case, to the affordances of powerful external resources. Rather than focusing on the simplistic question of whether the Internet is good or bad for, for example, human memory, the emerging literature suggests a more nuanced set of questions about how cognition transforms to adapt to digital contexts and how people coordinate internal and external resources while performing particular cognitive tasks. We anticipate that there are many theoretical and methodological discoveries to be made in this domain.

References

Anderson, M. C. (2003). Rethinking interference theory: Executive control and the mechanisms of forgetting. *Journal of Memory and Language, 49*, 415–445.

Anderson, M. C., Bjork, R. A., & Bjork, E. L. (1994). Remembering can cause forgetting: Retrieval dynamics in long-term memory. *Journal of Experimental Psychology: Learning, Memory, and Cognition, 20*, 1063–1087.

Barber, S. J., & Rajaram, S. (2011). Exploring the relationship between retrieval disruption from collaboration and recall. *Memory, 19*(5), 462–469.

Barr, N., Pennycook, G., Stolz, J. A., & Fugelsang, J. A. (2015). The brain your pocket: Evidence that smartphones are used to supplant thinking. *Computers in Human Behavior, 48*, 473–480.

Benjamin, A. S., Bjork, R. A., & Schwartz, B. L. (1998). The mismeasure of memory: When retrieval fluency is misleading as a metamnemonic index. *Journal of Experimental Psychology: General, 127*, 55–68.

Bilgin, E., & Wang, Q. (2023). Remembering and forgetting information about the COVID-19 vaccine on Twitter. *Memory, 31*, 247–258.

Bjork, R. A. (1975). Retrieval as a memory modifier: An interpretation of negative recency and related phenomena. In R. L. Solso (Ed.), *Information processing and cognition: The Loyola Symposium* (pp. 123–144). Erlbaum.

Bjork, R. A., & Bjork, E. L. (1992). A new theory of disuse and an old theory of stimulus fluctuation. In A. F. Healy, S. M. Kosslyn, & R. M. Shiffrin (Eds.), *From learning processes to cognitive processes: Essays in honor of William K. Estes* (Vol. 2, pp. 35–67). Erlbaum.

Clark, A., & Chalmers, D. (1998). The extended mind. *Analysis, 58*, 7–19.

Coman, A., & Hirst, W. (2015). Social identity and socially shared retrieval-induced forgetting: The effects of group membership. *Journal of Experimental Psychology: General, 144*, 717–722.

Conway, M. A. (2005). Memory and the self. *Journal of Memory and Language, 53*, 594–628.

Cuc, A., Koppel, J., & Hirst, W. (2007). Silence is not golden: A case for socially shared retrieval-induced forgetting. *Psychological Science, 18*, 727–733.

Fawns, T. (2019). Blended memory: A framework for understanding distributed autobiographical remembering with photography. *Memory Studies, 13*, 901–916.

Ferguson, A. M., McLean, D., & Risko, E. F. (2015). Answers at your fingertips: Access to the Internet influences willingness to answer questions. *Consciousness and Cognition, 37*, 91–102.

Firth, J., Torous, J., Stubbs, B., Firth, J., Steiner, G. Z., Smith, L., Alvarez-Jimenez, M., Gleeson, J., Vancampfort, D., Armitage, C. J., & Sarris, J. (2019). The "online brain": How the Internet may be changing our cognition. *World Psychiatry, 18*, 119–129.

Fisher, M., Goddu, M. K., & Keil, F. C. (2015). Searching for explanations: How the Internet inflates estimates of internal knowledge. *Journal of Experimental Psychology: General, 144*, 674–687.

Fisher, M., & Oppenheimer, D. M. (2021). Harder than you think: How outside assistance leads to overconfidence. *Psychological Science, 32*, 598–610.

Fisher, M., Smiley, A. H., & Grillo, T. L. (2022). Information without knowledge: The effects of Internet search on learning. *Memory, 30*, 375–387.

Gick, M. L., & Holyoak, K. (1983). Schema induction and analogical transfer. *Cognitive Psychology, 15*, 1–38.

Hupbach, A., Gomez, R., & Nadel, L. (2013). Episodic memory reconsolidation: An update. In C. M. Alberini (Ed.), *Memory reconsolidation* (pp. 233–247). Elsevier Academic Press.

Hutchins, E. (1995). *Cognition in the wild.* MIT Press.

Karpicke, J. D., Lehman, M., & Aue, W. R. (2014). Retrieval-based learning: An episodic context account. In B. H. Ross (Ed.), *Psychology of learning and motivation* (Vol. *61*, pp. 237–284). Elsevier Academic Press.

Koriat, A. (1993). How do we know that we know? The accessibility model of the feeling of knowing. *Psychological Review, 100*, 609–639.

Kornell, N., & Vaughn, K. E. (2016). How retrieval attempts affect learning: A review and synthesis. *Psychology of Learning and Motivation, 65*, 183–215.

Latour, B. (1996). Cogito ergo sumus! Or, psychology swept inside out by the fresh air of the upper deck: Review of Hutchins 1995. *Mind, Culture, and Activity, 3*, 54–63.

Lewis, K. (2003). Measuring transactive memory systems in the field: Scale development and validation. *Journal of Applied Psychology, 88*, 587–604.

Luchins, A. S. (1942). Mechanization in problem solving: The effect of Einstellung. *Psychological Monographs, 54*, i-95.

Marsh, E. J., & Rajaram, S. (2018). Cognition in the Internet age: What are the right research questions to ask? In an invited talk at the Annual Meeting of the Association for Psychological Science, May 26, 2018, San Francisco, CA.

Marsh, E. J., & Rajaram, S. (2019). The digital expansion of the mind: Implications of Internet usage for memory and cognition. *Journal of Applied Research in Memory and Cognition, 8*, 1–14.

McDaniel, M. A., & Masson, M. E. (1985). Altering memory representations through retrieval. *Journal of Experimental Psychology: Learning, Memory, and Cognition, 11*, 371.

Menary, R. (2007). *Cognitive integration: Mind and cognition unbounded.* Springer.

Menary, R. (2013). Cognitive integration, enculturated cognition and the socially extended mind. *Cognitive Systems Research, 25–26*, 26–34. https://www.sciencedirect.com/science/article/pii/S1389041713000326?via%3Dihub

Michaelian, K., & Sutton, J. (2013). Distributed cognition and memory research: History and current directions. *Review of Philosophy and Psychology, 4*, 1–24.

Morris, C. D., Bransford, J. D., & Franks, J. J. (1977). Levels of processing versus transfer appropriate processing. *Journal of Verbal Learning and Verbal Behavior, 16*, 519–533.

Murayama, K., Miyatsu, T., Buchli, D., & Storm, B. C. (2014). Forgetting as a consequence of retrieval: A meta-analytic review of retrieval-induced forgetting. *Psychological Bulletin, 140*, 1383–1409.

Nestojko, J. F., Finley, J. R., & Roediger, H. L. (2013). Extending cognition to external agents. *Psychological Inquiry, 24*, 321–325.

Rajaram, S., & Barber, S. J. (2008). Retrieval processes in memory. *Learning and Memory: A Comprehensive Reference, 2*, 261–283.

Risko, E. F., Ferguson, A. M., & McLean, D. (2016). On retrieving information from external knowledge stores: Feeling-of-findability, feeling-of-knowing and Internet search. *Computers in Human Behavior, 65*, 534–543.

Risko, E. F., & Gilbert, S. J. (2016). Cognitive offloading. *Trends in Cognitive Science, 20*, 676–688.

Roediger, H. L., III, & Guynn, M. J. (1996). Retrieval processes. In E. L. Bjork & R. A. Bjork (Eds.), *Memory* (pp. 197–236). Academic Press.

Roediger, H. L., & Karpicke, J. L. (2006). Test-enhanced learning: Taking memory tests improves long-term retention. *Psychological Science, 17*, 249–255.

Roediger, H. L., III, & Karpicke, J. D. (2006). The power of testing memory: Basic research and implications for educational practice. *Perspectives on Psychological Science, 1*, 181–210.

Runge, Y., Frings, C., & Tempel, T. (2019). Saving-enhanced performance: Saving items after study boosts performance in subsequent demanding tasks. *Memory, 27*, 1462–1467.

Runge, Y., Frings, C., & Tempel, T. (2021). Specifying the mechanisms behind benefits of saving-enhanced memory. *Psychological Research, 85*, 1633–1644.

Runge, Y., Frings, C., Tempel, T., & Pastötter, B. (2021). Electrophysiological correlates of saving-enhanced memory: Exploring similarities to list-method directed forgetting. *European Journal of Neuroscience, 54*, 6060–6074.

Schacter, D. L. (1999). The seven sins of memory: Insights from psychology and cognitive neuroscience. *American Psychologist, 54*, 182–203.

Schacter, D. L. (2022). Media, technology, and the sins of memory. *Memory, Mind & Media, 1*, e1.

Schooler, J. N., & Storm, B. C. (2021). Saved information is remembered less well than deleted information, if the saving process is perceived as reliable. *Memory, 29*, 1101–1110.

Schwartz, B. L., Benjamin, A. S., & Bjork, R. A. (1997). The inferential and experiential bases of metamemory. *Current Directions in Psychological Science, 6*, 132–137

Sparrow, B., Liu, J., & Wegner, D. M. (2011). Google effects on memory: Cognitive consequences of having information at our fingertips. *Science, 333*, 776–778.

Stone, C. B., Coman, A., Brown, A. D., Koppel, J., & Hirst, W. (2012). Towards a science of silence: The consequences of leaving a memory unsaid. *Perspectives on Psychological Science, 7*, 39–53.

Stone, C. B., & Wang, Q. (2019). From conversations to digital communication: The mnemonic consequences of consuming and producing information via social media. *Topics in Cognitive Science, 11*, 774–793.

Stone, S. M., & Storm, B. C. (2021). Search fluency as a misleading measure of memory. *Journal of Experimental Psychology: Learning, Memory, and Cognition, 47*, 53–64.

Storm, B. C., Angello, G., Buchli, D. R., Koppel, R. H., Little, J. L., & Nestojko, J. F. (2015). A review of retrieval-induced forgetting in the contexts of learning, eye-witness memory, social cognition, autobiographical memory, and creative cognition. In B. Ross (Ed.), *The psychology of learning and motivation* (pp. 141–194). Academic Press of Elsevier.

Storm, B. C., James, K. K., & Stone, S. M. (2022). Pretesting can be beneficial even when using the Internet to answer questions. *Memory, 30*, 388–395.

Storm, B. C., & Levy, B. J. (2012). A progress report on the inhibitory account of retrieval-induced forgetting. *Memory & Cognition, 40*, 827–843.

Storm, B. C., & Soares, J. S. (in press). Memory in the digital age. In A. Wegner & M. Kahana (Eds.), *The Oxford handbook of human memory*. https://global.oup.com/academic/product/the-oxford-handbook-of-human-memory-two-volume-pack-9780197746141?cc=us&lang=en&#

Storm, B. C., & Stone, S. M. (2015). Saving-Enhanced Memory. *Psychological Science, 26*(2), 182–188.

Storm, B. C., Stone, S. M., & Benjamin, A. S. (2017). Using the Internet to access information inflates future use of the Internet to access other information. *Memory, 25*, 717–723.

Sutton, J. (2010). Exograms and interdisciplinarity: History, the extended mind, and the civilizing process. MIT Press (pp. 189–225).

Tsai, P., Sachdeva, C., Gilbert, S., & Scarampi, C. (2023). An investigation of the saving-enhanced memory effect: The role of test order and list saving. *Applied Cognitive Psychology, 37*, 736–748.

Tulving, E. (2002). Episodic memory: From mind to brain. *Annual Review of Psychology, 53*, 1–25.

Wang, Y., Wu, L., Luo, L., Zhang, Y., & Dong, G. (2017). Short-term Internet search using makes people rely on search engines when facing unknown issues. *PloS One, 12*, e0176325.

Ward, A. F. (2013). Supernormal: How the Internet is changing our memories and our minds. *Psychological Inquiry, 24*, 341–348.

Watkins, O. C., & Watkins, M. J. (1975). Buildup of proactive inhibition as a cue-overload effect. *Journal of Experimental Psychology: Human Learning and Memory, 1*, 442–452.

Wegner, D. M. (1987). Transactive memory: A contemporary analysis of the group mind. In B. Mullen & G. R. Goethals (Eds.), *Theories of Group Behavior. Springer Series in Social Psychology* (pp. 185–208). Springer.

Wegner, D. M. (1995). A computer network model of human transactive memory. *Social Cognition, 13*, 319–339.

Wegner, D. M., Erber, R., & Raymond, P. (1991). Transactive memory in close relationships. *Journal of Personality and Social Psychology, 61*, 923–929.

Wegner, D. M., Guiliano, T., & Hertel, P. T. (1985). Cognitive interdependence in close relationships. In W. J. Ickes (Ed.), *Compatible and incompatible relationships* (pp. 253–276). Springer-Verlag.

7
Photography, Digital Media, and Technology

Moving from Effects on Memory to Entanglements in Remembering Activity

Tim Fawns

Research on memory in relation to photography, digital media, and technology tends to skate on thin evidence. Photography, in particular, has a long relationship with memory. Now that images pervade social media and the wider Internet, this relationship is becoming an increasingly important area of research (Schacter, 2022). Yet, the results of such research, and of research into memory, digital media, and the Internet more broadly, are frequently distorted through a mix of hyperenthusiasm and moral panic (see, e.g., Clowes, 2015). Consider the following headlines in online articles and blog posts:

"8 Ways Technology Makes You Stupid" (Hiscott, 2014)
"Is Modern Media Destroying Our Memories?" (Horvath, 2020)
"Want to Remember a Special Moment? Put Down the Camera" (Perry, 2018)
"Unplugged Weddings: Stopping Guests from Taking Photos Could Be Good for You and Them" (Wong, 2020)
"There's Now a Scientific Reason Why You Shouldn't Take Pictures at Gigs" (Tamblyn, 2018)

These posts, among many others, can be linked to a relatively small set of research studies and scholarly works. Two studies in particular have been widely cited in an emerging field of psychological research into the relationship between memory and technology. Sparrow et al. (2011) found that participants thought of technologies such as Google's search engine when asked difficult questions and were less likely to recall information that they believed would be stored on a computer. Henkel (2014) found that participants could recognize and recall fewer details for those museum objects they had photographed. I highlight these articles because they are important exemplars of a dominant approach within this emerging field, not because they are more deserving of critique than others.

Tim Fawns, *Photography, Digital Media, and Technology* In: *The Remaking of Memory in the Age of the Internet and Social Media.* Edited by: Qi Wang and Andrew Hoskins, Oxford University Press. © Oxford University Press 2024.
DOI: 10.1093/oso/9780197661260.003.0007

The findings of Sparrow et al. have been brought into question by several subsequent studies (Camerer et al., 2018; Hesselmann, 2020; Kahn & Martinez, 2020; Marsh & Rajaram, 2019), and other studies have shown the impairment of recall to be conditional or complicated (Grinschgl et al., 2021; Runge et al., 2019, 2021; Storm & Stone, 2015). Similarly, a range of studies are in tension with or, at least, add nuance to, Henkel's findings (e.g., Barasch et al., 2017; Koutstaal et al., 1998, 1999; Loveday & Conway, 2011; Soares & Storm, 2018), with the overall implication that recall is both helped and hindered by photography, depending on the practices and contexts involved (see Fawns, 2022a, for a more detailed discussion). As Schacter (2022) notes in his review for the new journal *Memory, Mind & Media*, the emerging evidence in this area does not support simple conclusions but instead "paints a more complex picture" in which effects depend on a range of factors. Nonetheless, these narrow and contested effects were quickly and widely extrapolated by journalists and bloggers as evidence for technologically driven stupidity and the ruination of memory for special moments, weddings, gigs, and holidays; and much more.

Whether the authors of those research papers intended to or not, they may have encouraged such extrapolation through their choices of language. Sparrow et al.'s (2011) finding that when participants knew they could look up information later, they were less likely to recall that information, was labeled the "Google effect". In reality, their experiments had little to do with the search engine or the ways in which people engage with it. By extrapolating from a task-specific finding (typing into a static computer document) to a domain-specific conclusion (this effect applies to all uses of computers and the Internet), they misinterpreted the significance of their research (see Schacter, 2022). The implications were then further extrapolated, within the conclusions of their paper, to a domain-general dependency "on our gadgets" (Sparrow et al., 2011, p. 778). Henkel (2014), finding that taking photographs impaired recall for the details of objects in a museum tour, attributed this "photo-taking-impairment effect" to "cognitive offloading." Citing Sparrow et al. (2011), Henkel (2014) argued that "the act of photographing the object appears to enable people to dismiss the object from memory, thereby relying on the external devise [sic] of the camera to 'remember' for them" (p. 401). While she was careful to put "remember" in quotes, the suggestion lingers that memory is either human or technological (but not both in combination) and can be transferred from one to the other. In this language of outsourcing meaning-making processes to technology, there is a notable resemblance to that used in the marketing of photography-related products (e.g., from Kodak's references to capturing "memories" [Paster, 1992] to Apple's labeling of algorithmically organized "memories" [Pereira, 2019]).

Such language signals a lack of conceptual precision that has implications for the relevance of the findings to other kinds of photography. For example,

Henkel suggested that new digital practices and trends (e.g., "ubiquitous" photo-taking and an apparent reduction in "in person sharing" among families) make the photo-impairment effect a more urgent phenomenon of study. Yet the participants' personal photography practices were not examined: Participants were told what to do and were not able to view or share photos. Where Sparrow and colleagues conflated typing information into a computer with using Google or "gadgets," Henkel reinforced an overly simplistic conception of the relationship between technology and memory by implying that the effects of photography are independent of actual practices, contexts, and situated meaning. Framing it as something that can be impaired or offloaded separates remembering not only from the contexts in which it happens, but also from the people on whose experiences it is based.

Metaphors and Conceptions of Memory and Remembering

Despite some promising interdisciplinary work (discussed under "Mixing Things Up: Disciplines, Methods, Data, and Conceptions", below), the most prominent studies of media and memory within psychology and cognitive science remain those that use numerical data and isolate interacting elements to look for a pure relation between independent and dependent variables. In seeking clarity, this creates a view of memory that foregrounds certain qualities and relations (e.g., number of recalled details, quantifiable ideas of accuracy, self-ratings of qualitative characteristics such as vividness or valence) and supresses others (e.g., agency, context, habits, and practices). These kinds of data, and their associated methods, can reinforce a conception of memory, whether implicitly or explicitly, as a set of objects that are stored and retrieved. In other words, memory is metaphorically framed in particular ways in order to make sense of "it," as an entity to study empirically and in a controlled manner. While researchers may recognize that any instance of recall can only ever be a situated manifestation of that object (Klein, 2015), this underlying framing is important.

Leary (1990) argues that metaphors have both shaped and reflected dominant conceptions of the mind over time, and a rich history of memory metaphors has unfolded within psychology. Roediger (1980) describes the evolution of, primarily spatial, metaphors, from Plato's wax tablets and aviaries, to Freud's mystic writing pad, a gramophone, a computer, a filing cabinet, variously composed stores (e.g., long term vs. short term), and more. Attempts to understand different aspects of memory have also resulted in metaphors of time travel (Michaelian, 2016; Suddendorf & Corballis, 2007); scene construction (Hassabis & Maguire, 2007); narrative (Brockmeier, 2010); dinosaur bones (Neisser, 2014); or a tennis forehand (Bartlett, 1932). Elsewhere, memory has been a tabula rasa (Locke,

1847); Odin's raven (Hermann et al., 2014); a "blunderer" (Clampitt, 1985); a photographic plate (Draaisma, 2000); and a hologram (Gibson, 1993). No metaphor is ever a perfect fit. The issue is not so much that we need to find the best metaphor, but that we should be careful not to believe too strongly in any metaphor or to use a single metaphor to define memory in its entirety. The value of metaphors is in their utility for helping us to think about, and interrogate, a phenomenon: They are there to be tested, stretched, and torn as we compare them with our experiences and evidence. Each metaphor is potentially useful but narrow, highlighting some aspects of memory but eliding others. Indeed, we learn from not only the ways in which metaphors explain something, but also where they fall short.

According to Lakoff and Johnson (1980), each metaphor constrains possibilities for thinking about what it stands for. Roediger (1980, p. 232) argues that spatial metaphors have reinforced views, in scientific and lay contexts, of the mind as "an actual physical space, with memories and ideas as objects in the space" (see also Koriat & Goldsmith, 1996, for a discussion of the implications of the "storehouse" metaphor of memory). Marsh and Rajaram (2019) point out that ideas of offloading memories to the Internet or external media (e.g., Kelly & Risko, 2021; Risko et al., Chapter 5, this volume; Sparrow et al., 2011; Storm et al., Chapter 6, this volume) continue this "long tradition of thinking about memories as things stored in a physical space." Yet a particular quandary is created: "Offloading" may be a handy label, but it does not adequately allow for combining internal memory with external resources. Where does memory go when we offload it? Is it, somehow temporarily transferred into the technology? Is all of it offloaded or only part of it? Perhaps there are internal and external stores, and, if we only access the internal one, as in the experiments discussed, the memory is less likely to be there. While retrieved instances of memory objects can be distorted or faded through media interactions, it is unclear—within this storehouse conception—whether or how media content can be part of the stored memory object. Do photographs, videos, or diary entries merely influence, during the process of retrieval, some distortion of a preexisting, internal memory object? Literature on false memory and doctored photographs suggests that photographs can form integral elements of what is remembered (Garry & Gerrie, 2005; Nash et al., 2009; Strange et al., 2008; see also Smit, Chapter 13, this volume).

An alternative explanation is that media, such as photographs, neither stand in for nor have an effect on memory. Instead, they are dynamically mixed into a range of ingredients that inform the construction of instances of remembering. The meaning attached to interactions with media can then also be part of this mix. For example, in my research (Fawns, 2019a, 2020, 2022a), which used photo-elicitation interviews to generate qualitative data about the relationship between photography and autobiographical memory, participants' feelings and beliefs about media shaped how they experienced and paid attention to the scenes and scenarios of their lives, and also their engagement with photos and stories afterward. Participants could often remember the circumstances of taking a photo. Some found analogue photography more conducive to reminiscing or were offended by other people's use of social media around personal events. Their accounts were rich with the spontaneous mixing of devices (e.g., traditional albums and frames, digital photo frames, phones, desktop computers, tablets); media (e.g., printed photos, digital photos, video, text); and synchronous ("real time") and asynchronous (fragmented over longer periods of time) conversation via social media, text messaging, email, and video chat. All of this varied widely across participants, with some preferring analogue photos and others digital, some feeling that cameras got in the way of experience and others using photography as part of the way they engaged with life as it unfolded around them. Many of these entanglements were contextual: Participants' choices of which media to engage with within our interviews and their discussions of their histories with a particular device or album contributed to which photos were looked at and talked about, what conversations happened, and, ultimately, what was remembered (Fawns, 2020).

Such rich accounts require us to move past metaphors of storage and retrieval and ideas of memories stored as fully formed objects. As I have argued elsewhere (Fawns, 2019a, 2022b), they also require switching focus from memory to *remembering activity* (see also the concept of "memory work" [e.g., Kuhn, 2010; Lohmeier & Pentzold, 2014; van Dijck, 2007] for related arguments). In mainstream psychology, remembering is assumed to happen inside the brain, and external factors merely have effects on this brain-bound activity (Manier, 2004). However, the self-reports, narratives, and even brain scans that researchers study are actually external manifestations of remembering. Shifting the unit of analysis to remembering activity cuts out an interpretative step that is often implicit in memory studies and allows for more active metaphors. For example, remembering can be seen as detective work (where the rememberer actively makes sense of different information sources); the weaving of a tapestry (where different elements, internal and external, are woven together into rich pictures of the past); or a dance (with brain, body, and external world engaged in dynamic negotiation). I introduced the metaphor of blended memory (Fawns, 2019a) to explain how ingredients of remembering (different categories of memory; external media; social, digital, and material activity; context) are inseparably mixed together in the moment. Each of these metaphors allows for complex, overlapping engagement with external resources and illustrates how controlled experiments constrain conceptions of memory. In "staging" events and behaviors (Neisser, 1981), experimental research obstructs the dance, provides impersonal subjects and impoverished materials for the tapestry, cuts off sources and personal relevance for detective work, and limits and sanitizes the ingredients that are blended together.

Rethinking Ecological Validity

Even where confounding variables are eliminated or minimized and conditions are uniform, remembering—the activity that we actually experience and observe in lieu of "memory"—is always, inevitably, deeply contextual. We cannot remove confounding variables without introducing new ones (e.g., the somewhat peculiarly prescriptive setting, the directives from the researchers, the fact of being observed and having one's data analyzed for research purposes). In any case, those noisy elements of context are not things to be isolated or controlled for; rather, they are constituent elements of the remembering activity being observed (Bietti et al., 2014). These arguments may seem familiar. Neisser (1978, p. 4) famously drew the ire of many psychologists when he announced that "If X is an interesting or socially important aspect of memory, then psychologists have hardly ever studied X." Media practices and remembering are both produced in social contexts that are partly contingent on technological possibilities and human agency—they do not simply occur, they are performed (intentionally or unintentionally, individually and collectively) by people in response to, and in relation to, social, digital, and material environments (Fawns, 2019b).

All of this does not discount the work of Sparrow et al. (2011), Henkel (2014), and others. Rather, it obliges us to interrogate the contexts in which the particular remembering activity of their participants is located. All remembering activity is both contrived and natural: Even remembering that happens in experimental studies can be regarded as ecologically valid, provided the ecology in which it occurs is appreciated within the analysis, conclusions, and reporting (Fawns, 2019a). Experimental settings are just another context in which remembering activity happens. Indeed, the same can be said of my own photo-elicitation interviews, even if they allowed greater agency to participants and acknowledged the role of the researcher and environment (see Fawns, 2020). There is no clear-cut, authentic, naturally occurring, or representative context for the wider field of digital media, the Internet, and memory. The answer, then, is not simply to move outside the laboratory (as Henkel, 2014, has done, to some extent, by using a museum setting), but to consider ways of taking explicit account of the media/memory ecologies (Brown & Hoskins, 2010; Hoskins, 2016) in which remembering is observed (Bietti et al., 2014).

Brown and Reavey (2016) suggest that Neisser, by holding onto aspirations of identifying clear effects on internal memory, just in ecologically richer settings, "appeared to be attempting to prolong an ageing paradigm beyond its natural lifespan by proposing a move outside the laboratory" (p. 219). Rather than sticking to systematic approaches, Brown and Reavey advocate for messier explorations that both broaden our understandings of memory and situate interactions within these broader flows of experience. As they argue, this will require going beyond "purely technical questions" and involve theoretical as well as empirical work and an interdisciplinary negotiation of methodological and epistemic differences. For this, we do not need to ask cognitive psychologists to "'let go' of the paradigmatic basis on which their intellectual commitments, and indeed careers, are formed" (Brown & Reavey, 2016, p. 216), but we should not let them off without having to explain and justify the epistemic and theoretical basis for their study designs and the interpretation of their results. To be sure, each of the experimental studies mentioned above shows *something interesting*. But the findings are not principles by which we can understand the entirety of the relationships between memory and the Internet, or digital media, or photography. They are drops in the ocean. In practice, understanding the individual and collective implications, for memory, of engagement with digital media and technology will involve the integration of multiple methodologies, forms of data, and disciplines.

Certainly, there have been many welcome and important developments since Neisser made his argument for ecological validity. The work of Brown and Reavey (2015a, 2015b); Keightley and Pickering (2012; Pickering & Keightley, 2015); Fivush (2019; Fivush & Merrill, 2016); Harris and colleagues (e.g., Harris et al., 2014, 2021); Stone and colleagues (Bietti et al., 2014; Stone & Jay, 2019); Manier (Hirst & Manier, 2008; Manier, 2004); Wang (2013); and many others (see, e.g., Singer & Conway, 2014) has developed the ways in which we understand and study the psychology of memory. These authors have benefited from looking across disciplines and from their preparedness to expand memory studies outward, beyond numerical data and purely internal, individual memory systems that are only ever influenced, distorted, reinforced, or damaged by the external world. They have shown us the value of going further in our quest for ecological validity than simply studying memory in the same old ways, albeit in richer settings. Their work is illustrative of a reconsideration of what ecological validity means and how that relates to the models and metaphors of memory we can use for a more meaningful examination of the influence of digital media going forward.

Photography and Remembering as Complex, Entangled Phenomena

It could be argued that we simply need more empirical data from controlled studies, and that it is this lack of data that leads to conclusions from existing research being exaggerated, over-extrapolated, and disproportionately influential. (Indeed, this need for data led to Qi Wang's recent call for empirical papers for a special issue in *Memory* on "Memory Online: Remembering in the Age of the Internet and Social Media"). However, it is my position that, while they are undoubtedly interesting, the papers by Sparrow et al. (2011), Henkel (2014), and others in this growing field can only be stepping stones toward a more ambitious and meaningful, interdisciplinary account of our relations with media, technology, and practices. They are indicative rather than conclusive, fuel for wider and richer conversations, rather than standalone findings that can be meaningfully generalized to broad populations and domains.

There is an appeal to simple and striking answers, such as that Google "is making us stupid" (Carr, 2008) or impeding recall (Sparrow et al., 2011); or that taking digital photographs impairs our ability to recall related information (e.g., Henkel, 2014). However, as Schacter (2022) demonstrates, broad claims often do not stand up to close scrutiny. In particular, Schacter laments the lack of specificity or conceptual precision around claims of technology-mediated impairment (e.g., what exactly does it mean to say that "Internet use is killing your memory"?). Across a range of studies, Schacter sees evidence only for *task-specific impairment* (i.e., impairment for the specific task being studied, such as recall or recognition of objects that are photographed, for that sample of participants) and not for all instances of that form of memory (e.g., recall or recognition) (*domain-specific impairment*) or all forms of memory (*domain-general impairment*). Part of the issue is that it is unclear what the effects found in such studies, aimed at statistical generalization, are being generalized to. First, it's not clear who the effects can be generalized to since the studies do not employ random sampling or specify which population is being represented. Psychological studies often use students, recruited by offering course credit, from Western, educated, industrialized, rich, and democratic (WEIRD) societies (Henrich et al., 2010). Perhaps the assumption is that these participants represent everyone (i.e., the human species), but do we know if all people's memories work in the same way? Wang (2013), for example, through examining the cultural, social, political, and economic forces that act on autobiographical remembering, shows that this is not the case (also see Wang, Chapter 2, this volume). Second, it's not clear what media or technology the effects can be generalized to. I have argued that Henkel's (2014) prescriptive photographing of museum objects and Sparrow et al.'s (2011) prescriptive entering of trivia into a computer are not representative of the wider domains of photography or Internet usage. Third, it's not clear what kinds of remembering the effects can be generalized to. What is being asked of those participants in terms of recognition or recall is very unlike many forms of everyday remembering.

In my research, everyday photography and remembering was chaotic, spontaneous, social, cultural, and idiosyncratic all at once (Fawns, 2019a, 2022a). Participants also described how their technological landscape was always changing, with new cameras and new and overlapping ways of producing, distributing, and consuming material and digital photos. Encounters with media are part of our life experiences and part of how we pay attention to and imagine the world (Keightley & Pickering, 2012). Remembering is not a self-contained activity; it is embedded in wider communication and sense-making, which, in turn, are located in yet broader historical patterns and trajectories (Fawns, 2019a). It is always situated at different and multiple social contexts; as well as in culture, the material, political, and economic environments; and across multiple timescales (Bietti & Sutton, 2015). How could an effect found in a controlled study be representative of all photography and photographic practices, in different contexts, across time?

It will not be surprising to those who see context as a fundamental ingredient of remembering, that controlled studies of media and memory are problematic to replicate or produce inconsistent or ambiguous findings in different contexts. As Neisser (1982) argues, all effects must be contextually framed, and there is likely to be a diversity of effects across contexts. This problem cannot be addressed simply by conducting more controlled studies in more settings with different populations. Clear answers to questions like "What is the effect of prolific photo-taking on autobiographical memory?," for example, require a view of photography and memory in which each is separate and can be clearly and narrowly defined and where one acts on the other in a linear direction. This is a view from which it is possible to set up identical situations for participants, tell them what cameras to use, what kinds of photos to take, what to do with those photos, and to ask very specific questions about what they can remember without those parameters changing the process of remembering beyond the specific effect they are looking for. In contrast, the picture from outside of psychology (e.g., Pickering & Keightley, 2015; Sarvas & Frohlich, 2011; van Dijck, 2008; Whittaker et al., 2010) shows a diversity of interconnected practices (the situated ways that people take, share, organize, and view photos) that are integrated elements of everyday remembering activity.

Arguments that technology and media are making us less able to remember neglect the ways that the Internet, social media, and photography are sources of learning about experiences and the wider world; are used by people in processing their experiences; and are, themselves, part of those experiences. Photography cannot *have an effect on* everyday memory because remembering is not something that happens *after* interaction; it happens *during* interaction, and it cannot be disentangled from the other activity (current and historical) in which it is embedded (Fawns, 2019a). In my research, recall and photography practices were intertwined in chains of remembering, along with inference, meaning making, and the construction of wide-ranging narratives (Fawns, 2022a). For instance, as my participants recalled something (perhaps prompted by a photograph), they would search their physical or digital collections for related photographs. Thus, it was not a question of *a* (media or photography) acting on *b* (memory). *a* and *b* are both very diverse categories, interdependent with the context in which they are situated and fundamentally entwined in broader cognitive and communicative, individual and collective, activity.

Mixing Things Up: Disciplines, Methods, Data, and Conceptions

Technology, digital media, and remembering are so integrated, in such diverse and overlapping ways, that we might as well ask: What is the effect of language on memory? The diversity of practices and contexts, and their implications for how and what we remember, means that we cannot lump all photography, or the whole Internet, or all methods of information searching into meaningful constructs that can be measured. It is also not a matter of just adding caveats to the claims that are made in publications (though this is important, and Henkel and others are careful to do so). We also need to work harder to understand the caveats for they are as important as the effects. They tell us where we might look next.

Controlled studies can contribute to a broader, interdisciplinary picture, in part by giving us contained contexts that can be interrogated through other conceptions, methods, and data. As Sutton (2010) argues, combining methods and traditions can open up new avenues of exploration, and the results from one method can inform studies that use another. Wang (2013), Pickering and Keightley (2015), van House et al. (2005), and others have shown the potential of ethnography and interviews to both build on and contribute to psychological research by exploring everyday practices over longer periods and investigating how they might reinforce, contrast, mitigate, or reframe the results of experimental studies. Conversely, work by Soares and Storm (2022) draws on the blended memory framework (Fawns, 2019a) in designing experiments that take into account personal goals and beliefs about the relationship between photography and memory. Barnier and Hoskins (2018) show how "ongoing conversations (between a cognitive scientist and a sociologist) force us to confront some of our basic assumptions about what memory is and what memory does" (p. 386). Such interdisciplinary interplay is very appropriate: Understanding the diverse ways in which practices, technology, media, and memory interrelate will require studying a large range of scenarios, over longer time frames, while taking account of the ecological settings in which they happen.

Kath Bicknell and colleagues (in progress) provide an exemplar by using both experimental and ethnographic methods at the same time. Extending a program of research on collaborative remembering (Harris et al., 2011, 2021), they take the experiment itself as the unit of analysis, attending to embodied, emotional, and ecological factors that shape the way that couples remember together but are not easily captured by standard coding procedures (J. Sutton, personal communication, 16 November 2021). This ethnographic approach is an interesting example of working across disciplines, using one method to interrogate another. The aim is not to dismiss experiments as invalid but to develop a more nuanced and reflexive understanding of how the situation, and its social and material context, matters to the data that are generated and of what is not captured within those data. The result, I am hopeful, will be a very rich understanding of the meaning of these particular experiments, which will help with both our understanding of the kinds of remembering that went on in that setting and our design of future studies.

In my own research, the use of alternative methods of data generation (photo elicitation interviews) and analysis (qualitative framework analysis, underpinned by a distributed cognition lens) allowed me to develop different kinds of insights from those produced by typical psychological approaches (Fawns, 2019a, 2020, 2022a). These insights are not statistically generalizable, but they can inform new ways of understanding how diverse, ecologically and historically situated photography practices are implicated in remembering. Combining disciplinary approaches can help us to define what it is that we need to understand. That is, the context in which remembering happens is a constitutive part of that remembering, and engagement with "the Internet" or "digital photography" is actually made up of a wide and nebulous set of practices.

Although some of what I have written in this chapter is challenging and critical, I hope that readers will take these arguments in the constructive spirit they are intended. As Manier (2004) points out, it may not be possible to achieve consensus, across the disciplines, on the meaning of experimental findings, or indeed, other kinds of memory research, or even on what memory is. This is a problem if we are set on finding a single shared conception, but perhaps we can live with some ambiguity and, instead, embrace a multiplicity of conceptions, metaphors, methodologies, and interpretations in order to see a richer, if not always clearer, picture of remembering with photography, digital media, and the Internet. Perhaps there are no simple answers, and we may need versatility in our conceptions of memory to allow the integration of different kinds of available information, in different ways, at the point of remembering.

Conclusions

Amid a general mix of overexcitement and moral panic about how technology is affecting our minds, researchers, journalists, and bloggers have extrapolated from the results of a small set of controlled studies to speculate about universal effects of the wider domains of photography and the Internet. In this chapter, I have argued that this issue is related to underlying conceptions and metaphors of memory and how these accommodate interactions with media and technology. Metaphors of storage and retrieval, in particular, cannot adequately account for our versatile and collective, historically situated, media practices. Thus, studies showing linear effects of technology on memory must be interpreted very cautiously when applying them beyond the specific practices and contexts in which those findings are produced (Fawns, 2019a).

Shifting the research focus from memory to remembering activity opens up alternative metaphors that take the contribution of engagement with media to be more fundamental and that can appreciate the diversity of everyday media practices. Multiple metaphors can provide a richer picture, as each picks up relevant aspects missed by the others. This can help us to design research that goes beyond simply moving the lab into the world and that generates alternative data and interpretations. Such moves require crossing disciplinary bounds for a more expansive view of psychology (Barnier & Hoskins, 2018; Brown & Reavey, 2015a; Sutton, 2010), which in turn will be necessary to take account of the diversity, dynamism, and complexity of real-world entanglements of mind and technology.

Acknowledgments

Thanks to Kath Bicknell and John Sutton for discussions about their exciting ethnography of memory experiments. For metaphorical help (i.e., help with metaphors), particular thanks to Lucas Bietti, Ceila Harris, Stephen Hill, Sarah Honeychurch, Suzy Houston, Ira Hyman, Alun Kirby, Stephen D Lindsay, Marina Trakas, and Lyn Tribble. Thanks to Linda Henkel, Betsy Sparrow, Jenny Lieu, and the late Daniel Wegner (whose work inspired that of Sutton, Harris, and others) for their work that I have critiqued here. I have tried to do so respectfully while also highlighting areas where I think new directions are required.

References

Barasch, A., Diehl, K., Silverman, J., & Zauberman, G. (2017). Photographic memory: The effects of volitional photo taking on memory for visual and auditory aspects of an experience. *Psychological Science, 28*(8), 1056–1066. https://doi.org/10.1177/0956797617694868

Barnier, A. J., & Hoskins, A. (2018). Is there memory in the head, in the wild? *Memory Studies, 11*(4), 386–390. https://doi.org/10.1177/1750698018806440

Bartlett, F. C. (1932). *Remembering: A study in experimental and social psychology.* Cambridge University Press.

Bietti, L. M., Stone, C. B., & Hirst, W. (2014). Contextualizing human memory. *Memory Studies, 7*(3), 267–271. https://doi.org/10.1177/1750698014530617

Bietti, L. M., & Sutton, J. (2015). Interacting to remember at multiple timescales: Coordination, collaboration, cooperation and culture in joint remembering. *Interaction Studies, 16*(3), 419–450. https://doi.org/https://doi.org/10.1075/is.16.3.04bie

Brockmeier, J. (2010). After the archive: Remapping memory. *Culture & Psychology, 16*(1), 5–35. https://doi.org/10.1177/1354067x09353212

Brown, S. D., & Hoskins, A. (2010). Terrorism in the new memory ecology: Mediating and remembering the 2005 London bombings. *Behavioral Sciences of Terrorism and Political Aggression,* 2(2), 87–107. https://doi.org/10.1080/19434471003597399

Brown, S. D., & Reavey, P. (2015a). Turning around on experience: The "expanded view" of memory within psychology. *Memory Studies, 8*(2), 131–150. https://doi.org/10.1177/17506 98014558660

Brown, S. D., & Reavey, P. (2015b). *Vital memory and affect: Living with a difficult past.* Routledge.

Brown, S. D., & Reavey, P. (2016). Dilemmas of memory: The mind is not a tape recorder. In C. Tileagă & E. Stokoe (Eds.), *Discursive psychology: Classic and contemporary issues* (pp. 210–223). Routledge.

Camerer, C. F., Dreber, A., Holzmeister, F., Ho, T. H., Huber, J., Johannesson, M., Kirchler, M., Nave, G., Nosek, B. A., Pfeiffer, T., Altmejd, A., Buttrick, N., Chan, T., Chen, Y., Forsell, E., Gampa, A., Heikensten, E., Hummer, L., Imai, T., . . . Wu, H. (2018). Evaluating the replicability of social science experiments in nature and science between 2010 and 2015. *Nature Human Behaviour, 2*(9), 637–644. https://doi.org/10.1038/s41562-018-0399-z

Carr, N. (2008, July). Is Google Making Us Stupid? *The Atlantic.* https://www.theatlantic.com/magazine/archive/2008/07/is-google-making-us-stupid/306868/.

Clampitt, A. (1985). A procession at Candlemas. In A. Knopf (Ed.), *The kingfisher* (pp. 15–20). Knopf.

Clowes, R. (2015). Thinking in the cloud: The cognitive incorporation of cloud-based technology. *Philosophy and Technology, 28*(2), 261–296. https://doi.org/10.1007/s13 347-014-0153-z

Draaisma, D. (2000). *Metaphors of Memory: A history of ideas about the mind.* Cambridge University Press.

Fawns, T. (2019a). Blended memory: A framework for understanding distributed autobiographical remembering with photography. *Memory Studies, 13*(6), 901–916. https://doi.org/10.1177/1750698019829891

Fawns, T. (2019b). Postdigital education in design and practice. *Postdigital Science and Education, 1*(1), 132–145. https://doi.org/10.1007/s42438-018-0021-8

Fawns, T. (2020). The photo-elicitation interview as a multimodal site for reflexivity. In P. Reavey (Ed.), *A handbook of visual methods in psychology: Using and interpreting images in qualitative research* (2nd ed., pp. 487–501). Routledge.

Fawns, T. (2022a). Cued recall: Using photo-elicitation to examine the distributed processes of remembering with photographs. *Memory Studies, 16*(2), 264–279. https://doi.org/10.1177/17506980211073093.

Fawns, T. (2022b). Remembering in the wild: Recontextualising and reconciling studies of media and memory. *Memory, Mind & Media, 1,* e11. https://doi.org/10.1017/mem.2022.5

Fivush, R. (2019). *Family narratives and the development of an autobiographical self: Social and cultural perspectives on autobiographical memory.* Routledge.

Fivush, R., & Merrill, N. (2016). An ecological systems approach to family narratives. *Memory Studies, 9*(3), 305–314. https://doi.org/10.1177/1750698016645264

Garry, M., & Gerrie, M. P. (2005). When photographs create false memories. *Current Directions in Psychological Science, 14*(6), 321–325. https://doi.org/10.1111/j.0963-7214.2005.00390.x

Gibson, W. (1993). *Neuromancer.* Harper.

Grinschgl, S., Papenmeier, F., & Meyerhoff, H. S. (2021). Consequences of cognitive offloading: Boosting performance but diminishing memory. *Quarterly Journal of Experimental Psychology, 74*(9), 1477–1496. https://doi.org/10.1177/17470218211008060

Harris, C. B., Barnier, A. J., Sutton, J., & Keil, P. G. (2014). Couples as socially distributed cognitive systems: Remembering in everyday social and material contexts. *Memory Studies, 7*(3), 285–297. https://doi.org/10.1177/1750698014530619

Harris, C. B., Keil, P., Sutton, J., & Barnier, A. J. (2011). We remember, we forget: Collaborative remembering in older couples. *Discourse Processes, 48*(4), 267–303. https://doi.org/https://doi.org/10.1080/0163853X.2010.541854

Harris, C. B., Sutton, J., & Barnier, A. J. (2021). Autobiographical forgetting, social forgetting, and situated forgetting: Forgetting in context. In J. Rummel (Ed.), *Current Issues in Memory: Memory Research in the Public Interest* (pp. 144–178). Routledge. https://doi.org/10.4324/9781003106715-9

Hassabis, D., & Maguire, E. A. (2007). Deconstructing episodic memory with construction. *Trends in Cognitive Sciences, 11*(7), 299–306. https://doi.org/10.1016/j.tics.2007.05.001

Henkel, L. (2014). Point-and-shoot memories: The influence of taking photos on memory for a museum tour. *Psychological Science, 25*(2), 396–402. https://doi.org/10.1177/0956797613504438.

Henrich, J., Heine, S. J., & Norenzayan, A. (2010). The weirdest people in the world? *Behavioral and Brain Sciences, 33*(2–3), 61–83; discussion, 83–135. https://doi.org/10.1017/S0140525X0999152X

Hermann, P., Mitchell, S. A., & Arnórsdóttir, A. S. (Eds.). (2014). *Memory in medieval Nordic culture.* Brepols.

Hesselmann, G. (2020). No conclusive evidence that difficult general knowledge questions cause a "Google Stroop effect." A replication study. *PeerJ, 8*, e10325. https://doi.org/10.7717/peerj.10325

Hirst, W., & Manier, D. (2008). Towards a psychology of collective memory. *Memory, 16*(3), 183–200. https://doi.org/10.1080/09658210701811912

Hiscott, R. (2014, July 29). 8 ways technology makes you stupid. *Huffington Post.* https://www.huffingtonpost.co.uk/entry/technology-intelligence_n_5617181

Horvath, J. C. (2020, May 1). Is modern media destroying our memories? *The Scientist.* https://www.the-scientist.com/critic-at-large/is-modern-media-destroying-our-memories--67483

Hoskins, A. (2016). Memory ecologies. *Memory Studies, 9*(3), 348–357. https://doi.org/10.1177/1750698016645274

Kahn, A. S., & Martinez, T. M. (2020). Text and you might miss it? Snap and you might remember? Exploring "Google effects on memory" and cognitive self-esteem in the context of Snapchat and text messaging. *Computers in Human Behavior, 104*(March 2020), 106166. https://doi.org/10.1016/j.chb.2019.106166

Keightley, E., & Pickering, M. (2012). *The mnemonic imagination: Remembering as creative practice.* Palgrave Macmillan.

Kelly, M. O., & Risko, E. F. (2021). Revisiting the influence of offloading memory on free recall. *Memory and Cognition, 50*, 710–721. https://doi.org/10.3758/s13421-021-01237-3

Klein, S. B. (2015). What memory is. *Wiley Interdisciplinary Reviews: Cognitive Science, 6*(1), 1–38. https://doi.org/10.1002/wcs.1333

Koriat, A., & Goldsmith, M. (1996). Memory metaphors and the real-life/laboratory controversy: Correspondence versus storehouse conceptions of memory. *Behavioral and Brain Sciences, 19*, 167–228. https://doi.org/10.1017/S0140525X00042114

Koutstaal, W., Schacter, D., Johnson, M. K., Angell, K. E., & Gross, M. S. (1998). Post-event review in older and younger adults: Improving memory accessibility of complex everyday events. *Psychology and Aging, 13*(2), 277–296. http://psycnet.apa.org/journals/pag/13/2/277/

Koutstaal, W., Schacter, D. L., Johnson, M. K., & Galluccio, L. (1999). Facilitation and impairment of event memory produced by photograph review. *Memory & Cognition, 27*(3), 478–493. http://www.ncbi.nlm.nih.gov/pubmed/10355237

Kuhn, A. (2010). Memory texts and memory work: Performances of memory in and with visual media. *Memory Studies, 3*(4), 298–313. https://doi.org/10.1177/1750698010370034

Lakoff, G., & Johnson, M. (1980). *Metaphors we live by*. University of Chicago Press.

Leary, D. E. (1990). Psyche's muse: The role of metaphor in the history of psychology. In D. E. Leary (Ed.), *Metaphors in the history of psychology* (pp. 1–78). Cambridge University Press.

Locke J. (1847). *An essay concerning human understanding*. Kay & Troutman.

Lohmeier, C., & Pentzold, C. (2014). Making mediated memory work: Cuban-Americans, Miami media and the doings of diaspora memories. *Media, Culture & Society, 36*(6), 776–789. https://doi.org/10.1177/0163443713518574

Loveday, C., & Conway, M. A. (2011). Using SenseCam with an amnesic patient: Accessing inaccessible everyday memories. *Memory, 19*(7), 697–704. https://doi.org/10.1080/09658211.2011.610803

Manier, D. (2004). Is memory in the brain? Remembering as social behavior. *Mind, Culture, and Activity, 11*(4), 251–266. https://doi.org/10.1207/s15327884mca1104_2

Marsh, E. J., & Rajaram, S. (2019). The digital expansion of the mind: Implications of Internet usage for memory and cognition. *Journal of Applied Research in Memory and Cognition, 8*(1), 1–14. https://doi.org/10.1016/j.jarmac.2018.11.001

Michaelian, K. (2016). *Mental time travel: Episodic memory and our knowledge of the personal past*. MIT Press.

Nash, R. A., Wade, K. A., & Lindsay, D. S. (2009). Digitally manipulating memory: Effects of doctored videos and imagination in distorting beliefs and memories. *Memory & Cognition, 37*(4), 414–424. https://doi.org/10.3758/MC.37.4.414

Neisser, U. (1978). Memory: What are the important questions? In M. M. Gruneberg, P. E. Morris, & R. N. Sykes (Eds.), *Practical aspects of memory* (pp. 3–19). Academic.

Neisser, U. (1981). John Dean's memory: A case study. *Cognition, 9*(1), 1–22.

Neisser, U. (1982). *Memory observed*. W. H. Freeman.

Neisser, U. (2014). *Cognitive psychology*. Classic edition. Psychology Press.

Paster, J. (1992). Advertising immortality by Kodak. *History of* Photography, 16(2), 135–139. https://doi.org/10.1080/03087298.1992.10442537

Pereira, G. (2019, October 2–5). *Apple memories and automated memory-making: Marketing speak, chip-engineering, and the politics of prediction* [Paper presentation]. Association of Internet Researchers Conference, Brisbane, Australia. https://www.gabrielpereira.net/AppleMemoriesAoIR2019Gabriel.pdf

Perry, S. (2018, June 28). Want to remember a special moment? Put down the camera. *MinnPost*. https://www.minnpost.com/second-opinion/2018/06/want-remember-special-moment-put-down-camera/

Pickering, M., & Keightley, E. (2015). *Photography, music and memory: Pieces of the past in everyday life*. Palgrave Macmillan.

Roediger, H. L. (1980). Memory metaphors in cognitive psychology. *Memory & Cognition, 8*(3), 231–246. https://doi.org/10.3758/BF03197611

Runge, Y., Frings, C., & Tempel, T. (2019). Saving-enhanced performance: saving items after study boosts performance in subsequent cognitively demanding tasks. *Memory, 27*(10), 1462–1467. https://doi.org/10.1080/09658211.2019.1654520

Runge, Y., Frings, C., & Tempel, T. (2021). Specifying the mechanisms behind benefits of saving-enhanced memory. *Psychological Research, 85*(4), 1633–1644. https://doi.org/10.1007/s00426-020-01341-0

Sarvas, R., & Frohlich, D. M. (2011). *From snapshots to social media—The changing picture of domestic photography*. Springer. https://doi.org/10.1007/978-0-85729-247-6

Schacter, D. L. (2022). Media, technology, and the sins of memory. *Memory, Mind & Media, 1*, e1. https://doi.org/10.1017/mem.2021.3

Singer, J. A., & Conway, M. A. (2014). The varieties of remembered experience: Moving memory beyond the bounded self. *Memory Studies, 7*(3), 385–392. https://doi.org/10.1177/1750698014530626

Soares, J. S., & Storm, B. C. (2018). Forget in a flash: A further investigation of the photo-taking-impairment effect. *Journal of Applied Research in Memory and Cognition, 7*, 154–160. https://doi.org/10.1016/j.jarmac.2017.10.004

Soares, J. S., & Storm, B. C. (2022). Exploring functions of and recollections with photos in the age of smartphone cameras. *Memory Studies, 15*(2), 287–303. https://doi.org/10.1177/17506980211044712

Sparrow, B., Liu, J., & Wegner, D. M. (2011). Google effects on memory: Cognitive consequences of having information at our fingertips. *Science, 333*(6043), 776–778. https://doi.org/10.1126/science.1207745

Stone, C. B., & Jay, A. C. V. (2019). From the individual to the collective: The emergence of a psychological approach to collective memory. *Applied Cognitive Psychology, 33*(4), 504–515. https://doi.org/10.1002/acp.3564

Storm, B. C., & Stone, S. M. (2015). Saving-enhanced memory: The benefits of saving on the learning and remembering of new information. *Psychological Science, 26*(2), 182–188. https://doi.org/10.1177/0956797614559285

Strange, D., Hayne, H., & Garry, M. (2008). A photo, a suggestion, a false memory. *Applied Cognitive Psychology, 22*, 587–603. https://doi.org/10.1002/acp.1390

Suddendorf, T., & Corballis, M. C. (2007). The evolution of foresight: What is mental time travel, and is it unique to humans? *Behavioral and Brain Sciences, 30*(3), 299–313. https://doi.org/10.1017/S0140525X07001975

Sutton, J. (2010). Exograms and interdisciplinarity: history, the extended mind, and the civilizing process. In R. Menary (Ed.), *The extended mind* (pp. 189–225). MIT Press.

Tamblyn, T. (2018, June 1). There's now a scientific reason why you shouldn't take pictures at gigs. *Huffington Post*. https://www.huffingtonpost.co.uk/entry/theres-now-a-scientific-reason-why-you-shouldnt-take-pictures-at-gigs_uk_5b110559e4b010565aaaee5c

van Dijck, J. (2007). *Mediated memories in the digital age*. Stanford University Press.

van Dijck, J. (2008). Mediated memories: A snapshot of remembered experience. In P. P. & W. S. J. Kooijman (Ed.), *Mind the screen: Media concepts according to Thomas Elsaesser* (pp. 71–81). Amsterdam University Press.

van House, N. A., Davis, M., Ames, M., Finn, M., & Viswanathan, V. (2005). The uses of personal networked digital imaging: An empirical study of cameraphone photos and sharing. In *CHI '05 Extended Abstracts on Human Factors in Computing Systems* (pp. 1853–1856). Association for Computing Machinery. https://doi.org/10.1145/1056808.1057039

Wang, Q. (2013). *The autobiographical self in time and culture*. Oxford University Press.

Whittaker, S., Bergman, O., & Clough, P. (2010). Easy on that trigger dad: A study of long term family photo retrieval. *Personal and Ubiquitous Computing, 14*(1), 31–43. https://doi.org/10.1007/s00779-009-0218-7

Wong, L. (2020, December 16). Unplugged weddings: Stopping guests from taking photos could be good for you and them. *ABC Everyday*. https://www.abc.net.au/everyday/unplugged-weddings-give-couples-more-control/10440830

PART IV

FAKE NEWS AND FALSE MEMORIES

8

Memories for Public Events in the Internet Age

Fake News, False Memories, and Filter Bubbles

Gillian Murphy, Rebecca Egan, and Ciara M. Greene

Social media has changed how people get their news. While social media platforms like Facebook may have been designed with the aim of connecting people and allowing them to share personal information, they have since become one of the principal sources of information about issues of public concern. Indeed, more than half of all adults surveyed globally report getting their news from social media at least some of the time (Kennedy & Prat, 2019).

The rise of social media platforms as a primary source of news for many people has changed the face of public events profoundly and rapidly. Where public events previously may have been reported once a day in newspapers, or on the hour, in television or radio bulletins, consumers now receive second-by-second live updates of public events. This evolution of news consumption has been aided by a rise in citizen journalism, allowing for a rich and varied flow of news updates through a variety of platforms. While this ever developing approach to information dissemination has facilitated the broadcasting of alternative perspectives and amplification of otherwise marginalized voices (Allan & Thorsen, 2009), the impact has not been entirely positive, with some blaming the Internet for increasing threats to democracy around the world (Lewandowsky & Pomerantsev, 2022). Consider, for example, the efforts by Reddit users to identify the perpetrators of the 2013 Boston Marathon. The Reddit community reacted enthusiastically to this new method of "crowdsourcing" investigations, and quickly narrowed their focus to an entirely innocent missing student, Sunil Tripathi. The speed with which suppositions about Sunil's involvement spread through social media serves as an object lesson about the dangers of online misinformation. Sunil had gone missing a month before the attack in Boston and had died by suicide. His body was found several days after the real perpetrators were identified by police. By this time, the damage was done; Sunil's family had been bombarded with racial slurs and relentlessly hounded by journalists and

Gillian Murphy, Rebecca Egan, and Ciara M. Greene, *Memories for Public Events in the Internet Age* In: *The Remaking of Memory in the Age of the Internet and Social Media*. Edited by: Qi Wang and Andrew Hoskins, Oxford University Press.
 DOI: 10.1093/oso/9780197661260.003.0008

members of the public in an effort to find him (Madrigal, 2013; National Public Radio [NPR], 2016). There are growing concerns also about the emergence of cheap and easy-to-use deepfake software, which allows average Internet users to create highly realistic doctored media that features a person doing or saying something they never did (Nightingale & Wade, 2022), potentially distorting memory (Murphy & Flynn, 2022).

Social media has become a primary vector for online misinformation (Allcott et al., 2019), with more and more research focusing on the problem of online "fake news." Fake news can be defined as "fabricated information that mimics news media content in form but not in organizational process or intent" (Lazer et al., 2018, p. 1094). One consequence of exposure to online misinformation may be the formation of false memories for the events described (i.e., fabricated memories of events that never occurred). Research has identified a range of factors that increase the likelihood that an individual will develop a false memory. These include presentation of the misinformation alongside an accompanying image (Garry et al., 2007; Sacchi et al., 2007); multiple presentations of a story (Pennycook et al., 2018); and alignment of the misinformation with the individual's personal views and beliefs (Montgomery & Rajagopal, 2018; Murphy et al., 2019; O'Connell & Greene, 2017). On the Internet, and particularly on social media, these factors can often occur simultaneously, creating an environment that is highly conducive to the formation of false memories for misinformation. This new landscape for the reporting of public events has therefore yielded new and pertinent opportunities for research into the impact of memory distortion.

This chapter describes the wealth of established research on the relationship between the Internet and formation of false memories for public events. We consider the role of social media "filter bubbles" and the impact of individual ideology and report on what we know about the effect of online interactions on offline behavior. We also consider key methodological challenges and pressing issues that require further contemplation in future research.

Ideology and Memory Distortion

A common concern about consuming information via the Internet is that we may live our online lives in "ideological echo chambers" (Eady et al., 2019; Guess, 2021) where our ability to curate our newsfeeds means that we may experience reality differently from those with opposing ideologies. In particular, we may be more likely to be exposed to ideologically congruent information due to filter bubbles that can form on social media (Pariser, 2011, though see Bruns, 2019, for an opposing view). Social media users are exposed to a personalized stream of information, in part because we tend to follow like-minded people (Lazer et al., 2018). Consuming a diet of primarily ideologically congruent information may make individuals more susceptible to misinformation (Rhodes, 2021). Some studies have found that partisan polarization is a key motivation for sharing misinformation on social media (Osmundsen et al., 2021), and that corrections of misinformation (e.g., fact checks) may be less effective for ideologically congruent stories (Grady et al., 2021).

The nature of human memory also affects how we experience and remember information gleaned from these online environments. Many decades of research have demonstrated the ease with which our memories can be distorted (Loftus, 2005); from inserting misleading details into our memories of a witnessed event (Loftus & Palmer, 1974; Zaragoza & Lane, 1994) to implanting entirely fabricated memories of events that never occurred (Hyman & Billings, 1998; Loftus & Pickrell, 1995; Wade et al., 2002). More recent research has established that false memories can form after exposure to misleading news articles or headlines (Greene & Murphy, 2020; Murphy, Lynch, et al., 2021; Polage, 2012). This phenomenon can be interpreted through the lens of the source-monitoring framework (SMF; M. K. Johnson et al., 1993). The SMF posits that our memories are not arranged like libraries: We do not have a collection of individual files with tags that identify their source, such as "this is a memory of a conversation you had with Susan last Tuesday." Instead, we distinguish between true and false memories based on the apparent qualities of the putative memory. When we encounter a news story and consider whether we remember this event as having really happened, we evaluate the memory using two parallel judgments. The first is a relatively quick, heuristic judgment, in which we assess the amount and quality of perceptual information available and compare the features of the mental experience with the characteristics of a typical true memory (e.g., in terms of vividness, clarity, detail, etc.). The second judgment involves a slower, more systematic evaluation of whether the details of the memory are plausible, in line with prior knowledge, and so on. Both of these processes can lead individuals to incorrectly categorize a mental experience (e.g., a mental image of a fabricated event described in a headline) as a real memory. Readers may then draw on their existing knowledge of the topic and previously encountered news stories to unwittingly manufacture a detailed and realistic false memory of the event. False memories are therefore likely to be constructed in line with our existing opinions: The congruency between the event and our attitudes, knowledge, and schemas may generate a misplaced sense of familiarity, biasing these source-monitoring judgements (Montgomery & Rajagopal, 2018; Murphy et al., 2019; O'Connell & Greene, 2017). A number of studies in recent years have established this ideological congruency effect in false memories for online fake news, providing insight into the interaction of memory and the Internet.

In 2013, Frenda and colleagues conducted an experiment with *Slate* magazine where over 5,000 readers were exposed to fake news stories featuring doctored political images. Approximately half of their participants reported remembering these fabricated stories, such as an account of President George W. Bush entertaining a famous athlete at his ranch during the aftermath of Hurricane Katrina in 2005. Readers who encountered a news story that was in line with their existing beliefs were especially likely to report a false memory for that story (see Figure 8.1a). This applied to both political parties; liberal voters were more likely to "remember" a story that reflected poorly on conservatives (e.g., the President Bush story), and likewise, conservative voters were more likely to "remember" a story that reflected poorly on liberals.

This ideological congruency effect for political false memories was replicated during a real-world political campaign. In 2018, Ireland held a national referendum on abortion, with voters asked whether they wished to remove a highly restrictive amendment in the constitution that outlawed abortion in almost all circumstances. One week before polling day, over 4,000 readers of an online news site completed a survey where they viewed true and fake news stories related to the campaign (Murphy et al., 2019). This included a story describing how campaign posters had to be destroyed after it emerged that they were purchased using funds from foreign lobbyists. Participants viewed either a version of the story that reflected poorly on the side they were supporting (e.g., a Yes voter reading that the Yes campaign was forced to destroy posters) or a version of the story that reflected poorly on the side they were not supporting (e.g., a Yes voter reading that the No campaign was forced to destroy posters). As in the Frenda et al. (2013) study, the findings demonstrated the ease with which online news readers formed false memories for these fake stories. Individuals were more susceptible to fake news stories that aligned with their existing political opinions (see Figure 8.1b). Many participants named the outlet where they had encountered this story and described their feelings at the time (e.g., "I had my mind made up prior to these posters; however, after this story I was disinterested in the No campaign as I didn't agree with the involvement of other countries in our country's decisions"). When warned at the end of the study that they may have been exposed to misinformation, participants were less likely to successfully identify the fake story if it was in line with their beliefs, demonstrating the difficulty in overcoming this form of bias.

A study with UK voters in the wake of the Brexit referendum found that, once again, Leave voters were more likely to report false memories for fabricated news stories that reflected poorly on Remain voters and vice-versa (Greene et al., 2021). There was some evidence that effects of ideological congruency were even stronger if the participants were first exposed to a threat to their social identity as a "Leaver" or "Remainer." This served to further reinforce the finding that false memories for fake news tend to form nonrandomly and may be used to shore up

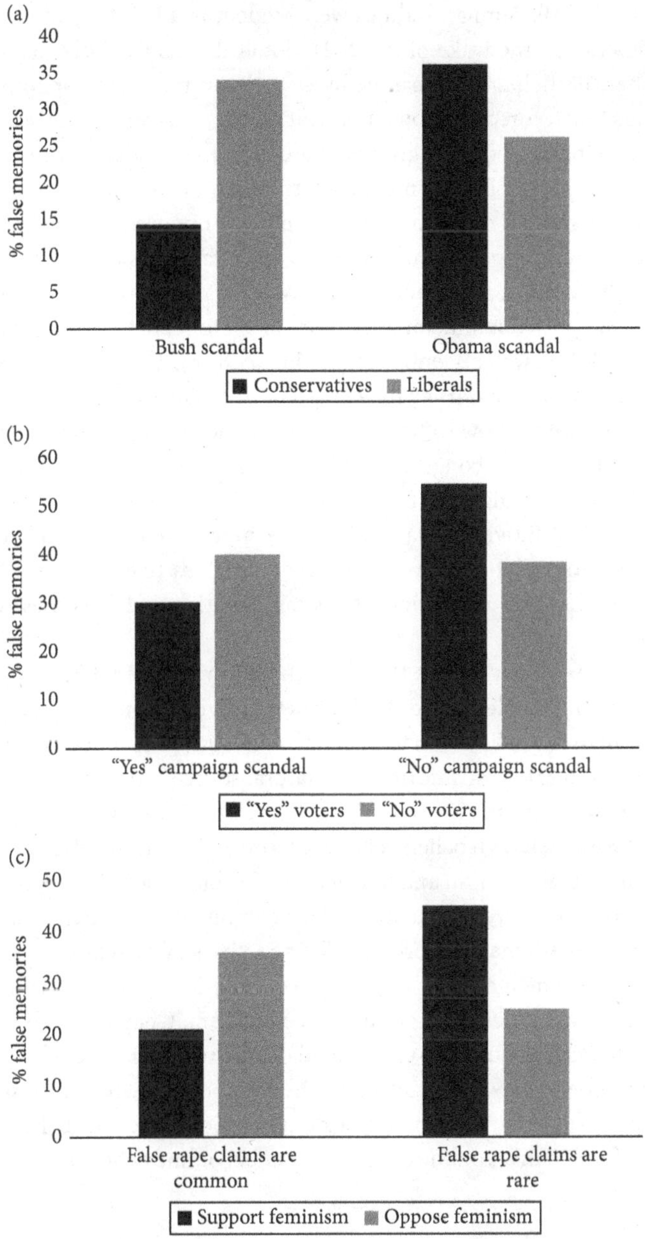

Figure 8.1 A simplified representation of results from three false memory experiments demonstrating the ideological congruency effect. (a) Percentage of liberal and conservative respondents who falsely remembered fabricated scandals about Presidents Bush and Obama (Frenda et al., 2013). (b) Percentage of Yes and No voters in the Irish abortion referendum who remembered fabricated scandals about the Yes and No campaigns (Murphy et al., 2019). (c) Percentage of participants who either oppose or support feminism who falsely remembered a fabricated news story claiming that false rape claims are very common or very rare (Murphy, Murray & Gough, 2021).

our existing beliefs. Similar findings were evident in a US study of Republicans and Democrats in the wake of the 2021 riot at the US Capitol (Calvillo et al., 2022), where participants were more likely to report memories for both true and false events that favored their own political party.

Outside of binary political groups, there is further evidence for the ideological congruency effect in false memory formation. In a study assessing attitudes toward feminism, the more strongly participants opposed feminism, the more likely they were to report a false memory for a fake news story that reflected poorly on the feminist movement (Murphy, Murray & Gough, 2021). Likewise, those who supported feminism were more likely to report a false memory for a story that reflected well on feminists (see Figure 8.1c). This effect persisted even when participants were warned they may have seen fabricated news stories, once again demonstrating how difficult this congruency effect can be to overcome. Finally, this ideological congruency effect was also observed in relation to misinformation concerning COVID-19 vaccines (Greene et al., 2022). Individuals with preexisting antivaccine attitudes were more likely to falsely remember a fabricated story that negatively portrayed vaccines (e.g., "The mRNA technology in the COVID-19 vaccine affects cell mutation and decreases your bone density").

Research has clearly shown then that there is a unique interaction between human memory, ideology, and the Internet. Individuals may be more likely to view content that is in line with their beliefs when they consume information online. On encountering misinformation, natural source-monitoring mechanisms of memory leave Internet users particularly vulnerable to misinformation that is consistent with their own beliefs. They are more likely to form false memories for this kind of misinformation and less likely to be able to detect it, even if they are warned about exposure to fake news. This combination of Internet algorithms and memory biases may exacerbate polarized views of current events and even distort collective memories of important community histories (for further discussion of social influence on memory, see Rajaram, Chapter 12, this volume). Further research is required to understand the nature of this kind of memory distortion and how it may be enhanced by the Internet. Perhaps the most pressing issue we must consider, though, is the extent to which inaccurate beliefs and false memories formed in an online context may affect offline behavior.

How Do Misinformation and False Memories Affect Offline Behaviors?

A key methodological challenge in this area is assessing the offline consequences of online misinformation. For example, to what extent does exposure to fake news about vaccines affect vaccine uptake? If an Internet user develops a false memory for a fake news story involving a particular politician, is this likely to affect their voting behavior? A wealth of research has examined responses to fake news exposure (Murphy, de Saint Laurent, et al., 2023). As discussed above, a number of studies have examined false memory formation after fake news exposure (Frenda et al., 2013; Murphy et al., 2019); however, the most commonly used outcome measures include how accurate a participant believes the information in question to be (Clayton et al., 2020; Pennycook et al., 2018), and how willing they would be to share the information online (Fazio, 2020; Mosleh et al., 2020). Interestingly, these two measures are not always tightly correlated. Pennycook et al. (2021) demonstrated that while true headlines are rated as more accurate than fake headlines, Internet users make decisions on what to share online based on factors other than accuracy. In addition to a genuine desire to educate or inform, social media users' motivations for sharing misinformation have been found to include efforts to engage in "collective fact-checking," the formation or maintenance of social relationships, advertisement of one's political leanings, and, very commonly, a desire to entertain others (Metzger et al., 2021). A prime example of this was provided by rapper Nicki Minaj in September 2021, when she tweeted: "My cousin in Trinidad won't get the [COVID-19] vaccine cuz his friend got it & became impotent. His testicles became swollen. His friend was weeks away from getting married, now the girl called off the wedding. So just pray on it & make sure you're comfortable with ur decision, not bullied." Minaj's post spread across the Internet like wildfire—garnering over 100,000 retweets within the first week—but it does not follow that this reflected a high level of serious engagement with or belief in the content of the tweet. In fact, a cursory examination of replies and quote tweets reveals that a high proportion of responses consisted of jokes at Minaj's expense or corrections of the misinformation contained in her tweet. Given the range of motivations for sharing misinformation described above (and also discussed by Stone et al., Chapter 1, in this volume), it seems clear that sharing intentions cannot be considered a valid proxy for real-world behavioral effects. Investigating offline behavior is undoubtedly challenging, but very few studies have attempted to bridge this gap in the literature, despite its clear applied importance.

Drawing on a wealth of research in communication studies, health psychology, political science, and other disciplines, there is evidence that exposure to information can affect attitudes (Cialdini et al., 1981; Feldman, 2011). More recent research has considered if the same may be true for misinformation. Featherstone and Zhang (2020) exposed participants to misinformation about vaccines and assessed how this affected attitudes toward vaccination. The misinformation was either conspiratorial in nature (e.g., pharmaceutical companies are deceiving us to make a profit) or described medical uncertainty about vaccines (e.g., scientists are not sure about the link between the measles-mumps-rubella [MMR] vaccine and autism). Both misinformation messages modestly decreased pro-vaccination attitudes in comparison to a control group, but did not increase vaccine safety concerns. Other studies have also found smaller or nonsignificant effects. Drummond et al. (2020) exposed participants to fake news headlines concerning climate change (e.g., "'Nearly All' Recent Global Warming Is Fabricated, Study Finds"; "Global Warming 'Vanishes' After Australia Adjusts Climate Data Error"). They found small reductions in belief in climate change due to human activity and lower estimates of the scientific consensus. Drummond et al. note that the very small effect sizes call into question the notion that misinformation is a primary driver of climate change skepticism in the United States, with their data demonstrating stronger effects of ideology and political party affiliation. These studies suggest that the kind of misinformation encountered online may affect attitudes that are relevant for real-world behaviors, but these effects may not be large when assessed after a single exposure.

Beyond attitudes, a recent study examined the effect of misinformation and false memories on behavioral intentions (Greene & Murphy, 2021). In a large online study conducted with a media outlet in May 2020, participants ($N = 3{,}746$) were presented with real and fake news stories concerning COVID-19. Fake stories included claims that eating spicy foods could boost immunity to the virus, and that the designers of a national contact-tracing app had previously been involved in a data privacy scandal. Participants were asked about their memories for these stories and their intention to engage in related behaviors (e.g., intentions to eat more spicy food, to download the contact-tracing app). About a quarter of participants reported a false memory for at least one of the two fake stories they were shown. Exposure to the fake news stories had small but inconsistent effects on behavioral intentions—for example, those who viewed the fake story about the contact-tracing app were 5% less willing to download the app than those who did not view the story (see Figure 8.2). Small but inconsistent effects of forming a false memory were also observed: For some fake stories, those who reported a false memory indicated significantly different behavioral intentions than those who did not. Finally, after being warned that they may have been exposed to fake news, participants were asked to rate the truthfulness of the stories. Those who had formed false memories for the fake stories rated those stories as considerably more truthful, even after this warning.

While there is a well-documented gap between intentions and behaviors (Rhodes & de Bruijn, 2013), intentions are a critical first step for behavior change. Although the effects of fake news exposure observed in this study were small, these changes in behavioral intention might be sufficient to "nudge" public behavior in a particular direction. This study was among the first to explore the

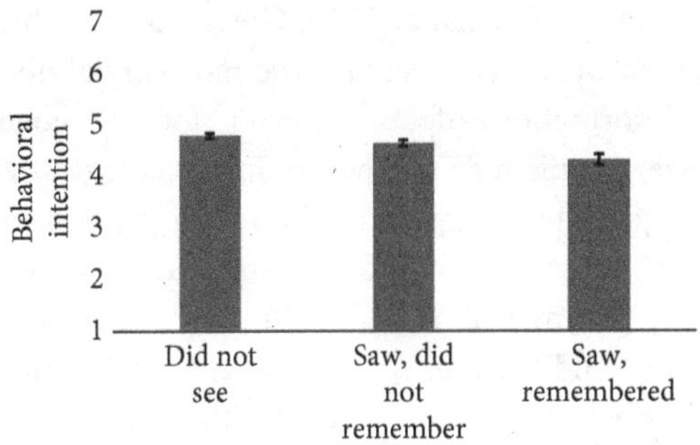

Figure 8.2 Intention to download a COVID-19 contact tracing app among participants who did or did not see a fabricated story about privacy concerns with the app. Intention to download the app was slightly reduced among participants who saw the story relative to those who didn't and further reduced among those who formed a false memory for the events described in the fake news story (Greene & Murphy, 2021).

effects of online misinformation on offline health behaviors by assessing behavioral intentions. There is now an urgent need for further research exploring offline effects of online misinformation. In particular, how does memory distortion via Internet misinformation actually change behavior? Despite its importance, this question comes with a number of methodological challenges.

Key Methodological Challenges

In assessing some of the most pressing methodological challenges in research in this area, we note that our perspective (as cognitive psychologists) means that we are considering memory from a human individual perspective ("memory in the head"), rather than a collective, sociocultural perspective ("memory in the wild") (Barnier & Hoskins, 2018). Both perspectives have much to offer, and interdisciplinary conversations should continue in this regard (also see Hoskins, Chapter 3, this volume, for further insight into technology-mediated memory in the wild).

Assessing the Effect of Multiple Exposures

In the vast majority of studies relating to misinformation effects on attitude and intention change, participants are exposed to misinformation very briefly, in a single session (Aftab & Murphy, 2022; de Saint Laurent et al., 2022; Drummond et al., 2020; Featherstone & Zhang, 2020; Greene & Murphy, 2020). For ethical and practical reasons, this is perhaps the most straightforward method of investigating misinformation effects, allowing for immediate debriefing of participants. However, this may not be the most ecologically valid approach. On social media, individuals may see the same fake news story multiple times, and research has shown that just two exposures to misinformation increases perceived accuracy (Pennycook et al., 2018). The challenge for researchers is balancing ecological validity (letting participants view misinformation multiple times, allowing time between exposures, etc.) with ethical concerns—we must be cognizant of the possibility that our research may result in participants retaining false beliefs that may affect their behavior or be shared with other individuals. We propose two complementary solutions to this issue: First, researchers may investigate effects of multiple exposures to potentially harmful misinformation in tightly controlled experiments, in which participants are carefully followed up and rigorously debriefed. Second, this approach may be combined with "field" studies, in which participants are exposed to harmless misinformation, and their real-world behavior tracked with experience-sampling methods. It is our contention that converging results from these studies may provide more accurate measures of the effects of online misinformation exposure.

Assessing the Role of Information Source

Online misinformation is often encountered in a social context. Individuals read stories from trusted friends and colleagues, from well-regarded news outlets, and similar. This is difficult to emulate in an experimental context. Given that experimental evidence suggests that trust in the source (Griffin et al., 2017; Pena et al., 2017) and presentation format (Fenn et al., 2014) affect false memory formation, our explorations of online memory distortion (and its potential offline consequences) need to be considered in context. Individuals may find groups of like-minded individuals on the Internet who provide a sense of community; this may lead to the formation of an in-group/out-group mentality on social media, especially if there is a perception that the in-group is under threat from outside sources (Branscombe et al., 1999). This can be augmented through the interactional nature of the Internet and social media in particular, with its focus on sharing, commenting, and instant messaging. For those consuming a largely homogeneous information diet within so-called filter bubbles, this community interaction may add a particularly persuasive layer to the processing of news stories. This sense of group belonging has been reported to have powerful and sometimes sinister effects: Such online communities can both contribute to an individual's polarization or radicalization, and also provide shared norms against which those already in possession of contentious views can compare themselves (Bliuc et al, 2020). Evidence has suggested that individuals tend to follow and interact with material posted by people perceived to be in their in-group (Mosleh et al., 2020; Wojcieszak et al., 2021) at a higher rate than members of their out-group (Rathje et al., 2021). The social contagion effect seen on social media, in which information spreads quickly through social networks, means that information can spread more rapidly in an online context than via offline networks (Brady et al., 2020). The potential power of this component of the Internet poses an additional methodological challenge to research in this area: How can this social interactional aspect of the Internet and in particular social media be replicated in an experimental context? Recreating these participatory aspects of the online world in empirical studies represents a key step toward more coherent investigation of the implications for offline behavior and subsequent memory distortion.

Appropriate Debriefing

Deception is often necessary when we study online misinformation and false memories. We typically do not tell participants in advance that they are about to encounter falsehoods, and we often expose them to realistic and convincing misinformation that they may believe to be true. It is of critical importance that we appropriately debrief our participants after they take part in such a study, ensuring that we don't inadvertently spread misinformation in the course of our research. This is especially important for false memory research that presents fake news stories concerning current events, where lingering false beliefs may have real consequences for participants' health behaviors, voting intentions, or other consequential decisions. As discussed in Tay and Ecker (Chapter 9, this volume), many studies have shown a "continued influence effect" (H. M. Johnson & Seifert, 1994), whereby retracting information does not entirely remove its effects (De Keersmaecker & Roets, 2017; Ecker et al., 2010). A crucial methodological challenge in this area of research is establishing guidelines for best practice in debriefing participants (Greene et al., 2023). To achieve this, we need further data on how well our current practices are working. This may involve following up with participants to assess whether they are more likely to believe information they were previously exposed to during our experiments (Greene & Murphy, 2023; Greene et al., 2024) or asking participants how they felt about the study and whether they perceived the debriefing procedure as sufficient and appropriate (Murphy, Maher, et al., 2023).

In a follow-up to the false memory study concerning the abortion referendum described in the section "Ideology and Memory Distortion" (Murphy et al.,

2019), Murphy et al. (2020) examined the effectiveness of the debriefing procedure and how participants felt about the study. There were 630 participants followed up six months after the original study and presented with true and fake news stories, some of which had appeared in the original study and some of which were novel. These returning participants' memories were compared with 474 newly recruited participants who had not taken part in the original study. The original participants were less likely than new recruits to report a false memory for a previously seen fake story, but more likely to report a memory for a previously seen true story, indicating that the debriefing procedure was effective. Both groups of participants also reported enjoying the experiment and feeling confident that they understood the deception that had been used.

Further research has emphasized the importance of appropriate debriefing in misinformation studies. Greenspan and Loftus (2021) found that when using a standard debriefing procedure following an eyewitness misinformation experiment, many participants continued to endorse the misinformation one week later. However, in a second study, they employed an enhanced debriefing procedure, where more information was given to participants, and found that this eliminated the misinformation effect at follow-up. Furthermore, participants who underwent enhanced debriefing also reported a more positive experience.

Future research concerning online misinformation must ensure that participants are appropriately debriefed (Murphy & Greene, 2023). We would encourage the use of follow-up studies to assess persistent false beliefs following debriefing. This is essential from an ethical standpoint, but will also provide insight into effective retractions of misinformation generally.

These findings have important applications in real-world online settings. Consider, for example, recent attempts by social media companies to curb the spread on their platforms of misinformation relating to the COVID-19 pandemic. The typical approach to combatting this misinformation includes corrective declarations on posts that may contain misinformation in combination with links to more reliable information on the topic. Further development of the optimal debriefing process in experimental settings could in turn influence the effectiveness of online procedures for reducing the harm associated with misinformation and the formation of false memories.

Conclusion

The rise of the Internet has changed the way in which we experience public events, whether a local political contest, national terrorism, or a global pandemic. The average consumer now has access to more information than ever before; by extension, we are also exposed to a greater quantity of misinformation, with the potential for significant effects on public health and political process. While the Internet has changed the way we get our news, it has also offered new opportunities to researchers hoping to study the impact of misinformation on cognition. In this chapter, we outlined recent research describing the effects of online misinformation on both cognitive processing—including the formation of false memories—and offline behavior. We identified key areas for future research, with a particular focus on the importance of connecting offline behavior to online misinformation exposure. We believe that the time is now ripe to develop a comprehensive and evidence-based model of the real-world effects of fake news and to further our understanding of human memory in the context of the Internet.

References

Aftab, O., & Murphy, G. (2022). A single exposure to cancer misinformation may not significantly affect related behavioural intentions. *HRB Open Research*, *5*(82), 82.

Allan, S., & Thorsen, E. (Eds.). (2009). *Citizen journalism: Global perspectives* (Vol. 1). Peter Lang.

Allcott, H., Gentzkow, M., & Yu, C. (2019). Trends in the diffusion of misinformation on social media. *Research & Politics*, *6*(2), 2053168019848554.

Barnier, A. J., & Hoskins, A. (2018). Is there memory in the head, in the wild? *Memory Studies*, *11*(4), 386–390.

Bliuc, A. M., Betts, J., Vergani, M., Iqbal, M., & Dunn, K. (2020). *The growing power of online communities of the extreme-right: Deriving strength, meaning, and direction from significant socio-political evens "in real life."* International Centre for Counter-Terrorism. https://doi.org/10.97812345/2020.4.3, http://www.jstor.org/stable/resrep25261

Brady, W. J., Crockett, M. J., & Van Bavel, J. J. (2020). The MAD model of moral contagion: The role of motivation, attention, and design in the spread of moralized content online. *Perspectives on Psychological Science*, *15*(4), 978–1010.

Branscombe, N. R., Ellemers, N., Spears, R., & Doosje, B. (1999). The context and content of social identity threat. In N. Ellemers, R. Spears, & B. Doosje (Eds.), *Social Identity: Context, Commitment, Content* (pp. 35–58). Blackwell Science.

Bruns, A. (2019). *Are filter bubbles real?* John Wiley & Sons.

Calvillo, D. P., Harris, J. D., & Hawkins, W. C. (2022). Partisan bias in false memories for misinformation about the 2021 US Capitol riot. *Memory*, *31*(1), 137–146. https://doi.org/10.1080/09658211.2022.2127771.

Cialdini, R. B., Petty, R. E., & Cacioppo, J. T. (1981). Attitude and attitude change. *Annual Review of Psychology*, *32*(1), 357–404.

Clayton, K., Blair, S., Busam, J. A., Forstner, S., Glance, J., Green, G., Kawata, A., Kovvuri, A., Martin, J., Morgan, E., Sandhu, M., Sang, R., Scholz-Bright, R., Welch, A. T., Wolff, A. G., Zhou, A., & Nyhan, B. (2020). Real solutions for fake news? Measuring the effectiveness of general warnings and fact-check tags in reducing belief in false stories on social media. *Political Behavior*, *42*(4), 1073–1095. https://doi.org/10.1007/s11109-019-09533-0

De Keersmaecker, J., & Roets, A. (2017). "Fake news": Incorrect, but hard to correct. The role of cognitive ability on the impact of false information on social impressions. *Intelligence*, *65*, 107–110.

de Saint Laurent, C., Murphy, G., Hegarty, K., & Greene, C. M. (2022). Measuring the effects of misinformation exposure and beliefs on behavioural intentions: A COVID-19 vaccination study. *Cognitive Research: Principles and Implications, 7*(1), 87.

Drummond, C., Siegrist, M., & Árvai, J. (2020). Limited effects of exposure to fake news about climate change. *Environmental Research Communications, 2*(8), 081003.

Eady, G., Nagler, J., Guess, A., Zilinsky, J., & Tucker, J. A. (2019). How many people live in political bubbles on social media? Evidence from linked survey and Twitter data. *Sage Open, 9*(1), 2158244019832705.

Ecker, U. K., Lewandowsky, S., & Tang, D. T. (2010). Explicit warnings reduce but do not eliminate the continued influence of misinformation. *Memory & Cognition, 38*(8), 1087–1100.

Fazio, L. (2020). Pausing to consider why a headline is true or false can help reduce the sharing of false news. *Harvard Kennedy School Misinformation Review, 1*(2). https://misinforeview.hks.harvard.edu/article/pausing-reduce-false-news/

Featherstone, J. D., & Zhang, J. (2020). Feeling angry: The effects of vaccine misinformation and refutational messages on negative emotions and vaccination attitude. *Journal of Health Communication, 25*(9), 692–702.

Feldman, L. (2011). The opinion factor: The effects of opinionated news on information processing and attitude change. *Political Communication, 28*(2), 163–181.

Fenn, K. M., Griffin, N. R., Uitvlugt, M. G., & Ravizza, S. M. (2014). The effect of Twitter exposure on false memory formation. *Psychonomic Bulletin & Review, 21*(6), 1551–1556.

Frenda, S. J., Knowles, E. D., Saletan, W., & Loftus, E. F. (2013). False memories of fabricated political events. *Journal of Experimental Social Psychology, 49*(2), 280–286.

Garry, M., Strange, D., Bernstein, D. M., & Kinzett, T. (2007). Photographs can distort memory for the news. *Applied Cognitive Psychology, 21*(8), 995–1004.

Grady, R. H., Ditto, P. H., & Loftus, E. F. (2021). Nevertheless, partisanship persisted: Fake news warnings help briefly, but bias returns with time. *Cognitive Research: Principles and Implications, 6*(1), 1–16.

Greene, C. M., de Saint Laurent, C., Hegarty, K., & Murphy, G. (2022). False memories for true and false vaccination information form in line with pre-existing vaccine opinions. *Applied Cognitive Psychology, 10*, 10022.

Greene, C. M., de Saint Laurent, C., Murphy, G., Prike, T., Hegarty, K., & Ecker, U. K. (2023). Best practices for ethical conduct of misinformation research: A scoping review and critical commentary. *European Psychologist, 28*(3), 139–140.

Greene, C. M., & Murphy, G. (2020). Individual differences in susceptibility to false memories for COVID-19 fake news. *Cognitive Research: Principles and Implications, 5*(1), 1–8.

Greene, C. M., & Murphy, G. (2021). Quantifying the effects of fake news on behavior: Evidence from a study of COVID-19 misinformation. *Journal of Experimental Psychology: Applied, 27*(4), 773.

Greene, C. M., & Murphy, G. (2023). Debriefing works: Successful retraction of misinformation following a fake news study. *PloS One, 18*(1), e0280295.

Greene, C. M., Nash, R. A., & Murphy, G. (2021). Misremembering Brexit: Partisan bias and individual predictors of false memories for fake news stories among Brexit voters. *Memory, 29*(5), 587–604.

Greene, C. M., Ryan, K. M., Ballantyne, L., Barrett, E., Cowman, C. S., Dawson, C. A., Huston, C., Maher, J. and Murphy, G. (2024). Unringing the bell: Successful debriefing following a rich false memory study. *Memory & Cognition*, 1–14. https://doi.org/10.3758/s13421-024-01524-9

Greenspan, R. L., & Loftus, E. F. (2021). What happens after debriefing? The effectiveness and benefits of postexperimental debriefing. *Memory & Cognition, 50*(4), 696–709.

Griffin, N. R., Fleck, C. R., Uitvlugt, M. G., Ravizza, S. M., & Fenn, K. M. (2017). The tweeter matters: Factors that affect false memory from Twitter. *Computers in Human Behavior, 77*, 63–68.

Guess, A. M. (2021). (Almost) everything in moderation: New evidence on Americans' online media diets. *American Journal of Political Science, 65*(4), 1007–1022.

Hyman, I. E., & James Billings, F., Jr. (1998). Individual differences and the creation of false childhood memories. *Memory, 6*(1), 1–20.

Johnson, H. M., & Seifert, C. M. (1994). Sources of the continued influence effect: When misinformation in memory affects later inferences. *Journal of Experimental Psychology: Learning, Memory, and Cognition, 20*(6), 1420.

Johnson, M. K., Hashtroudi, S., & Lindsay, D. S. (1993). Source monitoring. *Psychological Bulletin, 114*(1), 3.

Kennedy, P. J., & Prat, A. (2019). Where do people get their news? *Economic Policy, 34*(97), 5–47.

Lazer, D. M., Baum, M. A., Benkler, Y., Berinsky, A. J., Greenhill, K. M., Menczer, F., Metzger, M. J., Nyhan, B., Pennycook, G., Rothschild, D., Schudson, M., Sloman, S. A., Sunstein, C. R., Thorson, E. A., Watts, D. J., & Zittrain, J. L. (2018). The science of fake news. *Science, 359*(6380), 1094–1096. https://www.jstor.org/stable/26401620

Lewandowsky, S., & Pomerantsev, P. (2022). Technology and democracy: A paradox wrapped in a contradiction inside an irony. *Memory, Mind & Media, 1*, e5.

Loftus, E. F. (2005). Planting misinformation in the human mind: A 30-year investigation of the malleability of memory. *Learning & Memory, 12*(4), 361–366.

Loftus, E. F., & Palmer, J. C. (1974). Reconstruction of automobile destruction: An example of the interaction between language and memory. *Journal of Verbal Learning and Verbal Behavior, 13*(5), 585–589.

Loftus, E. F., & Pickrell, J. E. (1995). The formation of false memories. *Psychiatric Annals, 25*, 720–725.

Madrigal, A. C. (2013, April 19). #BostonBombing: The anatomy of a misinformation disaster. *The Atlantic*, 203. https://www.theatlantic.com/technology/archive/2013/04/-bostonbombing-the-anatomy-of-a-misinformation-disaster/275155/

Metzger, M. J., Flanagin, A. J., Mena, P., Jiang, S., & Wilson, C. (2021). From dark to light: The many shades of sharing misinformation online. *Media and Communication, 9*(1), 134–143.

Montgomery, N. V., & Rajagopal, P. (2018). Motivated reconstruction: The effect of brand commitment on false memories. *Journal of Experimental Psychology: Applied, 24*(2), 159.

Mosleh, M., Pennycook, G., & Rand, D. G. (2020). Self-reported willingness to share political news articles in online surveys correlates with actual sharing on Twitter. *PloS One, 15*(2), e0228882.

Murphy, G., de Saint Laurent, C., Reynolds, M., Aftab, O., Hegarty, K., Sun, Y., & Greene, C. M. (2023). What do we study when we study misinformation? A scoping review of experimental research (2016-2022). *Harvard Kennedy School Misinformation Review*. https://doi.org/10.37016/mr-2020-130

Murphy, G., & Flynn, E. (2022). Deepfake false memories. *Memory, 30*(4), 480–492.

Murphy, G., & Greene, C. M. (2023). Conducting ethical misinformation research: Deception, dialogue, & debriefing. *Current Opinion in Psychology, 54*, 101713. https://doi.org/10.1016/j.copsyc.2023.101713

Murphy, G., Loftus, E. F., Grady, R. H., Levine, L. J., & Greene, C. M. (2019). False memories for fake news during Ireland's abortion referendum. *Psychological Science, 30*(10), 1449–1459.

Murphy, G., Loftus, E., Grady, R. H., Levine, L. J., & Greene, C. M. (2020). Fool me twice: How effective is debriefing in false memory studies? *Memory, 28*(7), 938–949.

Murphy, G., Lynch, L., Loftus, E., & Egan, R. (2021). Push polls increase false memories for fake news stories. *Memory, 29*(6), 693–707.

Murphy, G., Maher, J., Ballantyne, L., Barrett, E., Cowman, C. S., Dawson, C. A., Huston, C., Ryan, K. M., & Greene, C. M. (2023). How do participants feel about the ethics of rich false memory studies? *Memory, 31*(4), 474–481. https://doi.org/10.1080/09658211.2023.2170417.

Murphy, G., Murray, E., & Gough, D. (2021). Attitudes towards feminism predict susceptibility to feminism-related fake news. *Applied Cognitive Psychology, 35*(5), 1182–1192.

Nightingale, S. J., & Wade, K. A. (2022). Identifying and minimising the impact of fake visual media: Current and future directions. *Memory, Mind & Media, 1*, e15.

NPR. (2016, April 18). How social media smeared a missing student as a terrorism suspect. *NPR Code Switch*. https://www.npr.org/sections/codeswitch/2016/04/18/474671097/how-social-media-smeared-a-missing-student-as-a-terrorism-suspect

O'Connell, A., & Greene, C. M. (2017). Not strange but not true: Self-reported interest in a topic increases false memory. *Memory, 25*(8), 969–977.

Osmundsen, M., Bor, A., Vahlstrup, P. B., Bechmann, A., & Petersen, M. B. (2021). Partisan polarization is the primary psychological motivation behind political fake news sharing on Twitter. *American Political Science Review, 115*(3), 999–1015.

Pariser, E. (2011). *The filter bubble: What the Internet is hiding from you*. Penguin UK.

Pena, M. M., Klemfuss, J. Z., Loftus, E. F., & Mindthoff, A. (2017). The effects of exposure to differing amounts of misinformation and source credibility perception on source monitoring and memory accuracy. *Psychology of Consciousness: Theory, Research, and Practice, 4*(4), 337.

Pennycook, G., Cannon, T. D., & Rand, D. G. (2018). Prior exposure increases perceived accuracy of fake news. *Journal of Experimental Psychology: General, 147*(12), 1865.

Pennycook, G., Epstein, Z., Mosleh, M., Arechar, A. A., Eckles, D., & Rand, D. G. (2021). Shifting attention to accuracy can reduce misinformation online. *Nature, 592*(7855), 590–595.

Polage, D. C. (2012). Making up history: False memories of fake news stories. *Europe's Journal of Psychology, 8*(2), 245–250.

Rathje, S., Van Bavel, J. J., & van der Linden, S. (2021). Out-group animosity drives engagement on social media. *Proceedings of the National Academy of Sciences of the United States of America, 118*(26), e2024292118.

Rhodes, R. E., & de Bruijn, G. J. (2013). How big is the physical activity intention–behaviour gap? A meta-analysis using the action control framework. *British Journal of Health Psychology, 18*(2), 296–309.

Rhodes, S. C. (2021). Filter bubbles, echo chambers, and fake news: how social media conditions individuals to be less critical of political misinformation. *Political Communication, 39*(1), 1–22.

Sacchi, D. L., Agnoli, F., & Loftus, E. F. (2007). Changing history: Doctored photographs affect memory for past public events. *Applied Cognitive Psychology, 21*(8), 1005–1022.

Wade, K. A., Garry, M., Read, J. D., & Lindsay, D. S. (2002). A picture is worth a thousand lies: Using false photographs to create false childhood memories. *Psychonomic Bulletin & Review, 9*(3), 597–603.

Wojcieszak, M., Casas, A., Yu, X., Nagler, J., & Tucker, J. A. (2021). *Echo chambers revisited: The (overwhelming) sharing of in-group politicians, pundits and media on Twitter*. https://doi.org/10.31219/osf.io/xwc79

Zaragoza, M. S., & Lane, S. M. (1994). Source misattributions and the suggestibility of eyewitness memory. *Journal of Experimental Psychology: Learning, Memory, and Cognition, 20*(4), 934.

9

Continued Influence of Misinformation and the Information Disorder

Li Qian Tay and Ullrich K. H. Ecker

Justice Oliver Wendell Holmes Jr. famously argued in *Abrams v. United States* (1919): "The best test of truth is the power of the thought to get itself accepted in the competition of the market." This appeal has been invoked frequently by the public and courts alike, at least in certain parts of the world, to illustrate the value of free and unrestricted speech (e.g., *Matal v. Tam, 2017*). A century later, rapid technological advancements and the Internet promised a new age of utopia for the marketplace of ideas: The barriers to entry have been substantially lowered, with the production, dissemination, and consumption of information easier than ever before. Yet, instead of arriving at a world in which truth is valued and erroneous claims routinely discarded, we appear to have edged toward a "post-truth" society. Efforts to combat climate change are hindered by individuals and vested-interest industries downplaying the threat (e.g., Cook et al., 2014; van der Linden et al., 2017); baseless fraud accusations can cast doubt on presidential election results (e.g., Pennycook & Rand, 2021); and public health directives, even during the COVID-19 pandemic, can be undermined by media personalities and fraudsters with no relevant expertise (Loomba et al., 2021; Simonov et al., 2022; Van Bavel et al., 2020). Indeed, misinformation, hereby defined as any information that is false or otherwise misleading irrespective of intent, appears to proliferate online and have wide-ranging consequences across a range of domains (Ecker et al., 2022; Lewandowsky et al., 2017). This pollution of the (online) information environment and its impacts has been termed "information disorder" (e.g., Hansson et al., 2021; Wardle & Derakhshan, 2017).

From a psychological perspective, one factor contributing to the information disorder is the *continued influence effect*—the finding that information, once encoded in memory, can influence individuals' reasoning and decision-making even if subsequently corrected. The continued influence effect has been demonstrated across a range of topics (e.g., fictitious event reports, common myths, and politicized misinformation) and settings (e.g., online and in the laboratory) and arises even if individuals are forewarned that they

Li Qian Tay and Ullrich K. H. Ecker, *Continued Influence of Misinformation and the Information Disorder* In: *The Remaking of Memory in the Age of the Internet and Social Media*. Edited by: Qi Wang and Andrew Hoskins, Oxford University Press.
 DOI: 10.1093/oso/9780197661260.003.0009

may be misled (Ecker et al., 2010; for a recent meta-analysis, see Walter & Tukachinsky, 2020).

This chapter aims to provide a synthesis of research on the continued influence and the information disorder in the context of the Internet and social media. We first introduce the standard paradigm used to investigate continued influence, as well as factors that can contribute to misinformation's persistence. We then present a novel model that outlines the causal paths that misinformation and contributing factors may take at the level of the information disorder. We align existing interventions along the model and argue that causal considerations at the information disorder level are required to appreciate the full impacts of interventions. Finally, we discuss key methodological challenges and speculate on future directions.

The Continued Influence Effect

With huge amounts of information now available online, individuals can easily be exposed to misinformation, which can contribute to the formation of false beliefs (Ecker et al., 2022). Information that is repeatedly encountered may also be judged as true regardless of veracity simply due to its familiarity (Dechêne et al., 2010). Although corrective information may likewise be readily available, the continued influence literature demonstrates that belief revision is no easy task.

In a typical continued influence study (e.g., Johnson & Seifert, 1994; Wilkes & Leatherbarrow, 1988), participants are asked to read a fictitious article about an event that unfolds over time (e.g., a warehouse fire). This use of fictitious materials allows researchers to minimize the influence of prior attitudes and motivations to examine the cognitive underpinnings of the effect. Critically, participants are randomly allocated into a control condition (no misinformation), a misinformation condition (e.g., with information alleging the warehouse fire was caused by negligent storage of flammable materials), or an intervention condition (e.g., a retraction stating that no flammable materials were in the warehouse). Self-report questionnaires, which can involve both open-ended inference questions (e.g., "What might be a good headline for a report about the fire?") and rating scale items (e.g., "Negligence contributed to the fire"; *strongly agree—strongly disagree*; see Connor Desai & Reimers, 2019) are then used to assess and compare participants' reliance on misinformation. Results generally show that retractions tend to reduce but not eliminate misinformation influence (e.g., many participants that read the retraction, when questioned, still refer to negligently stored flammable materials as a cause of the fire). Figure 9.1 presents a graphical overview of the standard paradigm and typical results.

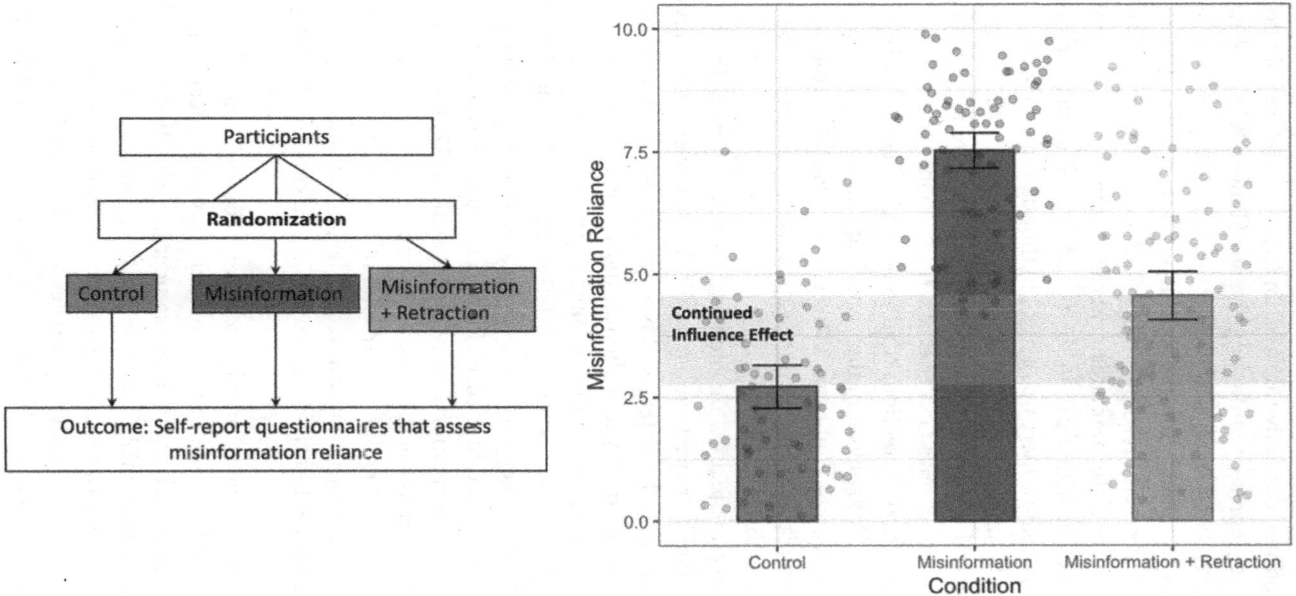

Figure 9.1 Graphical overview of the continued influence paradigm and typical results.

Note. Plotted data are hypothetical and on an arbitrary scale with a minimum score of 0 and maximum score of 10, representing a typical continued influence study with rating scale outcomes. Greater scores indicate greater misinformation reliance. The continued influence effect is the difference in misinformation reliance between the Misinformation + Retraction condition and the Control condition. The paradigm sometimes also uses a within-subjects design (e.g., Ecker et al., 2017).

Two theoretical accounts of the continued influence effect have been proposed. One account focuses on failures in memory integration when individuals encounter corrective details. Individuals are thought to build mental models to represent unfolding events (Bower & Morrow, 1990; Johnson & Seifert, 1994; Wilkes & Leatherbarrow, 1988). Whenever new information is encountered, the mental models are updated (Albrecht & O'Brien, 1993). If the new information includes a correction of prior information (e.g., there were no flammable materials at the warehouse), however, individuals may be left with a gap in their model—that is, they are left in a situation where they know there was a fire, but they do not know what started it. Such gaps can be uncomfortable (Susmann & Wegener, 2022), and to reduce the experienced discomfort individuals may prefer to rely on incorrect models over incomplete ones (Ecker et al., 2011). Evidence for this account includes the finding that corrections tend to be more effective when they include an alternative explanation of the event (e.g., there were no flammable materials at the warehouse, but arson materials were found), presumably because alternative explanations can fill the gaps in mental models (Ecker et al., 2010; Johnson & Seifert, 1994).

The second account focuses on memory processes during the retrieval stage, when individuals are performing tasks that require access to previously encoded information. In basic terms, this account explains continued influence through selective retrieval of the misinformation without the corrective information. One variant of this account draws on dual-process theories of memory (Yonelinas, 2002; Zimmer & Ecker, 2010), positing that cues in the environment can trigger automatic retrieval of familiar misinformation, which can cause continued influence effects if there is no concurrent recollection of corrective information (Swire, Ecker et al., 2017; also see Ayers & Reder, 1998). This account is supported by, among others, the finding that specific warnings promoting the suppression of misinformation and the activation of corrective information can reduce misinformation reliance (e.g., providing individuals with brief explanations of the continued influence effect; Ecker et al., 2010).

The two accounts are not mutually exclusive. Failures in memory integration and retrieval can both contribute to continued influence, depending on the misinformation, correction, and outcomes under consideration (e.g., whether factual alternatives to the misinformation exist; the amount of cognitive resources available at retrieval; etc.). Moreover, a range of factors exist that can impact the extent to which one ultimately relies on misinformation; thus, to fully understand the role of continued influence for information disorder, broader considerations of causal relations are important.

A Causal Model of the Information Disorder in the Internet Age

Figure 9.2 presents a causal model of the information disorder using a directed acyclic graph. Nodes represent variables of interest, and edges represent direct causal effects. For all connections, changes in one node are assumed to cause changes in downstream nodes. Such graphs allow researchers to map out causal effect chains that represent states of knowledge within a given domain (e.g., Pearl, 2009; Rohrer, 2018). Here, we use the graph as a thinking aid to organize a morass of findings in a parsimonious manner; as we discuss in subsequent sections, this can clarify areas in which current research is lacking and inspire future research.

Effects of Misinformants and Misinformation on Beliefs and Behaviors

The model posits that misinformants—broadly defined as individuals or institutions that create or introduce (intentionally or inadvertently)

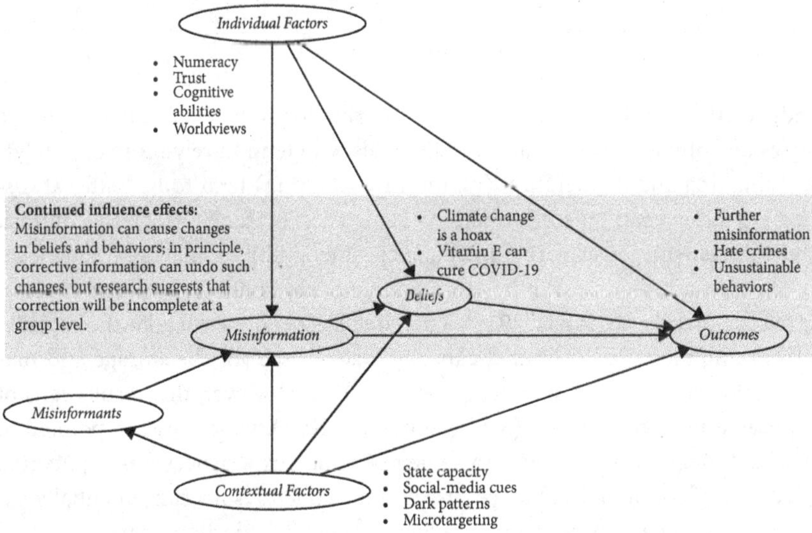

Figure 9.2 Directed acyclic graph illustrating factors within the information disorder.

Note. Nodes represent variables of interest, and edges represent direct causal effects. Continued influence effects mean that the effects of misinformation on beliefs and behaviors can be difficult to reverse. Bulleted lists provide examples of beliefs and behaviors, as well as individual and contextual factors (they are non-exhaustive).

misinformation to the information landscape or amplify it—cause misinformation in the system. Misinformation can, in turn, cause changes in beliefs if individuals fail to discern false from true information or are otherwise persuaded by the misinformation. In principle, corrective information can undo misinformation-driven belief change, but it is assumed that at a group level such correction will be incomplete (i.e., there will be continued influence). Further, once beliefs in misinformation have taken a hold in individuals' memory, they can have behavioral consequences. These include unsustainable behaviors in the context of climate change (e.g., Ding et al., 2011) or vaccine hesitancy and risky health behaviors at odds with official guidance in the context of COVID-19 (e.g., Loomba et al., 2021; Simonov et al., 2022; Van Bavel et al., 2020). However, behaviors can also be impacted by misinformation even when beliefs are not. For example, one may decide to share misinformation without believing in it, perhaps to signal group membership, as a tactic to enrage out-group members, or simply out of inattention (e.g., Lewandowsky, 2021; Pennycook & Rand, 2021). The observation that belief (change) and behavior (change) are often decoupled is known as the attitude-behavior gap, which has been documented across a wide range of behaviors (e.g., health behaviors; McEachan et al., 2011). Both individual and contextual factors are proposed to shape this core process chain.

Individual Factors

Individual factors that are related to misinformation influence include cognitive styles and abilities. For instance, individuals who tend to rely more on analytical thinking and deliberation (vs. intuitive thinking) tend to be better at discerning false versus true information (Pennycook & Rand, 2021). By contrast, individuals with lower verbal intelligence—the ability to engage in language-based reasoning—appear to be more susceptible to continued influence effects (De keersmaecker & Roets, 2017). The same has been shown with the capacity of working memory—a limited-capacity system used for the storage and manipulation of information (Brydges et al., 2017). However, this result was not replicated in a recent study (Sanderson et al., 2021), which instead pointed to episodic memory—the ability to remember one's experiences—as a potential predictor of continued influence susceptibility. Such results can potentially explain why older adults, perhaps experiencing cognitive decline, share more misinformation on social media than other age groups (Grinberg et al., 2019) and demonstrate greater continued influence effects (Swire, Ecker et al., 2017; see also Brashier & Schacter, 2020). Further, individuals who are less trusting of scientists have been found to be more susceptible to COVID-19 misinformation (e.g., Roozenbeek et al., 2020), and there is a long line of research on motivated reasoning demonstrating that individuals tend to preferentially search for, assess, as well as better remember attitude-consistent information (e.g., Bartels, 2002; Leeper & Slothuus, 2014).

Contextual Factors

Contextual factors refer to the entire environment in which information operates, as well as the individual components that make up such an environment. For example, different countries can have varying state capacities as well as historical contexts that are more or less conducive to misinformants and misinformation. In Indonesia, for instance, misinformation has previously been used to manufacture fear of minority groups and justify discriminatory legislation; these outcomes, in turn, have led to a volatile environment that facilitates further misdirection, sectarian violence, and ethnic conflicts (Osman & Waikar, 2018).

Critically, there are characteristics of the Internet that can make misinformation even more concerning. For instance, as information overload is now common, one may increasingly rely on heuristics to make judgments (Sundar, 2008). Social cues such as the number of "likes" a piece of content has on social media have been shown to impact individuals' judgments of veracity, such that content with greater social endorsement is more likely to be judged as true (e.g., Avram et al., 2020; Butler et al., 2023; Vlasceanu & Coman, 2022). Comments on news articles and blog posts can work in a similar manner (e.g., Lewandowsky et al., 2019). This means that misinformants with large followings (e.g., celebrities, politicians, or online influencers) can have outsized influence—any false content that they promote can amass a large number of "likes" that then impact further judgments in a cycle of misinformation. Such social cues may also be artificially inflated by bad actors, potentially via coordinated bot and spam accounts, if platforms are not sufficiently proactive or capable of detection (e.g., Cresi et al., 2019).

In addition, Internet spaces can be dynamically altered, potentially in nontransparent ways that undermine individuals' autonomy. For instance, organizations can implement dark patterns on their web pages; these are interface design architectures that can lead individuals into making unintended or unwanted decisions that benefit service providers (e.g., hidden defaults that exploit individuals' tendencies to opt for the first available choice; Brignull, 2011; Jachimowicz et al., 2019; Kozyreva et al., 2020). Machine learning methods can also be employed to track and learn individuals' preferences over time in order to maximize engagement (Yesilada & Lewandowsky, 2022). When such algorithms are intentionally exploited, microtargeting may be used to persuade and manipulate vulnerable individuals (e.g., targeting fear-based political messages to individuals inferred to be high on neuroticism; Venturini & Rogers, 2019). Targeted misinformation can also contribute to polarization and facilitate the formation of echo chambers, or environments in which individuals tend to only interact with others with similar views (Bakshy et al., 2015). Although online echo chambers may not be as common as initially thought (A. Guess et al., 2018), topic- and context-specific echo chambers can still cause substantial harm and contribute to radicalization (e.g., Del Vicario et al., 2016).

A Synthesis of Misinformation Interventions

Although an exhaustive discussion of all relevant factors is beyond the scope of this chapter, the selection of reviewed factors now allows us to turn to interventions. Critically, each of the aforementioned factors within the information disorder model can be individually or jointly targeted. For instance, interventions not only can have proximal targets, such as misinformation, but also can target individual factors and (both online and offline) contextual factors that serve as mechanisms of change for further influence on beliefs and behaviors. Moreover, interventions may have ancillary impacts, some of which may be undesirable, particularly if they ultimately negatively affect the targets. We elaborate on these possible targets in turn.

Targeting Misinformants and Misinformation

Common interventions such as de-platforming target misinformants (e.g., routine removal of bot and spam accounts; the suspension of Donald Trump from Twitter). At the governance level, there are also laws and legislative tools that aim to hold misinformants accountable (e.g., the Protection from Online Falsehoods and Manipulation Act, which has been in effect in Singapore since October 2019, allows misinformants to be convicted for the spread of misinformation with malicious intent). However, interventions can also directly target misinformation without necessarily impacting misinformants. This includes manual removal of misinformation by moderators or fact-checking teams. Machine learning and natural language processing models can also be trained to identify features of misinformants and misinformation (e.g., co-occurrence networks to detect bot-propagated content; semantic content representations of misinformation for classification; Shu et al., 2017). This then allows interveners to algorithmically down-rank (i.e., automatically reduce the visibility of) the identified misinformation. While still in the early stages (e.g., algorithms still routinely struggle to contextualize sarcasm and humor), such interventions hold potential to efficiently counteract the spread and effects of misinformation.

However, misinformation may not always be explicitly false; there can be implied misinformation that is true in a literal sense but is nevertheless misleading (Rich & Zaragoza, 2016; Tay et al., 2022). For instance, Joseph Goebbels, a propagandist for the Nazis during World War II, utilized the (factually accurate) existence of misinformation about Germany during World War I to undermine allegations of German war atrocities against the Jewish community (Marlin, 2013; Van Alstyne, 2023). Such implied misinformation can even be inadvertent and ironically result from attempts to address misinformation. The American Diabetes Association's web page on "Diabetes Myths," for instance, contains information that may be inaccurate only when interpreted ungenerously or out of context (e.g., "Myth: People with diabetes can't eat sweets or chocolates"). Labeling such information as myths—although technically correct—has been demonstrated to reduce readers' understanding of diabetes (Powell et al., 2020). On the one hand, such implied misinformation allows for plausible deniability and poses a challenge to professional fact checkers and neutral arbiters, and especially attempts to algorithmize the fact-checking process (Lim, 2018). On the other hand, there is also the critical concern that allowing governments and media platforms to be unilateral arbiters of truth can result in legal and ethical issues. For instance, governments and platforms may use an anti-misinformation stance as justification to suppress unfavorable narratives; specific countries where key social media companies are based may exert an outsized influence on content moderation (e.g., the Twitter Files revealed significant enmeshment between Twitter and US national security agencies; Marcetic, 2022).

Targeting Individual Factors

Interventions can target individual factors (e.g., information- and media-literacy training). When informed by the psychological and behavioral sciences, such an approach is known as "boosting" (Guess et al., 2020; Hertwig & Grüne-Yanoff, 2017). A more specific example involves inoculation against misinformation. Inoculation is a technique drawn from psychological research into persuasion and can be used to preemptively reduce misinformation's persuasiveness (Compton, 2013; Cook et al., 2017; Lewandowsky & van der Linden, 2021; Maertens et al., 2021). The technique involves warning individuals that there may be impending threats to their beliefs and refuting an example piece of misinformation to help individuals gain critical thinking skills and the ability to spot misleading strategies. Web applications and interactive games have been designed for this purpose. For example, the *Bad News Game*, a browser-based game that allows individuals to take on the role of misinformants, is designed to inoculate individuals against a variety of misleading strategies (Roozenbeek et al., 2020). Interventions of this type can potentially reduce the influence of misinformation on individuals even if they are exposed. This is not a trivial advantage, as a key challenge to combating misinformation in today's world is that fact-checking can often struggle to keep pace with the circulation of new misinformation (e.g., Vraga & Bode, 2021).

Targeting Contextual Factors

Contextual interventions, naturally, should involve efforts to address societal challenges that may give rise to both misinformation and problematic behaviors (e.g., improving economic conditions as well as transparency in science, media, and governance; resolving ethnic conflicts and grievances; reducing inequality and disenfranchisement; etc.). Further, "technocognition," an interdisciplinary approach that combines psychological insights with technological solutions, should also be incorporated (Kozyreva et al., 2020; Lewandowsky et al., 2017). For example, relatively minor prompts in the environment can help improve individuals' ability to discern misinformation or reduce its sharing (e.g., Twitter's introduction of a prompt for individuals to read articles before retweets, or brief interventions prompting individuals to consider content accuracy; Pennycook et al., 2020). The effectiveness of this approach has recently been demonstrated in a large-scale field experiment deployed directly on Twitter, in which a bot account was used to send users a message asking them to rate a politically neutral article on its accuracy; in a period following the message, these users reduced their sharing of misinformation on the platform (Pennycook et al., 2021). Another option may be interventions that alter context such that reputational concerns become more salient (e.g., a brief prompt at time of share indicating that sharing of misinformation can hurt one's reputation; Altay et al., 2022; also see Prike et al., 2023). As with interventions that target individual factors, this category of interventions also has the advantage of not requiring interveners to have a priori knowledge of information veracity.

Targeting Beliefs and Behaviors

Finally, a range of interventions target false beliefs and associated behaviors even more directly. On the side of behaviors, interventions can include financial incentives and mandates (e.g., vaccine mandates; Attwell et al., 2018); on the side of beliefs, interventions can include information campaigns, articles, or social-media posts by organizations, journalists, or individuals including policymakers, scientists, and science communicators. While this chapter focuses on misinformation, it is important to note that proper communication of facts continues to be a powerful antidote to information disorder (e.g., see Hyland-Wood et al., 2021). For communication-based interventions that do target misinformation, research on continued influence has shown that mere retractions that simply negate a piece of misinformation can be quite ineffective. Efficacy can be enhanced by incorporating more detailed refutations; these clarify why something is false, that is, they draw attention to a discrepancy between misinformation and facts (e.g., Kendeou et al., 2019). Ideally, refutations should come from a trustworthy source (e.g., Ecker & Antonio, 2021; Guillory & Geraci, 2013) and include a normative element, such as highlighting a relevant norm or consensus (e.g., Prike et al., 2023; van der Linden et al., 2017). If available, a factual alternative and a dissection of the misleading arguments used by misinformants should also be provided (e.g., MacFarlane, Tay, et al., 2021; Paynter et al., 2019). The recommendations can potentially be implemented in automated solutions that use machine learning and natural-language processing; for example, individuals previously exposed to misleading content can be automatically shown verified facts on the topic in optimized formats.

As of the time of writing, there is already a large collection of resources available online, although none has implemented all the above. See Table 9.1 for a small selection of the available options, ranging from less to more automated. Another relevant development is the emergence of AI-based generative language models such as ChatGPT (https://openai.com/blog/chatgpt), which can generate texts that mimic those written by humans. As with all technology, it poses both risks and opportunities. On the negative side, such models can facilitate production of maximally persuasive misinformation at scale. On the positive side, they may potentially provide a way to both reduce the workload of manual fact-checking and maximize fact-checking effectiveness (e.g., automatic dissection of misleading arguments and creation of detailed refutations).

Nontarget Ancillary Impacts

Interventions can have ancillary impacts beyond the targets; such impacts can be both positive and negative. For example, if the impacts include reinforcement of societal norms that value accuracy and truth (see also Lazer et al., 2018), the total effects of the interventions may be enhanced. On the contrary, undesirable impacts may negatively affect targets. In such cases, the overall effects of

Table 9.1 Examples of Online Fact-Checking Resources

URL	Description
politifact.com	Politifact checks claims made by individuals relevant to politics. This can include politicians, pundits, and other members of the media. Claims are rated on a scale of "True" to "Pants-on-Fire" by researchers employed by Politifact.
snopes.com	Snopes is a fact-checking website that covers a wide range of misinformation, including common myths, political misinformation, urban legends, and Internet memes. Each false claim is dissected in an article-style report by Snopes researchers and given considerations over "What's True," "What's False," and "What's Uncertain."
metafact.io	Metafact aims to provide easy-to-access estimates of scientific consensus by allowing verified researchers and academics to answer questions submitted by the public. For example, in response to the question "Are vitamin C supplements necessary for maintaining good health?," the current consensus estimate is 80% negative.
factcheckassistant.socialmedialab.ca	Fact Check Assistant is a chatbot that uses OpenAI's large language model to facilitate fact checking. Users can ask the chatbot to verify information. For example, in response to the claim. "Obama wasn't born in the US," the chatbot will respond "False. Barack Obama was born in Honolulu, Hawaii, on August 4, 1961."

the interventions may not be as anticipated, or as demonstrated in controlled environments where the causal path for ancillary impacts is not considered or assumed to be negligible. In practice, this may happen if interventions decrease public trust or raise concerns over censorship. For example, Twitter's efforts to combat misinformation were perceived as censorship by some, leading to sharp increases in the popularity of Parler, a social-media platform marketed as a less-regulated alternative to Twitter. In turn, activities on Parler were linked to the planning of the 2021 attack on the US Capitol, suggesting that ancillary impacts of Twitter's actions ultimately drove further radicalization (Otala et al., 2021). Increased polarization may also ensue; to illustrate, a large-scale field experiment demonstrated that exposure to opposing viewpoints on social media may exacerbate rather than resolve disagreements (Bail et al., 2018). Such examples highlight the need for researchers to go beyond individual-level misinformation reliance as a benchmark for intervention effectiveness, and systematically examine the range of possible effects. In the same vein, practitioners need to be mindful of any possible ancillary impacts, taking into account the psychological processes involved.

Open Questions and Future Considerations

Despite recent progress on both theories and interventions, open questions remain, some of which are summarized in the following:

First, what are the effects of implied versus explicit misinformation? Explicit misinformation, as is often used in laboratory research, may be increasingly easier to detect and overcome as technology develops. However, as aforementioned, using machine-learning methods to uncover implied misinformation can be almost impossible. Also, from a psychological perspective, there are reasons to believe that implied misinformation may be harder to correct. For example, an article may only insinuate that an individual committed a crime without explicit accusation, leaving it to readers to "connect the dots" and generate their own inferences regarding the perpetrator; this can lead to a richer and more enduring representation of the misinformation in memory (Rich & Zaragoza, 2016). Although a recent study showed that participants tend to rely more on explicit misinformation than implied misinformation post-correction (Tay et al., 2022), the study implemented best-practice interventions that are not always feasible in practice. No study has yet tested the correction of implied misinformation with light-touch interventions such as reputation prompts. To the extent that reputation concerns may be alleviated if the misinformation shared is literally true, such prompts may be rendered ineffective.

Second, what are the behavioral impacts of misinformation and its interventions? Misinformation research has, to date, relied mainly on self-report questionnaire measures. However, as aforementioned, attitudes and beliefs tend to predict behaviors only weakly and indirectly (McEachan et al., 2011), and the most concerning consequences of misinformation in the real world may often be behavioral in nature. Future experimental studies should therefore consider adopting behavioral measures (e.g., consumer choices; Hamby et al., 2020; MacFarlane, Hurlstone, et al., 2021). In a similar vein, real-world data should also be considered, although access to such data can be difficult. For example, social-media companies, whose motivations are misaligned with consumers and researchers, can act as gatekeepers. To this end, researchers might need to rely on creative use of observational causal-inference approaches, such as instrumental-variable analysis. Briefly, instrumental variables are variables that affect outcomes only through the primary variable of interest. For example, contextual factors such as the ordering of cable-TV channels (which in the U.S. at least can differ randomly across different localities) can affect outcomes via a change in misinformation exposure (e.g., if a low-quality news channel happens to be in a prime line-up position, this can increase viewing of that channel and thus exposure to misinformation; see Ash et al., 2024; Bursztyn et al., 2020). The use of such analyses allows researchers to test for causal effects in the presence of unmeasured confounds (Marinescu et al., 2018).

Third, can interventions lead to negative ancillary impacts, such as greater polarization and greater volume of circulating misinformation? Alternatively, can there be ancillary impacts that are positive, such as enhanced societal norms of valuing truth? How can such impacts be assessed? In our view, the first step to address such questions is to consider variables of interest at the scale of the information disorder (e.g., applying the model presented in this chapter). This allows researchers to clearly map out all assumptions, and test potential causal-effect paths in a systematic manner (e.g., studies that include not only misinformation reliance as an outcome measure, but also measures that assess potential ancillary impacts). Computational methods, such as agent-based models that model interactions between entities, may also be valuable additions to researchers' arsenal (Smaldino et al., 2015). For instance, one could combine individual-cognitive models of the continued influence effect (e.g., Ecker et al., 2011) with agent-based modelling to examine at scale the overall impacts of changes in misinformants, misinformation, and individual and contextual factors.

Fourth, are findings obtained in today's information landscape generalizable to landscapes of the future? As Wellman (2001) aptly put it, "an internet year is like a dog year, changing approximately seven times faster than normal human time". Thus, even assuming internal and external validity of findings (i.e., results from studies are causally interpretable and can generalize to the real world), temporal validity may be a concern given the rapid rate of technological change (see also Munger, 2019). Moreover, as hinted at earlier, technological advances that can help combat misinformation can also be useful for misinformants—for example, use of generative language models to generate misinformation that is tailored specifically to persuade specific audiences or to maximize continued influence effects.

Finally, what are the ethical implications of misinformation research? There are two dimensions to this question. First, researchers need to weigh the risk of harm of providing participants with misinformation, particularly if potentially harmful content is involved (e.g., vaccine misinformation). This is less of a concern for the standard continued influence paradigm, as studies with this paradigm tend to use fictional event reports. However, as research ventures into real-world topics to achieve greater generalizability and relevance, at the very least, a detailed debriefing process needs to be included (e.g., asking participants to demonstrate in post-debrief questionnaires that they understand the presented misinformation to be false; MacFarlane, Tay, et al., 2021; see also Greene et al., 2023). The second dimension, on a more general level, relates to the fact that researchers should respect individual differences. This can include differences in cognitive styles, abilities, but also worldviews. Although we have highlighted these factors as potential determinants of misinformation reliance, the solution is not to discriminate against individuals or to otherwise remove such individual differences (e.g., change worldviews; see also Lewandowsky et al., 2017). Rather, further research is needed to identify interventions that support those most at risk while retaining their autonomy.

Conclusion

The internet has fundamentally altered the information landscape and the information disorder represents a major challenge facing societies. There is a wide array of potential interventions, and a burgeoning literature on how these interventions may (or may not) be effective. Critically, however, the challenge requires not just technological or psychological solutions in isolation; to address the problem at scale, interdisciplinary work is required. In this chapter, we presented a causal-graphical approach to synthesizing disparate findings and interventions. We hope that this will help inspire future research to address the many open questions.

Acknowledgments

We thank Mark J. Hurlstone for helpful discussions. This work was supported by a University Postgraduate Award and a UWA International Fees Scholarship awarded to the first author and Australian Research Council Future Fellowship FT190100708 awarded to the second author.

References

Abrams v. United States, 250 U.S. 616, 40 S. Ct. 17, 63 L. Ed. 1173 (1919).

Albrecht, J. E., & O'Brien, E. J. (1993). Updating a mental model: Maintaining both local and global coherence. *Journal of Experimental Psychology: Learning, Memory, and Cognition*, *19*(5), 1061–1070. https://doi.org/10.1037/0278-7393.19.5.1061

Altay, S., Hacquin, A. S., & Mercier, H. (2022). Why do so few people share fake news? It hurts their reputation. *New Media & Society*, *24*(6), 1303–1324. https://doi.org/10.1177/1461444820969893

Ash, E., Galletta, S., Hangartner, D., Margalit, Y., & Pinna, M. (2024). The effect of Fox News on health behavior during COVID-19. *Political Analysis*, *32*(2), 285–284. https://doi.org.10.1017/pan.2023.21

Attwell, K., Navin, M. C., Lopalco, P. L., Jestin, C., Reiter, S., & Omer, S. B. (2018). Recent vaccine mandates in the United States, Europe and Australia: A comparative study. *Vaccine, 36*(48), 7377–7384. https://doi.org/10.1016/j.vaccine.2018.10.019

Avram, M., Micallef, N., Patil, S., & Menczer, F. (2020, July 28). Exposure to social engagement metrics increases vulnerability to misinformation. *Harvard Kennedy School Misinformation Review, 1*(5). https://doi.org/10.37016/mr-2020-033. https://misinforeview.hks.harvard.edu/article/exposure-to-social-engagement-metrics-increases-vulnerability-to-misinformation/

Ayers, M. S., & Reder, L. M. (1998). A theoretical review of the misinformation effect: Predictions from an activation-based memory model. *Psychonomic Bulletin & Review, 5*(1), 1–21. https://doi.org/10.3758/BF03209454

Bail, C. A., Argyle, L. P., Brown, T. W., Bumpus, J. P., Chen, H., Fallin Hunzaker, M., Lee, J., Mann, M., Merhout, F., & Volfovsky, A. (2018). Exposure to opposing views on social media can increase political polarization. *Proceedings of the National Academy of Sciences of the United States of America, 115*(37), 9216–9221. https://doi.org/10.1073/pnas.1804840115

Bakshy, E., Messing, S., & Adamic, L. A. (2015). Exposure to ideologically diverse news and opinion on Facebook. *Science, 348*(6239), 1130–1132. https://doi.org/10.1126/science.aaa1160

Bartels, L. M. (2002). Beyond the running tally: Partisan bias in political perceptions. *Political Behavior, 24*(2), 117–150. https://doi.org/10.1023/A:1021226224601

Bower, G. H., & Morrow, D. G. (1990). Mental models in narrative comprehension. *Science, 247*(4938), 44–48. https://doi.org/10.1126/science.2403694

Brashier, N. M., & Schacter, D. L. (2020). Aging in an era of fake news. *Current Directions in Psychological Science, 29*(3), 316–323. https://doi.org/10.1177/0963721420915872

Brignull, H. (2011). *Dark patterns: Deception vs. honesty in Ui Design, A List Apart.* https://alistapart.com/article/dark-patterns-deception-vs-honesty-in-ui-design/ (Accessed: 29 June 2024).

Brydges, C. R., Gignac, G. E., & Ecker, U. K. H. (2018). Working memory capacity, short-term memory capacity, and the continued influence effect: A latent-variable analysis. *Intelligence, 69*, 117–122. https://doi.org/10.1016/j.intell.2018.03.009

Bursztyn, L., Rao, A., Roth, C. P., & Yanagizawa-Drott, D. H. (2020). *Misinformation during a pandemic.* National Bureau of Economic Research. https://doi.org/10.3386/w27417

Butler, L. H., Fay, N., & Ecker, U. K. H. (2023). Social endorsement influences the continued belief in corrected misinformation. *Journal of Applied Research in Memory and Cognition, 12*(3), 364–375. https://doi.org/10.1037/mac0000080

Compton, J. (2013). Inoculation theory. In J. P. Dillard & L. Shen (Eds.), *The Sage handbook of persuasion: Developments in theory and practice* (2nd ed., pp. 220–237). Sage.

Connor Desai, S., & Reimers, S. (2019). Comparing the use of open and closed questions for Web-based measures of the continued-influence effect. *Behavior Research Methods, 51*(3), 1426–1440. https://doi.org/10.3758/s13428-018-1066-z

Cook, J., Bedford, D., & Mandia, S. (2014). Raising climate literacy through addressing misinformation: Case studies in agnotology-based learning. *Journal of Geoscience Education, 62*(3), 296–306. https://doi.org/10.5408/13-071.1

Cook, J., Lewandowsky, S., & Ecker, U. K. H. (2017). Neutralizing misinformation through inoculation: Exposing misleading argumentation techniques reduces their influence. *PLoS One, 12*(5), e0175799. https://doi.org/10.1371/journal.pone.0175799

Cresci, S., Lillo, F., Regoli, D., Tardelli, S., & Tesconi, M. (2019). Cashtag piggybacking: Uncovering spam and bot activity in stock microblogs on Twitter. *ACM Transactions on the Web, 13*(2), 1–27. https://doi.org/10.1145/3313184

Dechêne, A., Stahl, C., Hansen, J., & Wänke, M. (2010). The truth about the truth: A meta-analytic review of the truth effect. *Personality and Social Psychology Review, 14*(2), 238–257. https://doi.org/10.1177/1088868309352251

De keersmaecker, J., & Roets, A. (2017). "Fake news": Incorrect, but hard to correct. The role of cognitive ability on the impact of false information on social impressions. *Intelligence, 65*, 107–110. https://doi.org/10.1016/j.intell.2017.10.005

Del Vicario, M., Vivaldo, G., Bessi, A., Zollo, F., Scala, A., Caldarelli, G., & Quattrociocchi, W. (2016). Echo chambers: Emotional contagion and group polarization on Facebook. *Scientific Reports, 6*(1), article 37825. https://doi.org/10.1038/srep37825

Ding, D., Maibach, E. W., Zhao, X., Roser-Renouf, C., & Leiserowitz, A. (2011). Support for climate policy and societal action are linked to perceptions about scientific agreement. *Nature Climate Change, 1*(9), 462–466. https://doi.org/10.1038/nclimate1295

Ecker, U. K. H., & Antonio, L. M. (2021). Can you believe it? An investigation into the impact of retraction source credibility on the continued influence effect. *Memory & Cognition, 49*(4), 631–644. https://doi.org/10.3758/s13421-020-01129-y

Ecker, U. K. H., Hogan, J. L., & Lewandowsky, S. (2017). Reminders and repetition of misinformation: Helping or hindering its retraction? *Journal of Applied Research in Memory and Cognition, 6*(2), 185–192. https://doi.org/10.1016/j.jarmac.2017.01.014

Ecker, U. K. H., Lewandowsky, S., & Tang, D. T. W. (2010). Explicit warnings reduce but do not eliminate the continued influence of misinformation. *Memory & Cognition, 38*(8), 1087–1100. https://doi.org/10.3758/MC.38.8.1087

Ecker, U. K. H., Lewandowsky, S., Cook, J., Schmid, P., Fazio, L. K., Brashier, N., Kendeou, P., Vraga, E. K., & Amazeen, M. A. (2022). The psychological drivers of misinformation belief and its resistance to correction. *Nature Reviews Psychology, 1*(1), 13–29. https://doi.org/10.1038/s44159-021-00006-y

Ecker, U. K. H., Lewandowsky, S., Swire, B., & Chang, D. (2011). Correcting false information in memory: Manipulating the strength of misinformation encoding and its retraction. *Psychonomic Bulletin & Review, 18*(3), 570–578. https://doi.org/10.3758/s13423-011-0065-1

Greene, C. M., de Saint Laurent, C., Murphy, G., Prike, T., Hegarty, K., & Ecker, U. K. H. (2023). Best practices for ethical conduct of misinformation research: A scoping review and critical commentary. *European Psychologist, 28*(3), 139–150. https://doi.org/10.1027/1016-9040/a000491

Grinberg, N., Joseph, K., Friedland, L., Swire-Thompson, B., & Lazer, D. (2019). Fake news on Twitter during the 2016 US presidential election. *Science, 363*(6425), 374–378. https://doi.org/10.1126/science.aau2706

Guess, A., Nyhan, B., Lyons, B., & Reifler, J. (2018). *Avoiding the echo chamber about echo chambers: Why selective exposure to like-minded political news is less prevalent than you think*. Knight Foundation.

Guess, A. M., Lerner, M., Lyons, B., Montgomery, J. M., Nyhan, B., Reifler, J., & Sircar, N. (2020). A digital media literacy intervention increases discernment between mainstream and false news in the United States and India. *Proceedings of the National Academy of Sciences of the United States of America, 117*(27), 15536–15545. https://doi.org/10.1073/pnas.1920498117

Guillory, J., & Geraci, L. (2013). Correcting erroneous inferences in memory: The role of source credibility. *Journal of Applied Research in Memory and Cognition, 2*, 201–209. https://doi.org/10.1016/j.jarmac.2013.10.001

Hamby, A., Ecker, U. K. H., & Brinberg, D. (2020). How stories in memory perpetuate the continued influence of false information. *Journal of Consumer Psychology, 30*, 240–259. https://doi.org/10.1002/jcpy.1135

Hansson, S., Orru, K., Torpan, S., Bäck, A., Kazemekaityte, A., Meyer, S. F., Ludvigsen, J., Savadori, L., Galvagni, A., & Pigrée, A. (2021). COVID-19 information disorder: Six types of harmful information during the pandemic in Europe. *Journal of Risk Research, 24*(3–4), 380–393. https://doi.org/10.1080/13669877.2020.1871058

Hertwig, R., & Grüne-Yanoff, T. (2017). Nudging and boosting: Steering or empowering good decisions. *Perspectives on Psychological Science, 12*(6), 973–986. https://doi.org/10.1177/1745691617702496

Hyland-Wood, B., Gardner, J., Leask, J., & Ecker, U. K. H. (2021). Toward effective government communication strategies in the era of COVID-19. *Humanities and Social Sciences Communications*, *8*(1), 1–11. https://doi.org/10.1057/s41599-020-00701-w

Jachimowicz, J. M., Duncan, S., Weber, E. U., & Johnson, E. J. (2019). When and why defaults influence decisions: A meta-analysis of default effects. *Behavioural Public Policy*, *3*(2), 159–186. https://doi.org/10.1017/bpp.2018.43

Johnson, H. M., & Seifert, C. M. (1994). Sources of the continued influence effect: When misinformation in memory affects later inferences. *Journal of Experimental Psychology. Learning, Memory, and Cognition*, *20*(6), 1420–1436. https://doi.org/10.1037//0278-7393.20.6.1420

Kendeou, P., Butterfuss, R., Kim, J., & Van Boekel, M. (2019). Knowledge revision through the lenses of the three-pronged approach. *Memory & Cognition*, *47*, 33–46. https://doi.org/10.3758/s13421-018-0848-y

Kozyreva, A., Lewandowsky, S., & Hertwig, R. (2020). Citizens versus the internet: Confronting digital challenges with cognitive tools. *Psychological Science in the Public Interest*, *21*(3), 103–156. https://doi.org/10.1177/1529100620946707

Lazer, D. M. J., Baum, M. A., Benkler, Y., Berinsky, A. J., Greenhill, K. M., Menczer, F., Metzger, M. J., Nyhan, B., Pennycook, G., Rothschild, D., Schudson, M., Sloman, S. A., Sunstein, C. R., Thorson, E. A., Watts, D. J., & Zittrain, J. L. (2018). The science of fake news. *Science*, *359*(6380), 1094–1096. https://doi.org/10.1126/science.aao2998

Leeper, T. J., & Slothuus, R. (2014). Political parties, motivated reasoning, and public opinion formation. *Political Psychology*, *35*(S1), 129–156. https://doi.org/10.1111/pops.12164

Lewandowsky, S. (2021). Conspiracist cognition: Chaos, convenience, and cause for concern. *Journal for Cultural Research*, *25*(1), 12–35. https://doi.org/10.1080/14797585.2021.1886423

Lewandowsky, S., & van der Linden, S. (2021). Countering misinformation and fake news through inoculation and prebunking. *European Review of Social Psychology*, *32*(2) 348–384. https://doi.org/10.1080/10463283.2021.1876983

Lewandowsky, S., Cook, J., Fay, N., & Gignac, G. E. (2019). Science by social media: Attitudes towards climate change are mediated by perceived social consensus. *Memory & Cognition*, *47*(8), 1445–1456. https://doi.org/10.3758/s13421-019-00948-y

Lewandowsky, S., Ecker, U. K. H., & Cook, J. (2017). Beyond misinformation: Understanding and coping with the post-truth era. *Journal of Applied Research in Memory and Cognition*, *6*, 353–369. https://doi.org/10.1016/j.jarmac.2017.07.008

Lim, C. (2018). Checking how fact-checkers check. *Research & Politics*, *5*(3). https://doi.org/10.1177/2053168018786848

Loomba, S., de Figueiredo, A., Piatek, S. J., de Graaf, K., & Larson, H. J. (2021). Measuring the impact of COVID-19 vaccine misinformation on vaccination intent in the UK and USA. *Nature Human Behaviour*, *5*(3), 337–348. https://doi.org/10.1038/s41562-021-01056-1

MacFarlane, D., Hurlstone, M. J., & Ecker, U. K. H. (2021). Countering demand for ineffective health remedies: Do consumers respond to risks, lack of benefits, or both? *Psychology and Health*, *36*(5), 593–611. https://doi.org/10.1080/08870446.2020.1774056

MacFarlane, D., Tay, L. Q., Hurlstone, M. J., & Ecker, U. K. H. (2021). Refuting spurious COVID-19 treatment claims reduces demand and misinformation sharing. *Journal of Applied Research in Memory and Cognition*, *10*(2), 248–258. https://doi.org/10.1016/j.jarmac.2020.12.005

Maertens, R., Roozenbeek, J., Basol, M., & van der Linden, S. (2021). Long-term effectiveness of inoculation against misinformation: Three longitudinal experiments. *Journal of Experimental Psychology. Applied*, *27*(1), 1–16. https://doi.org/10.1037/xap0000315

Marcetic, B. (2022, December). Why the twitter files are in fact a big deal. *Jacobin*. https://www.congress.gov/event/118th-congress/house-event/115901/text

Marinescu, I. E., Lawlor, P. N., & Kording, K. P. (2018). Quasi-experimental causality in neuroscience and behavioural research. *Nature Human Behaviour*, *2*(12), 891–898. https://doi.org/10.1038/s41562-018-0466-5

Marlin, R. (2013). *Propaganda and the ethics of persuasion.* Broadview Press.

Matal v. Tam. No. 15-1293, 582 U.S. ___, 137 S. Ct. 1744 (2017). https://www.supremecourt.gov/opinions/16pdf/15-1293_1o13.pdf

McEachan, R., Conner, M., Taylor, N., & Lawton, R. (2011). Prospective prediction of health-related behaviours with the theory of planned behaviour: A meta-analysis. *Health Psychology Review, 5*, 97–144. https://doi.org/10.1080/17437199.2010.521684

Munger, K. (2019). The limited value of non-replicable field experiments in contexts with low temporal validity. *Social Media + Society, 5*(3). https://doi.org/10.1177/2056305119859294

Osman, M. N. M., & Waikar, P. (2018). Fear and loathing: Uncivil Islamism and Indonesia's anti-Ahok movement. *Indonesia, 106*, 89–109.

Otala, J. M., Kurtic, G., Grasso, I., Liu, Y., Matthews, J., & Madraki, G. (2021). Political polarization and platform migration: A study of Parler and Twitter usage by United States of America Congress members. In *Companion Proceedings of the Web Conference 2021* (pp. 224–231). Association for Computing Machinery. https://doi.org/10.1145/3442442.3452305

Paynter, J., Luskin-Saxby, S., Keen, D., Fordyce, K., Frost, G., Imms, C., Miller, S., Trembath, D., Tucker, M., & Ecker, U. K. H. (2019). Evaluation of a template for countering misinformation—Real-world autism treatment myth debunking. *PLoS One, 14*(1), e0210746. https://doi.org/10.1371/journal.pone.0210746

Pearl, J. (2009). *Causality.* Cambridge University Press.

Pennycook, G., Epstein, Z., Mosleh, M., Arechar, A. A., Eckles, D., & Rand, D. G. (2021). Shifting attention to accuracy can reduce misinformation online. *Nature, 592*(7855), 590–595. https://doi.org/10.1038/s41586-021-03344-2

Pennycook, G., McPhetres, J., Zhang, Y., Lu, J. G., & Rand, D. G. (2020). Fighting COVID-19 misinformation on social media: Experimental evidence for a scalable accuracy-nudge intervention. *Psychological Science, 31*(7), 770–780. https://doi.org/10.1177/0956797620939054

Pennycook, G., & Rand, D. (2021). Examining false beliefs about voter fraud in the wake of the 2020 presidential election. *Harvard Kennedy School Misinformation Review 2*(1). https://doi.org/10.37016/mr-2020-51. https://misinforeview.hks.harvard.edu/article/research-note-examining-false-beliefs-about-voter-fraud-in-the-wake-of-the-2020-presidential-election/

Powell, D., Bian, L., & Markman, E. M. (2020). When intents to educate can misinform: Inadvertent paltering through violations of communicative norms. *PLOS ONE, 15*(5), e0230360. https://doi.org/10.1371/journal.pone.0230360

Prike, T., Butler, L., & Ecker, U. K. H. (2023, *April 1*). Source-credibility information and social norms improve truth discernment and reduce engagement with misinformation online. *Scientific Reports, 14*, article 6900. https://doi.org/10.31234/osf.io/dhx6f

Rich, P., & Zaragoza, M. (2016). The continued influence of implied and explicitly stated misinformation in news reports. *Journal of Experimental Psychology. Learning, Memory, and Cognition, 42*(1), 62–74. https://doi.org/10.1037/xlm0000155

Rohrer, J. M. (2018). Thinking clearly about correlations and causation: Graphical causal models for observational data. *Advances in Methods and Practices in Psychological Science, 1*(1), 27–42. https://doi.org/10.1177/2515245917745629

Roozenbeek, J., Schneider, C. R., Dryhurst, S., Kerr, J., Freeman, A. L. J., Recchia, G., van der Bles, A. M., & van der Linden, S. (2020). Susceptibility to misinformation about COVID-19 around the world: Susceptibility to COVID misinformation. *Royal Society Open Science, 7*, 201199. https://doi.org/10.1098/rsos.201199

Sanderson, J. A., Gignac, G. E., & Ecker, U. K. H. (2021). Working memory capacity, removal efficiency and event specific memory as predictors of misinformation reliance. *Journal of Cognitive Psychology, 33*(5), 518–532. https://doi.org/10.1080/20445911.2021.1931243

Shu, K., Sliva, A., Wang, S., Tang, J., & Liu, H. (2017). Fake news detection on social media: A data mining perspective. *ACM SIGKDD Explorations Newsletter, 19*(1), 22–36. https://dl.acm.org/doi/abs/10.1145/3137597.3137600

Simonov, A., Sacher, S., Dube, J.-P., & Biswas, S. (2022). The persuasive effect of Fox News: Noncompliance with social distancing during the COVID-19 pandemic. *Marketing Science, 41*(2), 230–242. https://doi.org/10.1287/mksc.2021.1328

Smaldino, P. E., Calanchini, J., & Pickett, C. L. (2015). Theory development with agent-based models. *Organizational Psychology Review, 5*(4), 300–317. https://doi.org/10.1177/2041386614546944

Sundar, S. S. (2008). *The MAIN model: A heuristic approach to understanding technology effects on credibility* (pp. 73–100). MacArthur Foundation Digital Media and Learning Initiative.

Susmann, M. W., & Wegener, D. T. (2022). The role of discomfort in the continued influence effect of misinformation. *Memory & Cognition, 50*(2), 435–448. https://doi.org/10.3758/s13421-021-01232-8

Swire, B., Berinsky, A. J., Lewandowsky, S., & Ecker, U. K. H. (2017). Processing political misinformation: Comprehending the Trump phenomenon. *Royal Society Open Science, 4*(3), 160802. https://doi.org/10.1098/rsos.160802

Swire, B., Ecker, U. K. H., & Lewandowsky, S. (2017). The role of familiarity in correcting inaccurate information. *Journal of Experimental Psychology. Learning, Memory, and Cognition, 43*(12), 1948–1961. https://doi.org/10.1037/xlm0000422

Tay, L. Q., Hurlstone, M. J., Kurz, T., & Ecker, U. K. H. (2022). A comparison of prebunking and debunking interventions for implied versus explicit misinformation. *British Journal of Psychology, 113*(3), 591–607. https://doi.org/10.1111/bjop.12551

Van Alstyne, M. W. (2023). *Free speech and the fake news problem.* SSRN. https://ssrn.com/abstract=4414261

Van Bavel, J., Baicker, K., Boggio, P. S., Capraro, V., Cichocka, A., Cikara, M., Crockett, M. J., Crum, A. J., Douglas, K. M., Druckman, J. N., Drury, J., Dube, O., Ellemers, N., Finkel, E. J., Fowler, J. H., Gelfand, M., Han, S., Haslam, S. A., Jetten, J., . . . Willer, R. (2020). Using social and behavioural science to support COVID-19 pandemic response. *Nature Human Behaviour, 4*(5), 460–471. https://doi.org/10.1038/s41562-020-0884-z

van der Linden, S., Leiserowitz, A., Rosenthal, S., & Maibach, E. (2017). Inoculating the public against misinformation about climate change. *Global Challenges, 1*(2), 1600008. https://doi.org/10.1002/gch2.201600008

Venturini, T., & Rogers, R. (2019). "API-based research" or how can digital sociology and journalism studies learn from the Facebook and Cambridge Analytica data breach. *Digital Journalism, 7*(4), 532–540. https://doi.org/10.1080/21670811.2019.1591927

Vlasceanu, M., & Coman, A. (2022). The impact of social norms on health-related belief update. *Applied Psychology: Health and Well-Being, 14*(2), 453–464. https://doi.org/10.1111/aphw.12313

Vraga, E. K., & Bode, L. (2021). Addressing COVID-19 misinformation on social media preemptively and responsively. *Emerging Infectious Diseases, 27*(2), 396–403. https://doi.org/10.3201/EID2702.203139

Walter, N., & Tukachinsky, R. (2020). A meta-analytic examination of the continued influence of misinformation in the face of correction: How powerful is it, why does it happen, and how to stop it? *Communication Research, 47*(2), 155–177. https://doi.org/10.1177/0093650219854600

Wardle, C., & Derakhshan, H. (2017). *Information disorder: Toward an interdisciplinary framework for research and policymaking* (Vol. 27, pp. 1–107). Council of Europe.

Wellman, B. (2001). Computer networks as social networks. *Science, 293*(5537), 2031–2034. https://doi.org/10.1126/science.1065547

Wilkes, A. L., & Leatherbarrow, M. (1988). Editing episodic memory following the identification of error. *Quarterly Journal of Experimental Psychology, 40*(2), 361–387. https://doi.org/10.1080/02724988843000168

Yesilada, M., & Lewandowsky, S. (2022). Systematic review: YouTube recommendations and problematic content. *Internet Policy Review, 11*(1), 1652–1652. https://doi.org/10.14763/2022.1.1652

Yonelinas, A. P. (2002). The nature of recollection and familiarity: A review of 30 years of research. *Journal of Memory and Language, 46*(3), 441–517. https://doi.org/10.1006/jmla.2002.2864

Zimmer, H. D., & Ecker, U. K. H. (2010). Remembering perceptual features unequally bound in object and episodic tokens: Neural mechanisms and their electrophysiological correlates. *Neuroscience and Biobehavioral Reviews, 34*(7), 1066–1079. https://doi.org/10.1016/j.neubiorev.2010.01.014

10

Is It Possible for Justice to Be Blind When Social Media Is Everywhere?

Heather M. Kleider-Offutt and Beth B. Stevens

In the American legal system, there is an expectation of innocence until proven guilty, and along with this idea is that the chain of justice, from suspect identification through trial, will be unbiased. However, the ubiquitous nature of social media and the seemingly immediate accessibility of almost any information, be it valid or not, has created a situation where law enforcement and lawyers may be unsure of the source of reported information from eyewitnesses as memory may be compromised. Best practices recommendations attempt to protect eyewitness reports, police procedures, and juror decisions from the influence of extraneous information on legal outcomes; however, the advent of social media has made application of these recommendations especially difficult. The new era of immediate search and tracking of personal and public information by anyone with a cell phone challenges the integrity of legal system–based decisions.

In this chapter we discuss the ways in which social media impacts the integrity of the legal process at key decision points, the eyewitness account, the search and arrest of the suspect, and the evaluation of evidence by the jurors. The convenience and availability of the Internet has advantages and disadvantages when it comes to expeditious suspect identification and arrest. Memory error or bias related to social media searches may influence outcomes and serve to thwart the underlying cognitive processes that facilitate accurate memory retrieval.

Social Media and Eyewitness Memory

The fallibility of eyewitness memory is well documented (Albright, 2017; Wixted et al., 2016), and many of the contributing factors to memory error result from contamination of the first episodic trace of the event details. This means that information presented post-crime has the potential to modify how individuals recall the original memory. Memory is not static, and it updates with new information. This is an adaptive feature of memory, such that the most recent information is part of the memory episode, but this process works against recalling

Heather M. Kleider-Offutt and Beth B. Stevens, *Is It Possible for Justice to Be Blind When Social Media Is Everywhere?* In: *The Remaking of Memory in the Age of the Internet and Social Media.* Edited by: Qi Wang and Andrew Hoskins, Oxford University Press. © Oxford University Press 2024. DOI: 10.1093/oso/9780197661260.003.0010 specific detailed information from that episode along with the source of the information (Chan et al., 2012; Gordon & Thomas, 2017; Paterson et al., 2011). Internet searches for a possible perpetrator or crime scene content by an eyewitness, can overwrite and confuse the initial and sometimes tenuous memory of what they actually saw at the crime (Kleider-Offutt et al., 2021). When witnesses conduct an Internet search for crime details prior to law enforcement interviews, the integrity of the lineup identification may be unreliable as the eyewitness's memory could be tainted from the previous search (Wixted & Wells, 2017).

Early psycholegal research investigating the fragility of memory established that post-event information may distort memory through a process of retroactive interference in which newly learned information interferes with the ability to recall old information (e.g., Davis & Schiffman, 1985; Loftus, 1975; Loftus & Palmer, 1974; Loftus & Pickrell, 1995). When misinformation is presented post-event, the way a person remembers the original information may be altered (see Loftus & Palmer, 1974; Pickrell et al., 2017). Decades of empirical studies have intentionally presented eyewitnesses with postevent misinformation about the details of an event. At recall, these witnesses frequently incorporate the introduced misinformation into their memory of the scene, and they do so with confidence and rich detail (see Loftus, 2005, for review), Recent work finds that misinformation from several different sources (*double misinformation*, e.g., other witnesses or social media) can be incorporated into the witnesses' memory suggesting that guarding against this memory error must be multifaceted (Blank et al., 2022). For example, a witness to bank robbery gave her initial statement to police when she was very upset; she reported a light-haired man in his twenties held a gun on the bank teller. That evening, she read posts about the robbery on a neighborhood blog wherein others discussed that the suspect had a red-colored neck tattoo associated with a gang. The witness did not report the tattoo in her initial statement to the police, but in a subsequent interview, she reported that the suspect had a red-colored neck tattoo. Later, fingerprints led to the arrest of a suspect who did not have a neck tattoo. In this situation, the witness may believe that she remembers the tattoo from the crime scene, but she gathered that information from the blog. This is indicative of source misattribution, such that a witness may forget where the source of a particular memory originated (Johnson et al., 1993; Mitchell & Johnson, 2000). A similar scenario plays out with disinformation, which is an intentional misrepresentation of facts, typically to sway public opinion on political issues or potentially when garnering sympathy for suspect to a crime (Zerback & Töpfl, 2022). For example, high-profile cases that garner a lot of interest from reputable and malicious news media can distribute errant case facts that influence the ways in which the public view outcomes.

While the suggestable and sometimes unreliable nature of memory may have only minor consequences in our everyday lives, such as misattributing information heard from a friend to a newspaper article, memory for the source of information becomes crucial when we consider its impact on the criminal justice system. In many real-world criminal cases, eyewitness memory error has led to mistaken perpetrator identifications, resulting in the wrongful conviction of individuals (Innocence Project, 2019). For example, in a case in Dekalb County, Georgia (2017), two suspects opened fire on a room of people during a drug deal, and eyewitnesses knew one of the suspects. After a social media search of the first suspect, an associate of his—a cousin—was put in a lineup based on the Internet search; however, witnesses did not have a good description of the second shooter. Eyewitnesses identified the cousin as one of the shooters from the lineup. However, physical evidence proved he was not present during the crime and was found not guilty. This is an example of source monitoring error wherein the witnesses misplaced their familiarity with the picture found on social media (and his association with the shooter) for having seen the cousin at the crime.

Such mistaken identifications—because of faulty eyewitness memory—have impacted the criminal justice system, contributing to 69% of the wrongful convictions that have been overturned by post-conviction DNA evidence (Innocence Project, n.d.). In wrongful conviction cases—often—the confidence related to the initial identification is low, but subsequent presentations of the possible suspect via multiple lineups or picture presentation bolsters the confidence in the misidentification.

Researchers and legal experts have attempted to circumvent eyewitness error by establishing protocols that may reduce memory contamination. One approach is to reduce the number of times that a witness reviews possible suspects (see Wixted et al., 2021). Empirical research suggests that witnesses perusing mugshot books and viewing multiple lineups or viewing a show-up may exacerbate incorrect identifications because the post-event information can confuse memory and increase confidence in misidentifications (see Brigham & Cairns, 1988; Deffenbacher et al., 2006; Dysart et al., 2001; Hinz & Pezdek, 2001; Memon et al., 2002). Another approach is for law enforcement to avoid leading questions or presenting information to witnesses that may influence what they remember or report. Procedural recommendations, such as the Cognitive Interview (CI), an interviewing technique that includes context reinstatement, perspective taking, reverse order of event reporting, and rapport building, is recommended for law enforcement to guard against memory interference effects during eyewitness identification (see Blank & Launay, 2014; Geiselman et al., 1984; Smith, Wells, Lindsay, & Myerson, 2017; Wells, 2014; Wixted et al., 2021). The CI has been revised and shortened over the years, making it manageable for in-field use (i.e., the Modified Cognitive Interview [MCI]), as some reports suggested components of the technique were difficult to use outside the lab

(Clarke & Milne, 2001; Dando et al., 2008; Kebbell et al., 1999). Overall, meta-analyses suggest that compared to the standard police interview techniques, the CI and MCI produce more information without increasing errors (Köhnken et al., 1999; Memon et al., 2010), and more recent studies suggest that police trainees found the MCI to be a useful tool for victim information gathering, an attitude that increased after a year of continued use (Colomb et al., 2013). Awareness and training of law enforcement about how to avoid influencing witness memory has made strides toward keeping witness memory intact in the arenas where law enforcement has control over the procedure, but what about outside of the police station?

The popularization of social media has introduced new complications to keeping eyewitness memory intact. Until recently, eyewitnesses were exposed to post-event information and potential suspects primarily in the police station via lineups or mug shots. Social media, however, now affords individuals the opportunity to do their own type of mug shot searches on popular social media sites such as Twitter (now called X), Facebook, and Instagram. Witnesses use online resources to complete their own amateur crime investigations, known as "web sleuthing," and several recent empirical studies have revealed that this form of uncontrolled and unmonitored vigilante investigation can influence eyewitness identifications (Elphick et al., 2021; Havard et al., 2023; Kleider-Offutt et al., 2021; Yardley et al., 2016). For example, Elphick and colleagues (2021) had participants view a mock crime followed by a mock social media web site. Following a one-week delay, the participants attempted to identify the perpetrator from a photo lineup. Within the intervening social media pages, researchers exposed participants to a perpetrator "look-alike." Of inherent interest was whether participants would identify the look-alike from the lineup. Counter to expectations—the lookalike was not falsely selected; however, seeing the individual in social media did decrease correct identifications of the perpetrator at recall (Elphick et al., 2021).

Similarly, Kleider-Offutt and colleagues (2021) investigated how post-crime social media exposure influences identification accuracy; however, they considered how the context of these social media images would influence eyewitness accuracy. Participants in the experiment were first asked to view a crime video followed by a time delay (presented via an irrelevant distraction task). After witnessing the video, participants were exposed to post-event social media images via a fake Twitter page (i.e., a screen capture of a fake Twitter account used to mimic the Twitter interface) that framed a guilty or innocent suspect in neutrally valenced photos (i.e., participating in philanthropic events, etc.) or negatively valenced photos (i.e., photos wherein the subject was performing lewd hand gestures, criminal activity, etc.). After a second time delay, the participants made a lineup identification (see Figure 10.1 for experimental design details).

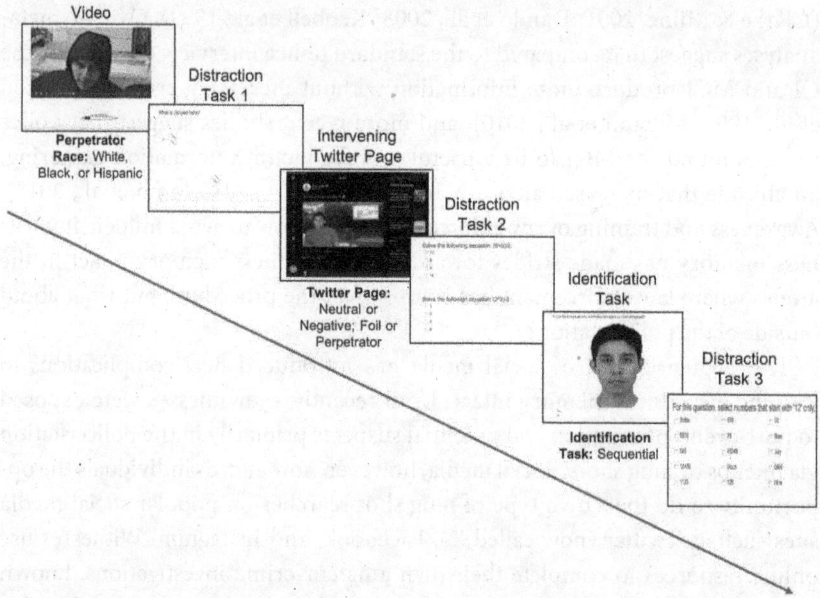

Figure 10.1 Example of eyewitness memory experimental design with intervening contextual information.
Note: The figure was taken from Kleider-Offutt et al. (2021) with permission from Taylor & Francis Ltd (www.tandfonline.com) and depicts screen captures of the experimental progress/procedure of the study.

The authors predicted that eyewitness exposure to post-event social media images via this fake Twitter interface would create a source confusion wherein eyewitnesses misattribute their familiarity of the innocent suspect to the scene of the crime rather than the correct location—the social media page/photos. In addition, researchers expected that framing the innocent or guilty suspect in the negative valenced photos on social media would activate criminal stereotypes and increase identifications regardless of the target's guilt. Framing them in the neutral valence, however, would mitigate misidentifications. Results showed that the context (i.e., neutral or negative) of the photographs on someone's social media did not have an impact on identifications. Seeing an innocent suspect on social media between witnessing a crime and making a lineup identification, however, did increase misidentifications of the suspect and decreased correct identifications to the actual perpetrator. Moreover, confidence generally was influenced by the intervening social media images/page, wherein eyewitness's confidence in their choice, whether they were correct or incorrect, decreased when they had viewed an innocent foil in the intervening pages. This suggests that viewing social media can impact not only the accuracy of an identification but also the confidence in a lineup selection.

Suspect Search and Arrest

Not only does social media influence the criminal justice system by directly impacting the memory of an eyewitness, but also real-world scenarios have indicated that social media postings can also contribute to suspect apprehension by providing police officers with evidence for an arrest. For instance, following the 2021 US Capitol insurrection, the US Federal Bureau of Investigation (FBI) encouraged members of the public to help in the identification of individuals who participated in entering the US Capitol building unlawfully (FBI, 2021). As a result, the FBI was able to identify and arrest several individuals when members of the public reported evidence of social media postings, live video streams, and images posted by those parties that initiated the violence at the Capitol (see National Public Radio [NPR], 2021; Yang, 2021).

While the use of social media in the apprehension of US Capitol rioters indicates how valuable it can be for suspect identification, there is still concern that it may have a biasing impact on suspect arrests and eyewitness memory. In the same way that memory is contaminated when witnesses look for suspects via social media, law enforcement officers may utilize social media in tandem with show-up procedures and unknowingly contaminate eyewitness memory. For example, officers may use utilize social media as a means of public information dissemination and communication, a set of common practices by law enforcement (see Beshears, 2017; Finklea, 2022; LexisNexis Risk Solutions, 2014; Lieberman et al., 2013). That is, officers may circulate a suspect's photo and information about the crime online through various media outlets (as was the case following the Capitol insurrection). Officers may then utilize show-up procedures where they show eyewitnesses a suspect alone rather than in a full lineup. This practice fosters two concerns. The first, disseminating information about suspect and crime online may bias public opinion of the alleged suspect's guilt and contaminate the memory of potential witnesses before case facts are reviewed (Ganga, 2021). Second, show-up procedures are inherently suggestive and do not protect against suspect misidentifications as there are no comparison suspects as while there are in a lineup (see Smith, Wells, Lindsay, & Penrod, 2017; Steblay et al., 2003; Wells et al., 2015). Therefore, the utilization of show-up procedures after the dissemination of suspect information in the media may further contaminate the memory of the eyewitness and lead to greater misidentifications. To prevent public bias and maintain the integrity of the information gathered throughout a criminal investigation, however, legislation is now being considered to prevent law enforcement from posting mug shots of suspects on social media as part of their suspect search (Cabanatuan, 2021).

Another growing concern with social media use by law enforcement is there are no legislative guidelines governing its use at the federal level (see Finklea,

2022). Therefore, many officers may have no formal training or guidance on utilizing social media as an investigative tool and are not trained in procedures to prevent their own memories and biases from influencing or guiding their investigations. For instance, it is possible that officers perusing social media may already be familiar with known criminals in an area—especially given that officers report a high prevalence of social media usage both formally and informally (see Kim et al., 2017; LexisNexis Risk Solutions, 2014). After an individual reports a crime, the acquired details about the suspect and the nature of the crime may direct officers' attention to known criminals that they have encountered on social media. This may benefit law enforcement by allowing for the identification and location of a criminal quickly; however, it may also contribute to the unjust arrest of an innocent individual based on an officer's social media–informed memory and biases toward them. Although arrests made from evidence obtained on or through social media is legal under the Fourth Amendment (see Schmidt, 2012), it does not mean the arrest and proceedings that follow (i.e., suspect interrogations, eyewitness lineups, suspect mental health evaluations, etc.) will be free of bias and memory errors.

Taken together, the information provided here suggests that the use of social media by law enforcement officials during a criminal investigation can benefit the criminal justice system; however, a lack of regulation/professional standards guiding its proper use can introduce biases into apprehension procedures that then facilitate memory errors, both for the officers themselves and the eyewitnesses. Regardless, once a suspect is arrested, the burden of whether the suspect is found guilty falls to the jury, with the expectation that the trial process is unbiased.

Juror Impartiality

In a perfect system, jurors weigh the evidence of a case and decide the guilt or innocence of the accused based on only the facts presented in the courtroom. To preserve impartiality, juror instructions ask jurors to set aside their individual existing biases about a defendant (i.e., race, gender, facial structure) before hearing evidence and to weigh only the facts as presented. For highly publicized trials, wherein there is local news coverage via the television news or newspaper, research has shown that exposure to pretrial publicity (PTP) can bias jurors' verdict decisions (see Steblay et al., 1999 for review); perceptions of the defendant's credibility (Otto et al., 1994; C. Ruva et al., 2007); and memory for trial evidence (C. L. Ruva, 2018; C. L. Ruva et al., 2011; C. L. Ruva & Guenther, 2015). PTP encompasses all media coverage of a case preceding the trial (Greene & Wade, 1988; Studebaker & Penrod, 1997). Importantly, substantial PTP that is prejudicial and antidefendant in nature can bias jurors' opinions of the defendant's character and increase the likelihood of a guilty verdict (see Steblay et al., 1999, for review) and affect the interpretation of trial evidence (Hope et al., 2004; C. L. Ruva et al., 2011). To avoid this exposure for local cases, attorneys may request a change of venue—which helps ensure that possible jurors are not biased by extraneous information presented outside of a courtroom about a case (Garfield Tenzer, 2019). The presence of social media exposure, however, complicates such attempts at mitigating the introduction of biases to jurors.

Moreover, from a memory standpoint, PTP creates a source-monitoring issue for jurors as they may be confused by whether remembered case information was recalled from case facts presented in the courtroom or from television news (C. L. Ruva & Guenther, 2015; Steblay et al., 1999). To add to the issue, when PTP has occurred, judicial admonishments asking jurors to disregard information presented outside the courtroom may not correct the way in which a juror recalls information (C. L. Ruva & Guenther, 2015). In a recent study, jurors given antidefendant PTP were more likely to give a guilty verdict than those given antiprosecution publicity or no PTP, regardless of deliberations suggesting that it is difficult to correct misinformation once encoded (C. L. Ruva & Coy, 2020). Recently, attorneys have requested that case information presented via social media exposure should also be considered biasing for the same reasons as television news (Garfield Tenzer, 2019). However, because social media is relatively new, the court system is slow to apply rules of PTP to include Internet publicity (*United States v. Tsarnaev*, 2015).

This is especially concerning as social media is universally available, beyond the reach of local news, as 67% of US adults are getting some news from social media (Shearer & Gottfried, 2017). Moreover, television and print news outlets have some modicum of fact-checking, whether it is via the editor or producer at a minimum. Alternatively, some social media platforms, such as Facebook, have taken strides toward monitoring misinformation (see Mosseri, 2016, 2017), but not all platforms have these safeguards in place, which has raised concern about people's consumption of fake news or slanted/biased news and how the information impacts memory (for review, see Pennycook & Rand, 2021). Pretrial information is important to monitor as it may impact what a juror remembers and ultimate trial outcomes. For example, in the highly publicized Trayvon Martin case, a young Black man was shot by a civilian security guard for trespassing. The news media and social media biased people's view, of the case, by how the facts were presented (Aizenman, 2012); later retractions or correction of errant reporting likely did not influence how people viewed either the victim or the accused. Even when people can identify information as coming from a reliable or unreliable source, they often fail to apply that knowledge when asked to determine whether something is true (Henkel & Mattson, 2011). The reason for this difficulty is that if information comes from a credible source, regardless of whether the source is remembered, it is deemed truthful (Marsh & Yang, 2017). However, a low-credibility source (e.g., a possible suspect posted on Instagram by an anonymous person) that is not persuasive initially becomes more impactful as the source is forgotten (Did I see that picture at the police station?; Underwood & Pezdek, 1998). From a juror's memory perspective, trial information that is gathered from even an unreliable social media site may have a lasting impact on how information at the actual trial is remembered and judged.

Once misinformation is incorporated into memory, it is very difficult to disentangle that information from fact (Frenda et al., 2011; Loftus, 2005; C. L. Ruva & Coy, 2020). Once exposed to biased social media, a juror's decision about a defendant's guilt may not be based solely on case facts (see Aizenman, 2012). General memory processes that work to tie memory episodes to the source of the information (e.g., is this face familiar from the crime or the newspaper?) may be unreliable when thematically similar information is presented via multiple sources (Johnson et al., 1993). Moreover, when a juror remembers a face or information as familiar, they may try to reconstruct the source of where the information was first encountered based on probable options (Kuhlmann et al., 2021 for review). For example, a juror may attribute their knowledge about the heinous nature of a crime to detective testimony in court, rather than a social media site, as being more probable, when in fact, they are mistaken (they saw it on Twitter)—a source-monitoring error. Although jurors are instructed to avoid media during a trial, pretrial information has already been stored in memory. Source-monitoring errors of this ilk can be reduced if the juror/witness is encouraged to engage a strict criterion of whether they saw information or read it, for example (Lindsay, 1994; Zaragoza & Koshmider, 1989). However, an increased criterion is only as successful as the difficulty of the source-monitoring context, and highly vivid, suggestible, or contextually similar information may be retrieved with the same source memory cues (Johnson et al., 1993, Loftus & Pickrell, 1995).

Although the courts are equipped to handle the suggestibility and bias presented from PTP via sequestering juries or change of venue, the current challenges presented by social media and the speed with which information is made available have created a new set of problems regarding ensuring a fair trial for the defendant.

Conclusion

The broad reach of social media and Internet news, more globally, has created an advantage for law enforcement in many situations, such as finding a suspect quickly by referencing posted pictures for eyewitnesses or disseminating "wanted" pictures of a suspect who is alluding capture. While memory is fresh and noncontaminated by outside information, an eyewitness can potentially retrieve the picture of a known perpetrator from a social media post, which expedites identification and potential arrest. The speed with which information is made available has been an advantage in many aspects of the legal system, although there are trade-offs for this immediate access to information by anyone with a cell phone.

A preeminent issue with ensuring a valid identification from an eyewitness is to guard the memory for the crime against contamination, whether from suggestive questioning by law enforcement, poor lineup procedures, or misinformation from other sources (Wells, 1978, 2020; Wells et al., 2020). Much of the eyewitness memory literature focuses on understanding system variables. These are procedural factors in the legal system that are controlled by law enforcement or triers of fact (Wells, 1978, 2020; Wells et al., 2006). To that end, several iterations of *best practices* for law enforcement have been culled (Wells et al., 1998, 2006, 2020) to ensure witness memory is valid. Some of these directives include using double-blind lineups, recording lineup identifications, measuring the confidence of the identification, avoiding the presentation of multiple lineups, and avoiding the use of the show-up procedure. Unfortunately, if an eyewitness has conducted a social media search and contaminated their memory for the suspect, then these procedural safeguards may be ineffective. That is, if an eyewitness searches the Internet before viewing a lineup, then the memory they had for the perpetrator may be replaced by the face of the person they found on social media (Kleider-Offutt et al., 2021). While the exact prevalence rate of this phenomenon is unknown, there are noted instances of its occurrence globally. In Australia, between 2013 and 2014 at least five known cases occurred wherein memory contamination via social media, specifically Facebook, contributed to innocent suspect misidentifications (see McGorrery, 2015). Additionally, recent criminological research suggests that practices of web sleuthing, wherein amateurs take to social media in attempts to identify a perpetrator, happens across the globe, most notably in the United States, the United Kingdom, Canada, and Australia (Yardley et al., 2016).

Given its global prevalence, this is a growing concern among lawyers who must rely on the veracity of witness memory when other evidence is circumstantial. Potentially, the way forward is for law enforcement to supervise any searches, to the extent possible, and require other incriminating evidence before conducting a social media search (see recommendations similar for lineup procedures; Wells et al., 2020). In the recent best practices directives from Wells and colleagues (2020), a key suggestion is for there to be evidence suggesting guilt or association with the crime before an individual's picture can be put in a lineup. This guards against identifications based solely on familiarity from social media searching.

Interestingly, some criminals post information about their crime, including photos of the actual commission of the crime or details about what they have done (Parker, 2017). In these instances, law enforcement searching for suspects is assisted by the perpetrators themselves. The boasting about crimes one has committed via social media opens the door for law enforcement to use that information. The Department of Justice even outlines ways law enforcement can use social media to their advantage (Department of Justice, 2017). The difficulty with ensuring that a person is not misidentified in a real-world case, unlike a laboratory experiment, is that law enforcement does not know who the perpetrator is, and they must rely on the memory of the eyewitness when other evidence is lacking. In the situation where the perpetrator self-incriminates via posting pictures or information about the crime they committed, law enforcement has *ground truth*, meaning that they know who the perpetrator is, and thus a subsequent eyewitness identification is supporting evidence. It is seemingly impossible to keep people from being influenced by PTP, on the Internet, for highly publicized trials. Once information about alleged perpetrators is disseminated, people may be biased to whatever information is available regardless of whether it is factual (Daftary-Kapur et al., 2014). From a courtroom procedures' standpoint, the judicial system will need to be amenable to attorney's pleas for a change of venue based on social media influencing the jury pool. In addition, the reluctance to include laws for these procedures that include social media as publicity must change as many people now get their news from the Internet in addition to other outlets (Aaronson & Patterson, 2013; Simpler, 2012).

What Can Be Done for Justice to Stay "Blind"?

As mentioned, there must be evidence to warrant the inclusion of a person in a lineup beyond just an Internet search. Another safeguard is to query witnesses about any Internet searches they have conducted on their own before police questioning or viewing a sanctioned lineup. This allows law enforcement to become aware of the potential memory contamination and calibrate subsequent identifications accordingly. One potential difficulty when asking people whether they did an Internet search for a suspect or read information about a case is that some people are constant Internet searchers, meaning that they intertwine their daily living with social media searches on their cell phones. Because there is no actual demarcation of what was seen on the Internet versus "real life," some people may be unable to report searches that could have biased their memory for crime events. That said, asking questions about Internet searches and familiarity with crime details is one step forward to deal with potential contamination.

Another new development for suspect identification and capture that is creating issues in the legal system is the facial recognition software used by everything from cell phone security to identifying criminal perpetrators (see Committee on Oversight and Reform, 2017). It is well established that eyewitness memory is fallible due to how the human memory system operates. Potentially, reliance on a system that is not vulnerable to suggestion or contamination per se is an alternative approach. Facial recognition software has shown some advantages in identifying people from crime videos, even those of the Capitol insurrection in 2021, even though it also has its own problems with mismatching/confusing people similar in appearance (Klare et al., 2012; Nawara, 2011). Whether this aspect of law enforcement in the Internet age is an advantage over human eyewitnesses is still being determined.

Overall, the Internet and social media have created a situation wherein witness memory for events may never be pristine/free of contamination, and witnesses may not be clear about the source of remembered information. Considering potential misidentifications and contaminating of jury pools via social media posts, the legal system must create laws and procedures to query search behavior before lineup identifications. Potentially, modifying the CI to accommodate this line of questioning could provide a calibration regarding how reliable a person's memory is and whether it is based on what was seen during the crime. In all segments of the legal system, professional guidelines for dealing with social media content are an important next step.

References

Aaronson, D. E., & Patterson, S. M. (2013). Modernizing jury instructions in the age of social media. *Criminal Justice, 27*(4). 26–35

Aizenman, H. C. (2012). Pretrial publicity in post-Trayvon Martin world. *Criminal Justice, 27*(3), 12–17.

Albright, T. D. (2017). Why eyewitnesses fail. *Proceedings of the National Academy of Sciences of the United States of America, 114*(30), 7758–7764. https://doi.org/10.1073/pnas.1706891114

Beshears, M. I. (2017). Effectiveness of police social media use. *American Journal of Criminal Justice, 42*, 489–501. https://doi.org/10.1007/s12103-016-9380-4

Blank, H., & Launay, C. (2014). How to protect eyewitness memory against the misinformation effect: A meta-analysis of post-warning studies. *Journal of Applied Research in Memory and Cognition, 3*(2). 77–88. https://doi.org/10.1016/j.jarmac.2014.03.005

Blank, H., Panday, A., Edwards, R., Skopicz-Radkiewicz, E., Gibson, V., & Reddy, V. (2022). Double misinformation: Effects on eyewitness remembering. *Journal of Applied Research in Memory and Cognition, 11*(1), 97–105. https://doi.org/10.1016/j.jarmac.2021.08.001

Brigham, J. C., & Cairns, D. L. (1988). The effect of mugshot inspections on eyewitness identification accuracy. *Journal of Applied Social Psychology, 18*(16), 1394–1410. https://doi.org/10.1111/j.1559-1816.1988.tb01214.x

Cabanatuan, M. (2021, July 24). Newsom signs bill banning police from posting mug shots of nonviolent suspects on social media. *San Francisco Chronical.* https://www.sfchronicle.com/crime/article/Bay-Area-lawmaker-wants-to-keep-mugshots-of-16335621.php

Chan, J. C. K., Wilford, M. M., & Hughes, K. L. (2012). Retrieval can increase or decrease suggestibility depending on how memory is tested: The importance of source complexity. *Journal of Memory and Language, 67*(1), 78–85. https://doi.org/10.1016/j.jml.2012.02.006

Clarke, C., & Milne, R. (2001). *National evaluation of the PEACE investigative interviewing course.* Home Office

Colomb, C., Ginet, M., Wright, D., Demarchi, S., & Sadler, C. (2013). Back to the real: Efficacy and perception of a modified cognitive interview in the field. *Applied Cognitive Psychology, 27*(5), 574–583.

Committee on Oversight and Reform. (2017, March 22). Committee to review law enforcement's policies on facial recognition technology. Committee on Oversight and Reform. https://republicans-oversight.house.gov/hearing/law-enforcements-use-facial-recognition-technology/

Daftary-Kapur, T., Penrod, S. D., O'Connor, M., & Wallace, B. (2014). Examining pretrial publicity in a shadow jury paradigm: Issues of slant, quantity, persistence and generalizability. *Law and Human Behavior, 38*(5), 462–477. https://doi.org/10.1037/lhb0000081

Dando, C., Wilcock, R., & Milne, R. (2008). The cognitive interview: Inexperienced police officers' perceptions of their witness/victim interviewing practices. *Legal and Criminological Psychology, 13*(1), 59–70. https://doi.org/10.1348/135532506X162498

Davis, J. M., & Schiffman, H. R. (1985). The influence of the wording of interrogatives on the accuracy of eyewitness recollections. *Bulletin of the Psychonomic Society, 23*, 394–396. https://doi.org/10.3758/BF03330194

Deffenbacher, K. A., Bornstein, B. H., & Penrod, S. D. (2006). Mugshot exposure effects: Retroactive interference, mugshot commitment, source confusion, and unconscious transference. *Law and Human Behavior, 30*(3), 287–307. https://doi.org/10.1007/s10979-006-9008-1

Department of Justice. (2017). Use of third-party social media tools to communicate with the public. Department of Justice. https://www.justice.gov/d9/pages/attachments/2021/08/19/thirdpartysocialwebservicespia_final_7-25-17.pdf

Dysart, J. E., Lindsay, R. C. L., Hammond, R., & Dupuis, P. (2001). Mug shot exposure prior to lineup identification: Interference, transference, and commitment effects. *Journal of Applied Psychology, 86*(6), 1280–1284. https://doorg/10.1037/0021-9010.86.6.1280

Elphick, C., Philpot, R., Zhang, M., Stuart, A., Pike, G., Strathie, A., Havard, C., Walkington, Z., Frumkin, L. A., Levine, M., Price, B. A., Bandara, A. K., & Nuseibeh, B. (2021). Digital detectives: Websleuthing reduces eyewitness identification accuracy in police lineups. *Frontiers in Psychology, 12*. https://doi.org/10.3389/fpsyg.2021.640513

Federal Bureau of Investigation. (2021, February 21). US Capitol violence. FBI. https://www.fbi.gov/wanted/capitol-violence

Finklea, K. (2022). Law enforcement and technology: Using social media. Congressional Research Service. https://sgp.fas.org/crs/misc/R47008.pdf

Frenda, S. J., Nichols, R. M., & Loftus, E. F. (2011). Current issues and advances in misinformation research. *Current Directions in Psychological Science, 20*(1), 20–23. http://dx.doi.org/10.1177/0963721410396620

Ganga, M. L. (2021, June 29). Police take "wanted" posters onto social media, nabbing suspects and ruining lives. *Los Angeles Times.* https://www.latimes.com/california/story/2021-06-29/police-social-media-wanted-posts-help-cases-ruin-lives

Garfield Tenzer, L. Y. (2019). Social media, venue, and the right to a fair trial. *Baylor Law Review, 71*(2), 421–465. https://dx.doi.org/10.2139/ssrn.3328959

Geiselman, R. E., Fisher, R. P., Firstenbrg, I., Hutton, L. A., Sullivan, S., Avetissian, I., & Prosk, A. (1984). Enhancement of eyewitness memory: An empirical evaluation of the cognitive interview. *Journal of Police Science & Administration, 12*(1), 74–80.

Gordon, L. T., & Thomas, A. K. (2017). The forward effects of testing on eyewitness memory: The tension between suggestibility and learning. *Journal of Memory and Language, 95*, 190–199. https://doi.org/10.1016/j.jml.2017.04.004

Greene, E., & Wade, R. (1988). Of private talk and public print: General pre-trial publicity and juror decision-making. *Applied Cognitive Psychology, 2*(2). 123–135. https://doi.org/10.1002/acp.2350020204

Havard, C., Strathie, A., Pike, G., Walkington, Z., Neww, H., & Harrison, V. (2023). From witness to web sleuth: Does citizen enquiry on social media affect formal eyewitness identification procedures? *Journal of Police and Criminal Psychology, 38*, 309–317. https://doi.org/10.1007/s11896-021-09444-z

Henkel, L. A., & Mattson, M. E. (2011). Reading is believing: The truth effect and source credibility. *Consciousness and Cognition: An International Journal, 20*(4), 1705–1721. https://doi.org/10.1016/j.concog.2011.08.018

Hinz, T., & Pezdek, K. (2001). The effect of exposure to multiple lineups on face identification accuracy. *Law and Human Behavior 25*(2), 185–198. https://psycnet.apa.org/doi/10.1023/A:1005697431830

Hope, L., Memon, A., McGeorge, P. (2004). Understanding pretrial publicity: Predecisional distortion of evidence by mock jurors. *Journal of Experimental Psychology Applied, 10*(2). 111–119. http://dx.doi.org/10.1037/1076-898X.10.2.111

Innocence Project. (2019, June 27). Innocence project. https://www.innocenceproject.org.

Innocence Project. (n.d.). Eyewitness memory reform. https://innocenceproject.org/eyewitness-misidentification/

Johnson, M. K., Hashtroudi, S., & Lindsay, D. S. (1993). Source monitoring. *Psychological Bulletin, 114*(1), 3–28. https://doi.org/10.1037/0033-2909.114.1.3

Kebbell, M., Milne, R., & Wagstaff, G. (1999). The cognitive interview: A survey of its forensic effectiveness. *Psychology Crime & Law, 5*(1–2), 101–115. https://doi.org/10.1080/10683169908414996

Kim, K., Mohr, A. O. N. E., & Oglesby, A. (2017, February). 2016 Law enforcement use of social media survey. International Association of Chiefs of Police and the Urban Institute. http://www.urban.org/sites/default/files/publication/88661/2016-law-enforcement-use-of-social-media-survey.pdf

Klare, B. F., Burge, M. J., Klontz, J. C., Vorder Bruegge, R. W., & Jain, A. K. (2012). Face recognition performance: Role of demographic information. *IEEE Transactions on Information Forensics and Security, 7*(6). 1789–1801. https://doi.org/10.1109/TIFS.2012.2214212

Kleider-Offutt, H. M., Stevens, B. B., & Capodanno, M. (2021). He did it! Or did I just see him on Twitter? Social media influence on eyewitness identification. *Memory, 30*(4). 493–504. https://doi.org/10.1080/09658211.2021.1953080

Köhnken, G., Milne, R., Memon, A., & Bull, R. (1999). A meta-analysis on the effects of the Cognitive Interview. *Psychology, Crime and Law, 5*, 3–27.

Kuhlmann, B. G., Symeonidou, N., Tanyar, H., & Wulff, L. (2021). Remembering and reconstruction episodic context: An overview of source monitoring methods and behavioral findings. *Psychology of Learning and Motivation, 75*, 79–124. https://doi.org/10.1016/bs.plm.2021.06.002

Loftus, E. F. (1975). Leading questions and the eyewitness report. *Cognitive Psychology, 7*(4), 560–572. https://doi.org/10.1016/0010-0285(75)90023-7

Loftus, E. F. (2005). Planting misinformation in the human mind: A 30-year investigation of the malleability of memory. *Learning & Memory, 12*(4), 361–366. https://doi.org/10.1101/lm.94705

Loftus, E. F., & Palmer, J. C. (1974). Reconstruction of automobile destruction: An example of the interaction between language and memory. *Journal of Verbal Learning & Verbal Behavior, 13*(5), 585–589. https://doi.org/10.1016/S0022-5371(74)80011-3

Loftus, E. F., & Pickrell, J. E. (1995). The formation of false memories. *Psychiatric Annals, 25*(12), 720–725. https://doi.org/10.3928/0048-5713-19951201-07

LexisNexis Risk Solutions. (2014). Survey of law enforcement personnel and their use of social media [Infographic]. https://risk.lexisnexis.com/insights-resources/infographic/law-enforcement-usage-of-social-media-for-investigations-infographic

Lindsay, D. S. (1994). Memory source monitoring and eyewitness testimony. In D. F. Ross, J. D. Read, & M. P. Toglia (Eds.), *Adult eyewitness testimony: Current trends and developments* (pp. 27–55). Cambridge University Press. https://doi.org/10.1017/CBO9780511759192.003

Lieberman, J. D., Koetzle, D., & Sakiyama, M. (2013). Police departments' use of Facebook: Patterns and policy issues. *Police Quarterly, 16*(4), 438–462. https://doi.org/10.1177%2F1098611113495049

Marsh, E. J., & Yang, B. W. (2017). A call to think broadly about information literacy. *Journal of Applied Research in Memory and Cognition, 6*(4). 401-404. https://doi.org/10.1016/j.jarmac.2017.09.012

McGorrery, P. (2015). The limited impact of Facebook and the displacement effect on the admissibility of identification evidence. *Criminal Law Journal, 39*(4). 207–218.

Memon, A., Hope, L., Bartlett, J., & Bull, R. (2002). Eyewitness recognition errors: The effects of mugshot viewing and choosing in young and old adults. *Memory & Cognition, 30*(8), 1219–1227. https://doi.org/10.3758/BF03213404

Memon, A., Meissner, C., & Fraser, J. (2010). The Cognitive Interview: A meta-analytic review and study space analysis of the past 25 years. *Psychology, Public Policy, and Law, 16*(4), 340–372. https://psycnet.apa.org/doi/10.1037/a0020518

Mitchell, K. J., & Johnson, M. K. (2000). Source monitoring: Attributing mental experiences. In E. Tulving & F. I. M. Craik (Eds.), *The Oxford handbook of memory* (pp. 179–195). Oxford University Press.

Mosseri, A. (2016, December 15). *Addressing hoaxes and fake news.* Facebook. https://newsroom.fb.com/news/2016/12/news-feed-fyi-addressing-hoaxes-and-fake-news/

Mosseri, A. (2017, April 6). *A new educational tool against misinformation.* Facebook. https://newsroom.fb.com/news/2017/04/a-new-educational-tool-against-misinformation/

National Public Radio. (2021, January 7). Law enforcement and social media identifying US Capitol mob members. https://www.npr.org/sections/insurrection-at-the-capitol/2021/01/07/954518782/law-enforcement-and-social-media-identifying-u-s-capitol-mob-members

Nawara, J. (2011). Machine learning: Face recognition technology evidence in criminal trials. *University of Louisville Law Review, 49*(4), 601–622.

Otto, A. L., Penrod, S. D., & Dexter, H. R. (1994). The biasing impact of pretrial publicity on juror judgments. *Law and Human Behavior, 18*(4), 453–469. https://doi.org/10.1007/BF01499050

Parker, M. (2017, April 19). Criminal suspects' social media use has pros, cons, for police. *Observer-Dispatch.* https://www.uticaod.com/news/20170419/criminal-suspects-social-media-use-has-pros-cons-for-police

Paterson, H. M., Kemp, R. I., & Kemp, J. R. Ng. (2011). Combating co-witness contamination: Attempting to decrease the negative effects of discussion on eyewitness memory. *Applied Cognitive Psychology, 25*(1), 43–52. https://doi.org/10.1002/acp.1640

Pennycook, G., & Rand, D. G. (2021). The psychology of fake news. *Trends in Cognitive Sciences, 25*(5). 388–402. https://doi.org/10.1016/j.tics.2021.02.007

Pickrell, J. E., McDonald, D.-L., Bernstein, D. M., & Loftus, E. F. (2017). Misinformation effect. In R. F. Pohl (Ed.), *Cognitive illusions: Intriguing phenomena in thinking, judgement and memory* (2nd ed., pp. 406–423). Routledge/Taylor & Francis Group.

Ruva, C., McEvoy, C., & Bryant, J. B. (2007). Effects of pre-trial publicity and jury deliberation on juror bias and source memory errors. *Applied Cognitive Psychology, 21*(1), 45–67. https://doi.org/10.1002/acp.1254

Ruva, C. L. (2018). From the headlines to the jury room: An examination of the impact of pretrial publicity on jurors and juries. In M. K. Miller & B. H. Bornstein (Eds.), *Advances in psychology and law* (Vol. 3, pp. 1–39). Springer International Publishing. https://doi.org/10.1007/978-3-319-75859-6_1

Ruva, C. L., & Coy, A. E. (2020). Your bias is rubbing off on me: The impact of pretrial publicity and jury type on guilt decisions, trial evidence interpretation, and impression formation. *Psychology, Public Policy, and Law, 26*(1), 22–35. https://doi.org/10.1037/law0000220

Ruva, C. L., & Guenther, C. C. (2015). From the shadows into the light: How pretrial publicity and deliberation affect mock jurors' decisions, impressions, and memory. *Law and Human Behavior, 39*(3), 294–310. https://doi.org/10.1037/lhb0000117

Ruva, C. L., Guenther, C. C., & Yarbrough, A. (2011). Positive and negative pretrial publicity: The roles of impression formation, emotion, and predecisional distortion. *Criminal Justice and Behavior, 38*(5), 511–534. https://doi.org/10.1177/0093854811400823

Schmidt, L. A. (2012). Social networking and the Fourth Amendment: Location tracking on Facebook, Twitter, and Foursqaure. *Cornell Journal of Law and Public Policy, 22*(2), 515–536. https://scholarship.law.cornell.edu/cjlpp/vol22/iss2/7

Shearer, E., & Gottfried, J. (2017, September 7). News use across social media platforms 2017. Pew Research Center. https://www.pewresearch.org/journalism/2017/09/07/news-use-across-social-media-platforms-2017/

Simpler, M. F. III. (2012). The unjust "web" we weave: The evolution of social media and its psychological impact on juror impartiality and fair trials. *Law & Psychological Review, 36*, 275–296.

Smith, A. M., Wells, G. L., Lindsay, R. C. L., & Myerson, T. (2017). Eyewitness identification performance on showups improves with an additional-opportunities instruction: Evidence for present-absent criteria discrepancy. *Law and Human Behavior, 42*(3), 215–226. https://doi.org/10.1037/lhb0000284

Smith, A. M., Wells, G. L., Lindsay, R. C. L., & Penrod, S. D. (2017). Fair lineups are better than biased lineups and showups, but not because they increase underlying discriminability. *Law and Human Behavior, 41*(2), 127–145. https://psycnet.apa.org/doi/10.1037/lhb0000219

Steblay, N. M., Besirevic, J., Fulero, S. M., & Jimenez-Lorente, B. (1999). The effects of pretrial publicity on juror verdicts: A meta-analytic review. *Law and Human Behavior, 23*(2), 219–235. https://doi.org/10.1023/A:1022325019080

Steblay, N. M., Dysart, J., Fulero, S., & Lindsay, R. C. L. (2003). Eyewitness accuracy rates in police showup and lineup presentations: A meta-analytic comparison. *Law and Human Behavior, 27*(5), 523–540. https://doi.org/10.1023/A:1025438223608

Studebaker, C. A., & Penrod, S. D. (1997). Pretrial publicity: The media, the law, and common sense. *Psychology, Public Policy, and Law, 3*(2–3). 428–460. https://psycnet.apa.org/doi/10.1037/1076-8971.3.2-3.428

Underwood, J., & Pezdek, K. (1998). Memory suggestibility as an example of the sleeper effect. *Psychonomic Bulletin & Review, 5*(3), 449–453. https://doi.org/10.3758/BF03208820

United States v. Tsarnaev, 157 F. Supp. 3d 57, 67 (2015). https://casetext.com/case/united-states-v-tsarnaev-15

Wells, G. L. (1978). Applied eyewitness-testimony research: System variables and estimator variables. *Journal of Personality and Social Psychology, 36*(12), 1546–1557. https://doi.org/10.1037/0022-3514.36.12.1546

Wells, G. L. (2014). Eyewitness identification: Probative value, criterion shifts, and policy regarding the sequential lineup. *Current Directions in Psychological Science, 23*(1), 11–16. https://doi.org/10.1177/0963721413504781

Wells, G. L. (2020). Psychological science on eyewitness identification and its impact on police practices and policies. *American Psychologist, 75*(9), 1316–1329. https://doi.org/10.1037/amp0000749

Wells, G. L., Kovera, M. B., Douglass, A. B., Brewer, N., Meissner, C. A., & Wixted, J. T. (2020). Policy and procedure recommendations for the collection and preservation of eyewitness identification evidence. *Law and Human Behavior, 44*(1), 3–36. https://doi.org/10.1037/lhb0000359

Wells, G. L., Memon, A., & Pernod, S. D. (2006). Eyewitness evidence. Improving its probative value. *Psychological Science in the Public Interest, 7*(2), 45–75. https://doi.org/10.1111%2Fj.1529-1006.2006.00027.x

Wells, G. L., Small, M., Pernod, S. J., Malpass, R. S., Fulero, S. M., & Brimacombe, C. A. E. (1998). Eyewitness identification procedures: Recommendations for lineups and photospreads. *Law and Human Behavior, 22*, 603–647. https://doi.org/10.1023/A:1025750605807

Wells, G. L., Yang, Y., & Smalarz, L. (2015). Eyewitness identification: Bayesian information gain, base-rate effect equivalency curves, and reasonable suspicion. *Law and Human Behavior, 39*(2), 99–122. https://doi.org/10.1037/lhb0000125

Wixted, J. T., Mickes, L., Dunn, J. C., Clark, S. E., & Wells, W. (2016). Estimating the reliability of eyewitness identifications from police lineups. *Proceedings of the National Academy of Sciences of the United States of America, 113*(2), 304–309. https://doi.org/10.1073/pnas.1516814112

Wixted, J. T., & Wells, G. L. (2017). The relationship between eyewitness confidence and identification accuracy: A new synthesis. *Psychological Science in the Public Interest, 18*(1), 10–65. https://doi.org/10.1177/1529100616686966

Wixted, J. T., Wells, G. L., Loftus, E. F., & Garrett, B. L. (2021). Test a witness's memory of a suspect only once. *Psychological Science in the Public Interest, 22*(1, Suppl), 1S–18S. https://doi.org/10.1177/15291006211026259

Yang, A. (2021, January 11). Many capitol rioters implicated by their own social media posts [News report]. American Broadcasting Company (ABC). https://abcnews.go.com/Technology/capitol-rioters-implicated-social-media-posts/story?id=75177672

Yardley, E., Thomas Lynes, A. G., Wilson, D., & Kelly, E. (2016). What's the deal with "websleuthing"? News media representations of amateur detectives in networked spaces. *Crime Media Cult, 14*(1), 81–109. https://doi.org/10.1177/1741659016674045

Zaragoza, M. S., & Koshmider, J. W. (1989). Misled subjects may know more than their performance implies. *Journal of Experimental Psychology, 15*(2), 246–255. https://psycnet.apa.org/doi/10.1037/0278-7393.15.2.246

Zerback, T., & Töpfl, F. (2022). Forged examples as disinformation: The biasing effects of political astroturfing comments on public opinion perceptions and how to prevent them. *Political Psychology, 43*(3), 399–418. https://doi.org/10.1111/pops.12767

11
Fake History
Digital Memory and the Specter of National Socialism in the Capital Riot

Jennifer V. Evans and Brandon Rigato

Even before Donald Trump was elected forty-fifth president of the United States in the fall of 2016, journalists, scholars, and politicians drew on historical analogies to arm a nervous electorate with lessons from the past. It was always a mediatized affair. Yet although pundits agreed on the pernicious threat to democracy, they differed on where to locate Trump and Trumpism in relation to history. Masha Gessen made parallels to Weimar Germany; New York University Italian History Professor Ruth Ben-Ghiat looked to strongmen like Mussolini (Ben-Ghiat, 2016; Gessen, 2016), while Yale Historian Tim Snyder gave instruction on how to thwart creeping authoritarianism to blunt its force before it fully takes hold (Snyder, 2017). First-term Congresswoman Alexandria Ocasio-Cortez took a different tack with her Instagram story likening Immigration and Customs Enforcement (ICE) migrant internment facilities to not only concentration camps but also internment facilities that housed Japanese Americans during World War II (CNN, 2019). White supremacy was not just a European phenomenon, she argued; it was part of the very fabric of American identity.

While scholars were preoccupied with comparison and context, a parallel fixation with analogies was taking place on other parts of social media from TikTok to Telegram (Gordon, 2020; Smith, 2020). Citizen journalists snapped images of police sporting odal rune tattoos, typically associated with neo-Nazism, at Black Lives Matter demonstrations. QAnon supporters perpetuated pedophilia conspiracy theories that drew on centuries old antisemitic blood libel myths (Evans, 2020). And antivaxxers ludicrously adopted the yellow star or the syringe swastika as the symbol of their outrage. In the months and days leading up to the 2021 inauguration, even the conservative, fringe, and radical right circulated the long-debunked tropes that National Socialism was itself a left-wing ideology. Analogies, in other words, circulated high and low, across media, and on all sides of the political spectrum.

Jennifer V. Evans and Brandon Rigato, *Fake History* In: *The Remaking of Memory in the Age of the Internet and Social Media.* Edited by: Qi Wang and Andrew Hoskins, Oxford University Press. © Oxford University Press 2024. DOI: 10.1093/oso/9780197661260.003.0011

This chapter asks how might we make sense of the role of historical analogies in the ebb and flow of digital memory, where meaning changes "on the fly" (Hoskins, 2011). It questions the role analogies play in the creation of networked publics, spaces of shared values forged through the affordances of social media (boyd, 2010; Papacharissi, 2017). Particularly, it shifts the focus away from intellectual elites to everyday people and argues that we may view Twitter (currently called X) as a site of quotidian memory making around the repetitive call to historical analogy and the legacy of fascism. Using a mixed-method approach combining network visualizations with discourse and visual analysis, we argue that an analysis of historical analogies on Twitter before, during, and after the Capitol insurrection on January 6, 2021, reveals that networked memory formations coalesced into specific media templates over the course of the latter weeks and months of the Trump presidency (Marres, & Weltevrede, 2013, Kitzinger, 2000; Wu, Hofman, Mason, & Watts, 2011). These simplified forms of explanation filtered out nuance and opposing views, forging the parameters of engagement with the past in the present. We argue that these media templates, grounded in historical analogy, became internalized as a kind of schemata for how people made sense of, in this case, the rightist turn in American politics (Brown & Hoskins, 2010). Yet, this is no simple top-down process. Our study suggests everyday people served as critical memory entrepreneurs in their own right, pushing this agenda forward. By focusing on select Twitter data sets, we argue that tweets serve as a vital, if fraught, site of collective identity, emotion, and claims making at the intersection of participatory media and civic engagement, with the meaning people assign to the past playing a critical role (Bolter & Grusin, 1999).

Going with the Flow

A survey of the shifts and changes in online historical analogies requires a mixed-method approach that accounts for anarchic sociotechnical and representational qualities of social media texts, one attuned to the shifting, fluid nature of digital memory, that "goes with the flow" of information (Bolter, 2019; Erll, 2011; Latour, 2008). Visualization tools capture moments in the data stream that help us gauge the relationships generated between networked publics, platforms, and content production amid the freneticism of the claims themselves. By focusing on the "scenographies" that emerged out of particular hashtags, which we selected to represent a spectrum of possible political affiliations, we demonstrate that the technical and representational staging of historical analogies are best understood as creative modes of social and political inquiry emerging out of fluid affiliative assemblages (Marres, 2017). This allows us to see the way users mobilize historical time itself to tap into specific moral, cultural, and intellectual foundations from which to launch their claims. Analogies orient users toward the like-minded and against others, solidifying crucial social and ideological affinities within an "emotional and affective circuit of relationality" (Boler & Davis, 2018, p. 83; Papacharissi, & Oliveira, 2012; Robinson, 2016). Memory is the tie that binds, turning stand alone "matters of fact"—in this case data points—into actionable "matters of concern," media templates with particular relevance to political culture and daily life in the era of Trump (Latour, 2008).

One of the biggest challenges to social media research comes from the technology itself and whether artificial intelligence (AI) or social bots are at the root of misinformation and hate (Gray et al., 2020; Knight Foundation, 2018; Lewis & Marwick, 2017; Törnberg, 2018). Instead of viewing fake history in terms of its veracity and saturation, there is more to be gained by focusing on the sociotechnical practices and emotions attached to the conjuring of particular memory formations as plausible if untrue (Highfield, 2018). The merits of doing so are twofold. For one, it forces us to ask what is distinctive and new about today's media landscape, considering that fake news has a history of its own in the analog era (Freelon & Wells, 2020; Tworek, 2019; Warwick et al., 2021). Media templates operate in a way that is time specific and bound; they reflect both the technological affordances of the day combined with the socio-political-psychological context influencing which analogies coalesce, become internalized, and are taken up in wider discourse. Viewing fake history as a distinct part of today's media landscape lends insight into the political as something constituted, in this instance, by a struggle over the narration of the past in a changing, multimodal universe. In this instance, hashtags and tweets conjuring fake historical claims are not empty or abstract signifiers or knee jerk reactions to the cause of the day. Rather, they serve as important framing devices that help align people affectively around claims to memory, turning the cacophony of the crowd into the claims of the networked public (Garde-Hansen & Gorton, 2013; Papacharissi, 2016, p. 309; van Dijck, 2013).

Data Flows and Digital Grammatization

On Twitter, social commentators and individuals invoke historical references to discuss the behavior and values of the leaders and supporters of both the Democrat and Republican Parties. This was even more pronounced during the Capital riot. To capture such conversations, we utilized an open-source Twitter tracking platform,[1] which allowed us to harvest 1% of all keywords, hashtags, individual users, and any metadata associated with a tweet. These form part of our digital archive of tabular data from before, during, and after the 2020 US presidential election and the January 6 Capitol Hill attack. We settled on the hashtags #GoPComplicitTraitors (GOP, Grand Old Party [Republicans] and #StopTheSteal due to their high profile and the likelihood for differences of political allegiance among those utilizing them. #GoPComplicitTraitors was employed chiefly by Democrats to shame the Republicans for standing with Trump, while #StopTheSteal was used by Republicans who believed Trump won the 2020 election.

Due to the million plus tweets gathered in these data sets, our analysis required selective sampling to make the data set manageable. Accordingly, we focused on four core analogies that circulated in response to the 2020 US presidential election: (1) Trump/Republicans as a fascist(s); (2) Biden/Democrats as socialist(s) and/or communist(s); (3) comparisons to the Holocaust and Kristallnacht; and (4) comparisons to the history of Nazism or Communism, generally including references to both concentration camps and gulags. To parse through the tweets we narrowed our findings further still by using basic keyword searches in Excel with the terms Stalin, communist, Antifa, fascist, Hitler, and Nazi. While there are other terms one might use, these generated a manageable subset of 60,000 tweets across two data sets.

Data visualizations were generated in Tableau from the archived Twitter data. They illustrate the dynamic conversations in the sampled Twitterstream, including when analogies rose and fell in prominence. We then analyzed the highest frequency peaks per data set to narrow the focus and conduct a critical discourse analysis on the most frequent retweets. This time series analysis showed how keywords coalesced into a form of digital grammatization, giving traces of thought and action visual representation (Auroux, 1994).

Long before the Capitol insurrection, our data sets showed evidence of historical analogy. The top two peaks in the #GoPComplicitTraitors data set made reference to Hitler on December 14, 2020, with twenty-five utterances, and January 7, 2021, with fifty-five. While the January 7 peak is understandable given the unfolding of the insurrection the previous day, December 14 is significant in that it marked a trifecta of outcomes with the Electoral College finally certifying Trump's defeat and the resignation of Attorney General William Barr, with COVID deaths reaching a grim 300,000 persons (Casey, 2020). These data helps make plain what America and the world was seeing in the weeks between the US election and the Capitol riot. Analogies to fascism already served as a vernacular to signal the challenge to democracy. A discourse analysis of historical analogies captured by these hashtags not only speaks to the political and individual leanings of the tweeters and retweeters but also shows how power is being both challenged and sought after by the two political parties in the United States, with memory at the fulcrum.

The Mediated Crowd

When visualized with Tableau, hashtags provide a lens into the shape and face of the mediated crowd in the networked public (boyd, 2010; Burgess & Baym, 2020; Bruns, & Burgess, 2011). Far from the homogeneous mass theorized by le Bon in the nineteenth century, with a common set of emotions, the technical affordances of Twitter reinforce a level of individuated social reflexivity amid the shared symbols and affective climate of the Trump era (le Bon, 1895; Papacharissi 2016). Twitter provides a degree of creativity, with storytelling, camp, and myth making central to how users interact. Mindful of the work of play and subterfuge in self-representation online, we are nevertheless able to glean a surprising number of interpersonal markers that help differentiate individual voices from the cacophony of the crowd.

When we examine highly active accounts—those accounts that contribute the most tweets and show high levels of engagement with the hashtag—we find that the hashtag is being fueled primarily by everyday Twitter users, many of whom do not have a high follower count but constitute the networked public forming around these hashtags. These users have legitimate profiles and are people seeking to amplify conversations regarding the Republican response to Trump's defeat but are not necessarily the most popular Twitter accounts. However, the top ten most visible accounts—those that are being tweeted *at*—are almost entirely Republican politicians. Visualization illustrates that the users utilizing this hashtag are actively attempting to call out Republican leadership for their response. Twitter allows us to see what for them was most worthy of engaging.

To explore how the conversation within the data set #GoPComplicitTraitors looks, we analyzed the top ten retweets from across the entirety of our data set, ranging from November 8, 2020, to January 14, 2021 (Figure 11.1).

The broad sentiment extends from tweeting at politicians such as Mitch McConnell, Matt Gaetz, and Marsha Blackburn to mock their defeat in the 2020 election, to retweets labeling Trump and his party as criminals paid off by Russia and Saudi Arabia. The broad conversation identified in these retweets can provide a sense of what the general tone of the conversation is when relying on #GoPComplicitTraitors. A closer examination reveals the underlying sentiment captured alongside the primary hashtag with terms like "betrayed," "corruption," "seditious," "Moscow," and "hypocrisy" all used to describe the GOP. The affective language in the hashtags themselves suggests that #GoPComplicitTraitors is an echo chamber of comments designed to promote intense affective reactions for politically aligned Twitter users (Bail, 2021). Even prior to close examination of the tweet texts, we see that most of the individuals using this hashtag are ideologically opposed to Donald Trump and the Republican Party.

#GopComplicitTraitors – Top 10 Retweets

1. #GOPComplicitTraitors
2. The @gop will forever smell like Trump trash #GOPComplicitTraitors
3. @mattgaetz Hey Matt it's over! 270 Joe hit it! 214 Frumps been there all week! #ByeDon #GOPComplicitTraitors
4. @senatemajldr And... THAT is how you LOST #MoscowMitch #FairAndSquare #VotersDecided #GOPComplicitTraitors #GOPCorruptionOverCountry Now for the #Senate #GEORGIA
5. @VoteMarsha You're up in the next election Marsha. Start packing sweetheart. #GOPComplicitTraitors #GOPHypocrisy
6. #GOPComplicitTraitors
7. I want an advent calendar with all the little Trump criminals behind each door.#TrumpTantrum #TrumpIsALoser #Election2020 #2020Election #ElectionResults #GOPComplicitTraitors
8. RT #JailThemALL Never forget #GOPBetrayedAmerica Remember their names and #VoteThemAllOut #Resistance ... our job is not finished! We still need to #DrainTrumpsSwamp!Undo his damage!#GOPComplicitTraitors!
9. RT Clearly being spokesmen for Russian Army attacking and undermining us democracy pays well.Texas oilmen sucking wind must be so proud - @gop's all in on Russia; 1st Trump let Putin & Saudi dump all that oil, now this.#GOPComplicitTraitors
10. Guess They Don't Know Every #Tweet Is Forever!#MORONS #GOPComplicitTraitors #gopIdiots

Figure 11.1 #GoPComplicitTraitors: top ten retweets.

#StopTheSteal

We applied the same analysis to #StopTheSteal and found, here also that the most active accounts are all Republican politicians and/or Trump supporters. These accounts have hundreds of thousands of followers and have well-established online political profiles that campaign and support Trump and Republican politicians. The top ten retweets across the #StopTheSteal data set, ranging from November 6, 2020, to January 14, 2021, discuss several areas of concern, including "absentee ballots," "ballot counting," "censorship," and the Democrat Party "cheating" (Figure 11.2). We also see mainstream media outlets CNN and Fox News criticized for reporting "fake news" regarding their reports on election fraud. The overview of these top ten retweets provides a sense of the general affect one can expect when interacting with the #StopTheSteal data set.

The analysis of secondary hashtags extends the analysis beyond mere slogans to an actual *cris de coeur* ("cry of the heart") that presages the Capitol insurrection. For instance, "MarchForTrump," "MillionMagaMarch," "Jan 6," "SaveTheRepublic," and "ReReadQ" are all activist banners and calls to action. In fact, the secondary hashtag "Jan 6" is first used on December 28, 2020,

#StopTheSteal – Top 10 Retweets

1. RT @LizRNC: "Democrats hide the evidence and then turn to you and say you have no evidence."Magically at almost exactly the same moment on election night that a series of key states quit counting, almost as though they were coordinating what they were doing." #StopTheSteal
2. RT @MattBatzel: Throw these illegal absentee ballots out and Trump could win Wisconsin #stopthesteal #wiright #maga
3. RT @LadyRedWave: SHARE SHARE SHARE ThisVideo As USUAL The TRUTH is being Censored! But They can NOT Censor every last 1 of us! #BackDateGate #StopTheSteal#StopTheCheating
4. I'M WITH @realDonaldTrump AND THE RULE OF LAW - I DESPISE CHEATERS AND LIARS AND THOSE WHO PUT POWER AHEAD OF THEIR BROTHER'S LIBERTY!#StopTheCheating#STOPTHESTEAL#GodBlessAmerica
5. I'M WITH @realDonaldTrump AND THE RULE OF LAW - I DESPISE CHEATERS AND LIARS AND THOSE WHO PUT POWER AHEAD OF THEIR BROTHER'S LIBERTY!#StopTheCheating #STOPTHESTEAL#GodBlessAmerica
6. #TwitterCensorship at work right here, right now. #StopTheSteal
7. @realDonaldTrump @BreitbartNews #StopTheSteal#Election2020#Trump2020#MAGA #MIGA#Restart_opposition #RestartLeader
8. Trump won, we fight the cheat. #StopTheSteal
9. @CNNPolitics They're lesbians.#StopTheSteal
10. @foxnewspolitics When did you loose your balls? Seems you have gone the way of "Fake News". #stopthesteal

Figure 11.2 #StopTheSteal: top ten retweets.

in preparation for the election protest that would unfold on January 6, 2021. These hashtags illustrate that Trump followers on Twitter are inspired by, and supportive of, Trump's attack on objective reality itself by pushing the idea the election was stolen from him (McIntyre, 2018). This is what McIntyre (2018) describes as the "post-truth" politics of the Trump presidency itself. Schertzer and Woods (2021) argue that part of Trump's ethnonationalist appeal is the way in which he makes the white majority that elected him feel they are perpetual victims, cheated out of the re-election of "their" president. Like the #GoPComplicitTraitors hashtag, we see an excessive affective appeal through the rhetoric of "saving," "stopping the steal," and other terminology designed to not only propel voters in the direction of feeling cheated, but also encourage an emotional reaction to continue their efforts offline (Bucy et al, 2020; Hoyng, 2020; Keener, 2019). The secondary hashtags show the underlying currents of an actualized post-truth media template that mobilizes an offline campaign aimed at keeping Trump as president.

What this broad overview of the data shows is a highly politicized and divided electorate engaging with itself on Twitter. While #GoPComplicitTraitors is centered on condemning the Republican Party, it turns to the affective appeals that are so prevalent in populist rhetoric (Keener, 2019; Schertzer & Woods, 2021). Deliberate attempts to evoke a visceral reaction from potential supporters can be seen by the evocation of analogy in our data set with terms such as "Moscow Mitch," "seditionists," and "traitors" mixing colonial American tropes with Cold War rhetorical flare. Whereas the pro-Democrat hashtag #GoPComplicitTraitors targeted elected officials in what is likely an attempt to "name and shame," we see the pro-Republican hashtag #StopTheSteal used to shore up support and momentum among its base leading up to the January 6 Capitol attack. This hashtag and the circulating discourses are also seen to motivate Trump's base through ethnonationalist appeals to their prevailing sense of victimhood (Schertzer & Woods, 2021). The reaction to Trump's defeat is a crescendo to the totality of his lies about mainstream media, his oft-repeated fallacies about the mainstream media, and the Democratic party itself engaged in deceptive practices (Schertzer & Woods, 2021). The foregoing analysis shows that both hashtags reveal the way these media templates begin to hold in advance of the Capital riot.

The Different Scenographies of the Capitol Attack

While the sheer volume of tweets in the Twitter data set makes it impossible to fully mine the ebbs and flows of analogies within a single chapter, we are able to discern specific instances where analogies to Hitler and Stalin peak before and after the January 6, 2021, Capitol Hill attack, showcasing the negotiation between liberal and illiberal memory formation around partisan interpretations of contemporary events (Rosenfeld, 2023). When mapped across time, they also illustrate changing sentiments within the mediascape itself. To demonstrate this change in register and tone, we conducted a keyword search and examined the most retweeted tweets prior to and following the Capitol Hill attack. While we captured thousands of tweets, this microanalysis of key terms allows us to see how history is not only being drawn on as a barometer of the events of the day, but also weaponized as a template to stoke fear through social media.

As we saw in Figure 11.1 with #GoPComplicitTraitors, well before the Capital attack the concern among users was that Trump's actions were in some way similar to Hitler's regime. Indeed, the most popular retweet in the December 14, 2020, time series was:

> Be on the lookout for #Gleiwitz incidents. Remember Hitler had his own men dress as Polish soldiers to create the appearance of a Polish aggression against Germany in order to justify the invasion of Poland. #FalseFlag #ProudBoysAreTerrorists #GoPComplicitTraitors. (Author name withheld, December 14, 2020)

This an analogy to not only the Nazi past, but also an attempt to signal through the use of popular memory the deceptive tactics used to justify militarism to prepare Americans for the possibility that Trump and his supporters may attempt something similar. The fear seems to be that groups that support Trump, like the Proud Boys, may disguise themselves as Democrat supporters to justify a police and National Guard crackdown on political opponents. At the same moment that Trump and the Republican Party were contesting the results of the 2020 US presidential election, the fear of America's descent into dictatorship was blatant enough to circulate widely on Twitter (Bucy et al., 2020; Hoyng, 2020; Keener, 2019).

By January 7, 2021, this generalizable fear around Trump and the far-right groups that supported him crystalized into a commentary on the entire American population and its susceptibility to fascist takeover. The most popular retweet witnessed comparisons to Hitler that vilified not only Trump supporters but also American democracy in general:

> Trump's lies and the American radical Right's extremism are tearing our country apart. We now know for certain how millions of Americans would have reacted under Hitler. #GoPComplicitTraitors MAGA= #TrumpsTraitors. (Author name withheld, January 7, 2021)

What this tweet and those that embraced its message were trying to convey is a sense of urgency and condemnation that the Republican base was increasingly synonymous with Nazi supporters. A week later, the comparisons continued:

> Over a week later, still just as sickening and disheartening to see how many Americans Trump misled through hype, fear and religious tactics. He has masterfully copied Hitler's misinformation campaign tactics. And still #GOP is defending him. #GoPComplicitTraitors. (January 14, 2021)

Tellingly, there are several neologisms that reflect that this analogy is rooted in the memory and not the actual history of National Socialism. Hitler used propaganda, not misinformation, and media manipulation was a core feature of all early journalism, Heidi Tworek has argued (Tworek, 2019). And yet, this binary is also problematic in other ways because the rhizomatic nature of connective memory of the Capitol riot has also, in its own way, become an important if amorphous site of national reckoning; it is a place where we witness the quickening or acceleration of the past for use in the present (Rothberg, 2009).

How exactly did proponents of the hashtag #StopTheSteal utilize the Hitler analogy within their tweets? As with #GoPComplicitTraitors, we picked our examples from two dates: December 15, 2020, and January 7, 2021. The most popular tweet during the December 15, 2020, peak appears as a reaction against how Democrat supporters mobilized the day before to call for unity following Biden's 2020 victory. The most retweeted comment reflects this sentiment:

> #KamalaHitler did you resign your senate seat yet? @JoeBiden make sure you keep an eye on that one she has it out for you! @RealDonaldTrump is our true president!! #StopTheSteal. (Name withheld, December 14, 2020)

Although this quote does not draw parallels to the history of National Socialism, vice President–Elect Kamala Harris is herself referred to as Hitler. This tweet is not as invested in establishing a link to Nazi Germany as much as it is designed to defame Harris through comparisons to Hitler. Following along after the Capitol riot, we see an even starker contrast in the usage of the term *Hitler* within this hashtag's data set. The most popular retweet on January 7, 2021, using the term *Hitler* was a clarion call for supporters to view the Democrats as the true inheritors of National Socialist demagoguery:

> #StopTheSteal #StopTheCoup we will not be destroyed from within like Hitler took Germany: thug violence to terrorize an old man, Hindenburg, into making him Chancellor. #Antifa #BLM constructs of the DEMOCRAT SOCIALISTS to end our #USA. (Name withheld, January 7, 2021)

Tellingly, the link in the tweet references an article that suggests Antifa was behind the Capitol Hill attacks disguised as Trump supporters to justify a crackdown against Trump and his proponents (Scarborough, 2021). The inference is that Black Lives Matter and Antifa are organizations endorsed and possibly established by the Democratic Party to intimidate and harass conservative Republican voters to bring down democracy.

Tweet "hijacking" of this sort allows opponents to adopt and repurpose the hashtags of political and ideological rivals to redirect the conversation in support of their ends. One such Tweet reads:

> Many have routinely referred to the #TeaParty as "The Beer Hall Putsch" because it's a movement of delusional people led by lunatics, grifters, and thugs. Here is Wikipedia's entry on Hitler's failed coup. #CapitolRiot #StopTheSteal #FightforTrump #trump. (January 11, 2021)

Here, #StopTheSteal tweets compared the failed Trump and Republican coup to the storied Beer Hall Putsch that brought a halt to early Nazi aspirations of power. In this bizarre amalgam of fake history and fact is a core rhetorical strategy within illiberal memory, which cultivates a sense of shared victimhood (Rosenfeld, 2023). Interestingly, Nazi Germany is drawn on across both data sets to condemn ideological opponents on either side of the political spectrum as surreptitiously working through political disguises and front organizations to bring about harm to their opposition. Yet, the differences are temporal as much as they also revolve around competing constructions of the historic past. The Democratic supporters argued *prior* to the Capitol attack that Democratic and progressive supporters need to be on the lookout for political violence that can be blamed on groups tangentially connected to the Democratic Party, such as Black Lives Matter, whereas we see the same sentiment expressed by Trump supporters *during* and after the Capitol attack as a legitimizing argument to view Antifa and BLM as the true destabilizers of American democracy. In this first successful use of hashtag hijacking in the data set, Republican opponents deliberately inserted their conversations into the Democratic Twittersphere by appropriating their use of history and hashtags.

Revanchism

Compulsive connectivity means our digital textual archives are by their very nature restless, ephemeral, and fleeting (Hoskins, 2018). It bears asking if the utterances captured in networked publics remain persistent after the fact, that is, if they carry heft and meaning as when first recorded. What is amplified, what sticks, and what remains elusive? Further still, what might visualization software allow us to see? We tend to assume that social media amplifies the guttural and banal, and perhaps we pay most attention to the signals and not the noise (Landshear & Knobel 2007). But one of those lost bits of ephemera is the fact that analogies to National Socialism were not the only ones in evidence in the data sets. Indeed, both hashtags saw references to Stalin in ways unexpected in both the pro-Democrat and pro-Republic stream, although only #StopTheSteal displayed a significant peak after the Capitol riot. "Stalin" was used by tweeters in November 2020 under the hashtag #GoPComplicitTraitors. Unlike the Hitler analogy, which spiked after the Capitol attack, Stalin does not serve the same purpose for those wishing to condemn the Republican Party and Trump. The most popular tweet prior to the January attack articulates:

> Trump's dangerous disorder is clear. The dangerous nature of GOP should now be spotlighted. Read the blueprint that Stalin used for dismantling democracy in Eastern Europe and spot the similarities. #GoPComplicitTraitors. (Name withheld, November, 10, 2020)

Like the historical narratives drawn on to disparage Trump and the Republican base by referencing Hitler, we see the use of Stalin drawn on as a warning. The fear is that as Stalin destroyed opposition and labeled opponents enemies of the state, so will Trump and his party follow a similar trajectory. Following the Capitol attack, the most popular retweet on January 7, 2021, characterizes Stalin in the following manner:

> Listening to #CapitolBuilding coverage, #GOPHypocrisy refusing to condemn Trump and his coup attempt. #Republicans saying "Millions of Americans believe the election was stolen" as if the issue were legit? MILLIONS OF RUSSIANS BELIEVED STALIN, TOO. #GoPComplicitTraitors #Amerikkka. (Name withheld, January 7, 2021)

As with the analogies to Hitler, the historical memory of Stalin serves the purpose of condemning not only Trump and the Republican Party, but also their base of supporters. Here, the analogy suggests that the gruesome dictatorship of Stalin and his political sycophants was not possible without the laypeople that supported their worldview. This condemnation of supporters is to suggest that the most horrific parties and leaders throughout time have found support from common people as well. This, in effect, is to brand those that do not condemn Trump as equally complicit with his crimes (Bucy et al., 2020; Hoyng, 2020; Keener, 2019). In a sense, it sees the everyday appropriation of the populist imaginary wielded back against itself in recognizing not only the elites but also the common man as morally suspect and compromised (Müller, 2016).

Following the same process, we examined the #StopTheSteal data set with this question in mind. There, the term *Stalin* is used much more frequently. The largest peak prior to the Capitol attack was on December 1, 2020, with the most popular retweet arguing:

> "It's not who votes, it's who counts the votes!" Joseph Stalin #StopTheSteal. (Name withheld, December 1, 2020)

Although it has been disproven that Stalin ever uttered these words, the memory of communism drawn on here is meant to form a direct parallel between Stalin and Biden and those that enabled each leader's political ascent. In the aftermath of the Capitol attack, the term *Stalin* peaks again on January 7, 2021, with a dramatic change in tone:

> #StopTheSteal, listen to general Flynn put the army and homeland security on the streets and jail the communist trying to steal the presidency starting with

> Joe "Stalin" Biden and his communist Politburo. . . . America is the land of the free not the land of the communists. (Name withheld, January 7, 2021)

Here, not only is Biden and his party likened to Stalin's Communist Party, but also, in a classic us-them maneuver common in illiberal memory formations, those that support Biden are labeled as complicit in trying to overthrow the Trump presidency (Rosenfeld, 2023). The tweet actively calls for these enemies of the state to be dealt with by the military and security agencies at Trump's disposal. In both instances we see a strong belief that Biden and his party are as corrupt as Stalin and the Bolsheviks. However, the tone and active calls for military engagement to halt Biden's ascension change drastically in the days after the attack, as the riot fails and all eyes turn on the insurrectionists.

Conclusion

There are two distinct strategies revealed in the various scenographies mapped out in the Twitter data sets. One is that the Republican base seems to be much more likely to argue that they have been wrongfully treated by the rest of the country (McIntyre, 2018). Such claims are common, as Schertzer and Woods (2021) argue, given the defensive ethnonationalist populism that propelled Trump to power in the first place. We see that there is a strong sense of victimhood and a need to portray the polls, vote counters, and political opponents as conspirators in a concerted effort "to normalize the nationalism" of the Trump agenda (Stern, 2018, p. 111). Another is that there is no need for evidence on which to stake such claims. The Republican base is willing to wield history as a cudgel as long as it allows them to maintain their sense of victimhood and to increasingly dehumanize their opponents (Rosenfeld, 2023). Democratic supporters are not averse to using similar tactics of comparison. As Bucy et al. (2020), Hoyng (2020), and Keener (2019) have discussed, much of the affective language used through populist communication strategies across social media encourages communication patterns favoring intense appeals to emotion that serve as a galvanizing force within the networked public based on a sense of emotive retaliation. What we see here is the possibility that such continuous appeals to emotions permeate both halves of the American social political mediascape.

While the data we examined are a subset of the total tweets we captured, there are significant findings that reveal not only how affect is wielded on Twitter, but also how repeated deployment of historical analogies, coupled with the affective appeals of political communication in the digital realm, render the unfamiliar (the challenge to democracy) familiar (embedded in that democracy). The media templates forged through the last months of Trump's presidency illustrate that social media-based analogies have become more frequent, repetitive, and visceral, pushed along in the everyday and wielded as much by the crowd as its leaders. These two data sets reveal the length partisans are willing to go to demean their opponents, raising warning signs about historical claims making as part of the field of memory and misinformation.

What gets selected from history is not benign. It lends insight into how a society "sanction(s) itself, affirm(s) its forms of government, its institutions, and dominant morals" (Haselby, 2019). But if the facts of history "remain robust only when they are supported by a common culture, by institutions that can be trusted, by a more or less decent public life, by more or less reliable media" (Latour in Kofman, 2018), then the question becomes to what extent do "alternative facts"—fake truths, fake history—serve as an equally salient force of misinformation when they become standardized as media templates, powerful enough to serve as a touchstone of common identity? As Katharina Niemeyer and Emily Keightley argue in their Chapter 14 in this volume, sometimes the anchoring of memory amid the freneticism of the digital public sphere is achieved through the cultivation of nostalgia. Another way in is to think about claims to the past as fabricated and circulated within the particular sociotechnological affordances of social media to get at when and where they begin to stick. The goal, in other words, is not to debate the facts of history along the lines of answering the question "Is Trump a fascist?" Rather, it is to understand the logic, force, and functioning of historical analogy itself as a media template that stabilizes a particular kind of claims making within the freneticism of the digital field as a form of connective memory itself (Hoskins, 2011).

Note

1. Hawksey, M. Twitter Archiving Google Sheet (TAGS): https://tags.hawksey.info

References

Auroux, S. (1994). *La revolution technologique de la grammatisation: introduction à l'histoire des sciences du langage*. Mardaga.

Bail, C. (2021). *Breaking the social media prism: how to make our platforms less polarizing*. Princeton University Press. https://doi.org/10.1515/9780691216508

Ben-Ghiat, R. (2016, August 10). An American authoritarian. *The Atlantic*. https://www.theatlantic.com/politics/archive/2016/08/american-authoritarianism-under-donald-trump/495263/

Boler, M., & Davis, E. (2018). The affective politics of the "post-truth" era: Feeling rules and networked subjectivity. *Emotion, Space and Society*, *27*, 75–85. https://doi.org/10.1016/j.emospa.2018.03.002

Bolter, J. D. (2019, May 20). Social media are ruining political discourse. *The Atlantic*. https://www.theatlantic.com/technology/archive/2019/05/why-social-media-ruining-political-discourse/589108/

Bolter, J. D, & Grusin, R., (1999). *Remediation: Understanding new media*. MIT Press.

boyd, d. (2010). Social network sites as networked publics: Affordances, dynamics, and implications. Z. Papacharissi (Ed.), *In Networked self: Identity, community, and culture on social network sites* (pp. 39–58). Routledge.

Bucy, E. P., Foley, J. M., Lukito, J., Doroshenko, L., Shah, D. V., Pevehouse, J. C., & Wells, C. (2020). Performing populism: Trump's transgressive debate style and the dynamics of Twitter response. *NewMedia and Society*, *22*(4), 634–658. https://doi.org/10.1177/1461444819893984

Brown, S.D., & Hoskins, A. (2010). Terrorism in the new memory ecology: Mediating and remembering the 2005 London bombings. *Behavioral Sciences of Terrorism and Political Aggression*, *2*(2), 87–107.

Bruns, A., & Burgess, J. (2011). The use of Twitter hashtags in the formation of ad hoc publics. In A. Bruns & P. De Wilde (Eds.), *Proceedings of the 6th European Consortium for Political Research (ECPR) general conference 2011* (pp. 1–9). European Consortium for Political Research (ECPR).

Burgess, J., & Baym, N. K. (2020). *Twitter: A biography*. New York University Press.

Casey, J. (2020, December 15). December 14, 2020: The day the news cycle crashed. *Advocate*. https://www.advocate.com/commentary/2020/12/15/december-14-2020-day-news-cycle-crashed

CNN. (2019, June 18). Ocasio-Cortez compares migrant detention facilities to concentration camps. *CNN*. https://www.cnn.com/2019/06/18/politics/alexandria-ocasio-cortez-concentration-camps-migrants-detention/index.html

Erll, A. (2011). *Memory in culture*. Palgrave Macmillan.

Evans, J. (2020, October 25). Folk devils and fear: Qanon feeds into a culture of moral panic. Folk devils and fear: QAnon feeds into a culture of moral panic. La Société royale du Canada. https://rsc-src.ca/fr/voix-de-la-src/folk-devils-and-fear-qanon-feeds-into-culture-moral-panic

Freelon, D., & Wells, C. (2020). Disinformation as political communication. *Political Communication*, *37*(2), 145–156. https://doi.org/10.1080/10584609.2020.1723755

Garde-Hansen, J., & Gorton, K. (2013). *Emotion online: Theorizing affect on the Internet*. Palgrave Macmillan.

Gessen, M. (2017). The Reichstag fire next time. *Harper's Magazine*. https://harpers.org/archive/2017/07/the-reichstag-fire-next-time/

Gordon, P. E. (2020, June 25). Why historical analogy matters. *New York Review of Books*. https://nybooks.com/daily/2020/01/07/why-historical-analogy-matters/

Gray, J., Bounegru, L., & Venturini, T. (2020). "Fake news" as infrastructural uncanny. *New Media and Society*, *22*(2), 317–341. https://doi.org/10.1177/1461444819856912

Haselby, S. (2019, May 20). *Muslims of early America. Aeon*. https://aeon.co/essays/muslims-lived-in-america-before-protestantism-even-existed

Highfield, T. (2018). Emoji hashtags // hashtag emoji: Of platforms, visual affect, and discursive flexibility. *First Monday*, *23*(9). https://doi.org/10.5210/fm.v23i9.9398

Hoskins, A. (2009). The mediatisation of memory. In J. Garde-Hansen, A. Hoskins, & A. Reading (Eds.), *Save as . . . digital memories*. Palgrave Macmillan. https://doi.org/10.1057/9780230239418_2

Hoskins, A. (2011). Media, memory, metaphor: Remembering and the connective turn. *Parallax*, *17*(4), 19–31.

Hoskins, A. (2018). The restless past: An introduction to digital memory and media. In A. Hoskins (Ed.), Digital memory studies: Media pasts in transition (pp. 1–24). Routledge.

Hoyng, R. (2020). Platforms for populism? The affective issue crowd and its disconnections. *International Journal of Cultural Studies, 23*(6), 984–1001. https://doi.org/10.1177/1367877920931853

Keener, K. (2019). Alternative facts and fake news: Digital mediation and the affective spread of hate in the era of Trump. *Journal of Hate Studies, 14*(1), 137–151. https://doi.org/10.33972/jhs.128

Kitzinger, J. (2000). Media templates: Patterns of association and the)re)construction of meaning over time. *Media, Culture & Society, 22*(1), 61–84.

Knight Foundation. (2018). Disinformation, "fake news" and influence campaigns on Twitter. https://knightfoundation.org/reports/disinformation-fake-news-and-influence-campaigns-on-twitter

Kofman, A. (2018, October 25). Bruno Latour, the post-truth philosopher, mounts a defense of science. *New York Times.* https://www.nytimes.com/2018/10/25/magazine/bruno-latour-post-truth-philosopher-science.html

Lankshear, C., & Knobel, M. (2007). Sampling "the New" in New Literacies. In M. Knobel, & C. Lankshear (Eds.), *A new literacies sampler* (Vol. 29, pp. 1–24). Peter Lang.

Latour, B. (2008). *What is the style of matters of concern: Two lectures on empirical philosophy.* Van Gorcum.

Le Bon, G. (1895). *The crowd: A study of the popular mind.* Transaction.

Lewis, B., & Marwick, A. E. (2017). Media manipulation and disinformation online. Data and Society. https://datasociety.net/library/media-manipulation-and-disinfo-online/

Marres, N. (2017). Digital sociology: The reinvention of social research. Polity Press. https://www.wiley.com/en-ru/Digital+Sociology%3A+The+Reinvention+of+Social+Research-p-9780745684789

Marres, N., & Weltevrede, E. (2013). Scraping the social?: Issues in live social research. *Journal of Cultural Economy, 6*(3), 313–335. https://doi.org/10.1080/17530350.2013.772070

McIntyre, Lee C. (2018). *Post-truth.* MIT Press.

Müller, J.W. (2016) *What is populism?* University of Pennsylvania Press.

Papacharissi, Z. (2016). Affective publics and structures of storytelling: sentiment, events and mediality. Information, *Communication and Society, 19*(3), 307–324. https://doi.org/10.1080/1369118X.2015.1109697

Papacharissi, Z. (2017). Editor's report. *Journal of Broadcasting and Electronic Media, 61*(4), 723–724. https://doi.org/10.1080/08838151.2017.1379296

Papacharissi, Z., & Oliveira, M. de F. (2012). Affective news and networked publics: The rhythms of news storytelling on #Egypt. *Journal of Communication, 62*(2), 266–282.

Robinson, S. (2016). The vital network: An algorithmic milieu of communication and control. *Communication +1, 5*, 1–22. https://doi.org/10.7275/R5416V0R

Rosenfeld, G. D. (2023). The rise of illiberal memory. *Memory Studies, 16*(4), 819–836. https://doi.org/10.1177/1750698020988771

Rothberg, M. (2009). *Multidirectional memory remembering the holocaust in the age of decolonization.* Stanford University Press.

Scarborough, R. (2021, January 6). Facial recognition identifies extremists storming the Capitol. *Washington Times.* https://www.washingtontimes.com/news/2021/jan/6/xrvision-firm-claims-antifa-infiltrated-protesters/

Schertzer, R., & Woods, E. (2021). Nationalism: The ethno-nationalist populism of Donald Trump's Twitter communication. *Ethnic and Racial Studies, 44*(7), 1154–1173. https://doi.org/10.1080/01419870.2020.1713390

Smith, H. (2020, September 1). No, America is not succumbing to fascism. *Washington Post.* https://www.washingtonpost.com/outlook/2020/09/01/no-america-is-not-succumbing-fascism/

Snyder, T. (2017). *On tyranny: Twenty lessons from the twentieth century.* Tim Duggan Books.

Stern, A.M. (2019). *Proud boys and the white Ethnostate: How the alt-right is warping the American imagination.* Beacon Press.

Tworek, H. (2019). *News from Germany: The competition to control world communications, 1900–1945* (vol. 43). Harvard University Press.

van Dijck, J. (2013). *The culture of connectivity: A critical history of social media.* Oxford University Press.

Törnberg, P. (2018). Echo chambers and viral misinformation: Modeling fake news as complex contagion. *PLoS One, 13*(9), e0203958. https://doi.org/10.1371/journal.pone.0203958

Warwick, A., Kuo, R., Cameron, S. J., & Weigel, M. (2021, March 25). *Launching the critical disinformation syllabus.* Center for Information, Technology, and Public Life (CITAP). https://web.archive.org/web/20210402174749/https://citap.unc.edu/launching-the-critical-disinformation-syllabus/

Wu, S., Hofman, J. M., Mason, W. A., & Watts, D. J. (2011). Who says what to whom on Twitter. Proceedings of the 20th International Conference on World Wide Web (pp. 705–714). Association for Computing Machinery. https://doi. org/10.1145/1963405.1963504a

PART V

REMEMBERING THROUGH THE INDIVIDUAL AND THE NET

12

Exploring Online Social Interactions in the Remaking of Memory

*Suparna Rajaram**

The explosion of information on the Internet, with which our memory system must contend, is just a click away from our devices. The embedded links take us to even more information, and distracting advertisements dispersed throughout even the shortest of articles add to the cauldron of input we process daily. To understand memory making under these conditions, it is fruitful to explore certain properties of both the Internet and memory. Critically, neither the operations of memory nor the use of the Internet occurs in a social vacuum. As social creatures, we seek to form experiences with others and reminiscence about them together. In this digital age, the social context for memory making has transformed, with an explosion of social media platforms where millions of people post, connect, and share experiences, exerting its influence more than ever before and influencing not only memory in general but also the very construction of our sense of self (Stone & Wang, 2019; Wang, 2022). As Hoskins (2011) observed: "Memory is unmoored yet dominated by media" (p. 19). He coined this complex connection between memory and digital media "the connective turn."

In this chapter, I consider the influence of social connections on our memories in this new arena of the Internet and social media. To consider the remaking of memories within this new frontier, I take into account three facets of the Internet that are especially applicable for the influence they can have on memory making, and three key properties of memory, drawn from decades of experimental laboratory research, that operate in abundance in the digital space. Against this backdrop, I consider laboratory research on the social influences on memory that can be applied to the social media context. With ever-increasing social media platforms, people are exposed not only to their proximal others during information exchange but also to the distal others who exert their influence through a web of connections. I present illustrative research to show how these properties

* Author Note: The preparation of this chapter was supported by the Stony Brook research funds.

Suparna Rajaram, *Exploring Online Social Interactions in the Remaking of Memory* In: *The Remaking of Memory in the Age of the Internet and Social Media.* Edited by: Qi Wang and Andrew Hoskins, Oxford University Press.
 DOI: 10.1093/oso/9780197661260.003.0012

of the Internet and of human memory shape in tandem memory remaking in the digital era.

Three Facets of the Internet of Interest

There has been a surge of interest in the impact of the Internet on memory and cognition (e.g., K. A. Hamilton & Benjamin, 2019; Lewandowsky et al., 2017; Marsh & Rajaram, 2019; Rajaram & Marsh, 2019; Risko, 2019; Russell, 2019; Stone & Wang, 2019; Storm, 2019; Storm & Soares, in press; Wang, 2019; Willingham, 2019; Yamashiro & Roediger, 2019). In our target article, Elizabeth Marsh and I reflected on the phenomenon we called "the digital expansion of the mind" (Marsh & Rajaram, 2019, p. 1; also see Rajaram & Marsh, 2019). We organized several properties of the Internet into three facets that are particularly important for understanding the impact of Internet use on cognition. First is the *content* or the sheer explosion of information that is available on the Internet and social media, including a plethora of misinformation. The second facet is the *usage*—or the ease and speed of access. Rapid access to a vast array of information and misinformation that populate social media posts is a key ingredient for how usage can shape memories. Third is the *connectedness of online communities* where anyone can post anything—information, falsehoods, photos, videos—and depending on the platform just about anyone can access these postings.

Let's consider the first two properties first—the sheer explosion of content on the Internet and the ease and speed with which we can access this information. We have come to over-rely on the Internet as a source for information because so much is available so easily. A curious consequence of such over-reliance is a sort of cognitive laziness. For example, Storm et al. (2017) reported that after using the Internet to find answers to difficult questions, people began to use the Internet to answer easy questions also, whereas those who did not use the Internet before answered these questions from memory. In other words, easy and quick access to vast information promotes over-reliance on the Internet and can cultivate harmful cognitive habits. We also know from laboratory research that people are more likely to remember information from a "social" source than a "nonsocial" source (Reysen & Adair, 2008). As much of the online information that floods our cognitive space comes from posts and opinions on social media, the sociality of this information is likely to increase our memory more for this information than for information from more traditional sources such as news, textbooks, and articles (Bourne et al., 2020; Mickes et al., 2013; Peña et al., 2023).

Beyond dulling the habit of an internal search for information and promoting the habit of reviewing more informal and less researched sources, easy access to the incessant arrival of notifications, messages, likes/dislikes, and similar reactions promotes an even greater cognitive cost. In his book *The Organized Mind*, cognitive neuroscientist Daniel Levitin (2014) evaluates this cost in terms of the addictive pull of social media use. Drawing on cognitive and neuroscience research, Levitin unpacks the steep costs of multitasking on cognitive performance, as would manifest from constantly engaging with texts, emails, Instagram, and Twitter (now called X), which can destroy focus and attention and consequently the ability to engage in deep work (Newport, 2016). For example, constant task switching to browsing the Internet while performing a meaningful cognitive task not only impairs performance on the problem-solving tasks, but also increases stress (Levitin, 2014), and stress impairs memory performance (e.g., Vogel & Schwabe, 2016). In other words, habitually seeking information on the Internet and compulsively peeking at social sources of information such as texts, emails, tweets, and Instagram and Facebook posts amount to prime examples of cognitive lethargy. Coupled with multitasking, the compounding costs of these Internet-driven practices on learning, memory, and cognition can be substantial.

In other words, beyond the usual information overload and attention-demanding sources that impinge on us in our environment, these two properties of the Internet and social media—plethora of content and ease of access increasing usage—can have a strong impact on our memory and cognition. With the many ways in which social media meets our need for social connections, these properties further lead us to use digital tools and platforms in ways that can create unprecedented, negative consequences on our ability to solve problems, handle stress, and manage precious attentional resources. If attention suffers, can memory be far behind?[1]

The third property of Internet—the ability to connect with a vast number of people at once and at any time—is of particular interest in my research. Not only do news items typically allow us to post comments, read others' comments, and reply to these comments, and so on, but also the ever-increasing social media platforms such as Facebook, Instagram, Reddit, Twitter/X, and TikTok enable us to connect with an unprecedented number of people now than ever before. We can form more social connections online than in our traditional face-to-face contexts and post and share autobiographical information, opinions, and our works. Especially relevant to the propagation of content, Internet platforms people connect us not only with friends but also strangers—forming online social networks through which all this content transmits rapidly and widely (Maswood & Rajaram, 2019). This property of the Internet intersects in many interesting ways with how humans like to share memories and form social bonds

[1] In homage to Percy Bysshe Shelley (1792–1822; "If Winter comes, can Spring be far behind?" from *Ode to the West Wind*), albeit different temporal causation in valence from that in the poem.

(Berger & Milkman, 2012; Rime, 2009), making the remaking of memory a particularly rich topic for research.

Three Properties of Memory of Interest

If we are to understand the impact of the Internet and social media on remaking memories, we must also consider certain properties of human memory that make it particularly susceptible to the influence of the Internet. The three properties I consider here are (1) the efficiency of human memory and its reconstructive nature; (2) the fragility of human memory, including the role of attention and rehearsal on memory; and (3) the social influences on human memory.

Human Memory Is Efficient and Reconstructive

If there is a myth about memory that decades of fascinating research have now squarely put to rest, it is that memory is like a photograph or a video that we play to revisit the past. The efficiency of memory also makes it highly reconstructive. The roles of meaning, schemas, and goals are central to driving the efficient and reconstructive nature of memory. It is worth considering these related facets of memory in turn.

Memory Is Efficient. Decades of research show that when we focus on the meaning of what we process, we get better at recalling and recognizing that information later. Research on the classic levels-of-processing framework (Craik & Lockhart, 1972; Craik & Tulving, 1975) has repeatedly shown an advantage of processing meaning over processing surface-level features in improving recall and recognition memory. An advantage of focusing on meaning for memory extends even when we are not aware of accessing information from the past, as in the case of implicit memory tasks, if the task demands the use of conceptual or meaning-based processing of information (Blaxton, 1989; M. Hamilton & Rajaram, 2001; Roediger, 1990). In other words, meaning improves a wide range of memory functions.

Processing meaning improves memory for many reasons. Of interest here is that when we access meaning, memory becomes efficient. I present an example here to illustrate this point. Bransford and Franks (1971) reported a powerful demonstration of the abstraction of gist representation from reviewing a series of sentences. Participants heard sentences such as "The jelly was sweet," "The ants were in the kitchen," "The jelly was in the kitchen," "The jelly was on the table," and "The ants ate the sweet jelly on the table." Even though the sentences were not necessarily in a continuous order with respect to meaning, they lent themselves to creating a semantic structure. Participants not only recalled and recognized never-presented sentences that were consistent with the holistic semantic structure, but also expressed more confidence in their memory as the sentence complexity increased. In other words, people fill in and insert appropriate but never-presented details, drawing on the essence of the story and adjusting the details accordingly. This illustration of poor verbatim memory and good gist memory led Bransford and Franks to conclude that "[m]emory is primarily a function of . . . wholistic structures" (p. 213). Furthermore, participants also report memories for the never-presented but gist-consistent sentences to be vivid in nature, as measured using Remember/Know responses (Holmes et al., 1998; Rajaram, 1993; Tulving, 1985). These findings are particularly interesting when we consider the first two properties of the Internet and social media I discussed—vast content and the easy and near-instant access to this content. Given its efficiency and its propensity to extract gist, our cognitive system is designed to "take in" and rapidly extract all sort of information (and misinformation) that swirls around various official as well as social media sources on the Internet. An Internet user may read a post somewhere alerting people to a possible public demonstration and another story about a court ruling about to be announced, leading the user to "fill in" never seen, and potentially false, information, even leading to confident and vivid memory representations. For example, having read these disparate pieces of information, extracting the gist, and making inferences, this user may later post that they read "somewhere on the Internet" about traffic jams and gridlock in town in response to the court decision. Because the Internet is replete with incessant updates and we have constant access to them, this first property of memory, efficient extraction of gist, in concert with the third property of the Internet (connecting many at the same time) can accelerate, in this manner, the remaking of memories in the digital age.

Memory Is Reconstructive. The efficiency of memory illustrates a related and well-established facet of memory, namely, its reconstructive nature. We reconstruct our memories in many striking ways. For example, every time we retrieve an experience, we reconsolidate it, and this process of reconsolidation changes our memory representation yet again (Lee et al., 2017). A fascinating example about how selective retrieval changes memory comes from research on retelling memories (Marsh, 2007; Marsh & Tversky, 2004). When people retell a story, they do not simply recall this story. Their retelling is usually selective, leading also to rehearsal of only selective information. Retelling also involves distortion of information to tune it to the social context where it occurs because retelling changes in line with the goals behind it and for the audience for whom it is designed (Marsh, 2007; see Echterhoff et al., 2009, for audience tuning and memory). On social media, retelling is a big reason behind the posts and comments people make. We curate a particular life story and a particularly social identity, and we share, forward, and endorse others' stories in turn (see Wang, Chapter 2, this volume). In this way, classic memory research on the nature of memory retelling and the sociality of this memorial experience underpins the processing of remaking memories in the digital context.

Just like gist extraction, schemas lead to memory reconstruction. When people rely on beliefs and prior knowledge, that is, schemas that are developed over time for specific themes, topics, sequence of actions, and experiences (e.g., going to college, driving on streets, eating at restaurants, what a post office or a ball game is and what we do there), these schemas make it efficient to establish new memories. At the same time, schemas also drive us to incorporate related *false* information or generate related false information and thus alter our memories through a process of reconstruction. I consider the Deese-Roediger-McDermott or the DRM paradigm (Deese, 1959; Roediger III & McDermott, 1995) to illustrate this point. The DRM effect is a widely reported, powerful phenomenon of false remembering. In DRM experiments, participants read a list of related words such as *bed, rest, awake, tired, dream, wake, snooze, blanket,* and others and later recall these words or recognize the words when intermixed with some words they did not study earlier. Even though the word *sleep* is not presented on this list, participants show a high propensity to recall and recognize this never-presented critical lure as having been on the study list and even report vivid memory of having encountered it there (Roediger III & McDermott, 1995).

This powerful phenomenon of memory reconstruction shows how readily related information can trigger false memory, with implications for illusions of memory that the daily influx of information on the Internet can create for the user. For example, a surge of information on the Internet about the keto diet for weight loss may create enormous interest in what the diet is, how to follow it, and the pros and cons to consider. In processing voluminous information that includes personal opinions and anecdotes about this diet and the general dietary recommendations (akin to presented, related information), someone may make inferences from the general medical recommendations about the importance of protein and then post a memory reconstruction that medical experts opine the keto diet is good (or bad) for you (akin to a never-presented critical lure). Furthermore, such illusions of memory can take hold in the public mind through information transmission on social media platforms unless the illusions are scrutinized and verified, something not easily done.

Furthermore, repeated enough times, misinformation can also create *the illusory truth effect* for incorrect information. The illusory truth phenomenon refers to the finding that when people encounter information repeatedly, they give it higher truth ratings than new statements (Hasher et al., 1977). Strikingly, people report illusory truth for incorrect information that is repeatedly presented, neglecting their own accurate knowledge (Fazio et al., 2015), and specific interventions are needed to prevent such illusory truth from developing (Brashier et al., 2020). This collection of findings has striking implications for the digital age. The Internet and social media not only abound in information, but also are replete with related misinformation (see chapters in this volume by Evans and Rigato, Chapter 10; Kleider-Offutt and Stevens, Chapter 11; Murphy et al., Chapter 8; and Tay and Ecker, Chapter 9). The impact of the proliferation of related but erroneous information on the Internet would be considerable on memory reconstruction, especially when it is compatible with our schemas. Furthermore, its repetition circulating on social media can lead us to neglect our own accurate knowledge. These processes in turn can make schemas faulty, beliefs more polarized, and future information seeking to be guided by these alterations.

Human Memory Is Fragile

A key reason memory is so malleable is that memory is fragile. Theories and evidence explaining this reality abound. One way to protect memory and make it more robust is through rehearsal of information. Here, I consider the effects of multitasking and the impact of rehearsal, and I discuss the implications for how these properties may play out in the context of Internet use.

Distraction Impairs Memory. Extensive experimental research shows that when people perform a secondary task (e.g., counting a sequence of odd numbers presented in an auditory stream) while studying words for which their memory is tested later, they exhibit poorer recall and recognition of the studied words (e.g., Jacoby et al., 1989; Mulligan, 1997, 1998; Mulligan & Hartman, 1996). Performing two tasks at once, and multitasking, are all-too-common experiences in the digital age. When we attempt to learn information available on Internet sites (e.g., reading up on some features of the statistical tool R or reading a scientific paper online), we often must navigate a plethora of unrelated information that floods just about any Internet site. These sites are replete with advertisements and related links that take us down a rabbit hole even as we attempt to read the intended piece, creating some of the biggest cognitive costs of the use of the Internet and social media. In this context, Jiang et al.'s (2016) study shed important insights on how structural arrangements on microblogging sites (in their case, a simulation of the Chinese microblogging site Weibo) can create interference and reduce information comprehension. Furthermore, the author showed that when people repost information, this takes time away from them for deeper cognitive processing of the actual content and reduces their ability to comprehend the information. To borrow Hoskins's (2017) characterization of practices on social media platforms "sharing without sharing," the ever-pervasive practice of reposting or "sharing" can in fact undermine comprehension and memory rather than enhance it.

It is worth bearing in mind that some forms of memory survive the impairing effects of distraction. But this preservation can produce costs of its own when we consider how information on social media shapes memory. For example, older adults retain memories of information they were instructed to ignore more so than do young adults, a phenomenon attributed to a reduction in the ability to inhibit information and the broadening of attention in normal aging (Kim et al., 2007; Weeks & Hasher, 2018). Such broad attention can come with its own cost, where an overwhelming amount of information on the Internet could make it difficult for older adults to discriminate information that is of interest from everything else. Beyond this possibility, older adults' digital use may be fraught with additional memory, cognition, and social changes. An increasing deficit in remembering the source of the information as we age, along with changes such as an increase in trust and difficulty in detecting deception, has been attributed to why older adults may be more susceptible to fake news on the Internet (Brashier & Schacter, 2020).

Rehearsal Improves Memory. Experiments on recall and recognition memory have long shown that the more we rehearse information, the better we remember it (Rundus, 1971). This improvement occurs through the repeated study of information as well as through recalling it repeatedly. Furthermore, repeated recall organizes memories better and improves long-term retention of information relative to repeated studying (Congleton & Rajaram, 2012; Karpicke & Roediger, 2007; Roediger III & Karpicke, 2006; Zaromb & Roediger, 2010). These robust phenomena of memory improvement provide a counterpoint to the illusory truth effect I discussed in the previous section where repetition increases the truthiness of false information. How might rehearsal impact our memories in the age of social media? In a creative study, Wang et al. (2017) asked participants to complete a daily diary for a week about autobiographical experiences and asked them to report if they posted this information online. On a surprise memory test later, participants exhibited better autobiographical memories for events they posted online than for the ones they did not post. As the authors discussed, these findings offer intriguing implications for how rehearsal is particularly effective in the context of social media, where sharing memories online is a social experience (also see Barnier et al., 2004; Stone et al., 2013; Wang et al., 2015) and where the medium allows for meaning making in the construction of the autobiographical self (Wang, 2013, 2022). As the practice of externalizing autobiographical memory has exploded across social media platforms such as Facebook, Twitter/X, and

Instagram, it would be fascinating to ask how the basic processes of encoding, consolidation, and retrieval play out in the maintenance and remaking of autobiographical memories (Eliseev & Marsh, 2021).

Human Memory Is Social

People like to share memories, and memory sharing regulates emotions and facilitates social bonds (Berger & Milkman 2012; Rime, 2009). In line with these phenomena, people exhibit a propensity for remembering information that is social in nature (Reysen & Adair, 2008). Effects of sociality in memory can be seen in interesting ways for both the type of information that influences memory and the impact of recalling past experiences with others.

When people engage with a variety of information sources on the Internet and social media, their memory and their confidence in their false memories are shaped by the source of that information (Bourne et al., 2020; Fenn et al. 2014; Mickes et al., 2013). For example, people remember microblog information such as Facebook posts, typically a part of social exchanges and often about people and personal experiences, better than information from sources such as books (Mickes et al., 2013). Interestingly, the power of microblogs such as tweets over the more standard news headlines holds even when tweets and headlines convey *inconsistent* messages on the same topic; we found that people recall and recognize tweets better than headlines regardless of whether these sources provide inconsistent or consistent messaging (Peña et al., 2023). This microblog memory advantage is well explained by the informal language and the sociality of exchanges in microblogs that news headlines lack.

What we see then is that the Internet and social media create conditions where access to information is easy and information and misinformation abound (Marsh & Rajaram, 2019), where fake news can propagate for a variety of psychological reasons (e.g., Pennycook & Rand, 2018), where our attention to rapid notifications for microblogs (e.g., texts, emails, Instagram, and Twitter/X) makes the use of the Internet addictive (Levitin, 2014), and where the microblog style of composing information makes it so cognitively compelling that microblogs that conflict in messaging can override news headlines in memory even though people generally consider microblogs to be less credible (Mickes et al, 2013; Peña et al., 2023).

In light of these conditions where exposure to information and misinformation can be rampant and incessant, the social nature of online spaces, including the unprecedented rates at which we connect with friends and strangers when navigating the online spaces, is especially fascinating to consider for its impact on remaking memories. This process of forming social connections on the Internet includes the formation of groups, cliques, and echo chambers, at the same time giving access to thousands of followers to whom we can send our messages and from whom we can receive messages, all at the mere click of a button.

Social Sharing Shapes Memories

About 90 years ago, Bartlett (1932) published a book on the social transmission of memory. The thesis and findings reported in this book remain presciently relevant in today's age of social media, beyond the use of more traditional sources of information and face-to-face exchange of information that preceded the digital era. Bartlett's studies showed that when people recall narratives they read earlier and when they relay this information in a chain from one to another, the recalled information shows memory loss, insertions, alterations, and distortions, changes that also reflect their own cultural orientations. These findings reflect our reality that "remembering is often a social experience," as we share life's ups and downs and routinely chat about news and gossip with friends and family (Maswood & Rajaram, 2018, p. 687).

Laboratory research from the last quarter of a century, using experiments where people recall previously seen information together, has uncovered several cognitive processes that come into play when recalling and sharing past experiences in collaboration with others (e.g., Basden et al., 1997; Rajaram, 2022; Rajaram et al., 2022; Weldon & Bellinger, 1997). These cognitive processes engaged during collaboration include disrupting others' recall with our own output, correcting one another's memory errors, and augmenting mutual memories not only correctly but also often falsely—such that together these processes reshape the memories of each individual engaged in these conversational recalls (Rajaram & Pereira-Pasarin, 2010). While these processes can improve our memory (e.g., Blumen & Rajaram, 2008; Weldon & Bellinger, 1997), recalling the past with others also impairs memory (e.g., Barber et al., 2015; Cuc et al., 2007).

A particular important phenomenon to consider here is the social contagion effect (Meade & Roediger, 2002; Roediger et al., 2001), where people incorporate others' memory errors into their own memories. Social memory contagion can be sensitive to different types of social interactions (Maswood, et al., 2022; Thorley & Dewhurst, 2007). In one experimental study, we compared two different ways people can collaborate with others to recall the past, either by taking turns to recall one studied item at a time or by engaging in free-flowing exchange to contribute whenever studied items came to mind (Maswood et al., 2022). The turn-taking interaction style allows for fewer corrections, whereas the free-flowing style allows for higher interaction and more error correction. As such, free-flowing recall can decrease error contagion from social exchange compared to turn-taking recall.

This comparison bears parallels to the way many social media platforms are set up. Some platforms place restrictions on what one can post and the extent to which people can interact via their posts, for example, by not enabling the comment function on some sites or blogs. Without the option to post comments, users can lose the ability to correct potential errors in the posts, and these errors then go unnoticed by other users who are not aware of them. Other platforms such as Wikipedia may be at the other end of this spectrum, by requiring consensus and giving editing access to many, or there are platforms that give different extent of access for users to interact, communicate, and provide feedback (e.g., Twitter/X, Facebook, Reddit) (see Maswood & Rajaram, 2019).

In laboratory studies, turn taking particularly increases reports of false memory in group recall (Maswood et al., 2022; Thorley & Dewhurst, 2007), and both types of interactions promote greater false recall by group than no interaction, indicating powerful implications for how different types of communication allowed on the Internet sites can shape false memories of the users. In a follow-up recall in our study where participants from all three groups (turn taking, free flowing, no interaction) now recalled the studied information alone, the participants who had collaborated earlier, with either style of interaction, continued to exhibit greater false memory.

In this context, an even more striking finding we observed was the emergence of collective false memory (Maswood et al., 2022). Collective memory is a phenomenon that has captured the interests of social scientists across disciplines such as anthropology, history, and sociology for decades (Halbwachs, 1950/1980). Memory psychologists have become particularly interested in this phenomenon in recent years, where in the process of recalling the past together, people develop shared representations of the past, or collective memory (Hirst & Manier, 2008; Rajaram, 2022; Roediger & Wertsch, 2022; Wertsch & Roediger, 2008). Laboratory studies show that such joint remembering also creates shared structures of memory that have the potential to produce a greater impact on future remembering and learning (Choi et al., 2014; Congleton & Rajaram, 2014; Greeley et al., 2024; Rajaram, 2022; Rajaram et al., 2022). Like the formation of collective memory for true information, recalling with others, regardless of whether people use the turn-taking style or the free-flowing style for interaction, can also give rise to collective *false* memories (Maswood et al., 2022).

The implications for the emergence of collective memory through online interactions come from a recent study where we found that collective memories develop in not only face-to-face settings but also completely virtual, online settings (Greeley et al., 2022). In this experiment, participants joined from remote locations to form online collaborating groups and performed the memory tasks in a completely chat-based environment. We found that even in this modality, where collaboration occurred without any face-to-face interaction, those who collaborated during the initial recall, later exhibited collective memory compared to noncollaborating participants. Given the similarity between this chat-based environment and many social media platforms that mainly use text for social exchange, these findings provide intriguing insights into the formation of collective memory among online users who repeatedly interact with one another and are likely to become prone to recalling more of the same content and to shedding variety in their memories.

Further, groups can settle on different versions of collective memory depending on the group structure, for example, who their partners are, and how often they collaborated to recall past information (e.g., Choi et al., 2014, 2017; Geana et al., 2019). In a laboratory study, we found that when people engage in conversational recall, if they repeatedly recall with the same partners, they are more likely to collectively forget the same information, whereas if they engaged in recall the same number of times but with different partners each time, the group possesses more variety in reported information (Choi et al., 2014). These findings show that repeatedly interacting with the same partners prunes away memories not shared by others and has far-reaching implications for the way social network topology in social media forums can shape the collective memories and belief formation among the users. Together, these findings motivate research questions on the impact of online interactions among small groups as well as more complex social networks for the emergence of collective memory, echo chambers, broadcasting, online education, and work (Greeley et al., 2022; Rajaram et al., 2022).

Conclusion

I propose that to understand the remaking of memory in the digital era, we need to consider certain properties of both the Internet and human memory function, as well as social influences that shape our memories. These considerations are expected to provide insights into the novel and unique ways in which information consumption and sharing may shape memory in the age of the Internet and social media use.

References

Barber, S. J., Harris, C. B., & Rajaram, S. (2015). Why two heads apart are better than two heads together: Multiple mechanisms underlie the collaborative inhibition effect in memory.

Journal of Experimental Psychology: Learning, Memory, and Cognition, 41(2), 559–566. https://psycnet.apa.org/doi/10.1037/xlm0000037

Barnier, A. J., Hung, J., & Conway, M. A. (2004). Retrieval-induced forgetting of emotional and unemotional autobiographical memories. *Cognition & Emotion, 18*, 457–477. https://doi.org/10.1080/0269993034000392

Bartlett, F. C. (1932). *Remembering: A study in experimental and social psychology*. Cambridge University Press.

Basden, B. H., Basden, D. R., Bryner, S., & Thomas, R. L. (1997). A comparison of group and individual remembering: Does collaboration disrupt retrieval strategies? *Journal of Experimental Psychology: Learning, Memory, and Cognition, 23*(5), 1176–1189

Berger, J., & Milkman, K. (2012). What makes online content viral? *Journal of Marketing Research, 49*, 192–205.

Blaxton, T. A. (1989). Investigating dissociations among memory measures: Support for a transfer-appropriate processing framework. *Journal of Experimental Psychology: Learning, Memory, and Cognition, 15*(4), 657–668. https://doi.org/10.1037/0278-7393.15.4.657

Blumen, H., & Rajaram, S. (2008). Influence of re-exposure and retrieval disruption during group collaboration on later individual recall. *Memory, 16*(3), 231–244.

Bourne, K. A., Boland, S. C., Arnold, G. C., & Coane, J. H. (2020). Reading the news on Twitter: Source and item memory for social media in younger and older adults. *Cognitive Research: Principles and Implications, 5*(1), 1–13. https://doi.org/10.1186/s41235-020-0209-9

Bransford, J. D., & Franks, J. J. (1971). The abstraction of linguistic ideas. *Cognitive Psychology, 2*(4), 331–350. https://doi.org/10.1016/0010-0285(71)90019-3

Brashier, N. M., Eliseev, E. D., & Marsh, E. J. (2020). An initial accuracy focus prevents illusory truth. *Cognition, 194*, 104054. https://doi.org/10.1016/j.cognition.2019.104054

Brashier, N. M., & Schacter, D. L. (2020). Aging in an era of fake news. *Current Directions in Psychological Science, 29*(3), 316–323. https://doi.org/10.1177/0963721420915872

Choi, H. Y., Blumen, H. M., Congleton, A. R., & Rajaram, S. (2014). The role of group configuration in the social transmission of memory: Evidence from identical and reconfigured groups. *Journal of Cognitive Psychology, 26*(1), 65–80. https://doi.org/10.1080/20445911.2013.862536

Choi, H. Y., Kensinger, E. A., & Rajaram, S. (2017). Mnemonic transmission, social contagion, and emergence of collective memory: Influence of emotional valence, group structure, and information distribution. *Journal of Experimental Psychology: General, 146*(9), 1247–1265. https://psycnet.apa.org/doi/10.1037/xge0000327

Congleton, A. R., & Rajaram, S. (2012). The origin of the interaction between learning history and delay in the testing effect: The roles of processing and retrieval organization. *Memory & Cognition, 40*(4), 528–539.

Congleton, A. R., & Rajaram, S. (2014). Collaboration changes both the content and the structure of memory: Building the architecture of shared representations. *Journal of Experimental Psychology: General, 143*, 1570–1584. https://psycnet.apa.org/doi/10.1037/a0035974

Craik, F. I. M., & Lockhart, R. S. (1972). Levels of processing: A framework for memory research. *Journal of Verbal Learning and Verbal Behavior, 11*, 671–684.

Craik, F. I. M., & Tulving, E. (1975). Depth of processing and the retention of words in episodic memory. *Journal of Experimental Psychology: General, 104*(3), 268–294. https://doi.org/10.1037/0096-3445.104.3.268

Cuc, A., Koppel, J., & Hirst, W. (2007). Silence is not golden: A case for socially shared retrieval-induced forgetting. *Psychological Science, 18*(8), 727–733.

Deese, J. (1959). Influence of inter-item associative strength upon immediate free recall. *Psychological Reports, 5*, 305–312.

Echterhoff, G., Lang, S., Krämer, N., & Higgins, E. T. (2009). Audience-tuning effects on memory: The role of audience status in sharing reality. *Social Psychology, 40*(3), 150–163. https://doi.org/10.1027/1864-9335.40.3.150

Eliseev, E. D., & Marsh, E. J. (2021). Externalizing autobiographical memories in the digital age. *Trends in Cognitive Sciences, 25*, 1072–1081. https://doi.org/10.1016/j.tics.2021.08.005

Fazio, L. K., Brashier, N. M., Payne, B. K., & Marsh, E. J. (2015). Knowledge does not protect against illusory truth. *Journal of Experimental Psychology: General, 144*(5), 993–1002. https://doi.org/10.1037/xge0000098

Fenn, K. M., Griffin, N. R., Uitvlugt, M. G., & Ravizza, S. M. (2014). The effect of Twitter exposure on false memory formation. *Psychonomic Bulletin & Review, 21*(6), 1551–1556. https://doi.org/10.3758/s13423-014-0639-9

Geana, A., Duker, A., & Coman, A. (2019). An experimental study of the formation of collective memories in social networks. *Journal of Experimental Social Psychology, 84*, 103813. https://doi.org/10.1016/j.jesp.2019.05.001

Greeley, G. D., Chan, V., Choi, H.-Y., & Rajaram, S. (2024). Collaborative recall and the construction of collective memory organization: The impact of group structure. *Topics in Cognitive Science, 24*(2), 282–301.

Greeley, G. D., Peña, T., & Rajaram, S. (2022). Social remembering in the digital age: Implications for virtual study, work, and social engagement. *Memory, Mind, & Media, 1*, e3.

Halbwachs, M. (1980). *The collective memory* [La memoire collective]. (F. J. Ditter, Jr., & V. Y. Ditter, Trans.). Harper Row. (Original work published 1950)

Hamilton, K. A., & Benjamin, A. S. (2019). The human-machine extended organism: New roles and responsibilities of human cognition in a digital ecology. *Journal of Applied Research in Memory and Cognition, 8*(1), 40–45. https://doi.org/10.1016/j.jarmac.2019.01.001

Hamilton, M., & Rajaram, S. (2001). The concreteness effect in implicit and explicit memory tests. *Journal of Memory and Language, 44*(1), 96–117. https://doi.org/10.1006/jmla.2000.2749

Hasher, L., Goldstein, D., & Toppino, T. (1977). Frequency and the conference of referential validity. *Journal of Verbal Learning & Verbal Behavior, 16*, 107–112. http://dx.doi.org/10.1016/S0022-5371(77)80012-1

Hirst, W., & Manier, D., 2008. Towards a psychology of collective memory. *Memory, 16*(3), 183–200.

Holmes, J. B., Waters, H. S., & Rajaram, S. (1998). The phenomenology of false memories: Episodic content and confidence. *Journal of Experimental Psychology: Learning, Memory, and Cognition, 24*(4), 1026–1040. https://doi.org/10.1037/0278-7393.24.4.1026

Hoskins A (2011). Media, memory, metaphor: Remembering and the connective turn. *Parallax, 17*(4), 19–31. https://doi.org/10.1080/13534645.2011.605573

Hoskins, A. (2017) The restless past: An introduction to digital memory and media. In A. Hoskins (Ed.), *Digital Memory Studies* (pp. 1–24). Routledge.

Jacoby, L. L., Woloshyn, V., & Kelley, C. (1989). Becoming famous without being recognized: Unconscious influences of memory produced by divided attention. *Journal of Experimental Psychology: General, 118*, 115–125.

Jiang, T.-L., Hou, Y., & Wang, Q. (2016). Does micro-blogging make us "shallow"? Sharing information online interferes with information comprehension. *Computers in Human Behavior, 59*, 210–214.

Karpicke, J. D., & Roediger, H. L., III. (2007). Repeated retrieval during learning is the key to long-term retention. *Journal of Memory and Language, 57*, 151–162.

Kim, S., Hasher, L., & Zacks, R. T. (2007). Aging and a benefit of distractability. *Psychonomic Bulletin & Review, 14*, 301–305.

Lee, J. L. C., Nader, K., & Schiller, D. (2017). An update on memory reconsolidation updating. *Trends in Cognitive Sciences, 21*(7), 531–545. https://doi.org/10.1016/j.tics.2017.04.006

Lewandowsky, S., Ecker, U. K., & Cook, J. (2017). Beyond misinformation: Understanding and coping with the "post-truth" era. *Journal of Applied Research in Memory and Cognition*, *6*(4), 353–369. https://doi.org/10.1016/j.jarmac.2017.07.008

Levitin, D. J. (2014). *The organized mind: Thinking straight in the age of information overload*. Dutton Penguin.

Marsh, E. J. (2007). Retelling is not the same as recalling: Implications for memory. *Current Directions in Psychological Science*, *16*(1), 16–20.

Marsh, E. M., & Rajaram, S. (2019). The digital expansion of the mind: Implications of Internet usage for memory and cognition. *Journal of Applied Research in Memory and Cognition*, *8*(1), 1–14.

Marsh, E. J., & Tversky, B. (2004). Spinning the stories of our lives. *Applied Cognitive Psychology*, *18*, 491–503.

Maswood, R., Luhmann, C. C., & Rajaram, S. (2022). Persistence of false memories and emergence of collective false memory: Collaborative recall of DRM word lists. *Memory*, *30*, 465–479.

Maswood, R., & Rajaram, S. (2019). Social transmission of false memories in small groups and large networks. *Topics in Cognitive Science*, *11*(4), 1–23.

Meade, M. L., & Roediger, H. L. (2002). Explorations in the social contagion of memory. *Memory & Cognition*, *30*(7), 995–1009.

Mickes, L., Darby, R. S., Hwe, V., Bajic, D., Warker, J. A., Harris, C. R., & Christenfeld, N. J. S. (2013). Major memory for microblogs. *Memory and Cognition*, *41*(4), 481–489. https://doi.org/10.3758/s13421-012-0281-6

Mulligan, N. W. (1997). Attention and implicit memory tests: The effects of varying attentional load on conceptual priming. *Memory & Cognition*, *25*, 11–17.

Mulligan, N. W. (1998). The role of attention during encoding on implicit and explicit memory. *Journal of Experimental Psychology: Learning, Memory, & Cognition*, *24*, 27–47.

Mulligan, N. W., & Hartman, M. (1996). Divided attention and indirect memory tests. *Memory & Cognition*, *24*, 453–465.

Newport, C. (2016). *Deep work: Rules for focused success in a distracted world*. Grand Central Publishing.

Peña, T., Maswood, R., Chen, M., & Rajaram, S. (2023). Memory for Tweets versus headlines: Does message consistency matter? Applied Cognitive Psychology, *37*(4), 768–784.

Pennycook, G., & Rand, D. G. (2018). Lazy, not biased: Susceptibility to partisan fake news is better explained by lack of reasoning than by motivated reasoning. *Cognition*, *188*(C), 39–50.

Rajaram, S. (1993). Remembering and knowing: Two means of access to the personal past. *Memory & Cognition*, *21*(1), 89–102. https://doi.org/10.3758/BF03211168

Rajaram, S. (2022). Collective memory and the individual mind. *Trends in Cognitive Sciences*, *26*(12), 1056–1058.

Rajaram, S., & Marsh, E. M. (2019). Cognition in the Internet age: What are the important questions? *Journal of Applied Research in Memory and Cognition*, *8*(1), 46–49.

Rajaram, S., Peña, T., & Greeley, G. D. (2022). How collective memories emerge: A cognitive psychological perspective. In H. L. Roediger & J. Wertsch (Eds.), *National memories: constructing identity in populist times* (pp. 409–433). Oxford Academic Press.

Rajaram, S., & Pereira-Pasarin, L. P. (2010). Collaborative memory: Cognitive research and theory. *Perspectives on Psychological Science*, *5*(6), 649–663.

Reysen, M. B., & Adair, S. A. (2008). Social processing improves recall performance. *Psychonomic Bulletin & Review*, *15*(1), 197–201. https://doi.org/10.3758/PBR.15.1.197

Rime, B. (2009). Emotion elicits the social sharing of emotion: Theory and empirical review. *Emotion Review*, *1*, 60–85.

Risko, E. F. (2019). Examining the implications of Internet usage for memory and cognition: Prospects and promise. *Journal of Applied Research in Memory and Cognition, 8*(1), 36–39. https://doi.org/10.1016/j.jarmac.2018.12.006

Roediger, H. L. (1990). Implicit memory: Retention without remembering. *American Psychologist, 45*(9), 1043–1056. https://doi.org/10.1037/0003-066X.45.9.1043

Roediger, H. L., Meade, M. L., & Bergman, E. T. (2001). Social contagion of memory. *Psychonomic Bulletin & Review, 8*(2), 365–371.

Roediger, H. L., & Wertsch, J. V. (Eds.). (2022). *National memories: Constructing identity in populist times.* Oxford University Press.

Roediger, H. L., III, & Karpicke, J. D. (2006). Test-enhanced learning: Taking memory tests improves long-term retention. *Psychological Science, 17,* 249–255.

Roediger, H. L., III, & McDermott, K. B. (1995). Creating false memories: Remembering words not presented in lists. *Journal of Experimental Psychology: Learning, Memory, & Cognition, 21,* 803–814.

Rundus, D. (1971). Analysis of rehearsal processes in free recall. *Journal of Experimental Psychology, 89,* 63–77.

Russell, D. M. (2019). Commentary on: The digital expansion of the mind: Implications of Internet usage for memory and cognition. *Journal of Applied Research in Memory and Cognition, 8*(1), 33–35.

Stone, C. B., Barnier, A. J., Sutton, J., & Hirst, W. (2013). Forgetting our personal past: Socially shared retrieval-induced forgetting of autobiographical memories. *Journal of Experimental Psychology: General, 142*(4), 1084–1099. https://doi.org/10.1037/a0030739

Stone, C. B., & Wang, Q. (2019). From conversations to digital communication: The mnemonic consequences of consuming and sharing information via social media. *Topics in Cognitive Science 11,* 774–793. https://doi.org/10.1111/tops.12369

Storm, B. C. (2019). Thoughts on the digital expansion of the mind and the effects of using the Internet on memory and cognition. *Journal of Applied Research in Memory and Cognition, 8*(1), 29–32. https://doi.org/10.1016/j.jarmac.2018.12.003

Storm, B. C., & Soares, J. S. (in press). Memory in the digital age. In M. J. Kahana & A. D. Wagner (Eds.), *Handbook of human memory: Foundations and applications.* Oxford University Press.

Storm, B. C., Stone, S. M., & Benjamin, A. S. (2017). Using the Internet to access information inflates future use of the Internet to access other information. *Memory, 25,* 717–723.

Thorley, C., & Dewhurst, S. A. (2007). Collaborative false recall in the DRM procedure: Effects of group size and group pressure. *European Journal of Cognitive Psychology, 19*(6), 867–881.

Tulving, E. (1985). Memory and consciousness. *Canadian Psychology/Psychologie canadienne, 26*(1), 1–12. https://doi.org/10.1037/h0080017

Vogel, S., & Schwabe, L. (2016). Learning and memory under stress: implications for the classroom. *NPJ Science of Learning, 1,* 16011. https://doi.org/10.1038/npjscilearn.2016.11

Wang, Q. (2013). *The autobiographical self in time and culture.* Oxford University Press.

Wang, Q. (2019). The individual mind in the active construction of its digital niche. *Journal of Applied Research in Memory and Cognition, 8*(1), 25–28. https://doi.org/10.1016/j.jarmac.2018.12.005

Wang, Q. (2022). The triangular self in the social media era. *Memory, Mind & Media, 1,* e4. https://doi.org/10.1017/mem.2021.6

Wang, Q., Bui, V., & Song, Q. (2015). Narrative organization at encoding facilitated children's long-term episodic memory. *Memory, 23,* 602–611. https://doi.org/10.1080/09658211.2014.914229

Wang, Q., Lee, D., & Hou, Y. (2017). Externalizing the autobiographical self: Sharing personal memories online facilitated memory retention. *Memory, 25*(6), 772–776. https://doi.org/10.1080/09658211.2016.1221115

Weeks, J. C., & Hasher, L. (2018). Older adults encode more, not less: Evidence for age-related attentional broadening. *Aging, Neuropsychology & Cognition, 25*(4), 576–587. https://doi.org/10.1080/13825585.2017.1353678

Weldon, M. S., & Bellinger, K. D. (1997). Collective memory: Collaborative and individual processes in remembering. *Journal of Experimental Psychology: Learning, Memory, and Cognition, 23*(5), 1160–1175.

Wertsch, J. V., & Roediger, H. L., III. (2008). Collective memory: Conceptual foundations and theoretical approaches. *Memory, 16*(3), 318–326.

Willingham, D. T. (2019). The digital expansion of the mind gone wrong in education. *Journal of Applied Research in Memory and Cognition*, 8(1), 20–24. https://doi.org/10.1016/j.jarmac.2018.12.001

Yamashiro, J. K., & Roediger, H. L., III. (2019). Expanding cognition: A brief consideration of technological advances over the past 4000 years. *Journal of Applied Research in Memory and Cognition, 8*(1), 15–19. https://doi.org/10.1016/j.jarmac.2018.12.004

Zaromb, F. M., & Roediger, H. L., III. (2010). The testing effect in free recall is associated with enhanced organizational processes. *Memory & Cognition, 38*, 995–1008.

13
When Memories Become Data

Rik Smit

In a space resembling a nineteenth-century library or archive, an old man hunches over a filing cabinet filled with hundreds of drawers. There are no lights, save for the gray glow entering the space through magnificent domed windows. The light falls on the man's hands as he pulls open one of the drawers and takes out a photograph of a boy waving at the camera. A piano plays a slow, melancholic tune in the background. The old man sighs as he regards the picture in his hands, a sad look visible through his horn-rimmed glasses. As if by magic, the boy in the picture starts to wave as the old man puts the moving picture in a folder, on top of other photos. The scene shifts, and we see the old man standing on top of a small elevator in a vast room filled with numerous shelves, which are stacked with rows on rows of film reel cases. The man pulls out a case titled "Papa Hola 3/2/16" and brings it to another room. Here, we finally understand what the purpose of the old man's archival expedition has been. He starts to carefully edit the footage he has assembled into a movie. When he is done, he loads his film onto a projector, which starts to play. The first image we see is not what we might have expected, for it shows an image of a family of three, the word "Together" superimposed on it and a small loading icon with the words "Creating Movie . . . " next to it. When the loading is done, a female voice chimes in with the melancholic piano, which has been playing in the background all this time. The film the old man has so carefully edited is a collage of pictures and videos of a baby together with its family during its first year. The combination of visuals and audio makes the old man's film an emotionally charged trip down memory lane. Its sole purpose seems to be to invoke nostalgia and a longing, to paraphrase Proust, for a time we never get back.

The story of the old man and his film is actually a promotional video (Spiccia, 2018) for the technology company Apple. As its final twenty seconds make clear, it was made to promote the then-new software functionality Memories. Memories are, a text at the end of the video reads, "movies made for you on iPhone 7. Practically magic," followed by the Apple logo. As the feature's description on Apple's website puts it: "A Memories movie is a beautifully edited video, complete with transitions and music, featuring curated photos and videos from your library," and its purpose is to "[r]ediscover favorite and forgotten

Rik Smit, *When Memories Become Data* In: *The Remaking of Memory in the Age of the Internet and Social Media*. Edited by: Qi Wang and Andrew Hoskins, Oxford University Press. © Oxford University Press 2024.
DOI: 10.1093/oso/9780197661260.003.0013

moments from deep in your photo library. Memories automatically create curated collections of your most meaningful photos and videos" (Apple, 2020). The feature does this on the basis of date, place, and facial recognition. The old man, therefore, could actually stand for an Apple employee; or, perhaps, it is the personification of an algorithm or artificial intelligence (AI) designed by the company. The old man might even represent Apple itself, a company that aims to show it cares for you and your memories, and that demonstrates this care by making beautiful and thoughtful audiovisual collages of the past you recorded with their technology, your iPhone.

It is safe to say users' mediated memories have become a business interest to big tech (Google, Apple, Facebook, Amazon, and Microsoft [GAFAM]). Market research has estimated that about 1.12 trillion photographs were taken globally in 2020, factoring in an 18% pandemic-related drop (many photos are taken during travel) (Carrington, 2020). With these numbers projected to increase dramatically in the coming years, so does the need to develop software that effectively organizes and meaningfully re-presents mediated memories. The question is if we can call these memories even. Jacobsen (2021, p. 358) argues this is not the case:

> These photographs, videos and posts that have been uploaded on social media platforms are better conceptualized as "memory objects": objects that set the stage for various acts of remembering as well as various engagements with and reactions to these media objects. As traces of memory, these photographs evoke and set the stage for remembering, yet cannot be reduced to memories as such.

Here I agree with this theoretical observation but use the term *memories* in the way technology companies describe memory objects. Apple is not alone in developing software applications like Memories: Google, Facebook, Microsoft, and various other companies are offering similar algorithmic solutions to the "problem" of narrating users' pasts in an era of digital overabundance (Jacobsen, 2022). There seems to be a growing genre of software applications concerned with our memories, whether they are private and personal, public and collective, or what lies in between these heuristic dichotomies.

Social media, apps, and other digital services increasingly enable, shape, and constrain the various ways in which we remember our personal and collective pasts. Like other media before them, they can regarded as technologies of memory (Van House & Churchill, 2008) that help keep and communicate memories. Moreover, such software applications ease and capitalize on the "outsourcing" of memory (Pereira et al., 2022; Risko et al., 2019) or "cognitive offloading" (Gilbert et al., 2022; Risko & Gilbert, 2016), which impacts what and how we remember (see also Risko et al., Chapter 5, this volume). In that sense, they are active agents in "memory work" or "the transfer and reconstruction of knowledge and experience of the past into the present and future . . . through and by specific practices, technologies, and cultural forms and, often, for specific goals" (Smit, 2020, p. 86). Digital platforms such as social media are also structuring and steering memory work up to the point that these technologies automatically remember *with* and *for* us (Prey & Smit, 2019). As technologies that simultaneously keep and shape memory, they can be regarded as "platforms of memory" (Smit, 2018).

However, platforms are not "just" technical infrastructures comprising code, algorithms, and interfaces. They are also commercial enterprises that are part of "surveillance capitalist" (Zuboff, 2019) efforts to render experiences into behavioral data that can be packaged and sold to third parties. In other words, platforms are not neutral intermediaries in the construction of memory, whether this is cultural memory through YouTube, autobiographical memory through a diary app, or Apple's Memories. Hence, the politics and practices of memory are gradually but surely interweaving with what Gillespie (2010) has called the "politics of platforms," an increased dependence on technologies that present themselves as neutral intermediaries. This process of growing dependence on the keeping *and* automated re-presentation of memories, I argue, can be viewed as the "platformization" (Helmond, 2015; Nieborg & Poell, 2018) of memory, a concept I unpack in the following pages.

While developing an argument that builds on Sections II ("The Digital Self in the Making"), III ("Google Effect"), and VI ("From the Individual to the Community and Society") of the present volume, I aim to provide an overview of the literature on the topic of this chapter and bridge memory studies with critical platform, app, and software studies, a much-needed epistemological step within the field. In order to do so, I first discuss the terms platform and second platformization. Then I deliberate what the platformization of memory would entail and how it relates to mediatization. The word *platform* is conceptually problematic and connotes and denotes a number of meanings. Moreover, the term *platformization*, a concept mainly pertaining to the cultural industries and cultural production, requires some appropriation for it to become helpful in the context of memory. I conclude this chapter by thinking through some of the consequences of platformization and what it means for memory studies. Before all this, however, a very brief philosophical intervention is required for clarity.

From Mnemotechnics to Mnemotechnologies

I resist the idea that the categories "memory" and "technology" were once separated. As various philosophers of technology, memory, and cognition (e.g., Chun, 2011; Hayles, 2012; Stiegler, 2010) have argued, human and "non-human" actors co-construct memory, and memories have always partly resided in objects, places, and our (technological) environment. That is, memory has always been a *distributed*, entangled process, not "merely" residing "in the head" but also "in the wild" (Barnier & Hoskins, 2018). Memory is a matter of both the inside and outside, of biology and technology, of organism and environment. We are as shaped by our technologies as much as we are shaping our technologies. We are always already cyborgs (Harraway, 1985/1991).

However, as Stiegler demonstrates, the era of mnemotechnics is gradually eclipsed by one constituted by mnemotechnologies—those technological systems that automatically remember for us and that inscribe their own logic onto the mnemonic object (Lemmens & Stiegler, 2011; Prey & Smit, 2019; Stiegler, 2010). This concerns us consciously storing our mediated memories within a computational system (e.g., database), but Stiegler's thinking can be extended to include how our searches online are recorded, stored, and made sense of so they can later influence our behavior. The "platformization of memory," then, is a next step in the "systematic industrialization of human memory and cognition through digital technologies" (Lemmens & Stiegler, 2011, pp. 33–34). The result of this is a colonization of our personal and collective pasts for commercial benefit and an increased dependence on the colonizers, in terms of both memory's infrastructure and process. As a growing part of our everyday lives is turning digital, the more we will come to depend on technologies associated with "platform capitalism" (Srnicek, 2017; Zuboff, 2019) and the algorithms that help make sense of our past. For example, when we use a platform like Instagram to share our photos during a trip, the platform simultaneously stores it for us, and later, on the basis of its own algorithmic logic, re-presents them for us, which shapes how we view ourselves, often in relation to others (cf. in this volume chapters by Wang, Chapter 2; Hoskins, Chapter 3; and Stone et al., Chapter 4). But what is a platform in the first place?

Platform

As Gillespie (2010) has shown, discursively, the term *platform* is highly problematic and conceptually messy. "The term 'platform,'" he writes (2010, p. 348), "has emerged recently as an increasingly familiar term in the description of the online services of content intermediaries, both in their self-characterizations and in the broader public discourse of users, the press and commentators." That is, the term has, more or less, become a freely floating signifier that can be infused with new meaning depending on the context. Nevertheless, or despite this, it has both semantic and symbolic power because the term has occupied four territories of meaning: the computational, the architectural, the figurative, and the political—dimensions that are also associated with contemporary memory construction.

The computational meaning of the word is the latest. As a technical term, it originally refers to "an infrastructure that supports the design and use of particular applications, be they computer hardware, operating systems, gaming devices, mobile devices or digital disc formats" and also to "online environments that allow users to design and deploy applications they design or that are offered by third parties" (Gillespie, 2010, p. 349). The latter comes close to a definition of platform provided by political economist Nick Srnicek:

> At the most general level, platforms are digital infrastructures that enable two or more groups to interact. They therefore position themselves as intermediaries that bring together different users: customers, advertisers, service providers, producers, suppliers, and even physical objects. More often than not, these platforms also come with a series of tools that enable their users to build their own products, services, and marketplaces. (2017, p. 43)

In the older, architectural sense, platform "has been broadly used to describe human-built or naturally formed physical structures, whether generic or dedicated to a specific use" (Gillespie, 2010, p. 349). Both the computational and architectural meanings suggest that a platform can be used to "build on" or provide the basis for further activities.

From this literal, denotative meaning, the word developed into something that can be used figuratively. It came to connote "opportunity, action and insight" and "we might describe our entry-level job as a 'platform' for climbing the corporate ladder" (Gillespie, 2010, p. 350). Last, platform can also "refer to the issues a political candidate or party endorses" and a phrase often asked of politicians is how they "stand" on a political issue (Gillespie, 2010, p. 350). These different semantic dimensions of the word *platform* make it appealing to public relations and marketing in various lines of business because "it suggests a progressive and egalitarian arrangement, promising to support those who stand upon it. . . . 'Platform' could suggest a lot while saying very little" (Gillespie, 2010, p. 351).

This latter remark points precisely at where the politics of platforms come in. Platforms—in the sense of digital technological infrastructure—are not neutral intermediaries, even though the term suggests neutrality. The goal of platforms such as Facebook, YouTube, and Instagram is to seamlessly move into our everyday lives, to become habitual: not invisible, but seeming not to matter in our interactions with the content and others "on" them. Platforms are habitual media, and "our media matter most when they seem not to matter at all," as Chun

(2016, p. 1) reminds us. As Morris and Murray (2018, p. 8), building on the work of Chun (2016), put it: "As software becomes habit, it waffles between conscious routine and unconscious action, between the voluntary and the involuntary, the creative and the mechanical, and thus becomes a prime locus of power." In other words, they are designed to not seem to matter, to fully integrate within everyday life, whereas an older memory technology such as a photo album requires conscious effort and designated time.

In other words, when a medium presents itself as a neutral intermediary, it is exercising politics because media are always already engaged in representation, selection, and the shaping of the communicative act. Platforms are the newest addition to a long list of media that claim to provide an unfiltered and unbiased version of reality (cf. newspapers, radio, television), and the very word itself aids this project. This is also part of Zuboff's (2019) compelling argument about "surveillance capitalism" tracking our everyday activities and selling these as data profiles to third parties. It is a truism that our data are the new oil, and just as oil requires platforms to be mined, so does data.

In their highly influential article on platformization in the cultural industries, Nieborg and Poell (2018), advancing from Gillespie (2010), write that the discursive power of platforms "obfuscates as much as it reveals. It obscures how social media and other digital services, labeled as platforms, not just facilitate socioeconomic, cultural, and political interaction, but very much organize and steer this interaction" (p. 4276). Technically speaking, platforms comprise computer code and algorithms and hence are programmable to achieve specific outcomes or solve particular problems.

As a growing body of academic work has argued, this has consequences for how we engage with our personal, collective, private, and public pasts. Platforms such as Facebook, YouTube, Twitter, and Reddit are appropriated and have come to function as "platforms of memory" (Smit, 2018) for and by their users. These range from activists (Smit et al., 2018; Merrill et al., 2020) and witnesses of war (Smit et al., 2017) to popular culture fans (Burgess et al., 2019; De Kosnik, 2016; Esteve del Valle & Smit, 2021).

It is true that "the platform has emerged as a new business model, capable of extracting and controlling immense amounts of data" (Srnicek, 2017, p. 6), and that code and algorithms allow this. However, "'platforms' are 'platforms' not necessarily because they allow code to be written or run, but because they afford an opportunity to communicate, interact or sell" (Gillespie, 2010, p. 351). That is, platforms "set the stage"—to use another infrastructural metaphor—for human practices (e.g., memory practices) that result in particular cultural forms (e.g., a memory object such as a photo with a specific filter). However, users rarely interact directly with a platform, but rather with "apps" designed by or for a platform.

Application software—or, apps—can be part of or built on the infrastructure of platforms, whether they are hardware or software platforms. They are specific types of software designed to help users perform a particular activity. Word processors and web browsers are apps and so are email and a media player. Nieborg and Helmond (2019) conceptualize these user encounters with platforms through application software as "platform instances." Hence, in the case of Facebook, they write that "individual platform instances serve as standalone derivatives that each provide a distinct 'view' of the platform as a whole and offer different functionalities tailored to distinct user groups. Each platform instance contributes to Facebook's overall data work while simultaneously engaging in its own" (Nieborg & Helmond, 2019, p. 199). Therefore, in order to study platforms or platformization—a term I turn to next—it makes sense to scrutinize how their power is reified and executed through and by apps such as Apple's Memories, a diary app, or Facebook's On This Day (Prey & Smit, 2019; Smit, 2023).

Platformization: The Logics of Contingency

In her pioneering work on the platformization of the web, Helmond (2015, p. 5) defines the process as "the rise of the platform as the dominant infrastructural and economic model of the social web and the consequences of the expansion of social media platforms into other spaces online." Her conceptualization of the term describes the construction of a computational infrastructure where other parties can build their software and services. This is how a platform as a networked technology comprising different "instances" continually expands.

Thus, as Plantin and others (2018, p. 307) point out, major platforms such as Google, Apple, and Facebook have become the "modern-day equivalents of the railroad, telephone, and electric utility monopolies of the late 19th and the 20th centuries." Just like railroads and telephones, the more people use them, and the more services can be created on the basis of the infrastructure and the more attractive the infrastructure becomes. (Respectively, these processes are commonly called direct and indirect network effects in economics and business literature.) Moreover, platforms are interconnected and have created an "ecosystem of connective media" that led to a "transformation from networked communication to 'platformed' sociality, and from participatory culture to a culture of connectivity" (Van Dijck, 2013, pp. 4–5). That is, almost all our online social interactions and practices are directly or indirectly supported by a platform.

Picking up this argument and expanding it, Nieborg and Poell (2018, p. 4276) argue: "Cultural production is progressively 'contingent on,' that is, *dependent on* a select group of powerful digital platforms." That is, cultural producers are increasingly dependent on big tech (GAFAM), which not only offer infrastructural support but also provide insight into (media) consumption behavior and the circulation of cultural commodities.

This leads to the second use of the word contingent in their theorization: "Products and services offered and circulated via digital platforms are contingent in the sense that they are malleable, modular in design, and informed by datafied user feedback, open to constant revision and recirculation" (2018, p. 4276). This cybernetic, algorithmic-supported feedback loop is increasingly influencing what we watch, listen to, or read, ranging from the latest podcast to the next Netflix show. Gillespie (2014, p. 192) sees this as an emergent knowledge logic that "depends on the proceduralized choices of a machine, designed by human operators to automate some proxy of human judgment or unearth patterns across collected social traces." This "algorithmic logic" slowly but surely replaces a traditional "editorial logic," which relies on the choices of experts, across the cultural industries and beyond (Nieborg & Poell, 2018, p. 4280).

Taking this dual contingency on board, Nieborg and Poell define platformization as "the penetration of economic, governmental, and infrastructural extensions of digital platforms into the web and app ecosystems, fundamentally affecting the operations of the cultural industries" (2018, p. 4276). In order to study platformization, the authors argue, researchers should pay attention to not only the technical medium, but also how the larger market structures, platform governance, and material infrastructures of cultural production interoperate.

This also offers us roads into studying the platformization of memory work as a process of both cultural consumption and production. Appropriating the work by Helmond, Nieborg, and Poell for the purpose of memory studies, we can ask: How do the interrelated economic, governmental, and infrastructural dimensions of digital platforms—or, platform instances, to be more precise—affect memory work? What roles do data and algorithmic logic play in how we represent our personal and collective past and carry it over into the future? How do largely computational processes make sense of us, and how do we make sense of our past selves through them? What are the consequences of our memory work being *platformed*, to repeat Van Dijck's (2013) term. Such questions are too ambitious to fully answer in these pages, but a start can be made by outlining some of the structural aspects of the platformization of memory.

The Platformization of Memory

The platformization of memory can be regarded as a next step within the mediatization of memory (Hoskins, 2014). Exploring the concept of "deep mediatization," Couldry and Hepp (2017, p. 7) write: "The ways in which we make sense of the world phenomenologically become necessarily entangled with the constraints, affordances and power-relations that are features of media as infrastructures of communication." In line with this, Hoskins (2014, p. 662) argues the mediatization of memory entails "the process of shifting interconnected individual, social, and cultural dependency on media, for maintenance, survival, and growth." In other words, Couldry, Hepp, and Hoskins, like Nieborg and Poell, stress that individuals, cultures, and societies increasingly become *contingent* upon media.

If mediatization describes this expanding contingency, why would we need the concept of platformization? The answer lies in the fact that platforms, as not only software applications, but also data companies with specific business models, have become the "media of media" (Manovich, 2013): They provide the infrastructure for other media to operate on. This makes platformization simultaneously a more specific and wider lens through which we can view memory work. That is, we can scrutinize how a specific platform instance shapes memory work through its operations, mechanics, and technological affordances while also paying attention to how the platform serves as a basis for other businesses and technologies. But, to repeat, we should not see platforms as "merely" software comprising code. Platforms are also commercial enterprises with specific business models; they have specific visions and worldviews, and they draw from and add to specific discourses. In other words, they are ideological through and through. They are built with an architectural and infrastructural motive and hence generate growing dependence.

Taking all of the above into account, what implications does this have for memory work? What does the phrase "the platformization of memory" mean? In the first place, it entails an increased dependence on platforms and the many applications built on them for the ways in which we engage with our pasts—Nieborg and Poell's first use of the word contingency. From archiving documents in Google Drive to reminiscing with friends elsewhere on WhatsApp, we depend on platform infrastructures. From automatically generating Memories videos on an iPhone to Facebook's Year in Review or On This Day feature, we depend on platforms' algorithms. From making playlists of our children's video-recorded steps on YouTube, to commemorating a deceased family member on Instagram, we make use of platforms' interfaces and affordances. We might not lose our internal memories, but our attitudes toward and our practices related to them might very well be lost. This might have consequences for the ways in which we make sense of our current selves through our autobiographical memories (cf. Section II, this volume; Conway et al., 2005). Indeed, we still make our photos and videos ourselves. We have agency. However, as soon as we upload these photos and videos to platforms, we give part of this agency away to a computational system that, in its own way, interprets this material and processes it in a way a photo album never could and for purposes often unknown to users. Moreover, and more straightforward, what happens to these mediated memories when a platform deletes them (for any given reason) or is discontinued (e.g., MySpace)?

Second, the traces we leave on platforms, consciously or unconsciously, can emerge at any time and in any form. As Schwarz (2014, p. 17) has put it succinctly:

> Our memory does not rely merely on bodily neuronal networks and material objects but also on the structures of databases that store the growing number of digital memory objects and on the design of algorithms that mediate their retrieval, that is, the structure regulating our interaction with them.

Memory objects are malleable and revisable because they undergo a process of rendition (Zuboff, 2019) when entering the formatted structure of a platform or a software application: They become data. This second meaning of contingency contributes to the datafication of memory and thus how memory is simultaneously prepared for algorithmic processing and the product of this. Ultimately, this comes down to the datafication of what is essentially a qualitative, experiential process. It makes memories platform ready (Gillespie, 2014) in order to provide a personalized experience of the past. The technology developed for this is something that researchers at Facebook call "memory products" (Konrad, 2017), fitting memory objects within a corporate and commercial discourse. An example of this would be Facebook's Memories functionality (previously called On This Day) and how it is aimed at creating and maintaining an intimate connection with its users (see Prey & Smit, 2019, for a political-economic critique of this feature). When every single aspect of everyday life is mediated, making such "memory products" will eventually become a lucrative business or create a competitive edge.

How does the above translate into a research agenda for memory studies? Nieborg and Poell (2018) assert that in order to "understand how the platformization of cultural production unfolds we need to untangle the mutual articulation of market arrangements, infrastructures, and governance of content production, distribution, and advertising" (p. 4281). While the authors focus on large market structures, political-economic arrangements, and large-scale technological infrastructures, research could scrutinize how these dynamics are manifested or play out within a single app or platform instance. Appropriating this, an approach to the platformization of memory could investigate how the (1) business model; (2) technical features, affordances, algorithms, and interfaces; and (3) regulation and governance of a software application mutually shape memory work on, by, and with platforms and platform instances.

Conclusion: Platformization of Memory as a Research Agenda within Memory Studies

I have argued in this chapter that the economic, governmental, and infrastructural logics of platforms and apps extend into and affect digital memory work. That is, just as other media before them, platforms increasingly and idiosyncratically intertwine with and envelop digital memory work. Appropriating the original conceptualization of platformization, I contended that platforms—that group of simultaneously vague and specific digital media technologies/businesses—encapsulate this process through their technological infrastructures, interfaces, and business models. Platformization contributes to the datafication of memory and thus how memory is both prepared for algorithmic processing and the product of this. This differentiates platformization from the mediation (Erll & Rigney, 2009; Lohmeier & Pentzold, 2014) or mediatization of memory (Hoskins, 2014), while it is also an extension of such processes. That is, platforms increasingly constitute the *infrastructure* of memory's construction, while also shaping and taking part in the *process* of "making memories" by turning (mediated) experiences into data and data into "memories." This results in a cybernetic feedback loop in which our experiences (input) are represented to us as "memories" (output), which in turn shapes how we view ourselves and our pasts.

Memories, or better, "memory objects" (Jacobsen, 2021), become contingent when they enter the formatted structure of a software application. That is, memories are made "algorithm ready" (Gillespie, 2014) and "programmable" (Chun, 2011) in this process. They are rendered into data (Zuboff, 2019) that can be sorted, reorganized, and re-presented in various forms. In computational terms, memories are both the "input" and "output" of such algorithmic processes, but memories are rendered into something else in the process. In other words, they are subjected to a specific algorithmic logic, which changes the ways in which we construct and interact with, in the case of Apple's Memories, our autobiographical memory objects. This datafication of memory is one of the many consequences of platforms—and the application built on them—becoming habitually situated within our everyday routines and practices, among them those dealing with our pasts.

The platformization—and with that, the datafication—of memory does not come out of thin air. Apple's Memories consists of what Rieder (2020) has called "algorithmic techniques," the technical processes behind the smooth interfaces of our apps that have their own histories, are part of existing webs of knowledge, and have their own goals. Instead of being impartial and objective, all sorts of decisions, judgments, and constraints go into the design of software and the algorithms that are constitutive of it (Kitchin, 2017, p. 4). Software is a sociocultural product—or process, since it is contingent—that, in its turn, also impacts other sociocultural products and processes. As Neff and Nafus (2016, p. 27) aptly put it: "Engineers must contend with the brute facts of circuitry, but they also have their own social imaginations. There are many 'visions' circulating within the technology-building community, and these visions inform what eventually makes it to the marketplace." Digital memory studies, therefore, should scrutinize not only cultural "memory products," cognitive processes, or practices but also the underlying infrastructures that enable, shape, and constrain such symbolic objects and mental activity.

It is true that, on the one hand, lived experiences and memories of them cannot be captured in a computational system or medium. On the other hand, there is no such thing as unmediated memory (Prey & Smit, 2019; Smit, 2020). Memory is a distributed and relational process that is always situated and embedded in existing social and communicative environments. Today, this involves a whole range of new actors that facilitate and shape memory construction and the ways in which we make sense of ourselves. Among them, increasingly, are platforms that generate, process, and thrive on memories as data.

References

Apple. (2020). Use Memories in Photos on your iPhone or iPad. https://support.apple.com/en-us/HT207023

Barnier, A. J., & Hoskins, A. (2018). Is there memory in the head, in the wild? *Memory Studies, 11*(4), 386–390. https://doi.org/10.1177/1750698018806440

Burgess, J., Mitchell, P., & Münch, F. V. (2019). Social media rituals: The uses of celebrity death in digital culture. In Z. Papacharissi (Ed.), *A networked self and birth, life, death* (pp. 224–239). Routledge.

Carrington, D. (2020). How many photos will be taken in 2020? https://focus.mylio.com/techtoday/how-many-photos-will-be-taken-in-2020

Chun, W. H. K. (2011) *Programmed visions: Software and memory.* MIT Press.

Chun, W. H. K. (2016). *Updating to remain the same: Habitual new media.* MIT Press.

Conway, M. A., Wang, Q., Hanyu, K., & Haque, S. (2005). A cross-cultural investigation of autobiographical memory: On the universality and cultural variation of the reminiscence bump. *Journal of Cross-Cultural Psychology, 36*(6), 739–749.

Couldry, N., & Hepp, A. (2017). *The mediated construction of reality.* Polity Press.

De Kosnik, A. (2016). *Rogue archives: Digital cultural memory and media fandom.* MIT Press.

Erll, A., & Rigney, A. (2009). *Mediation, remediation, and the dynamics of cultural memory.* W. de Gruyter. https://doi.org/10.1515/9783110217384

Esteve del Valle, M., & Smit, R. (2021). *Moonwalking* together: Tracing Redditors' digital memory work on Michael Jackson. *Convergence, 27*(6), 1811–1832. https://doi.org/10.1177/13548565211003878

Gilbert, S. J., Boldt, A., Sachdeva, C., Scarampi, C., & Tsai, P.-C. (2022). Outsourcing memory to external tools: a review of "intention offloading." *Psychonomic Bulletin & Review, 30*(1), 60–76. https://doi.org/10.3758/s13423-022-02139-4

Gillespie, T. (2010). The politics of "platforms." *New Media & Society, 12*(3), 347–364.

Gillespie, T. (2014). The relevance of algorithms. In T. Gillespie, P. J. Boczkowski, & K. A. Foot (Eds.), *Media technologies: Essays on communication, materiality, and society* (pp. 167–193).MIT Press.

Harraway, D. (1991). A cyborg manifesto: Science, technology and socialist- feminism in the late twentieth century. In N. Wardrip-Fruin & N. Montfort (Eds.), The *new media reader* (pp. 515–547). MIT Press. (Original work published 1985)

Hayles, N. K. (2012). *How we think: Digital media and contemporary technogenesis.* University of Chicago Press.

Helmond, A. (2015). The platformization of the web: Making web data platform ready. *Social Media + Society,* 1(2), 1–11. https://doi.org/10.1177/2056305115603080

Hoskins, A. (2014). The mediatization of memory. In K. Lundby (Ed.), *The mediatization of communication* (pp. 661–679). De Gruyter Mouton.

Jacobsen, B. N. (2021). Sculpting digital voids: The politics of forgetting on Facebook. *Convergence, 27*(2), 357–370. https://doi.org/10.1177/1354856520907390

Jacobsen, B. N. (2022). Algorithms and the narration of past selves. *Information, Communication & Society, 25,* 1082–1097. https://doi.org/10.1080/1369118X.2020.1834603

Kitchin, R. (2017). Thinking critically about and researching algorithms. *Information, Communication & Society, 20*(1), 14–29. https://doi.org/10.1080/1369118X.2016.1154087

Konrad, A. (2017, September 6). Facebook memories: The research behind the products that connect you with your past. https://research.facebook.com/blog/2017/9/facebook-memories-the-research-behind-the-products-that-connect-you-with-your-past/

Lemmens, P., & Stiegler, B. (2011). "This system does not produce pleasure anymore." An interview with Bernard Stiegler. *Krisis,* 1, 33–41.

Lohmeier, C., & Pentzold, C. (2014). Making mediated memory work: Cuban-Americans, Miami media and the doings of diaspora memories. *Media, Culture and Society, 36*(6), 776–789. https://doi.org/10.1177/0163443713518574

Manovich, L. (2013). *Software takes command: Extending the language of new media.* Bloomsbury.

Merrill, S., Keightley, E. and Daphi, P. (Eds.). (2020). *Social movements, cultural memory and digital media: Mobilising mediated remembrance.* Palgrave Macmillan.

Morris, J. W., & Murray, S. (2018). Introduction. In J. W. Morris & S. Murray (Eds.), *Amplified: Culture in the age of apps* (pp. 1–22). University of Michigan Press.

Neff, G., & Nafus, D. (2016). *Self-tracking.* MIT Press.

Nieborg, D. B., & Helmond, A. (2019). The political economy of Facebook's platformization in the mobile ecosystem: Facebook messenger as a platform instance. *Media, Culture, and Society, 41*(2), 196–218. https://doi.org/10.1177/0163443718818384

Nieborg, D. B., & Poell, T. (2018). The platformization of cultural production: Theorizing the contingent cultural commodity. *New Media & Society, 20*(11), 4275–4292. https://doi.org/10.1177/1461444818769694

Pereira, A. E., Kelly, M. O., Lu, X., & Risko, E. F. (2022). On our susceptibility to external memory store manipulation: Examining the influence of perceived reliability and expected access to an external store. *Memory, 30*(4), 412–428. https://doi.org/10.1080/09658211.2021.1990347

Plantin, J.-C., Lagoze, C., Edwards, P. N., & Sandvig, C. (2018). Infrastructure studies meet platform studies in the age of Google and Facebook. *New Media & Society, 20*(1), 293–310. https://doi.org/10.1177/1461444816661553

Prey, R., & Smit, R. (2019). From personal to personalized memory: Social media as mnemotechnology. In Z. Papacharissi (Ed.), *A networked self and birth, life, death* (pp. 209–223). Routledge.

Rieder, B. (2020). *Engines of order: A mechanology of algorithmic techniques.* Amsterdam University Press.

Risko, E. F., & Gilbert, S. J. (2016). Cognitive offloading. *Trends in Cognitive Sciences, 20*(9), 676–688. https://doi.org/10.1016/j.tics.2016.07.002

Risko, E. F., Kelly, M. O., Patel, P., & Gaspar, C. (2019). Offloading memory leaves us vulnerable to memory manipulation. *Cognition, 191,* 103954. https://doi.org/10.1016/j.cognition.2019.04.023

Schwarz, O. (2014). The past next door: Neighbourly relations with digital memory artefacts. *Memory Studies, 7*(1), 7–21. https://doi.org/10.1177/1750698013490591

Smit, R. (2018). *Platforms of memory: Social media and digital memory work* [Unpublished doctoral dissertation]. University of Groningen.

Smit, R. (2020). *Connective memory work on* Justice for Mike Brown. In S. Merrill, E. Keightley, & P. Daphi (Eds.), *Social movements, cultural memory and digital media: Mobilising mediated remembrance* (pp. 85–108). Palgrave Macmillan.

Smit, R. (2023). Die Plattformisierung des Erinnerns. In C. Pentzold & C. Lohmeier (Eds.), *Handbuch kommunikationswissenschaftliche Erinnerungsforschung* (pp. 471–493). De Gruyter.

Smit, R., Heinrich, A., & Broersma, M. (2017). Witnessing in the new memory ecology: Memory construction of the Syrian conflict on YouTube. *New Media & Society, 19*(2), 289–307.

Smit, R., Heinrich, A., & Broersma, M. (2018). Activating the past in the Ferguson protests: Memory work, digital activism and the politics of platforms. *New Media & Society, 20*(9), 3119–3139. https://doi.org/10.1177/1461444817741849

Spiccia, M. (Dir.). (2018). Apple "Memories." https://vimeo.com/224517148

Srnicek, N. (2017). *Platform capitalism*. Polity Press

Stiegler, B. (2010). *For a new critique of political economy*. Polity.

Van Dijck, J. (2013). *The culture of connectivity: A critical history of social media*. Oxford University Press.

Van House, N., & Churchill, E. (2008). Technologies of memory: Key issues and critical perspectives. *Memory Studies, 1*(3), 295–310.

Zuboff, S. (2019). *The age of surveillance capitalism: The fight for a human futureat the new frontier of power*. Profile Books.

14

Between Coping and Commodification

Nostalgic Remembering in a Connected World

Katharina Niemeyer and Emily Keightley

The accumulation and increasing availability of images, texts, and sounds from the past (or at least from parts of the past) — especially since the development of Web 2.0, different forms of digital storage, collections, archives, and techniques to digitize analogue data—have been recognized as shaping memory work on an individual and collective level (Merrill et al., 2020; Wang & Hoskins, Chapter 1, this volume) such as new extensions of autobiographical memory (Wang, Chapter 2, this volume) and the increase sharing of personal memories (Stone et al., Chapter 4, this volume). Nostalgia, by virtue of the affordances of digital technology, has also enabled its embedding into processes of media production, content, and use, on an unprecedented scale, from the rebooting of film franchises (Steiner, 2020) to the circulation of retro photographs on social media (Abend et al., 2018). As a specific modality of remembering in which the past is construed in positive terms, digital media have also impacted the volume and nature of explicitly *nostalgic* relations to the past.

In this chapter we seek to trace the complex ways in which digital media have transformed both the cultural practices involved in mediated nostalgic remembering (also during the COVID crisis), and scholarly approaches to it, all by coming back to the historically important question of media as a remedy and a trigger of nostalgia (Niemeyer, 2014). In doing so, we highlight and explore the creative and progressive potentialities of (digital) nostalgia, while also acknowledging its (often simultaneous) corporatization as part of new digital economies. We conclude by signaling future directions for nostalgia research.

While certainly not exclusive in digital "attention" economies, the use of nostalgic relations with the past as part of a business model has intensified and deepened the paradox of nostalgia as having both the potential to enliven and attenuate productive transactional relations between past, present, and future. Taken in a broad historical perspective, new ways of digitally accessing and

Katharina Niemeyer and Emily Keightley, *Between Coping and Commodification* In: *The Remaking of Memory in the Age of the Internet and Social Media*. Edited by: Qi Wang and Andrew Hoskins, Oxford University Press. DOI: 10.1093/oso/9780197661260.003.0014 communicating the "restless past" (Hoskins, 2017) are particularly attractive for media institutions of all kinds: news media; media industries (video games, film, etc.); streaming platforms; social media networks; as well as traditional TV channels. Netflix is a prominent example of a platform that reruns old shows and creates new ones with nostalgic overtones (Pallister, 2019). Social media platforms such as Facebook host numerous groups and pages that are dedicated to the past, for example, those that focus on historical events, music history, personal childhood memories, or the architectural memory of cities bringing together "before-and-after" images. While most of these groups and pages are communities administrated by volunteers, in other instances companies create these groups to generate an advertising income and create an online business centered on the exploitation of memory and nostalgia (Niemeyer & Keightley, 2020). Most of these nostalgic media productions or online communities seek to exploit the potential of a nostalgic mode of remembering to monetize a longing for a lost past.

In these cultural forms and practices, the past becomes a commodified object of desire, often stripped of any negative traces. Nevertheless, the composite temporal dynamics of nostalgia (longing for a desired past, a sense of lack in the present, and the perception of loss over time) mean that these nostalgic cultural commodities inevitably imply a negative temporal other. In bridging the past, present, and (potentially) the future, these digital traces of a desired, even joyful, past provide a rich site for the exploration of the digital mobilization of what has gone before in response to the various crises that characterize late modern experience.

It is not only the deepening of commercial exploitation that has contributed to the ubiquity of nostalgia as a mode of engaging with the past in digital culture. The objects of contemporary nostalgic practice have also proliferated, at least in part enabled, by digital communication technologies. Numerous social, political, and ecological phenomena have triggered different types of nostalgia in recent years, ranging from sustainable nostalgia (Davies, 2010), environmental nostalgia (Howell et al., 2019), and political nostalgia (Landgrebe, 2020; Richards et al., 2020; Steenvoorden & Harteveld, 2018) to emancipatory (Kisukidi, 2014), motivational (Sedikides & Wildschut, 2020), as well as nostalgia for earlier media content and technologies (Menke, 2018; Niemeyer, 2014). This plethora of nostalgias (the plural here underpins the diversity of its forms, expressions, and meanings) are not necessarily new in terms of their form, but they have gained greater visibility and (un)popularity with their increasing entrenchment and accumulation in accelerated digital news cycles, in popular discourse, and via social media networks.

Nostalgia and the (COVID) Crisis

The turn to nostalgia in digital culture is therefore not reducible to technological change only but is produced in the interplay between broader trajectories of social change and contemporary events, alongside the communicative opportunities afforded by digital infrastructures. As for memory work and remembering in general, the recent COVID-19 pandemic has thrown this into sharp relief (Pogačar, Chapter 16, this volume; Worcman & Garde-Hansen, Chapter 18, this volume). While the broader digital conditions in which memory is communicated have been in place long before the recent pandemic, the emergence and entrenchment of various modalities of nostalgia as a way of relating to the past have become viral (Sampson, 2012) during the COVID crisis, underpinning—once again—that media can be not only a trigger but also a remedy for nostalgia in times of doubt and stagnation (Niemeyer, 2022). Memory has, for the last decade, been communicated via plurimedial constellations of cultural content and is articulated across and between platforms. It is the specific temporal valences of nostalgia that have allowed it to emerge as a prominent mode of relating to the past in the present in pandemic and postpandemic conditions. In other words, one of the key sentiments that has been expressed, experienced, and performed via social media networks, media companies, and "traditional" news media alike during months and years following the spate of lockdowns across the world is one of nostalgia, in which diverse prepandemic pasts are mobilized comparatively (implicitly and explicitly) in response to current conditions (Gibbs & Egermann, 2021; Martin, 2021). For quite some time, scholars such as Svetlana Boym (2001) have pointed out that feelings of nostalgia emerge as protective reactions to crises and to so-called progress—both inevitable historical companions to most of our societies and systems (Hartog, 2015). The spread of the virus, people being obliged to stay at home, and keeping distance from others have resulted in experiences of loss: the death of close others, limited or no physical relations in immediate or extended social groups, restricted freedom in public spaces, job losses, and so on. It is no surprise that pandemic conditions have led to a peak in informational and fictional media consumption (Lee & Koblin, 2020). During the COVID crisis, this sense of home itself has also been shattered. It was not a nostalgia for missing the home by being far away, but a nostalgia for what the home we were in used to be. This type of nostalgia is close to solastalgia, (preliminarily and broadly defined as the distress caused by the transformation and degradation of one's home environment) (Galway et al., 2019, p. 2662). Likewise, "nostalgic" leisure activities, from playing board games to watching old TV shows, have occupied the "free" time of those privileged enough to have the means to distract themselves and calm their anxiety (Gammon & Ramshaw, 2021). Media and media technologies are therefore not only communicative platforms of and for nostalgia, stimulating a desire for a lost past in moments of consumption, but also they can also serve to provoke and to "heal" the rift between a desired past and a lacking present, by not only providing a salve to painful experience but also resources for actively rethinking (Menke, 2017; Niemeyer, 2014).

It is in this context of digital nostalgia as produced in the complex interplay between media technologies and content on the one hand, and social and cultural experience on the other that, we trace the transformations in nostalgic practice and the analysis of it. In doing so we explore the paradoxical ways in which both opportunities and limits of digital nostalgia as a mode of mobilizing the past in the present in the interest of the future are produced in digital economies. We begin by considering the various assessments of nostalgia as a specifically mediated form of remembering and follow this with a critical reflection on the modalities of digital nostalgia and the numerous ways in which they configure cross-temporal relations.

Nostalgia and (Digital) Media—Between Historical Sickness and Coping

Without reprising the historical conceptualizations of nostalgia in other scholarly fields (for recent overviews, e.g., Becker, 2018; Dodman, 2018; Jacobsen, 2020), exploring some of the key historical aspects and interpretational shifts in relation to nostalgia leading up to the digital era is crucial in order to understand the specificities of nostalgia today. Recognized and expressed in Homer's *Odyssey*, the coining of the medical neologism "nostalgia" to signify homesickness first appeared in a medical thesis written by Johannes Hofer in 1688 in Switzerland, the author referring to a recurring sickness in the army. The Greek etymology of the concept thus comes from *nostos* ("to return home") and *algia* ("longing/ yearning or pain"). The homesick were cured when they went physically home or with the promise of returning there, when they were visited by members of their family, or when they listened to music or stories that evoked images and memories of their homeland (Bolzinger, 2007). Thus, in the seventeenth century, the power of narratives, images, and sounds acting as remedy made it possible to alleviate the symptoms of nostalgia as a condition, transporting one to another space/time. The notion that media and cultural representations of what is lost have the potential to ameliorate a sense of lack in the present continues to persist (Niemeyer, 2014), but the intensification of the commodification of cultural content, especially online, has seen the emergence of representations of lost pasts as the deliberate mobilization or stimulation of temporal desire to engage audiences and media users. In this sense, media representations of a lost past can also be positioned as the origin of the nostalgic feeling, stimulating temporal desire for what is no longer (Burman, 2010; Estévez, 2005; Menke, 2017; Niemeyer, 2014; Wulf et al., 2018). Sanitized, stylized representations of a desired past can be the origin of the nostalgic feeling and present its remedy all at once in a cycle of temporal desire for that which has been lost.

Nostalgia has mainly been understood as a Westernized, mostly regressive, or superficial modality of engaging with the past. Since the mid-2000s, this conceptualization has been challenged—coinciding with the widespread adoption of Web 2.0 and the possibility of an "accumulation" of the past and memories in online archives or digital storage media (Wang & Hoskins, Chapter 1, this volume; Hoskins, 2017; Niemeyer, 2016). Informed by wider reconceptualizations of media audiences and audience agency in the production of meaning, it was Sean Scanlan (2004) in cultural studies, as well as Emily Keightley and Michael Pickering (2006) in media sociology, who launched a call for rethinking nostalgia. Scholars in psychology also empirically demonstrated the more constructive and positive nature of nostalgia as a means for overcoming personal crises of the present (Arndt et al., 2006). Moreover, the publication of a special issue of the journal *Memory Studies*, focusing on historical misconceptions about nostalgia, finally paved the way toward a more constructive approach to individual and collective nostalgia (Dames, 2010). Thus, the transition toward the verb "nostalgize" became possible (Niemeyer 2014; Sedikides et al. 2015). Without attempting to deny nostalgia's potential mobilization as an object and tool that can be deployed in economic and political interests—its status has changed into a more complex and open conceptualization (Angé & Berliner, 2015; Bonnett, 2016; Lems, 2016). Media and communication scholars also began developing an interest in the changing perspectives on nostalgia and its more general relations to (digital) media (Lizardi, 2015; Niemeyer, 2014). Research dealing with the performative approach to nostalgia and "media texts" has been published during the last years with a focus on film (Dwyer, 2015; Fevry, 2017; Ochonicky, 2020; Sperb, 2015); digital and platform television (Pallister, 2019); cultural and media industries (Natterer, 2017); visual cultures and aesthetics (Bevan, 2019; Kay et al., 2017; Sielke, 2019); video games (Ivănescu, 2019; Toniolo & Giovannini, 2020); or media cultures in the broad sense of the term (Santa Cruz & Ferraz, 2019). Nostalgia has become a key theme in media and communication research with a profusion of special issues dedicated to the topics of media, memory, nostalgia, and retro/vintage cultures. The Italian publication *H-erme: Journal of Communication* (2016) embraces the general theme of nostalgia and memory as well as their historical, cultural, and communicational aspects. Kim Knowles (2015) edited a special issue on *vintage*. In the French journal *Le Temps des Médias*, Emmanuelle Fantin and Thibault Le Hégarat (2016) also devoted a special issue in which they question the historical and mnemonic media constructions of often-idealized times.

What this body of research reveals is that the expansion, intensification, and immersiveness in relation to "nostalgic" media and cultural texts and their circulation has been made possible by Web 2.0, digital archiving, cross-platform modes of media production, and the increasingly participatory nature of mediated experiences of nostalgia made possible through interactive platforms. This has stimulated new ways of thinking about the creative, agentic potential of mediated nostalgia. Thinking of media and digital technologies as tools for coping with contemporary crises, and as imaginative, creative resources for rethinking the lacking or uncertain present, has been empirically analyzed by Manuel Menke (2018), whose study reconfirms that nostalgia often appears in times of transition and doubt, that "recent" media changes from analogue to digital media, and even more recent changes in web-based technology have themselves triggered different types of nostalgia. During the COVID-19 panic, for example, explicitly digital forms of nostalgia ranged from the intensified sharing of childhood photos on Indian social media (Hussain, 2020) to the nostalgic quality that accumulated around the photographs shared online of the most recent of at this time prohibited activities, such as going to restaurants (Bose, 2020). The temporal range of nostalgic desire, as these examples suggest, is broadened by digital technologies, allowing for those experiences that have only just receded from the present moment to become objects of nostalgic longing and creative resources for the articulation of loss. In this sense, digital media texts clearly operate as both mechanisms for simple medications for both ameliorating a sense of loss and lack in the present and as symbolic markers of that loss and lack. While this this duality is not new, the *virality* (Sampson, 2012) of nostalgia in times of crisis is. The ability to share a sense of loss and the temporalized symbolic resources that may both stimulate a sense of loss and provide a temporary balm for it under current conditions of crisis allow for what Reading has called a globital field of memory (2011). While in memory studies more generally, this globital memory field has been considered with reference to the global, digital circulation of pasts and memories that are often painful or contested (see, e.g., Reading, 2011; Smit, 2019), what animates the analysis of the global-digital dynamics of nostalgia is a concern for the circulation and transmission of structures of feeling that are characterized by desire and longing with increasing rapidity and reach.

In the following section we discuss precisely how nostalgia has been operationalized as a concept and the modes of analysis that have been used in media, communication, and cultural studies.

Modalities of (Digital) Nostalgia

Recent research has increasingly moved beyond a straightforward notion of either media or their users as "being nostalgic" in their consumption of media and cultural texts toward a more complex characterization of how (often digital) media and their users are intertwined in a performative and dynamic process of multiply-mediated engagements with the past and memory (Fawns, Chapter 7, this volume; Merrill, Chapter 156, this volume; Wang, Chapter 2, this volume), through which emerge expressions and experiences of nostalgic longing. This understanding of nostalgia as produced in the active navigation of a complex media ecology involves various layers of analysis, which account for symbolic, technological, and institutional elements in the generation of nostalgia in digital culture, and affords both the pleasure of nostalgic cultural consumption (very often the content or experience of such "nostalgias" is related to not only the memory of media devices and their texts but also ritual leisure activities of the past shared with friends or family) alongside a more profound search for spatio-temporal "home."

Mediated Nostalgia as a Cultural Style

Media texts that use nostalgic aesthetics (black and white, sepia, grains, etc.) or narratives are not new. With his postmodern critique of nostalgia films, Frederic Jameson (1991) names such aesthetics *nostalgic modes*, whereas Paul Grainge (2000) reworks this concept and discusses in detail the role of *nostalgia as a cultural style* in the production of nostalgia as a feeling: a *nostalgic mood.*

Increasingly, researchers are engaging with an even broader analysis of *nostalgia as a cultural form* in relation to diverse media texts and objects of popular culture (advertising, TV shows, films, video games, etc.) by addressing questions of commodification in digital economies and interrogating the media technologies and tools that render those styles possible. As Baschiera and Caoduro note: "Revival styles, vintage fashions, retro phenomena, skeumorphs and remediations are common presences in our increasingly digital cultural landscape, which gives up the dreams of spotless perfection of the binary code for the indexical ruins of the analogical" (2017, p. 1). They consider the place of these styles in the context of media theory, media archaeology, and within (audio)visual media in general, and in doing so position the technical affordances and economic imperatives of digital media industries as allowing for a creative reanimation of the past in accordance with the specific aesthetics of nostalgia. Further exploration of the digital conditions that facilitate the embedding of nostalgic cultural styles are made a chapter that discusses various visual modes that represent or simulate the past (Menke & Niemeyer, 2019) and in a number of other recently published books that include reflections on nostalgic styles (see, e.g., Abend et al., 2018; Bevan, 2019; Kay et al., 2017). In addition, there are specific interrogations of amateur uses of digital filters in everyday photography (Bartholeyns, 2014; Chopra-Gant, 2016), for example, or the role of such nostalgic styles in media art (e.g., Schrey, 2017). While these nostalgic *modes* or *styles* do not automatically generate nostalgic feelings, these experimentations or creations can be described as ironic, playful, or serious performances of *analogue and digital (tech-)nostalgias*, which are a specific type of *media nostalgia in which the objects of nostalgia are the aesthetics of earlier media forms themselves.* The digital era and its digital tools can therefore trigger, accelerate, and diffuse nostalgic cultural styles and their specific symbolic features.

Analogue and Digital (Tech-)Nostalgias

Nostalgia for media technologies and devices, often labeled *tech-nostalgia*, is also not a new phenomenon (Böhn & Möser, 2010; van der Heijden, 2015). Moreover, tech-nostalgia can encompass a yearning for the rituals, practices, places, and ways of life associated with certain technologies (e.g., Ferraz, 2017; Magaudda & Minniti, 2019; Mehrvarz & Muliaee, 2020; Menke, 2017; Niemeyer, 2015). Why make a distinction here between *analogue and digital (tech-)nostalgia*? The "digital" in *digital nostalgia* is not in opposition to the analogue, of course. These two concepts are often misinterpreted historically and technologically, and their analytical separation is primarily a political and economic one in order to account for the specific affordances of digital culture in the production and articulation of nostalgia (Sterne, 2016). Indeed, the concept of digital (tech-)nostalgia seeks to emphasize the idea that "reality is just as analogue as it is digital" (Sterne, 2016, p. 41), rather than casting analogue nostalgia as more authentic than its digital counterpart. In this sense, the differentiation of these two types of nostalgia is heuristic, serving to not only distinguish between modalities of tech-nostalgia but also highlight their entanglement: Analogue nostalgia (e.g., Marks, 2002; Schrey, 2014, 2017) and digital nostalgia (Niemeyer, 2016, Wills, 2002) are bound. These two nostalgias converge particularly in terms of their emotional involvement, and, in both cases, the contraction and passage of time allows for a contrast with the past to manifest on an aesthetic or technological level.

Nostalgia is concerned with both analogue and digital objects; their technological functions and construction; and their contents and forms and the social rituals, personal narratives, and stories associated with them. While a Polaroid camera can materially bear traces of the time that passes, an animated GIF image does not age in the same way. It is with a temporal distance that a design appears "old," as is also the case with certain aesthetic forms and styles in general. Unlike retro objects that reproduce past designs as contemporary imitations, analogue vintage objects transport and depict the passage of time in and of themselves; they are essentially like "ruins" that travel through time (Niemeyer, 2015). Similarly, using new techniques to make content sound and appear old is no longer new, as demonstrated by the TV series *Stranger Things* (Steiner, 2020). A second form of analogue nostalgia concerns the vintage techniques and rituals connected with these objects. This type of nostalgia can be found dispersed across all media—in music, video games, television series, and more—and, once again, reiterates the importance of the technology or the tool in nostalgic production through a quest for authenticity or, at the very least, its simulation.

The notion that digital objects are sensorial agents, that they are at the same level or have the same symbolic value as objects that we can physically touch, is routinely overlooked in nostalgia research. And yet, nostalgic feeling can also be expressed for objects that have never been present to us in their analogue form. They are "digital icons" that transport us to a social space and time in the past, shared with friends or family, mostly online.

Media Nostalgia

Bringing the past back onto the smart TV screen can provide opportunities for those with experiential memories of the past being represented to articulate a sense of loss, lack, and longing, but at the same time the presence of the past on screen affords opportunities for attracting new, younger viewers and providing resources for them to create connections across generations in a secondhand way. For example, by running the remastered show *Friends* on Netflix, older fans can engage fondly with a previous moment of cultural consumption that has been revivified, sharpened, and made accessible in the present, stimulating the desire for an experience that is no longer. In contrast, younger people can access their parent's (nostalgic) past, where the fantasy freedoms of pre-smart media, financially independent twenty somethings become a creative space through which to reflect on their own contemporary cultural moment. Media institutions and industries use this potential of the past in different ways. For example, they reuse their own archives to put the past into the present. To define this special way of connecting to the past, Bourdon (2018) attributes the concept of *institutional nostalgia.* He not only refers mainly to programmers and researchers who long for former media organizational forms, but also examines the ways in which journalists worked, for example. Bourdon evokes the rebroadcast of television shows as potentially categorized within so-called media nostalgia. In a media archaeology perspective of remembering (Pogačar, 2016), Mehrvarz and Muliaee (2020) reflect less on the content of what is nostalgically remembered, but put into the forefront the ahistorical aspects and potentials of tech-nostalgia when it comes to work in media archives and more generally in archives.

Hagedoorn (2017) suggests a hybrid form of institutional and media nostalgia by coining the term *programmed nostalgia*. This type of nostalgia research mainly concerns the analysis of the production and cross-media work that public and private media and cultural institutions implement (e.g., Natterer, 2017). As a digital platform, Netflix occupies a very special double role here as it mediates nostalgia in the form of new homemade productions with nostalgic styles and tones while simultaneously implementing nostalgic programming (Avilés-Santiago, 2019; Pallister, 2019).

During the COVID crisis, nostalgic programming has become a way to offer the public a homelike journey back to the past by screening significantly more old films, even including productions usually reserved for Christmastime. On digital platforms such as Facebook, sharing joyful memories of the past were also part of a nostalgic way of coping within the stagnation of an eternal present that seemed, in its suspended social animation, devoid of possibilities to create new memories. Of course, this does not necessarily mean that viewers, readers, players, or users become automatically nostalgic from consuming content diffused by industries or institutions; "nostalgic reception" is more complicated than that. Some researchers are already assessing the value of *media nostalgia* in terms of psychological well-being, in ways that are certainly not always intentional or prefabricated. Media-induced nostalgia as triggers of well-being (Wulf et al., 2018) is positioned as an ideal function of nostalgia programming. However, the precise nature of the relationship between digital media, practices of cultural consumption, and individual affective dimensions of nostalgic desire require more interrogation. Further research is necessary to critically penetrate the nostalgia loops that might surface between production and reception standpoints. In other words, future work on the production and reception of media nostalgia is still needed because it implies the nostalgic a priori condition of not only media users and consumers, but also the media industries and institutions themselves.

Conclusions and Perspectives

If we continue to distinguish—without imposing a strict categorization—between the different nostalgias that are shared in, via, and with media and (new) information and communication technologies and recognize their creative and progressive potentialities, we must not uncritically accept their political or economic exploitation. The distinction between joyful, playful nostalgia and more deeply rooted yearnings is characterized by reciprocal dynamics of temporal desire and contemporary longings that are not exclusively governed by media industries or other institutions but are the product of a complex interplay of the practices of media users and the technological and symbolic provision of media industries. The heterogeneous nature of nostalgic feeling and the diversity of its expressions (Bonnett, 2016) have the potential to lead to an epistemological change in both the formulation of nostalgia as a concept and a common feeling in everyday life where it remains still colonized by regressive meanings and by its linkage to the attenuation of social action in the present, rather than a potential enabler of it. To enact this epistemological change requires a critical approach to the digital commodification of nostalgia that undermines the potential for deep-rooted yearnings for the past, present, and future that connect the desire for the past to a critique of the present in the interests of a yet-to-be determined future.

Nostalgia as a feeling and as a practice will not disappear in the future and will likely follow its usual historical waves and moments, linked to moments of contemporary crisis and transition. Media institutions and industries will always be able to rely on nostalgic cultural styles and content for use in their production strategies as a simple bittersweet comforting tactic, an amusing reminder of the past or an entertaining anachronism. The range of pasts that are routinely reproduced in digital culture represents a rather narrow range of interests, formats, and time periods. Many archives have either been lost or are unprofitable, which leads to the reiteration of patterns of cultural dominance and class, racial, sexual privilege as witnessed with the rerun of *Friends*, for example. Nevertheless, the critique of commodified forms nostalgic content and styles does not adequately account for the progressive potential of nostalgia that exists alongside its commercial exploitation.

One future possibility is to diversify the lens of nostalgia research in the interests of recognizing the extent to which digital spaces provide opportunities for the articulation of more diverse types of nostalgia, specifically those that stimulate temporal desires with the potential to inform new visions of the future, are shared "online" (mostly via social media networks). Recent efforts to connect digital nostalgia research to areas of inquiry that reach beyond cultural aesthetics, or media economies, such as environmental communications, memory politics in the Global South (Ahad-Legardy, 2021), and sexual politics (Kies & West, 2017; Padva, 2015), provide promising signs that the future of research on nostalgia in digital culture is sharpening its critical analytical potential.

References

Abend, P., Bonner, M., & Weber, T. (Eds.). (2018). *Just little bits of history repeating: Medien, Nostalgie, Retromanie* (vol. 28 of Medien'welten. Braunschweiger Schriften zur Medienkultur). LIT Verlag.

Ahad-Legardy, B. (2021). *Afro-nostalgia: Feeling good in contemporary Black culture* (vol. *1*). University of Illinois Press.

Angé, O., & Berliner, D. (Eds.). (2015). *Anthropology and nostalgia*. Berghahn Books.

Arndt, J., Routledge, C., Sedikides, C., & Wildschut, T. (2006). Nostalgia: Content, triggers, functions. *Journal of Personality and Social Psychology*, *91*(5), 975–993.

Avilés-Santiago, M. G. (2019). "This is it!" [Is it?]: The marketing of nostalgia on Netflix's *One Day at a Time*. *Journal of Latin American Communication Research*, *7*(1–2), 60–78.

Bartholeyns, G. (2014). The instant past: Nostalgia and digital retro photography. In K. Niemeyer (Ed.), *Media and nostalgia* (pp. 51–69). Palgrave Macmillan.

Baschiera, S., & Caoduro, E. (Eds.). (2017). The new old: Archaisms and anachronisms across media. *Alphaville: Journal of Film and Screen Media*, *12*, 1–7.

Becker, T. (2018). The meanings of nostalgia: Genealogy and critique. *History and Theory*, *57*(2), 234–250.

Bevan, A. (2019). *The aesthetics of nostalgia TV: Production design and the boomer era*. Bloomsbury Academic.

Böhn, A., & Möser, K. (Eds.). (2010). *Techniknostalgie und Retrotechnologie*. KIT Scientific Publishing.

Bolzinger, A. (2007). *Histoire de la nostalgie*. Campagne Première.

Bonnett, A. (2016). *The geography of nostalgia: Global and local perspectives on modernity and loss*. Routledge.

Bourdon, J. (2018). Is the end of television coming to an end? *VIEW Journal of European Television History and Culture*, *7*(13), 80–95.

Boym, S. (2001). *The future of nostalgia*. Basic Books.

Burman, J. (2010). *Transnational yearnings: Tourism, migration and the diasporic city*. UBC Press.

Chopra-Gant, M. (2016). Pictures or it didn't happen: Photo-nostalgia, iPhoneography and the representation of everyday life. *Photography and Culture*, *9*(2), 121–133.

Dames, N. (2010). Nostalgia and its disciplines: A response. *Memory Studies*, *3*(3), 269–275.

Davies, J. (2010). Sustainable nostalgia. *Memory Studies*, *3*(3), 262–268.

Dodman, T. (2018). *What nostalgia was: War, empire, and the time of a deadly emotion*. University of Chicago Press.

Dwyer, M. D. (2015). *Back to the fifties: Nostalgia, Hollywood film, and popular music of the seventies and eighties*. Oxford University Press.

Estévez, S. M. (2005). Transnacionalismo a la ecuatoriana: migración, nostalgia y nuevas tecnologías. In G. Herrera, M. C. Carrillo, & A. Torres (Eds.), *La migración ecuatoriana: transnacionalismo, redes e identidades* (pp. 481–492). FLACSO.

Fantin, E., & Le Hégarat, T. (Eds.). (2016). L'Âge d'or. *Le Temps des médias*, *27*(2), 5–15.

Ferraz, T. (2017). Activating nostalgia: Cinemagoers' performances in Brazilian movie theatres reopening and protection cases. *Medien & Zeit*, *4*(*2017*), 72–82.

Fevry, S. (2017). Sepia cinema in Nicolas Sarkozy's France: Nostalgia and national identity. *Studies in French Cinema*, *17*(1), 60–74.

Galway, L. P., Beery, T., Jones-Casey, K., & Tasala, K. (2019), Mapping the solastalgia literature: A scoping review study. *International Journal of Environmental Research and Public Health*, *16*, 2662.

Gammon, S., & Ramshaw, G. (2021). Distancing from the present: Nostalgia and leisure in lockdown. *Leisure Sciences*, *43*(1–2), 131–137.

Gibbs, H., & Egermann, H. (2021). Music-evoked nostalgia and wellbeing during the United Kingdom COVID-19 pandemic: Content, subjective effects, and function. *Frontiers in Psychology*, *12*, p. 787.

Grainge, P. (2000). *Monochrome memories: Nostalgia and style in 1990s America* [Doctoral thesis, University of Nottingham]. http://eprints.nottingham.ac.uk/12833/1/313203.pdf

Hagedoorn, B. (2017). Collective cultural memory as a TV guide: "Living" history and nostalgia on the digital television platform. *Acta Universitatis Sapientiae, Film and Media Studies*, *14*(1), 71–94.

Hartog, F. (2015): *Regimes of historicity: Presentism and experiences of time*. Columbia University Press.

Hoskins, A. (2017). The restless past: An introduction to digital memory and media in *Digital Memory Studies*. Routledge; pp. 1–24.

Howell, J. P., Kitson, J., & Clowney, D. (2019). Environments past: Nostalgia in environmental policy and governance. *Environmental Values, 28*(3), 305–323.

Hussain, F. (2020, March 27). *Lockdown opens the floodgates of nostalgia as netizens share old photographs. Times of India*. https://timesofindia.indiatimes.com/city/bengaluru/lockdown-opens-floodgates-of-nostalgia-as-netizens-share-old-photographs/articleshow/74841375.cms?utm_source=contentofinterest&utm_medium=text&utm_campaign=cppst

Ivănescu, A. (2019). *Popular music in the nostalgia video game: The way it never sounded*. Springer International Publishing.

Jacobsen, M. H. (Ed.). (2020). *Nostalgia now: Cross-disciplinary perspectives on the past in the present*. Routledge.

Jameson, F. (1991). *Postmodernism, or, the cultural logic of late capitalism*. Duke University Press.

Kay, J. B., Mahoney, C., & Shaw, C. (2017). *The past in visual culture: Essays on memory, nostalgia and the media*. Macfarland.

Keightley, E., & Pickering, M. (2006). The modalities of nostalgia. *Current Sociology, 54*(6), 919–941.

Kies, B., & West, T. J. III (Eds.). (2017). Queer nostalgia and queer histories in uncertain times. *Queer Studies in Media & Popular Culture, 2*(2), 161–165.

Kisukidi, N. Y. (2014). Nostalgia and postcolonial utopia in Senghor's négritude. In K. Niemeyer (Ed.), *Media and nostalgia* (pp. 191–202). Macmillan.

Knowles, K. (Ed.). (2015). Locating vintage. Special issue on vintage. *European Journal for Media Studies, 4*(2). https://necsus-ejms.org/locating-vintage/

Landgrebe, A. (2020). Between hatred and nostalgia: Creating a new vision of Polish jewry in the Third Polish Republic (1995–2005). *Nordisk Judaistik/Scandinavian Jewish Studies, 31*(1), 76–86.

Lee, E., & Koblin, J. (2020). Glued to TV for now, but when programming thins and bills mount . . . *New York Times*. https://www.nytimes.com/2020/03/17/business/media/coronavirus-television-netflix.html

Lems, A. (2016). Ambiguous longings: Nostalgia as the interplay among self, time and world. *Critique of Anthropology, 36*(40), 419–438.

Lizardi, R. (2015). *Mediated nostalgia: Individual memory and contemporary mass media*. Lexington Books.

Magaudda, P., & Minniti, S. (2019). Retromedia-in-practice: A practice theory approach for rethinking old and new media technologies. *Convergence, 25*(4), 673–693.

Marks, U. L. (2002). *Touch: Sensuous theory and multisensory media*. University of Minnesota Press.

Martin, J. (2021). Keep crafting and carry on: Nostalgia and domestic cultures in the crisis. *European Journal of Cultural Studies, 24*(1), 358–364.

Mehrvarz, M., & Muliaee, M. (2020). Media-as-things: A nonhistorical nostalgia through failure. In R. Lizardi (Ed.), *Subjective experiences of interactive nostalgia in media* (pp. 167–186). Peter Lang Publishing.

Menke, M. (2017). Seeking comfort in past media: Modeling media nostalgia as a way of coping with media change. *International Journal of Communication, 11*, 626–646.

Menke, M. (2018). *Mediennostalgie in digitalen Öffentlichkeiten: zum kollektiven Umgang mit Medien-und Gesellschaftswandel*. Herbert von Halem Verlag.

Menke, M., & Niemeyer, K. (2019). Retro, vintage, nostalgie: Zur visuellen Kommunikation des Vergangenen und des Vergehens. In K. Lobinger (Ed.), *Handbuch VisuelleKommunikationsforschung* (pp. 1–18). Springer.

Merrill, S., Keightley, E., & Daphi, P. (2020). Introduction: the digital memory work practices of social movements. In Merrill, Keightley, & Daphi (Eds.), *Social movements, cultural memory, and digital media*. Palgrave Macmillan.

Natterer, K. (2017). *Nostalgie als Zukunftsstrategie Fur Unterhaltungsmedien: Empirische Studien Zu Personlicher Und Historischer Nostalgie in Medien*. Springer.

Niemeyer, K. (2022). Nostalgia and media. Media philosophy and nostalgising in times of crisis. In M. H. Jacobsen (Ed.), *Intimations of nostalgia multidisciplinary explorations of an enduring emotion* (pp. 152–170). Bristol University Press.

Niemeyer, K. (Ed.). (2014). *Media and nostalgia: Yearning for the past, present and future*. Palgrave Macmillan.

Niemeyer, K. (2015). A theoretical approach to vintage, from oenology to media. *European Journal of Media Studies*, *4*(2), 85–102.

Niemeyer, K. (2016). Digital nostalgia. *Media Development*, *4*, 27–31.

Niemeyer, K., & Keightley, E. (2020). The commodification of time and memory: Online communities and the dynamics of commercially produced nostalgia. *New Media & Society*, *22*(9), 1639–1662.

Ochonicky, A. (2020). *The American Midwest in film and literature: Nostalgia, violence, and regionalism*. Indiana University Press.

Padva, G. (2015). *Queer nostalgia in cinema and popular culture*. Palgrave Macmillan.

Pallister, K. (Ed.). (2019). *Netflix nostalgia: Streaming the past on demand*. Rowman & Littlefield.

Pogačar, M. (2016). *Media archaeologies, micro-archives and storytelling: Re-presencing the past*. Springer.

Reading, A. (2011). Memory and digital media: Six dynamics of the global memory field. In M. Neiger, O. Meyers, & E. Zandberg (Eds.), *On media memory* (pp. 241–252). Palgrave Macmillan Memory Studies. Palgrave Macmillan. https://doi.org/10.1057/9780230307070_18

Richards, L., Heath, A., & Elgenius, G. (2020). Remainers are nostalgic too: An exploration of attitudes towards the past and Brexit preferences. *British Journal of Sociology*, *71*(1), 74–80.

Sampson, T. D. (2012). *Virality: Contagion theory in the age of networks*. University of Minnesota Press.

Santa Cruz, L., & Ferraz, T. (Eds.). (2019). *Nostalgias e mídia: No caleidoscópio do tempo*. e-papers.

Scanlan, S. (2004). Introduction: Nostalgia. *Iowa Journal of Cultural Studies*, *5*, 3–9.

Schrey, D. (2014). Analogue nostalgia and the aesthetics of digital remediation. In K. Niemeyer (Ed.), *Media and nostalgia* (pp. 27–38). Palgrave Macmillan.

Schrey, D. (2017). *Analoge Nostalgie in der digitalen Medienkultur*. Kadmos.

Sedikides, C., & Wildschut W. (2020). The motivational potency of nostalgia: The future is called yesterday. *Advances in Motivation Science*, *7*, 75–111.

Sedikides, C., Wildschut, T., Routledge, C., Arndt, J., Hepper, E.G., & Zhou, X. (2015). To nostalgize: Mixing memory with affect and desire. In *Advances in experimental social psychology 51* (pp. 189–273). Academic Press.

Sielke, S. (2019). Retro aesthetics, affect, and nostalgia effects in recent US-American cinema: The cases of *La La Land* (2016) and *The Shape of Water* (2017). *Arts*, *8*(3), 87.

Sperb, J. (2015). *Flickers of film: Nostalgia in the time of digital cinema*. Rutgers University Press.

Steenvoorden, E., & Harteveld, E. (2018). The appeal of nostalgia: The influence of societal pessimism on support for populist radical right parties. *West European Politics*, *41*(1), 28–52.

Steiner, J. (2020). Zum kreativen und progressiven Potenzial von Nostalgie in der Retro-Serie Stranger Things. *ffk Journal*, *5*, 366–386.

Sterne, J. (2016). Analog. In B. Peters (Ed.), *Digital keywords* (pp. 31–44). Princeton University Press.

Toniolo, F., & Giovannini, S. (2020). Gli elementi nostalgici dei punta-e-clicca italiani degli Anni Dieci = Nostalgic elements in Italian point-and-click video games of the 2010s. *H-ermes: Journal of Communication, 16*, 81–98.

van der Heijden, T. (2015). Technostalgia of the present: From technologies of memory to a memory of technologies. *European Journal of Media Studies, 4*(2), 103–121.

Wills, J. (2002): Digital dinosaurs and artificial life: Exploring the culture of nature in computer and video games. *Cultural Values, 6*(4), 395–417.

Wulf, T., Rieger, D., & Schmitt, J. B. (2018). Blissed by the past: Theorizing media-induced nostalgia as an audience response factor for entertainment and well-being. *Poetics, 69*, 70–80.

PART VI

FROM THE PERSON TO THE COMMUNITY AND SOCIETY

15

Hybrid Methodologies for Studying Social and Cultural Memory in the Postdigital Age

Samuel Merrill

It has been more than twenty years since Radstone noted that social science and humanities research about memory demands "not just combinations of, but, more accurately, hybridized methods" (2000, p. 13). One of the earliest attempts to foreground issues of methodology within social and cultural memory research, Radstone's edited volume, *Memory and Methodology*, conceptualized these hybridized methods primarily with respect to liminal understandings of memory that crossed academic disciplines. In this respect, the methods highlighted by the volume were more conceptually oriented than practically aligned, including, for example, integrating technological and psychoanalytic ideas of memory (see Locke, 2000).

Since then, we have witnessed the growing pervasiveness of internet and social media platforms, associated advances in digital technology and media, and the overall deepening of society and culture's mediatization, digitalization, and datafication. For some, the ubiquity of these platforms, technologies, media, and processes has rendered contemporary life in much of the world "postdigital." Rather than indicating the end of digitality per see, the *postdigital* term demarks "the immersive and disorientating experiences of computational infrastructures as they scale-up and intensify" (Berry & Dieter, 2015, p. 4) and pragmatically helps describe "either a contemporary disenchantment with digital information systems and media gadgets, or a period in which our fascination with these systems and gadgets has become historical" (Cramer, 2015, p. 13).

Recognizing that these developments have increased the need for, and appeal of, not only "hybridized methods" but also more appropriately "hybrid methodologies" suited to the study of social and cultural memory in the postdigital age, in this chapter I specify some of the different sorts of hybridity that such methodologies can target. In turn, I discuss some of the impulses and procedures on which these methodologies might rely. The general focus of the chapter, reflecting my own disciplinary background and research endeavors to

Samuel Merrill, *Hybrid Methodologies for Studying Social and Cultural Memory in the Postdigital Age* In: *The Remaking of Memory in the Age of the Internet and Social Media*. Edited by: Qi Wang and Andrew Hoskins, Oxford University Press.
 DOI: 10.1093/oso/9780197661260.003.0015

date, centers primarily on social and cultural forms of memory, but much of it arguably has relevance for the wider interdisciplinary study of memory, including in its cognitive forms. Overall, I aim to explore hybrid methodologies as a means of studying hybrid objects of analysis like memory, rather than hybridized methods as the combination of methods. To expand, while hybridized methods and hybrid methodologies certainly carry similar meanings, I use the latter term to refer to research procedures and rationales suited to the study of phenomena that can be considered to be ontologically hybrid and reserve the former for instances involving the amalgamation of research tools whether or not such tools are turned toward understanding ontologically hybrid phenomena.

I begin by discussing some of the social science and humanities literature on memory research methods. In this task, I foreground Radstone's volume (2000), alongside Keightley and Pickering's *Research Methods for Memory Studies* (2013) and Drozdzewski and Birdsall's *Doing Memory Research: New Methods and Approaches* (2019a) because these are the major book-length publications that are explicitly dedicated (in title at least) to methodological matters within the study of social and cultural memory published in the last 25 years. I do this not only to highlight a continuing deficit in explicit methodological discussions within the field of social and cultural memory studies but also to identify how hybridized and hybrid methods and methodologies have been conceived, if at all. In these initial efforts, as with the rest of the chapter, my focus remains on those methods and methodologies that engage digital technology and digital media. This does not mean to deny the possibility of non- or less-digital hybrid methodologies but rather reflects the goals of this volume and my own research interest in the digital memory practices of activists and social movements and the digital commemoration of traumatic events.

In the second section of this chapter, I suggest several trajectories of hybridity (technological, spatial, temporal, and agentic) that hybrid methodologies might target. Thereafter, in a third section I discuss some impulses and procedures that underpin my understanding of hybrid methodologies and which might serve to practically inform the methodological choices of others. Where possible and productive, the points covered in these two sections are illustrated through brief references to concepts and cases from my own research. The essay closes with a speculative consideration of the future of hybrid methodologies for social and cultural memory research.

Toward Hybrid Methodologies for Social and Cultural Memory Research

Within Radstone's volume, Locke's (2000) early discussion of the circularity of human and digital memory and the mnemonic influence of artificial intelligence and intelligent agents is the most relevant to the task at hand. His chapter is hybrid insofar as it conceptually shifts between technological and psychoanalytic registers, but not in a strictly methodological sense. In fact, as is mostly the case with the volume's other contributors who primarily use life story and narrative analysis approaches to understand memory's liminality, Locke's methodology is for the most part implicitly communicated rather than explicitly discussed. This reflects a general situation within social and cultural memory studies whereby the literature dedicated to memory research methods is arguably lacking relative to the continued expansion of the field.[1] Wulf Kansteiner noted around two decades ago: "The success of memory studies has not been accompanied by significant conceptual and methodological advances in the research of collective memory" (2002, p. 179). Social and cultural memory studies have since become characterized by varied and vibrant conceptual debates and developments, but this has not been matched in terms of explicit discussions of method and methodology. Illustrating this, at the time of (first) writing (in September 2021), searching the *Memory Studies* journal (published since 2008) for articles containing "method(s)," "methodology," or "methodologies" in their title or keywords list returned just five results.[2] Besides Radstone's volume, two further exceptions to this general situation are the edited volumes by Keightley and Pickering (2013) and Drozdzewski and Birdsall (2019a).

In the introduction to their volume, *Research Methods for Memory Studies,* Pickering and Keightley acknowledge that empirical work in memory studies "has usually been presented with little, if any, attention to the methods that have been employed, or the methodological implications of what has been studied" (2013, p. 2). While hybridized methods are not explicitly mentioned in the volume, they are conveyed to some degree by the emphasis placed on creative interdisciplinary exchange, mixed methods, and methodological pluralism. Of all its contributions, it is perhaps Basu's (2013) discussion of "multi-sited methods" that most encapsulates the hybrid sensibility I wish to foreground in this essay. Multi-sited methods, in opening up what constitutes a "site," pertain to the study of memories across numerous sites while appreciating that each site will require quite different research methods and thus their appropriate combination. Suited to investigating "associations and connections between the distributed sites of memory," multi-sited methods have the capacity to also accommodate digital sites of memory even if Basu does not discuss this explicitly (2013, p. 118). Besides a few brief mentions, the methodological implications of digital technology and media for memory research are not covered in the volume. This is not surprising given its aim to explicate some of the methods that had implicitly underpinned earlier memory research.

Where the contribution of Keightley and Pickering's volume is retrospective, Drozdzewski and Birdsall's later volume, *Doing Memory Research* (2019a; see also Drozdzewski & Birdsall 2019b), in its emphasis on new methods and approaches, is more forward looking. The contributions to their volume foreground new phenomenologically informed "emplaced methods" that support sensory-based memory research as well as memory-mapping techniques, including those that utilize digital technology and software or map digital content. While many of the contributions rely on what Rogers (2013) calls "digitized methods"—preexisting methods that have been applied to new digital settings and objects—others apply what he distinguishes as "digital methods" (those originating from digital settings and objects). The sorts of hybrid methodologies that I wish to stress in this chapter are hinted at by some contributors, including by Osborne (2019) in her use of biosensing technology to understand visceral remembering in urban conservation areas. However, appeals to hybridity remain mostly restricted to mixed-methods approaches (e.g., the combination of methods), and the only explicit reference to hybridity conceives it primarily in terms of research that crosses disciplinary boundaries.

While interdisciplinarity and mixed methods certainly connect with the use of hybridized methods, these are not synonymous with what I call hybrid methodologies. Hybrid methodologies, as I conceive them, often depend on the combination of methods drawn from across disciplines but, ultimately, exceed this by relating also to ontological assumptions about their objects of analysis. In addition, even if my focus here is turned toward "the digital," I also want to avoid simply equating digital methods with hybrid methodologies. At the same time, within social and cultural memory studies, developments in both can be anchored to the so-called third wave of memory research that has foregrounded new degrees of mnemonic mobility, dynamism, and plurality in an increasingly digitalized and globalized world. This wave has undoubtedly reinvigorated the field, partly by introducing the "trans" prefix to preexisting scales of analysis to emphasize memory's liminalities, percolations, exchanges, and alterations in ways that encourage its hybrid conceptualization and, in turn, the development of hybrid methodologies.

However, despite these theoretical advances, methodologically much social sciences and humanities research still seems to conceive memory in a paradoxically static manner. In other words, the analytical focus still often reverts to the product rather than its production, whereby the boundary crossing of memories is often retrospectively recounted, as if with a neat start and finish, in order to evidence the existence of transnational, transcultural, translocal, or transmedial remembrance rather than being wholeheartedly problematized and interrogated as an unfolding and ongoing process worthy of scrutiny in and of itself.[3] This is partly, I believe, because of the tendency to approach the internet as well as social media platforms primarily as digital archives or sites of memory. In short, social and cultural memory scholars still generally prefer digitized to digital methods and tend to mobilize "digital sources but not digital analysis" (Bernstein, 2016, p. 424; Rogers, 2013). While this is not wholly unproductive, it might inhibit the realization of the internet and social media's methodological promise. Even with the increased uptake of new "truly" digital methods by memory scholars, the further development of hybrid methodologies can help further address this shortcoming. The explication of such hybrid methodologies is necessary not only to counter social and cultural memory studies' long-standing methodological opacity but also because of the dynamic and complex qualities of the internet and its associated digital technologies and media. It is to this task of explication that I now turn by specifying some different trajectories of hybridity associated with society's continued mediatization, digitalization, and datafication.

Three Trajectories of Hybridity

Digital-Nondigital: Technological and Spatial Hybridity

Arguably, the most prominent trajectory of hybridity associated specifically with the internet relates to the ontological reconsideration of the societal conditions created by the continued advance of its associated digital technologies, media, and platforms. In short, in their ever more digitalized form society and culture are increasingly conceived of as hybrid themselves—constituted by a mix and amalgamation of both digitally and nondigitally imbricated elements. Recognition of this hybridity, which is usually conceived in technological or spatial terms (see Chadwick, 2013; Silva, 2006; see also Halstead, 2021; Merrill, 2017), has involved the revision of earlier academic attitudes that tended to separately conceive of, and often discretely study, the so-called "offline" and "online" or "real" and "virtual" with digital phenomenon originally regarded as somehow less authentic than their nondigital counterparts (see Lindgren et al., 2014). The popular and academic usage of terms like offline, online, real, and virtual, however, continues unabated, even as everyday life, particularly in some parts of the world, advances toward that postdigital state where the use of "digital" and "internet" as distinguishing prefixes becomes obsolete (Berry, 2014; Merrill & Lindgren, 2021).

An early, alternative vocabulary, which displays a greater hybrid sensitivity, is offered by Milgram and Kishino via their concept of the "reality-virtuality continuum" (1994), a concept that has framed the design of visual display technology for the last 25 years. Hybridity appears within this continuum as "mixed reality," itself split between augmented reality and augmented virtuality with all these points in the continuum also captured by the later notion of extended reality. The continued development and deployment of extended reality technology is likely to further highlight how "digitally (re)mediated memory remains spatially bound" (Merrill, 2017, p. 38) while having considerable impact on the formation of both individual and collective memory. Cultural memory studies research that relies on what can broadly be considered as a hybrid methodology has begun to explore such matters (see Reading et al., 2021). Meanwhile, with others (Merrill, 2017, 2019; Merrill & Lindgren 2021; Merrill et al., 2020), I have also sought to develop concepts and vocabularies that are sensitive to this technological and spatial hybridity not least through reference to "the more or/and less digital." This phrase seeks to encourage the conceptualization and study of the relationship between the digital and nondigital in graduated terms.[4]

Now-Before/After-Now: Temporal Hybridity

A further trajectory of hybridity I want to highlight relates to the blending of different temporalities created by society's digital mediatization and its associated processes of "time-space compression" (Harvey, 1989) and "time-space distanciation" (Giddens, 1990). Viriljo discusses this temporal hybridity in terms of the "acceleration of real time" that is caused by digital communication technologies and that leads to the disintegration of distinctions between past, present, and future (2005, p. 118; see Keightley, 2013). Similarly, Castells writes of a compressed and desequenced "timeless time" created under the conditions of instantaneous real-time digital communication (2010). In terms of memory, I have found it useful to approach this sort of temporal hybridity via the concept of "context collapse." This concept helps explain how digital technologies, platforms, and media can merge not only multiple spatial but also temporal and mnemonic contexts into one another (see Brandtzaeg & Lüders, 2018; Marwick & boyd, 2011; Merrill, 2020; see also Pogačar, Chapter 16, this volume). Attention to temporal hybridity is, as might be expected, quite marked within contemporary memory scholarship. Erll notes how the ongoing hybridization of so-called traveling memory "engenders complex temporal phenomena, such as time-space compression and anachronies" (2011, p. 13). Hoskins and Tulloch, meanwhile, highlight how the sense of immediacy created by an overabundance of digital information and connectivity leads to forms of mediatized hyperconnectivity that afford "temporal proximity (and distance) to the past and an emergent future" (2016, p. 9), creating a sort of "extended now" (see Hoskins, 2017b, p. 2). In this hybrid of the "now," "before-," and "after-now" the past and present not only merge but also can be projected forward in time as a future-oriented form of "prospective memory" (Tenenboim-Weinblatt, 2013).

While the generalized characterization of the temporal consequences of digital mediatization in terms of acceleration is often justified, digital immediacy it neither unrelenting nor inevitable.

An overfocus on the immediacy of digital media can obscure other forms of temporal hybridity related to the technological and spatial trajectories of hybridity already mentioned. Keightley (2013), for example, stresses how different intersecting temporal experiences are facilitated by an array of media technologies within various zones of intermediacy. She writes: "Digital technologies and their distinctive temporal logics interweave with older technologies and their temporal provisions" (2013, p. 63). Kaun (2015), meanwhile, has discussed how different internet and social media platforms create their own specific temporal regimes in much a similar way as nondigital spaces (cf. Till, 2004). As Pentzold has highlighted, these finer-grained understandings of digitally mediatized temporality also bridge notions of communicative and cultural memory and their commonly conceived time spans "It is a mistake to separate non-mediated lived memories and mediated distant memories, because our acts of imagining, constructing, and presenting the past usually involve communicative practices as well as media texts and technologies" (2018, p. 933). Similarly, the mediatization, digitalization, and datafication of memory erodes conceptual distinctions between individual and collective memory in ways that encourage memory's reconceptualization in a more connective and multitudinous manner (Hoskins, 2017a).

Human-Nonhuman: Agentic Hybridity

The final trajectory of hybridity associated with the internet and social media that I foreground relates to agency and its distribution between not only the individual and collective but also human and nonhuman actors. If we accept that ever-deepening forms of mediatization and digitalization have created new technologically, spatially, and temporally hybrid experiences, then it is also critical that we acknowledge that the processes of datafication that underpin the digital workings of this existence are hybrid in themselves insofar as they are influenced by the combined energies of human and nonhuman actors. Set against the backdrop of the wider adoption of Latour's actor network theory (2005), this sort of agentic hybridity has recently been highlighted by the broad wave of research dedicated to the social power and societal impacts of digital algorithms (see Beer, 2017). Digital algorithms are essentially mathematical procedures that underpin intelligent agent software and, in turn, artificial intelligence systems and that process data to produce new forms of data in response to specific tasks, including those of a mnemonic character (see Smit, Chapter 13, this volume) Recent research on them has placed renewed emphasis on how much of our contemporary digital labors have been delegated to algorithmically informed intelligent agents (see again Locke, 2000), especially in terms of navigating the sublimity of the internet. In turn, when algorithms are used in, for example, internet search engines and social media recommendation systems, "the social consequences can be far-reaching and devastating" (Lindgren, 2022, p. 203; see, e.g., Noble, 2018). Acknowledging the potential mnemonic agency of artificial intelligence and algorithms is important (see Merrill, 2023a), but also it is important to avoid thinking of them purely in nonhuman and abstract terms. Just as computers do not run without human assistance, algorithms are not simply "cold mechanisms"—they have been designed and are underpinned by "warm human and institutional choices," including those related to the data sets on which they are trained (Berry, 2014; Denton et al., 2021; Gillespie, 2014, p. 169; Lindgren, 2022).

Of specific relevance to social and cultural memory studies, sensitivity to this trajectory of hybridity (as well as the others) is conveyed by the media archaeology approach. Ernst, a leading proponent of that approach, for example, reminds us that the Internet should not be approached as an archive of digital and digitized material in the strictest sense but rather as a database of information. He writes: "The real archive on the Internet (in the sense of arché) is its systems of technological protocols" (2012, p. 85). Algorithms also remember and forget. For example, alongside, and again often in collaboration with, human content moderators, they lie behind the removal of copyright infringing, pornographic, or violent content from the search engine indexes that other algorithms scour according to individual retrieval requests (Gillespie, 2014). In this respect, not only distinguishing between but also appreciating the mixing of different "assemblages" and "constellations" created by algorithm-based systems like search engines can be productive because these concepts attribute agency to nonhuman and human actors in different measure (see Merrill, 2023b).

Hybrid Methodological Impulses and Procedures

On a general level, methodologies that aim to understand the trajectories of hybridity outlined above can be said to (1) approach the complex and challenging technological and spatial conditions of our increasingly digitalized lives without isolating the digital and nondigital or relying on vocabularies that imply a hierarchical relationship between them; (2) conceive of contemporary temporality as both folded in on itself and diversified through processes of mediatization that create an extended now that is cojoined to both the before-now and after-now;

and (3) be sensitive to the agentic hybridity created by society's mounting datafication in terms of not only their objects of study but also the methodological decisions on which they themselves rely. In these aims, it is worth noting that hybrid methodologies share commonalities with and can take inspiration from other methodological approaches. These include the "ambivalent" and "anarchistic methodologies" promoted by Lindgren that involve the pragmatic bricolage of automated computational methods (digital methods) with manual interpretative methods (digitized and nondigital methods) in ways that both invoke previous mixed-method approaches and break down divisions between so-called quantitative and qualitative methods (2021). They also include Back and Puwar's "live methods," which, among other things, stress the need for new modes of real-time investigation that enfold research processes of collection, analysis, and dissemination and are adept at conveying extended understandings of the mediatized present without being trapped by the now (2012). Finally, Marres and Gerlitz's "interface methods" should be mentioned for their incorporation of concerns related to the ambiguous methodological bias associated with research that involves digital platforms and data, as well as a sensitivity for the agencies involved in such research and their assumed hierarchies (2016).

While reference to these broader social sciences methodological agendas helps further pin down the idea of hybrid methodologies through association, it does not really help exemplify how such methodologies might look when deployed within the field of social and cultural memory studies. To this end, I use the remainder of this chapter to briefly draw attention to a couple of the impulses and procedures that I recognize to underpin my own hybrid methodological approach through reference to some of my empirical research. I do this not to position them as the only hybrid methodological impulses and procedures but rather to provide some examples of what such impulses and procedures might look like in practice.

Embracing Complexity and Messiness

One of the main impulses that underpins my own attempts to understand the influence of different trajectories of hybridity on issues relating to memory is the acceptance of the complexity or, perhaps more appropriately, the messiness surrounding the objects I study. Channeling Law and following others in their attempts to methodologically approach mess (2004; see also Lindgren, 2021; Postill & Pink, 2012), this impulse acknowledges that studying hybridity often involves points of inexactitude. While such inexactitude has been methodologically conventionalized in "less digital" settings (e.g., the acknowledgment that the traditional archive is selective), it still presents a stumbling block for many when they turn to the "more digital" elements of hybrid experiences (e.g., the desire to collect "all" the data). With respect to the latter, this messiness can pertain to the deletion of websites, "broken data" (see Pink et al., 2018), or inescapably personalized search engine results.

Accepting this mess as constitutive of hybrid complexity (see also Fawns, Chapter 7, this volume) might mean that a study cannot be easily reproduced but also provides new routes to knowing. This applies to memory research. Take, for example, the case of Silvio Meier, a left-wing activist who was killed in Berlin in 1992 by neo-Nazis and whose remembrance continues to spread across an array of more-or-less digital spaces in accordance with an array of competing and overlapping temporalities (Merrill & Lindgren, 2020). In the process of researching Meier's remembrance, one important digital space of his remembrance, an independent news website, was banned and taken offline by the German government. This, however, helped foreground not only some of the vulnerabilities of Meier's more digital spaces of remembrance but also the hybrid character of his memory in general—laws were consulted, police were dispatched, servers were seized, digital memory disappeared. As another example, the search engine personalization algorithms that through their very biases open up the opportunity to explore the agentic hybridity behind the results they provide and their influence on memory (see Merrill, 2023b).

Following Mnemonic Objects

On a more practical level, I have found that the procedure of following research objects can help in the task of approaching the complexity and messiness of the hybrid webs of connections in which such objects now sit and move. "Following," as an academic methodological praxis, is, of course, well established in an array of different disciplines (see, e.g., Appardurai, 1986; Latour, 2005) and its utility in terms of following specific memories has also been noted (see Basu, 2013; Erll, 2011). This utility increasingly relates to the fact that memories or perhaps more appropriately mnemonic objects circulate in a hybrid manner across and between technologies, spaces, temporalities, and agents, creating mnemonic assemblages and constellations that are both digitally and nondigitally imbricated; of the now, before-now, and after-now; and shaped by both human and nonhuman agents (Merrill, 2023b).

In practice, as I have demonstrated with regard to the activist appropriation of an historical protest photo (see Merrill, 2020, 2023b), the following method involves both "tracing" an object backward in time and "tracking" it forward in time while paying particular attention to moments when it "changes direction" due to, for example, processes of remediation, translation, translocation, or transduction. While most of these processes have been substantially explored in memory studies (see De Cesari & Rigney, 2014; Erll & Rigney, 2009; see also Evans & Rigato, Chapter 11, this volume), the idea of transduction, which foregrounds the networks of matter and energy underpinning the spread of digital content (see Kinsley, 2014), remains underapplied despite its hybrid sensitivity. In the case of the historical protest photo, my efforts to follow it over a period of three years using a combination of methods, including archival research, interviews, social media, and search engine analysis, and drawing on material including newspapers, artworks, books, ephemera, artifacts, Wikipedia entries, Google results, and tweets, helped to foreground moments of the photo's hybrid transduction, including when it appeared in street activism. In this instance, the procedure of following helped to spotlight transductive processes whereby activists, having been reminded of the photo by viral social media content, located it on the internet using a search engine; downloaded and digitally altered it to feature in a protest sticker using image-editing software; had the sticker mass printed; and sold it, leading it to "touch down" in (primarily) urban environments that included the campus building where I have my office (see Merrill, 2020).

Enrolling Computational Collaborators

The idea of enrolling computational collaborators in efforts to make sense of the complexity and messiness of hybrid objects of analysis and to aid us when we might lose sight of them in the thick of the crowd can indicate, at different levels, both a hybrid methodological procedure and impulse. Computers, software, code, algorithms, and more have been procedurally enrolled by numerous scholars interested in essentially hybrid phenomena if only through the contribution that digital and digitized methods have made to their methodologies. But, at a more speculative level, the impulse to consider such things as research collaborators and not merely tools, speaks to the sorts of twofold agentic hybridity mentioned above—that is the agency they have not only as objects of study but also the agency that they have as means of study. Illustrating this, as this essay was being reviewed by the volume's editors (November 2022), ChatGPT, an artificial intelligence chatbot developed by OpenAI, was launched. By January 2023, ChatGPT had already been listed as a coauthor on several academic papers.

While not presented in these exact terms or to this extent, a similar impulse can be discerned in Kozinets's redefined and expanded approach to netnography which highlights the possibility of integrating the sorts of computational methods more commonly associated with data science (2015; see Lindgren, 2021). The possibility to foreground the agency rather than intentionality of computational tools by explicitly thinking of them in terms of collaborators has presented itself to me most powerfully when I have been carrying out my own hybrid ethnographies (see Hine, 2015; Kozinets, 2015) during commemorative events that mark the anniversaries of terror attacks or other traumatic events (see Merrill, 2018, 2019; Merrill et al., 2020). For instance, when running automatic data collection tasks concurrently with embodied, team-based participant observation in both urban and digital space, it became persuasive to think of the programming code that was collecting social media content in real time as a nonhuman collaborator. The code was able to record tweets at a rate and for a duration that no other member of the research team could match, thus providing benefits related to extending the scope of our observations. But it was not infallible. Just as each of my human collaborators balanced participation and observation differently (see Gold, 1958) and focused on different elements of the hybrid field site and were inescapably selective in their note making, so did this nonhuman collaborator. Adopting a perspective closer to that of complete observer, the code focused specifically on a set of Twitter (now X) hashtags and generated notes that were thus also piecemeal and only partial.

Conclusion: The Future of Hybrid Methodologies for Social and Cultural Memory Research

In this chapter I have foregrounded some different trajectories of hybridity and several methodological impulses and procedures with the hope of aiding the future development of hybrid methodologies suited for the study of memory in the postdigital age. The pursuit of such methodologies is likely to become even more necessary in years to come. This will especially be the case if processes of mediatization, digitalization, and datafication continue apace with the result that memory's hybridity will increasingly exceed those technological, spatial, temporal, and agentic trajectories, which I have heuristically singled out here, and come to more accurately relate to their combined accretion and the emergence of even more cyborgian forms of remembrance: "a hybrid of machine and organism" (Haraway, 1991, p. 147; Merrill, 2023a). In this eventuality, human and digital memory will not merely supplement or characterize each other but constitute each other (see Locke, 2000).

Such predictions, given their corollary that soon almost everything might be more acutely perceived as relating to memory, also speak to the potential need to develop hybrid methodologies that are intrinsically memory oriented. In pursuit of such a methodology, perhaps we might start to distinguish "memory methods" from "memory-ized methods," echoing the differences between digital and digitized methods (cf. Rogers, 2013). After all, like the data underpinning digital memory, the memories at the center of human remembering are always incomplete.

Notes

1. It should be noted that the deficit in the explicit discussion of methods and methodologies does not characterize all disciplinary corners of the study of memory. The investigation of cognitive memory within psychology, for example, is underpinned by the rigorous discussion of methodological matters.
2. This does not mean that *Memory Studies* articles do not discuss method and methodology at all. Searches for these words anywhere in the journal returned 416 results. At the time of the search (September 14, 2021), there were 625 *Memory Studies* articles indexed in Scopus.
3. This observation was made in discussion with Rik Smit as part of our motivation for a 2016 European Communication Research and Education Association (ECREA) panel: "'From Transnational to Transnationalising Memory Work: The Mechanics of Mnemonic Movements."
4. Conceptual vocabularies are, of course, tricky. This attempt to avoid misleadingly dichotomous terms still somewhat relies on them. The explanation of the idea of "the more or/and less digital" often requires reference to "the digital" and "the nondigital," centering digitality and creating new hierarchies.

References

Appadurai, A. (Ed.). (1986). *The social life of things: Commodities in cultural perspective.* Cambridge University Press.

Back, L., & Puwar, N. (2012). A manifesto for live methods: Provocations and capacities. *Sociological Review*, 60(1), 6–17. https://doi.org/10.1111/j.1467-954X.2012.02114.x

Basu, P. (2013). Memoryscapes and multi-sited methods. In E. Keightley & M. Pickering (Eds.), *Research methods for memory studies* (pp. 115–131). Edinburgh University Press.

Beer, D. (2017). The social power of algorithms. Information, *Communication & Society*, *20*(1), 1–13. https://doi.org/10.1080/1369118X.2016.1216147

Bernstein, S. (2016). Remembering war, remaining Soviet: Digital commemoration of World War II in Putin's Russia. *Memory Studies*, *9*(4), 422–436. https://doi.org/10.1177/17506 98015605573

Berry, D. M. (2014). *Critical theory and the digital.* Bloomsbury.

Berry, D. M., & Dieter, M. (2015). Thinking postdigital aesthetics: Art, computation and design. In D. M. Berry & M. Dieter (Eds.), Postdigital *aesthetics* (pp. 1–11). Palgrave Macmillan.

Brandtzaeg, P. B., & Lüders, M. (2018). Time collapse in social media: Extending the context collapse. *Social Media + Society*, 4(1), 1–10. https://doi.org/10.1177/2056305118763349

Castells, M. (2010). *The rise of the network society* (2nd ed.). Wiley-Blackwell.

Chadwick, A. (2013). *The hybrid media system: Politics and power.* Oxford University Press.

Cramer, F. (2015). What is "post-digital"? In D. M. Berry & M. Dieter (Eds.), *Postdigital aesthetics* (pp. 12–26). Palgrave Macmillan.

De Cesari, C., & Rigney, A. (Eds.). (2014). *Transnational memory: Circulation, articulation, scales.* De Gruyter.

Denton, E., Hanna, A., Amironesei, R., Smart, A., & Nicole, H. (2021). On the genealogy of machine learning datasets: A critical history of ImageNet. *Big Data & Society*, 8(2). https://doi.org/10.1177/20539517211035955

de Souza e Silva, A. (2006). From cyber to hybrid: Mobile technologies as interfaces of hybrid spaces. *Space and Culture*, *9*(3), 261–278. https://doi.org/10.1177/1206331206289022

Drozdzewski, D., & Birdsall, C. (Eds.). (2019a). *Doing memory research: New methods and approaches*. Palgrave Macmillan.

Drozdzewski, D., & Birdsall, C. (2019b). Advancing memory methods. In D. Drozdzewski & C. Birdsall (Eds.), *Doing memory research: New methods and approaches* (pp. 1–20). Palgrave Macmillan.

Erll, A. (2011). Travelling memory. *Parallax*, 17(4), 4–18. https://doi.org/10.1080/13534645.2011.605570

Erll, A., & Rigney, A. (Eds.). (2009). *Mediation and remediation, and the dynamics of cultural memory*. De Gruyter.

Ernst, W. (2012). *Digital memory and the archive*. University of Minnesota Press.

Giddens, A. (1990). *The consequences of modernity*. Stanford University Press.

Gillespie, T. (2014). The relevance of algorithms. In T. Gillespie, P. J. Boczkowski, & K. A. Foot (Eds.), *Media technologies: Essays on communication, materiality and society* (pp. 167–194). MIT Press.

Gold, R. (1958). Roles in sociological field observation. *Social Forces*, 36, 217–213. https://doi.org/10.2307/2573808

Halstead, H. (2021). Cyberplace: From fantasies of placelessness to connective emplacement. *Memory Studies*, *14*(3), 561–571. https://doi.org/10.1177/17506980211010693

Haraway, D. J. (1991). *Simians, cyborgs and women: The reinvention of nature*. Free Association Books.

Harvey, D. (1989). *The condition of postmodernity*. Blackwell.

Hine, C. (2015). *Ethnography for the Internet: Embedded, embodied and everyday*. Routledge.

Hoskins, A. (2017a). Memory of the multitude: The end of collective memory? In A. Hoskins (Ed.), *Digital memory studies: Media pasts in transition* (pp. 85–109). Routledge.

Hoskins, A. (2017b). The restless past: An introduction to digital memory and media. In A. Hoskins (Ed.), Digital memory studies: Media pasts in transition (pp. 1–24). Routledge.

Hoskins, A., & Tulloch, J. (2016). *Risk and hyperconnectivity: Media and memories of neoliberalism*. Oxford University Press.

Kansteiner, W. (2002). Finding meaning in memory: A methodological critique of collective memory studies. *History and Theory*, *41*(2), 179–197. http://www.jstor.org/stable/3590762

Kaun, A. (2015). Regimes of time: Media practices of the dispossessed. *Time & Society*, *24*(2), 221–243. https://doi.org/10.1177/0961463X15577276

Keightley, E. (2013). From immediacy to intermediacy: The mediation of lived time. *Time & Society*, *22*(1), 55–75. https://doi.org/10.1177/0961463X11402045

Keightley, E., & Pickering, M. (Eds.). (2013). *Research methods for memory studies*. Edinburgh University Press.

Kinsley, S. (2014). The matter of "virtual" geographies. *Progress in Human Geography*, 38(3), 364–384. https://doi.org/10.1177/0309132513506270

Kozinets, R. (2015). *Netnography: Redefined*. Sage.

Latour, B. (2005). *Reassembling the social: An introduction to actor-network-theory*. Oxford University Press.

Law, J. (2004). *After method: Mess in social science research*. Routledge.

Lindgren, S. (2021). *Data theory*. Polity.

Lindgren, S. (2022). *Digital media and society* (2nd ed.). Sage.

Lindgren, S., Dahlberg-Grundberg, M., & Johansson, A. (2014). Hybrid media culture: An introduction. In S. Lindgren (Ed.), *Hybrid media culture: Sensing place in a world of flows* (pp. 1–15). Routledge.

Locke, C. (2000). Digital memory and the problem of forgetting. In S. Radstone (Ed.), *Memory and Methodology* (pp. 25–36). Berg.

Marres, N., & Gerlitz, C. (2016). Interface methods: Renegotiating relations between digital social research, STS and sociology. *Sociological Review*, *64*(1), 21–46. https://doi.org/10.1111/1467-954X.12314

Marwick, A. E., & boyd, danah. (2011). I tweet honestly, I tweet passionately: Twitter users, context collapse, and the imagined audience. *New Media & Society, 13*(1), 114–133. https://doi.org/10.1177/1461444810365313

Merrill, S. (2017). *Networked remembrance: Excavating buried memories in the railways beneath London and Berlin.* Peter Lang.

Merrill, S. (2018). The dead are coming: Political performance art, activist remembrance and dig(ital) protests. In A. Breed & T. Prentki (Eds.), Performance and *civic engagement* (pp. 159–186). Palgrave Macmillan.

Merrill, S. (2019). Walking together? The mediatised performative commemoration of 7/7's tenth anniversary. *Journalism: Theory, Practice and Criticism*, 20(10), 1360–1378.

Merrill, S. (2020). Following the woman with the handbag: The activist appropriation of an iconic historical photograph. In S. Merrill, E. Keightley, & P. Daphi, (Eds.), *Social movements, cultural memory and digital media: Mobilising mediated remembrance* (pp. 111–139). Palgrave Macmillan.

Merrill, S. (2023a) Artificial intelligence and social memory: Towards the cyborgian remembrance of an advancing mnemo-technic. In S. Lindgren (Ed.), *Handbook of critical studies of artificial intelligence* (pp. 173–186). Edward Elgar Publishing.

Merrill, S. (2023b). Memory, iconicity and virality in action: Exploring protest photos online. In A. Rigney & T. Smits (Eds.), *The visual memory of protest* (pp. 133–156). University of Amsterdam Press.

Merrill, S., & Lindgren, S. (2020). The rhythms of social movement memories: The mobilisation of Silvio Meier's activist remembrance across platforms. *Social Movement Studies*, *19*(5–6), 657–674.

Merrill, S., & Lindgren, S. (2021). Memes, brands and the politics of post-terror togetherness: Following the Manchester bee after the 2017 Manchester Arena bombing. *Information, Communication and Society*, 24(3), 2403–2421.

Merrill, S., Sumartojo, S., Closs Stephens, A., & Coward, M. (2020). Togetherness after terror: Commemorative public atmospheres during the Manchester bombing's first anniversary. *Environment and Planning D: Society and Space*, 38(3), 546–566.

Milgram, P., & Kishino, F. (1994). A taxonomy of mixed reality visual displays. *IEICE Transactions on Information and Systems*, 77, 1321–1329.

Noble, S. U. (2018). *Algorithms of oppression: How search engines reinforce racism.* NYU Press.

Osborne, T. (2019). Biosensing: A critical reflection on doing memory research through the body. In D. Drozdzewski & C. Birdsall (Eds.), Doing *memory research*: New *methods and approaches* (pp. 63–86). Palgrave Macmillan.

Pentzold, C. (2018). Between moments and millennia: Temporalising mediatisation. *Media, Culture & Society*, *40*(6), 927–937. https://doi.org/10.1177/0163443717752814

Pickering, M., & Keightley, E. (2013). Introduction: Methodological premises and purposes. In E. Keightley & M. Pickering (Eds.), *Research methods for memory studies* (pp. 1–9). Edinburgh University Press.

Pink, S., Ruckenstein, M., Willim, R., & Duque, M. (2018). Broken data: Conceptualising data in an emerging world. *Big Data & Society*, *40*(6). https://doi.org/10.1177/2053951717753228

Postill, J., & Pink, S. (2012). Social media ethnography: The digital researcher in a messy web. *Media International Australia*, *145*, 123–134. https://doi.org/10.1177/1329878X1214500114

Radstone, S. (2000). Working with memory: An introduction. In S. Radstone (Ed.), *Memory and methodology*. (pp. 1–22). Berg.

Reading, A., Bjork, J., Hanlon, J., & Jakeman, N. (2021). The labour of place: Memory and extended reality (XR) in migration museums. *Memory Studies*, *14*(3), 606–621. https://doi.org/10.1177/17506980211010697

Rogers, R. (2013). *Digital methods.* MIT Press.

Tenenboim-Weinblatt, K. (2013). Bridging collective memories and public agendas: Toward a theory of mediated prospective memory. *Communication Theory*, 23(2), 91–111. https://doi.org/10.1111/comt.12006

Till, K. E. (2004). Emplacing memory through the city: The new Berlin. *German Historical Institute Bulletin*, 35, 73–83.

Virilio, P. (2005). *The information bomb.* Verso.

16

Weaponization of Memory

Viruses and Affective Resonance

Martin Pogačar

The COVID-19 pandemic unfolded during the ongoing mediatization of everything (Livingstone, 2009) and further exposed the vulnerability of social systems of trust and care, aggravated by the onslaught of the neoliberal economic order and "democratic backsliding" (Hacker & Pierson, 2020, p. 25). It affected the conditions of living, work, and leisure and foregrounded the need to understand the psychosocial or economic effects crises have on individuals and societies. Not least, the need to understand how people remember the pandemic and what effects it may have on the future necessitated different research emphases across social sciences and humanities and spawned a new path in memory studies (Ebbrecht-Hartmann, 2020; Erll, 2020; Roigé et al., 2024; see also Worcman & Garde-Hansen, Chapter 18, this volume).

Where to (and From)

The medico-political uncertainty also affected the uses of memory of the twentieth century, a still dominant cultural, political, as well as media referential framework of the present. For example, after March 2020 political and media discourses in Slovenia saw an upsurge in the referencing of events from the Second World War (WWII; 1941–1945) and the socialist period (1945–1991) to make sense of the situation but predominantly to legitimize the struggle for power; the latter I call weaponization of memory. The discussion that follows is situated in a postsocialist Slovenian perspective, where the COVID-19 pandemic came next in a line of crises, following socialism's end in 1991, the ensuing Yugoslav wars (ending in 1995), and the 2008 economic crisis. All had severe repercussions for the sociopolitical structures and were marked by rising economic inequalities, the hollowing out of politics, and (neo)nationalism (Bergmann, 2020; Mihelj & Jiménez-Martínez, 2020). What is more, sociopolitical crises were also affected

Martin Pogačar, *Weaponization of Memory* In: *The Remaking of Memory in the Age of the Internet and Social Media.* Edited by: Qi Wang and Andrew Hoskins, Oxford University Press. © Oxford University Press 2024.
DOI: 10.1093/oso/9780197661260.003.0016

by technological innovations that upended life in myriad ways, including the systems of production, dissemination, and consumption of products and information, labor, and leisure.

The pandemic, I argue, acted as a catalyst for the weaponization of memory, which was driven by affective resonance, understood here as a dynamic force of moving and being moved by participating in mediated interaction (Anderson, 2009, p. 80; Mühlhoff, 2015; Riedel, 2019, p. 92; cf. Masumi, 2015). To explore the term *weaponization of memory*, I engage with how politics and memory became entangled in a selection of "pandemic media events" that resonated in 2020–2021 Slovenia. In doing so, I employ the concepts of context and temporal collapse (Davis and Jurgenson, 2014; Marwick & boyd, 2011; Meyrowitz, 1985) in relation to media memory (Neiger et al., 2011) and mnemonic imagination (Keightley & Pickering, 2012). Along the way, I set out the contours of a pandemic-conditioned methodology marked by "hovering attention," inflected by scrolling through and following content, which entails observers' affective engagement with selected content, which then undergoes a qualitative analysis (see Pogačar, 2016; see also Paasonen, 2015).

Media and digital communications technologies and their life-structuring, social, and political effects play an important role in mnemonic processes and practices (Erll, 2009; Garde-Hansen, 2011; Garde-Hansen et al., 2009). Jay Winter, for example, noted that since the 1960s and 1970s audiovisual and digital data banks preserved and protected the "voice" of victims. The media enabled their stories to be captured and accessed, through listening or viewing them, as well as coming into contact with people's lives in the past (Winter, 2007, p. 373). Media memory—or rather mediated collective pasts—and its studies (Neiger et al., 2011, p. 1) therefore facilitate insight into the interplay of humans and technology and media discourses and devices, always already conditioned by the capacity of media to hybridize previous media technologies (see Bolter & Grusin, 1999). Media memory is also affected by the hybridizing of experiential planes, reticulating the intimate, personal, collective, and public domains. These are co-shaped by re-presenced pasts, mediated by films, songs, voice recordings, newspapers, TV shows, social media posts, and more (see Pogačar, 2016). In turn, media memory influences how present-day sociopolitical phenomena are understood and made sense of, importantly in the context of the mnemonic imagination, understood as a synthesis of remembering and imagining as critical for our understandings of the relationship between past, present, and future (Keightley & Pickering, 2012, p. 7).

Media memory and mnemonic imagination become particularly relevant in the context of sociopolitical crises that shake and stir the prospect of societal stability and, in the search for renewed stability, rely on mediated re-presencing of past events, personalities, periods, and processes. But as digital media affect the scale and magnitude of the production of "stuff mnemonic," the questions arise: How much memory can we consume, or rather process? To what purposes is memory used? How are these purposes conditioned by media affordances and the psychosocial effects of a crisis? And how can we, humans, handle this? Retreat and curl up? Weaponize and prosper?

A brief contextual detour: Radio in the interwar period bombarded the ear with more information and structured and meaningful sound than ever experienced before (Biocca, 1988). It gave birth to new forms of communication and social engagement, dissemination of affective political speeches, and recorded music previously often consumed communally, with no way of keeping track of sounded (non)facts (see Adena et al., 2013). Digital media operate on a similar basis: Collective (mediated) engagement and high volumes of ephemeral content leave little chance to track media(ted) events (leaving aside deepfakes and uses of artificial intelligence): Immersed in the flux of the ever-new and the always-already obsolete, mediated realities (particularly in time of crisis) resonate unprecedentedly fast and furiously between individuals, groups, the here and there, and the then and now: The present is unhinged, narrative destabilized, the search for truth debased (see Murphy et al., Chapter 8, this volume).

Conflate (and Rewind)

Processes of mediated re-presencing of the past have been both limited and empowered by what Alice Marwick and danah boyd call context collapse, understood as the effect of "social media technologies that collapse multiple contexts and bring together commonly distinct audiences" (Marwick & boyd, 2011). Jenny Davis and Nathan Jurgenson see it as a way in which "people, information, and norms from one context seep into the bounds of another" (Davis & Jurgenson, 2014). These accounts emphasize the aspects of audiences and contexts and foreground the encounters between content and humans that otherwise might not have happened. The issue of context collapse was brought to an extreme during the pandemic, exemplified in memes showing people framed by screens in suits and off-screen body parts in pajamas or setting up generic backgrounds to mask the harsh reality of sitting on the toilet during a work meeting. Before the onslaught of digital media, context conflation was quite rare outside the more curated spaces, most obviously in cinema and music, literature, as well as archives and museums that brought together different imagined worlds or different places, cultures, and times; but the visual and the audible and the textual that we consume on handheld devices reformat the spatiality (and in fact invalidate the virtual/real distinction) and just as critically foreground the temporal aspects of experience (see Risko et al., Chapter 5, this volume).

Any discussion of context collapse thus also touches on the question of collapse of temporalities and the question of mnemonic imagination. Adding the temporal aspect to the spatial emphasis above, Petter Bae Brandtzaeg and Marika Lüders suggest that "social media, as enduring and sometimes unpredictable life-logs, are increasingly experienced as a collapsing of the past and the present." They emphasize that social media contribute "to a blurring of time and a muddling of past and present experiences." The time collapse draws attention to how old stuff can disrupt the present (Brandtzaeg & Lüders, 2018, p. 2, 4). The diachronic emphasis here refers to the intrusion of mediated past events—and by that also ideologies, collective dreams and traumas, images, people, music, art—into the present. This not only affects individual but also social imaginaries. Again, historically this is not new, but it is radically upscaled and enhanced by content consumption practices and the enabling devices and media affordances.

Projecting the past into the future has been essential in providing a transtemporal communicative framework for any collectivity. Yet, with technical capture of the past, particularly in audiovision, mediated past can readily migrate into the future, eliminating the symbolic temporal boundary; thus it gives way to what Boris Buden calls the "culture of the past," where the past becomes the utterly new terrain to be discovered in the present (Buden, 2012; see also Pogačar, 2017).

Time collapse therefore upends the (desired) linearity of historical progression by enabling the intrusion of the mediated past into the present, messing up the diachronicity of experience and affecting how we imagine the past, as well as the present. It contributes to the emergence of the extended now (Berlant, 2011; see Merrill, Chapter 15, this volume) or extended present (Nowotny, 1989; see also Pogačar, 2017). To illustrate, in a Facebook post from March 16, 2021, a Slovenian TV presenter and actress shared a meme, taken from a right-wing party FB post. It featured an image of a character from the Scooby Doo cartoon, with the added words: Q: "Who are you?" A: "A dissatisfied local [center-liberal] party committee." The person revealed is a former liberal politician, an alleged member of the communist deep state. The TV presenter framed it: "When I saw this poster I was reminded of fascist propaganda in Hitler's time! A blond boy, an Aryan or something, on the other side someone tied up . . . ! [Slovenian intellectuals, Slovenian politicians] YOU ARE ALL responsible! Do you really want us to kill each other? . . . No one trusts anyone anymore, you have used corona to trample human rights!"

I followed the post for some days, in a hoovering attention mode: scrolling and reading through the comments and related posts. I was following the flow of words, contextualized also by other news and political exchanges in social media at the time, which formed the affective context of this research (into which I was implicated). The presenter's post garnered over 1,200 comments and 180 shares and triggered a lively debate, mostly revolving around left–right political strife, aggravated during the pandemic, and the memory of the late twentieth century past. The memory of WWII prevailed with repeated references to the Nazi occupation and national ideological strife between the antifascist resistance movement and collaboration units (1941–1945).

One user shared an intimate memory of their grandmother brutally murdered by the partisans during WWII, "just because she was a landowner." In response, another user noted that their family members were killed by the Home Guard (Nazi collaborators) and the Fascists. "Can you answer which of our families suffered more?" The reference to indiscriminate suffering suggests an affective relationship to the past that is potentiated by a familial bond. This, in turn, makes clear that feelings of loss are transgenerationally resonant in the commenter's understanding of the past and present. What is more, the exchange exemplifies and subsumes the persistence of a divided memory of WWII within the population, further potentiated by the presence of this topic in daily politics that feeds on perpetuating it.

Affective Resonance (in a State of Emergency)

The ensuing debate included the recounting of WWII events and brought into discussion other historical traumatic events. Referring to the post author's note that offensive messages will be deleted, one commenter conflated different historical contexts and events: "In Nazi Germany, stickers were posted everywhere 'Jews are not allowed to enter,' in the American South during the segregation the sign 'Blacks are not allowed to enter' was hung everywhere." Another person replied that a political opinion is a choice, while being a Jew or African American is not. Such comments stretch back and across history and conflate historical contexts. Thus, they reveal the intensity of moral outrage over injustices, in response to social injustices or to the transgression of moral norms (Brady et al., 2021). Such exchanges appear even more resonant and powerful in the context of crisis, in this case the pandemic. During the lockdowns, (social) media, as elsewhere, was rife with heated political debate, outrage triggered by the "rule by decree" as an indication of "democratic backsliding," marked by rule breaking and thuggish practices (Hacker & Pierson, 2020, p. 25).

These contextualities also affected the selection of the approach and material for this chapter and influenced the hovering attention mode of qualitative analysis. In the context of practices of consuming online content, this approach takes into account the fact that "posts in a discussion thread are often skimmed through quickly, by skipping over sentences, messages, and even entire sections. Such skipping is directly supported, or even encouraged, by the information architecture of discussion platforms that regulates the format and order in which posts are rendered accessible to users" (Paasonen, 2015, p. 31; on platformization and economic, governmental, and infrastructural logic of platforms, see Smit, Chapter 13, this volume). While the hovering attention approach, which accommodates a desktop, on-the-fly mode of navigating between resonating tweets and videos, does affect the interpretative position, it also offers a way to detect and reflect on the resonance of observed events unfolding on screens, which feed on not only cultural and technical contexts and networks (cf. Rajaram, Chapter 12, this volume), but also biological and cognitive responses of the body.

Media events thus illustrate the mechanics of time collapse in the context of the politicized and mediated twentieth-century past perpetually remediated in social media and political conflicts. More specifically, time collapse is often further driven by outrage that, according to William Brady et al., is more common in ideologically more extreme networks (e.g., right-wing politics via Twitter [now called X]) and when social feedback is disregarded in deciding whether to express outrage (Brady et al., 2021, p. 8). As affectively resonating traumatic historical events enter users' interpretative planes, they structure their fields of experience.

Forcing social life to screens and social media newsfeeds, the pandemic further redefined the how and where we consume information and how and when we engage in mediated social contacts. It disturbed the relationship between the space of experience and horizon of expectation (cf. Keightley & Pickering, 2012; Koselleck, 2004). The field of experience became at once homebound and radically mediated, eliminating from view much of the haphazard encounters and unplanned, unstructured social engagements. Instead, it was replaced by, on the one hand, excessive f(ol)lowing of news and endless browsing and, on the other hand, the technologically structured spaces of encounter (scheduled meetings, socializing). The pandemic thus substantially reduced the horizon of experience.

In a state of pandemic emergency, then, the use of social media and digital technology in general led to the escalation in excessive consumption of mediated stuff to migration of some labor arrangements online. It also furthered the public proliferation of intimate and affective everyday activities, including reinterpretations of the past. Digital media, or rather the capacity of mediated content to invade the privacy of individual space, blurred the distinction between work and leisure, politics and the everyday, home and (mediated) public spaces. Along the way this was co-structured by the fusing of the sociopolitical and private roles of politicians (as powerful actors forming and driving public discourse) that blurred the distinction between their private and political personae. This was driven by, for example, tweeting: Some high-ranking politicians used Twitter for both expressing volatile personal opinions and communicating pandemic measures and other governmental decisions. In this hybridizing capacity, social media exchanges play a significant role in the formation of affective resonances between individuals and collectivities, politicians and individuals, articulated in a world of short and affectively charged statements that collapse historical complexities in explaining and subduing the present.

The disregard of (historical) complexity in social media communication codetermines and structures human action and engagement and thus plays an important role in the emergence of the culture of the past, as well as in driving mnemonic imagination. In mnemonic imagination, Keightley and Pickering argue: "Our engagements with the past move through a series of interactive dualities: the constitution of selfhood and the commission of social action; the interplay between experience and expectation, memory and possibility; the relations between lived first-hand experience and mediated or inherited second-hand experience" (Keightley & Pickering, 2012, p. 7).

This calls for a critical emphasis: Mnemonic imagination in digital media is influenced by the affective resonance that emerges out of the relationships between and among users and content, entangled as it is in the mediation of individual and collective syn- and diachronicities. Affective resonance, following Rainer Mühlhoff, is essentially an entanglement of relational forces that foreground interpersonal relatedness (Mühlhoff, 2015, pp. 1010, 1017). The latter is a critical component of mediated interaction as it contributes to the construction of an apparition of a collectivity, yet one based on mediated outrage that feeds back into cognitive processes as well. Susanna Paasonen, following Isobel Anderson, notes: "Texts and readers produce reciprocal feedback loops, where energies build up and are released through acts of interpretation. In online communication, such feedback loops broaden into affective networks that encompass writers/readers/users; platforms and their information architecture; textual, visual, and audiovisual messages; and sensory experience of connectivity and disconnection" (Paasonen, 2015, p. 31). Cognitive processes are inflected by individual and collective engagement with historical facts and interpretations, personal and familial histories, and traumas and pain mediated in political discourses and conditioned by day-to-day immersion in collapsed contexts and times.

Due to the nature of engagement (brevity, economy of attention, volume of information), the emergence of affective resonance is most effectively conditioned by powerful, publicly reverberating statements. These tend to skew, deny, or disregard prevalent historical interpretations and thus make a resonant statement by employing a joke, provocation, expression of intimate belief, anger, or outrage. In their tone, fierceness, and spontaneity, such statements invite a dynamic, if short lived, social attuning, not unlike those invited in live communication by gestures and speech (laughter, intonation, rhythm) (Mühlhoff, 2015,

p. 1010). Thus, it is the short and powerful statements (outrageous and product of outrage) that constitute the conditions of a relational dynamic of moving others and being moved by others, whereas the latter is only partly under an individual's control (Mühlhoff, 2015, p. 1011), if necessarily of the individual. Consequentially, mnemonic imagination is informed by the affective resonance driven by distilled and conflated re-presencing of the past in temporally and spatially collapsed mediated contexts.

Weaponize Distress (Postsocialist)

To see how the past, contextually and temporally mediated and collapsed, is driven by affective resonance, a contextual look at how WWII and the socialist past affects postsocialist memory politics in the former Yugoslavia proves useful (Atanasoski & Vora, 2018; Dujisin, 2021; Luthar et al., 2020). Post-1991 memory politics rest on the collapse of socialist ideology and the state of Yugoslavia, the failed integration of new states into the new symbolic and socioeconomic order, and the effects of digitalization (Pogačar, 2016).

On the brink of the digital era, postsocialist societies embarked on a transformation that, Dominik Bartmanski notes, during the 1990s represented a "microliminality, a rite of passage from the profane qualities of 'Eastern' Communism to the sacred values of 'Western' order" (Bartmanski, 2011, p. 214). Socialist past was subjected to what Svetlana Boym called reflective nostalgia (Boym, 2001), which was used to unmask the ideological clockworks of the emergent nationalist mythologies by making playful references to the socialist everyday (on Yugonostalgia, see Mihelj, 2017; Petrović, 2013; Pogačar, 2016; Velikonja, 2017; see also Bartmanski, 2011; Reifová, 2018). It challenged the anticommunist memory imperative and the confiscation of the memory and history of the 1980s democratization movement. However, inasmuch as the playful memory games were set against the co-optation of the 1980s democratization initiatives by ethnonationalists (see Dujisin, 2021), the process of postsocialist transformation nevertheless resulted in a version of restorative nostalgia aiming to reinstate the lost order (Boym, 2001): to elide socialism and repurpose the pre-WWII nationalism (on nostalgia and mobilization of the past in response to the various crises, see Niemeyer & Keightley, Chapter 14, this volume).

In the process, the socialist past was conflated into a uniform category of communist totalitarianism against which the ideal nation was presented as "some pure, authentic space of indigenousness that is outside of 'the state,' technological degradation, and history itself" (Nelson, 1996, p. 302). A yearning for a romanticized ethnos that never existed is a powerful political tool to affectively modulate the ethnonational imaginary, grafted onto the "symbolic capital of anticommunism, previously up for grabs in the political field, . . . now regulated and apportioned by institutions that seek to legitimate scientifically the 'unfinished revolution' (Mark, 2010)" (Dujisin, 2021, p. 91). Over the years, antisocialist ethnostalgia gained further impetus and translated during the pandemic into the practice of "weaponization of memory."

The concept builds on the scrutiny of the mechanics of mediated context and temporal collapse and affective resonance, which during the pandemic fueled and revealed a political turn toward the far right, renouncing the socialist, antifascist past, and leftist critical thought in general, while espousing neo-Nazi affiliations. This symptom of failed democratization, seen in attempts to dismantle the media system (the right-wing takeover of Slovenian national public TV), judiciary, and police (which during the pandemic were the takeover bounty), resonated intensely across social media and political discourses, where the socialist past was weaponized to not only delegitimize the center-left political opposition but also fuel mnemonic distress that emerged as a consequence of memory conflict and its daily-political abuse. Generating distress and feeding on context and temporal collapse, then, was used to attack and discredit any econopolitical alternative to neoliberalism and frame it as an ideological, cultural threat, and, as I discuss next, a viral intrusion and infection.

Viruses (Ideologically Speaking)

Biological and computer viruses are intrusive and are about information. They are interfacing humans, technologies, and natures (Parikka, 2007, p. 108). But viruses, or rather virality, are also linked to memes, as indicated in the example in section Conflate and Rewind above (see also Blackmore, 2000; Dawkins, 1977), which means, Jussi Parikka argues, that virality and contagion attain an explanatory social function (2007, p. 108). Virality, then, is also ideologically applicable, much like some animal characteristics were used to deride "lesser humans" (e.g., rats, swarms) or natural phenomena such as floods to stoke up hatred against migrants.

Shortly after taking office in March 2020, following the stepping down of a center-liberal government, the unelected right-wing government set up an official Crisis Headquarters Twitter account. One of its first (re)tweets was: "Psychiatrists are looking for 4 patients who escaped quarantine. They are infected with covid-Marx/Lenin virus." The tweet was directed against a number of critical Slovenian newspapers and leftist public figures, one of them the philosopher Slavoj Žižek. It subsumes the problematic of context and time collapse and makes clear from very early on in the pandemic that the right-wing government was fighting not only the biological virus, but also the "ideological" one. Alluding to the mental state of nutters running amok, the tweet—inscribed into the wider phenomenon of relating biology and culture in framing the "war against" the virus—drew an analogy between a virus as a biological entity that must be fought against appropriately and the virus of the ideological left, subsumed by the image of Žižek. War metaphor rhetoric was not at all uncommon elsewhere, with comparisons being drawn, as Tamara Banjeglav and Nicolas Moll discuss, to war as such or a specific war (e.g., the 1930s Spanish civil war or the recent wars in the former Yugoslavia) (Banjeglav & Moll, 2021; see Castro Seixas, 2021).

This tweet:event structured the field of engagement where the medically precarious situation was used to frame a battleground for a political and cultural war against left-wing politics, socialism, multiculturalism, intellectuals and artists, alternative collectives and autonomous spaces, LGBTQ (lesbian, gay, bisexual, transgender, queer or questioning), and migrants and refugees. At about the same time, a group of right-wing intellectuals published a "Memorandum of the Cathedral of Freedom." They drew an analogy between the time of Slovenian independence and the current crisis, emphasizing an "external enemy": "Thirty years ago it was an invasion of the JNA [Yugoslav People's Army] armed forces, today it is an invasion of a new corona virus. . . . The epidemic is not similar to socialism, but socialism is similar to an epidemic" (Jambrek, 2020).

The mediatized tweet:event—unfolding in the devices and the minds of individuals—illustrates the upsurge of exclusivist, nationalist, right-wing propaganda, in large part based on radical distancing from center/left as well as the socialist past, to the extent that any relation with socialism becomes politicized, indeed weaponized, in an ideological clash for political power. This is embedded in global trends of rising nativist populism and neonationalism, as Eirikur Bergmann calls it, that also sees mainstream parties abandon democratic values in the pursuit of voters (Bergmann, 2020, p. 215). Indeed, these processes reveal a trend toward what Jacques Rancière terms postdemocracy, a "paradox that, in the name of democracy, emphasises the consensual practice of effacing the forms of democratic action" (Rancière in Wilson & Swyngedouw, 2014, p. 13). Ruthlessly, this is extrapolated in a sociopolitical setup where an adversary is not someone you want to defeat, but rather someone you have to destroy (Ignatieff in Bergmann, 2020, p. 7).

The virus-socialism analogy thus entangles the users in a web of affective resonance that emerges out of circulating inflammatory tweets, particularly powerful when people in governmental positions take on the ordinary citizen persona. Framing the virus as an ideological entity thus posits any ideological alternative as an enemy, hence in need of destroying rather than defeating in debate, and, importantly, it drives and feeds on the radical flattening of historical complexity.

Fatigue (Unfolds)

Affective resonance acts a social force (building on antisocialism, emphasizing communist crimes and misdoings) arising out of individuals and groups participating in mediated encounters in the context of context and time collapse. What is more, the platformization of the ongoing social conflict takes any prospective future development out of the realm of public discourse and away from the processual, collective, societal defining of possibilities toward the field of conflicting tweet:events that relegate conflict resolution outside institutional structures onto "the streets" (as apparent in the clashes between protesters and the police that marked the pandemic). Not least, it posits an individual in the mediated network of outrage and disarticulated voices, conditioned in each new present by the invasion of contextually and temporally collapsed past events, overwritten and reinterpreted over time and on the fly, precisely through participating in, commenting, retweeting, and thinking about the heated now of a tweet:event.

The force of the weaponization of memory of the Slovenian past in daily political conflict detected during the writing of this chapter was thus marked by ceaseless re-presencing of collapsed snippets of the history of WWII, the antifascist resistance and Nazi-fascist collaboration, and the socialist period with the mythologization of 1991 independence (Pušnik & Luthar, 2020; Pogačar, 2020). During the pandemic, the postsocialist mnemonic distress was thus given a resonant medicopolitical framework for further politicization of the past and the weaponization of memory.

The interpretative and referential frameworks of human experience, embedded in a specific moment already affected by the contextual and time collapse radicalized by social media, further collapsed into the "dread of ever-now." In such situations, Astrid Erll notes, there is "little time for future-thinking or attention paid to those outside the narrow emergency-frames of collective (usually national) identity—such as, for example, the refugees on Europe's borders" (Erll, 2020, p. 863). The excessive nowness, fueling the urge to look back (nostalgic romanticism) and inward (nationalism), were enhanced by extreme measures: social distancing; restriction of movement and gathering; adaptations in domains of work, education, care, leisure, eating (Erll, 2020). The pervasive reliance on communications devices and screens hindered unstructured communication and promoted the monotonization of media diets, further adding to the already stressful situation.

In this context, Nathalie Theodore's observation is relevant: "Living with this chronic underlying stress means we have less bandwidth to deal with the ups and downs of daily life, or other emotional triggers," adding that "decision fatigue" could be causing excessive tiredness (Theodore in Karlis, 2021). This ties in, David Rand and Gordon Pennycock note, with

> "'lazy thinking' [instead of lazy that foregrounds conscious human (in)activity and is itself a decidedly capitalist-utilitarian term, I'd rather emphasize the econo-technological structural conditions that contribute to the stifling of social action], that is likely exacerbated in social media, where people scroll quickly, are distracted by a deluge of information, and encounter news mixed in with emotionally engaging baby photos, cat videos and the like." (Rand & Pennycock, 2021)

In the context of the pandemic, Theodore continues: "Any activity we choose to engage in requires a risk analysis, which is exhausting" (Theodore in Karlis, 2021).

Transposed to the realm of pandemic media contexts, encountering upsetting news or provocative content may contribute to taking recourse to the more energy efficient social practices, for example, consuming easily available, clear-cut topics, memories, references, allusions, interpretations, information that effects an immediate, volatile reaction (outrage). Similar can be said of sifting through and sharing historical sources and accounts, images, or texts for the expected thrill of outrage and outrageous response. This, paradoxically, reinforces consuming more content and aggravating the oppressiveness of media diets, triggering affective responses to images and content that one finds upsetting, overlooking along the way their affective mechanisms; and it reduces the urge for and the potential of debate.

The examples discussed above cannot be used to generalize the wider social sentiment, not least because they have relatively limited reach within some social strata (e.g. the elderly). But as they seep into other media, they nevertheless frame and drive the topics in daily politics and demonstrate the mechanisms of how intimate memories and individual remembering are employed in the mechanics of generating public, politicized affective resonance. Affective resonance emanates from the incessant flow of "outraging" information and "pumped-up" sentiment between the personal and public, the political and intimate information consumption across media. This has implications for how the past is treated and used when it is at the same time not only easily digestible, fixed, and neat, but also increasingly fragmented, multilayered, and malleable. Thus, the crisis and technology-driven exhausting mediated social engagement pushes already fringe positions to further extremes, enhances the postdemocratic hollowing out of politics and leads to participatory and cognitive numbness (as a response and driver of further instability).

Disremember

From early 2020, people were glued to their screens *en masse*, immersed in pandemic media diets and the heated-up media and political discourses. This contributed to not only exposing the underlying social, political, and economic flaws and failures, but also scrambled temporalities. The mediated synchronicity of the personal and intimate, professional, and political, the past and present, contributed to context and time collapse and potentiated affective resonance. Practically, this led to the weaponization of memory, in this case the memory of WWII and socialist Yugoslavia. The pandemic thus acted as a catalytic event that intensified the power of intimate diachronicities and further entangled the medical and political measures into the potentiating of affective resonance: conflated and conflictual histories and memories of traumatic twentieth-century periods were used as weapons in framing the pandemic and became the condition of mnemonic distress, which in turn was appropriated in culture-war politics.

In a time of crisis, the present is rendered instable while the past tends to appear a stable, if contentious, source of unresolved conflicts. However, its apparent stability works only to the extent that it can operate with notoriously simplified and radicalized categories and thematic tropes (socialism, resistance, the Holocaust, Nazism). In the pandemic digital culture of postsocialist Slovenia, the past, as used in politics or media and in private or public discourses, indeed became a new potentiality: ready to be remade and reexperienced anew, in participating in each new media event. It became a reinforced referential explanatory trope, tailored to one's liking. Thus, the past, when affectively reassembled, appropriated, and repurposed, reinvented and forgotten, can serve as not only a mode of explanation but also social dissonance. Despite its veneer of fixity, it can no longer be a source of desired collective stability but instead becomes a Heideggerian-like standing reserve (of facts, stories, myths, and lies) ready to be extracted and recombined in any new situation for any new purposes. The conflated, simplified past, history, and memory become a viral infection itself.

When uncertainty abounds, the future is hardly imaginable beyond the imminent catastrophe, and the recourse to the past and its uses—as a disposable, daily reinvented and discarded asset in media and political weaponization of crisis—affects interpersonal engagements and societies at large. Societal volatility and ideological strife enforce the forgetting of past events and further open the door to neonationalism, populism, postdemocracy. What is more, affective resonance, coupled with media:pandemic fatigue, not only shapes the conditions of mnemonic imagination, but also contributes to the paradox of living in the culture of the past: The exclusivist romanticizing of the national, the short-term weaponization of the past for political purposes or intimate consolation, facilitates a radical disremembering of the need for a planetary forward thinking in dealing with planetary crises.

References

Adena, M., Enikolopov, R., Petrova, M., Santarosa, V., & Zhuravskaya, E. (2013). *Radio and the rise of the Nazis in prewar Germany*. https://shs.hal.science/halshs-00858992

Anderson, B. (2009). Affective atmospheres. *Emotion, Space and Society, 2*, 77–81.

Atanasoski, N., & Vora, K. (2018). Postsocialist politics and the ends of revolution. *Social Identities, 24*(2), 139–154. https://doi.org/10.1080/13504630.2017.1321712

Banjeglav, T., & Moll, N. (2021). Outbreak of war memories? Historical analogies of the 1990s wars in discourses about the coronavirus pandemic in Bosnia and Herzegovina and Croatia. *Southeast European and Black Sea Studies, 21*(3), 353–372. https://doi.org/10.1080/14683857.2021.1942656

Bartmanski, D. (2011). Successful icons of failed time: Rethinking post-communist nostalgia. *Acta Sociologica, 54*(3), 213–231. https://doi.org/10.1177/0001699311412625

Bergmann, E. (2020). *Neo-nationalism. The rise of nativist populism*. Palgrave Macmillan.

Berlant, L. (2011). *Cruel optimism*. Duke University Press.

Biocca, F. A. (1988). The pursuit of sound: radio, perception, and utopia in the early twentieth century. *Media, Culture & Society, 10*(1), 61–67.

Blackmore, S. (2000). *The meme machine*. Oxford University Press.

Bolter, J. D., & Grusin, R. (1999). *Remediation: Understanding new media*. MIT Press.

Boym, S. (2001). *The future of nostalgia*. Basic Books.

Brady, W. J., McLoughlin, K., Doan, T. N., Crockett, M. J. (2021). How social learning amplifies moral outrage expression in online social networks. *Science Advances, 7*, 1–14.

Brandtzaeg P. B., & Lüders M. (2018). Time collapse in social media: extending the context collapse. *Social Media + Society, 4*(1), 1–10. https://doi.org/10.1177/2056305118763349

Buden, B. (2012). *Zona prelaska, O kraju postkomunizma*. Fabrika knjiga.

Castro Seixas, E. (2021). War metaphors in political communication on COVID-19. *Frontiers in Sociology, 5*. https://doi.org/10.3389/fsoc.2020.583680

Davis, J. L., & Jurgenson, N. (2014). Context collapse: Theorizing context collusions and collisions. *Information, Communication & Society, 17*(4), 476–485. https://doi.org/10.1080/1369118X.2014.888458

Dawkins, R. (1977). *The selfish gene*. Oxford University Press.

Dujisin, Z. (2021). A history of post-communist remembrance: From memory politics to the emergence of a field of anticommunism. *Theory and Society, 50*, 65–96. https://doi.org/10.1007/s11186-020-09401-5

Ebbrecht-Hartmann, T. (2020). Commemorating from a distance: the digital transformation of Holocaust memory in times of COVID-19. *Media, Culture & Society, 13*(6), 1095–1112.

Erll, A. (2009). Literature, film and the mediality of culture. In A. Erll & A. Nunning (Eds.), *Cultural memory studies: An international and interdisciplinary handbook* (pp. 389–398). Walter de Gruyter.

Erll, A. (2020). Afterword: Memory worlds in times of Corona. *Memory Studies, 13*(5), 861–874.

Garde-Hansen, J. (2011). *Media and memory*. Edinburgh University Press.

Garde-Hansen, J., Hoskins, A., & Reading, A. (Eds.). (2009). *Save as . . . Digital memories*. Palgrave Macmillan.

Hacker, J. S., & Pierson, P. (2020). *Let them eat tweets: How the right rules in an age of extreme inequality*. Liveright Publishing.

Jambrek, P. (2020, March 26). Spomenica katedrale svobode. Katedrala svobode. mailchi.mp/4701f591307b/povabilo-na-akademski-forum-nove-univerze-in-katedrale-svobode-konvencije-za-nacionalni-program-2710523

Karlis, N. (2021, March 18). It's not just you: Why everyone is super exhausted right now. *Salon*. https://www.salon.com/2021/03/18/its-not-just-you-why-everyone-is-super-exhausted-right-now/

Keightley, E., & Pickering M. (2012). *The mnemonic imagination, remembering as creative practice*. Palgrave Macmillan.

Koselleck, R. (2004). *Futures past: On the semantics of historical time*. Columbia University Press.

Livingstone, S. (2009). On the mediation of everything: Ica presidential address 2008. *Journal of Communication, 59*(1), 1–18. https://doi.org/10.1111/j.1460-2466.2008.01401.x

Luthar, O., Bieber, F., & Petrović, T. (2020). (De)colonising socialist experience—Understanding southeastern Europe and the former Yugoslavia. In S. Gruber, D. Gutmeyr, S. Jesner, E. Krasniqi, R. Pichler, & C. Promitzer (Eds.), *From the highlands to Hollywood: multidisciplinary perspectives on southeastern Europe festschrift for Karl Kaser and SEEHA* (pp. 95–104). Lit Verlag.

Mark, J. (2010). *The unfinished revolution: Making sense of the communist past in central-eastern Europe*. Yale University Press.

Marwick, A. E., & boyd, d. (2011). I tweet honestly, I tweet passionately: Twitter users, context collapse, and the imagined audience. *New Media & Society, 13*(1), 114–133. https://doi.org/10.1177/1461444810365313

Masumi, B. (2015). *Politics of affect*. Polity.

Meyrowitz, J. (1985). *No sense of place: The impact of electronic media on social behavior*. Oxford University Press.

Mihelj, S. (2017). Memory, post-socialism and the media: Nostalgia and beyond. *European Journal of Cultural Studies, 20*(3), 235–251. https://doi.org/10.1177/1367549416682260

Mihelj, S., & Jiménez-Martínez, C. (2020). Digital nationalism: Understanding the role of digital media in the rise of "new" nationalism (Version 1). *Nations and Nationalism, 27*(2), 331–346. hdl.handle.net/2134/12656252.v1

Mühlhoff, R. (2015). Affective resonance and social interaction. *Phenomenology and the Cognitive Sciences, 14*(4), 1001–1019.

Neiger, M., Meyers, O., & Zandberg, E. (Eds.). (2011). *On media memory collective memory in a new media age*. Palgrave Macmillan.

Nelson, D. M. (1996). Maya hackers and the cyberspatialized nation-state: Modernity, ethnostalgia, and a lizard queen in Guatemala. *Cultural Anthropology, 11*(3), 287–308.

Nowotny, H. (1989). Mind, technologies, and collective time consciousness: From the future to the extended present. In J. T. Fraser (Ed.), *Time and mind: Interdisciplinary issues* (pp. 197–216). Fraser International Universities Press.

Paasonen, S. (2015). A midsummer's bonfire: Affective intensities of online debates. In K Hillis, S. Paasonen, & M. Petit (Eds.), *Networked affect* (pp. 27–42). MIT Press.

Parikka, J. (2007). *Digital contagions: A media archaeology of computer viruses*. Peter Lang.

Petrović, T. (2013). The past that binds us: Yugonostalgia as the politics of future. In S. Pavlović & M. Živković (Eds.), *Transcending fratricide: Political mythologies, reconciliations, and the uncertain future in the former Yugoslavia* (pp. 129–147). Nomos.

Pogačar, M. (2016). *Media archaeologies, micro-archives, and storytelling: Re-presencing the past*. Palgrave Macmillan.

Pogačar, M. (2017). Culture of the past: Digital connectivity and dispotentiated futures. In A. Hoskins (Ed.), *Digital memory studies. Media pasts in transition* (pp. 27–48). Routledge.

Pogačar, M. (2020). Alterations of memory: Mediatising the interpretative void in post-Yugoslav Slovenia. In M. Pušnik & O. Luthar (Eds.), *The media of memory* (pp. 133–156). Brill.

Rand, D., & Pennycock, G. (2021, March 17). Most people don't actively seek to share fake news. *Scientific American*. https://www.scientificamerican.com/article/most-people-dont-actively-seek-to-share-fake-news/

Reifová, I. (2018). The pleasure of continuity: Re-reading post-socialist nostalgia. *International Journal of Cultural Studies, 21*(6), 587–602. https://doi.org/10.1177/1367877917741693

Riedel, F. (2019). Atmosphere. In J. Slaby & C. Von Scheve (Eds.), *Affective societies: Key concepts* (pp. 85–95). Routledge.

Roigé, X., Canals, A., & Rico, M. (2024). Creating memory of COVID-19: The actions of museums and archives in Spain. *Memory Studies, 17*(2), 193–212. https://doi.org/10.1177/17506980231155560

Velikonja, M. (2017). *Titostalgia: A study of nostalgia for Josip Broz*. Lambert.

Wilson, J., & Swyngedouw, E. (2014). Introduction: Seeds of dystopia: Post-politics and the return of the political. In J. Wilson & E. Swyngedouw (Eds.), *The post-political and its discontents. Spaces of depoliticization, spectres of radical politics* (pp. 25–48). Edinburgh University Press.

Winter, J. (2007). The generation of memory: Reflections on the "memory boom." *Contemporary Historical Studies, Archives & Social Studies, 1*(0), 363–397.

17
Understanding Holocaust Memory on Instagram and TikTok

Noam Tirosh

The opening song of Bob Dylan's latest album (*Rough and Rowdy Ways*, 2020) is titled: "I Contain Multitudes." Paraphrasing Walt Whitman, Dylan is celebrating the inherent contradictions of the self. According to Whitman, we are large enough, thus we contain multitudes.[1] Yet, what is at stake when our memory turns "large enough" and contains multitudes? Moreover, is the memory of the Holocaust capable of containing such multitudes? In this context, the notion of multitudes encompasses not only adaptability, flexibility, and tolerance but also conflicts, dissonance, and disharmony. Can we embrace a memory broad enough to reconcile these conflicting elements? This chapter employs Andrew Hoskins's perspectives on the "memory of the multitude" (Hoskins, 2017) to answer these questions and explore contemporary Holocaust memory.

To examine the relations between Holocaust memory and the memory of the multitude, two case studies are scrutinized. The first, the "Eva Stories," is an Instagram project from 2019 that presented the story of Éva Heyman, a young Jewish girl that was murdered in Auschwitz (Henig & Ebbrecht-Hartmann, 2022). The second, the #HolocaustPOVchallenge on TikTok, is a social media viral trend that became prominent on TikTok in 2020, in which users uploaded short videos of themselves as Holocaust victims (Ebbrecht-Hartmann & Divon, 2020).

Both projects were highly criticized worldwide in public discourse. Critics suggested that an Instagram account of a girl murdered in the Holocaust is not the proper way to commemorate the most tragic event in human history (Kershner, 2019; Scharf & Horowitz, 2019; Holmes, 2019). The TikTok trend attracted even harsher responses. The Auschwitz Museum, for example, stated that some of these videos are "dangerously close or already beyond the border of trivializing history" ("Auschwitz Museum Calls TikTok Holocaust Trend," 2020). In both of these cases, both the medium and the message faced criticism for being offensive. Critics not only contended that the content produced was

Noam Tirosh, *Understanding Holocaust Memory on Instagram and TikTok* In: *The Remaking of Memory in the Age of the Internet and Social Media*. Edited by: Qi Wang and Andrew Hoskins, Oxford University Press. © Oxford University Press 2024. DOI: 10.1093/oso/9780197661260.003.0017 insulting but also deemed the platforms on which it was presented as inappropriate for Holocaust-related material.

Both projects, however, are much more than a "low-brow" way to commemorate the Holocaust in our digital era. Using Hoskins's assumption about the memory of the multitude (2017), this chapter explores the logic behind two telling initiatives of digital Holocaust commemorations and analyzes their broader impact on Holocaust memory as a whole.

Digital Memory and Digital Holocaust Memory

Questions regarding Holocaust memory and its importance have a leading element on memory studies as a field (Rothberg, 2009). Indeed, our systematic attempts to understand how society remembers the Holocaust were the "central element of the memory boom and the rise of memory studies in the first place" (Kansteiner, 2017, p. 115). Indeed, Holocaust memory was understood as a prominent example of society's cultural memory (Assman & Czaplicka, 1995)—a memory in whose light we construct our sense of identity and community. Addressing Holocaust memory as a component of society's cultural memory leads scholars to explore mostly the institutionalized ways in which the memory of the Holocaust endures and how it crystalizes group identities through its prism. Today we consider such a group to be a transnational community of remembering individuals, unconstrained by geographical and cultural limitations. Indeed, Holocaust remembrance demonstrates the "transnational turn" of memory studies (Erll, 2011), in which historical events are shaped and remembered while traveling between various communities, borders, and national affiliations.

This process has not occurred in a social, political, and cultural vacuum. Erll (2018) claims: "Whenever we approach memory in culture . . . we are dealing with mediation" (p. 309). And indeed, the memory of the Holocaust has transcended familial, geographical, and national boundaries through mediation by the established media of the time. We are reminded of our individual and collective past through constant exposure to media content (Hoskins, 2011; Neiger et al., 2011). As part of this process, we externalize our own memories and internalize mediated "collective" memories (Erll, 2018; Neiger et al., 2011). Thus, there is no way to fathom a shared understanding of the Holocaust without widely circulated images, stories, and narratives that have become available through the media (Meyers et al, 2014). The 1978 NBC miniseries *Holocaust*; Claude Lanzmann's epic nine-hour *Shoah* documentary, released in 1985; and Steven Spielberg's 1993 *Schindler's List* all turned into cultural phenomena, which influenced audiences, transcending distinct geographical locations and distinct national affiliations or commitments.

However, the media are constantly in a state of flux, and the mediascape in which we engage and experience shared memory is continually changing. Digital media change the way we experience the past and alter the way we currently perceive the very meaning of memory, remembering, and forgetting (Reading, 2009). The digitalization of media is changing Holocaust memory as well (Frosh, 2018; Kansteiner, 2014; Walden, 2022). Holocaust witnesses are currently testifying as holograms (Frosh, 2018; Kansteiner, 2014); museums develop and stream online memorials (Trezise, 2012); and Holocaust memory institutions use social media (Commane & Potton, 2019) on a daily basis. These are all important examples of the "virtual Holocaust memory" culture (Walden, 2022), which has come to define our current memory sphere (Walden, 2022). During the COVID-19 pandemic, the transition to digitalization intensified as Holocaust memory moved online at an accelerated pace (Ebbrecht-Hartmann, 2021).

However, there is still a need to reveal the various meanings of this process in greater detail (Commane & Potton, 2019). Kansteiner (2014) called us to explore if the digitalization of Holocaust memory changes, or at least challenges, how we remember the Holocaust. He wondered if digital commemorations are simply a new method through which traditional, known, and accepted stories about the Holocaust and its consequences are communicated. In this chapter, I wish to address these questions by using Hoskins's (2017) discussion about the memory of the multitude. I adopt this framework as a methodological approach to help unpack current digital mnemonic projects.

The Memory of the Multitude as a Method

Digital media has changed how we engage with the memory of the Holocaust by reshaping social remembering and forgetting. Memory, claims Hoskins (2011), is now "lived through a media ecology wherein abundance, pervasiveness and accessibility of communication networks, nodes, and digital media content, scale pasts anew" (Hoskins, 2011, p. 29). This leads to a situation in which what we tend to perceive as our "collective memory," or the shared understanding of the past that shapes both individual and collective identity and sensibility, is no longer possible. Instead of the "collective" aspect of our memory, Hoskins (2017) claims that it is the "multitude" that serves as the "defining digital organizational form of memory beyond but also incorporating the self" (Hoskins, 2017, p. 85).

I use the memory of the multitude framework as an approach to explore novel forms of digital Holocaust commemoration. I focus on three elements of Hoskins's (2017) approach: (a) the changing parameters of memory and remembering that are causing the "softening of history"; (b) the decline of human capacity to remember that enhances a crisis of moral remembering; and (c) the transition of the audience from spectators to active participants in memory processes, which defies memory narrativity. These are, clearly, not the only factors at play when discussing the memory of the multitude. However, these three elements are fundamental to our understanding of the transition to a new form of memory and commemoration.

The Shifting Parameters of Memory

Discussions of collective memory often assume that society's remembrance is confined to official spheres of memory, those designated spaces where we are encouraged to recollect past events, contemplate their significance, and foster a shared sense of history and community. However, the advent of digital media has disrupted this paradigm. When we speak about the memory of the multitude, we speak of an all-encompassing memory sphere that we remain connected to, even in the most mundane aspects of our daily lives. According to Hoskins (2017), this new way of connecting to the past "softens history." Our meeting with "The" history is not confined any more to the traditional ways of commemorations. The memory of the multitude changes "the parameters of the who, what, when and why of remembering. With digital searching, accessing, participating, there is little unseen, untouched or uncommented on by the multitude" (p. 89). These parameters—*who remembers, what is being remembered, when we engage in such a remembering process*, and *why we do so*—are employed to explore the two case studies discussed in this chapter.

The Decline of the Human Capacity of Memory

In the past, memory environments were largely dominated by traditional one-way media and communication technologies, which provided limited external competition for the audience's attention. When reflecting on mnemonic messages in front of physical monuments, traditional media audiences were seen as spectators who maintained a high level of attention. Clearly, during that time, memory initiatives were designed without anticipating the bombardment of other information and competing messages that we now encounter when visiting monuments with our mobile devices.

The digital environment is different. As we have access to more platforms and abundance of information at the same time from the same device, and as various information about the past is just a click away from us at all times, it is becoming harder to discern among the pieces of information about the past that are now available to us. According to Hoskins (2017), this may create a decline in what he describes as normative remembering and forgetting. In this chapter, normative remembering and forgetting are framed by the questions posed by Thompson (2009): What should individuals or groups remember or forget? How can they actively facilitate these processes? And how should they respond to the demands that emerge from memory? These questions serve as a valuable framework for analyzing the various dimensions of the digital projects examined in this study and their moral value.

The Evolving Role of the Audience in the Digital Memory Environment

The traditional task of mass media outlets has been to shape and represent social memory by spreading and constructing a memory narrative to an audience of passive spectators (Neiger et al., 2011). This spectatorship, according to Hoskins (2017), "implies a focused gaze on a single text" (p. 100). In numerous popular digital platforms, audiences play a more active role than being mere onlookers. They actively participate in selecting the content they wish to be exposed to, contribute additional information about the events being described, and have agency in sharing the content with their friends and relatives.

This active participation transforms the very meaning and value of memory. Prior remembrance processes sought to provide a narrative of past events. By constructing coherent narratives, memory actors infused society mnemonic activities with a "lesson of morals that guide and instruct mnemonic communities in the present" (Neiger et al., 2011, p. 5). In the digital environment of the multitude, memory is perpetually in the making. Memory is constructed "on the fly" (Hoskins, 2009), and thus it is "characterized by its mediated or mediatized emergence through range of everyday digital media" (Hoskins, 2009, p. 94). As such, memory never congeals as a coherent, immutable narrative. On the contrary, the mere value of the memory of the multitude "is found in its perpetual becoming" (Hoskins, 2017, p. 95). As such, when analyzing the case studies in this chapter, I also explore issues of narratives and narrativity. I ponder whether the memory actors involved in these projects have created a new form of Holocaust narrative or whether these projects defy the construction of any kind of singular narrative regarding the Holocaust.

Eva Stories and the #HolocaustPOVchallenge

"Hello, my name is Eva," the sound of a young girl is heard. "That's me!" A smiling picture of Eva appears with her name written in sparkly purple underneath it. This is the opening scene of the first "story" published on the Instagram account: @Eva.stories. The account went online on May, 1, 2019, on Israel's official Holocaust Remembrance Day and was accompanied by an extensive public relations campaign asking: What if a girl in the Holocaust had Instagram?

One year later, a new viral trend spread in TikTok. Users posted videos of themselves acting as Holocaust victims. TikTok #HolocaustPOVchallenge had a different look and feel than the Eva Stories: a sad violin gently playing in the background, soft voices wailing. The embedded text represented a young girl's words:

> I was in my home making a stew. And the Nazis came, and they broke down my door.
> And starting kicking me and beating me out of my own home. They showed us on a train
> with a bunch of other people from my town. We were all going to the same place . . .
> Auschwitz. And we know we were never coming back.[2]

Thousands of teenagers worldwide participated in the Holocaust challenge, posing as Holocaust victims on clips produced and posted by them.

These two digital case studies appeared on different social media platforms—Instagram and TikTok, and they differ in content, style, and tone. Yet, despite their differences, both cases are emblematic examples of Holocaust memory culture in our current digital media environment and demonstrate the influence of short videos as prominent communication tools, particularly among young users (Kaye et al., 2022; Wang & Wu, 2021), on Holocaust memory. Before discussing both Eva Stories and the TikTok's #HolocaustPOVchallenge, it is worth highlighting some information about Instagram and TikTok as communication platforms. Instagram, launched in 2010 and now owned by Meta (formerly Facebook), is a platform primarily dedicated to sharing photos and videos. With over two billion monthly users in 2022, Instagram has been credited with initiating the "era of the influencer" (Eldridge, 2023). Additionally, Instagram has become a significant arena for political discourse, where politicians actively engage with the platform's users (Boulianne & Larsson, 2023; Filimonov et al., 2016; Turnbull-Dugarte, 2019). TikTok, with over a billion monthly users in 2023, is a platform solely focused on short video communication (DataReportal, 2023). It enjoys popularity among young adults aged 18–24 and is available in multiple countries and languages (Zeng, Crystal, & Schäfer, 2021; Zeng, Schäfer, & Allgaier, 2021).

Indeed, both Instagram and TikTok have faced criticism for their potential to host inappropriate content, spread fake news, provide misinformation and disinformation, as well as negatively impact the mental health of young adults

(Eldridge, 2023; Schellewald, 2021; Southerton, 2021). As Schellewald (2021) notes, these platforms are regarded as "communicative environments that afford merely simple entertainment made addictive through algorithmic means" (p. 1451). However, critical media scholarship emphasizes the importance of thoroughly exploring platforms like Instagram and TikTok from a perspective that examines how the unique attributes of these platforms create opportunities for users to "express their concerns, frustration and personal stake in what they perceive to be salient issues of their time" (Hautea et al., 2021, p. 12). This is also what this chapter is trying to do when exploring Eva Stories and the #HolocaustPOVchallenge.

The Eva Stories is a project that offered a digital adaptation of Éva Heyman's diary, written originally in Hungarian by a 13-year-old Jewish girl who perished in Auschwitz, as an Instagram "story." In 1945, Éva's mother found the diary and published it in its original language (Yad Vashem, n.d.). In 2019, Mati Kochavi, an Israeli high-tech entrepreneur, together with his daughter, Maya, who sponsored and initiated the project, decided to adapt Éva's diary into an Instagram "story" that eventually won the Webby award—the "Academy Awards" of digital content—for the "best use of social platform functionality to tell an ongoing story" (Webby Awards, 2020). Within the digital Holocaust memory literature, Instagram is described as an accessible medium that can play a significant role in the culture of Holocaust remembrance (Commane & Potton, 2019). Alongside the criticism discussed above, in an in-depth exploration of the Eva Stories, Henig and Ebbrecht-Hartmann (2022) claimed that it is a representative example of a new digital Holocaust memory initiative, creating a "responsive space for remembering the Holocaust" in which users are enabled to "inscribe themselves in mediated Holocaust memory."

The TikTok challenge is part of a point-of-view (POV) video genre that is popular in TikTok and other media (Ankel, 2020). In the POV genre, videos are taken from a first-person perspective, "making the viewers the main character of the video" (Ankel, 2020, n.p.). In an interview to *The Insider*, one creator of such a video claimed that she tried to "educate people" about the Holocaust (Ankel, 2020). However, the challenge was highly criticized by many official Holocaust memory institutions. This critique has arisen from the concerns of Holocaust memory institutions regarding new commemorative initiatives, primarily due to their novelty and deviation from established practices (Kansteiner, 2014). The discussion by Niemeyer and Keighley (Chapter 14, this volume) regarding the role of nostalgia can also provide a theoretical frame to understand such criticism as one can claim that there exists a nostalgia for a desired form of Holocaust commemorations, a feeling of absence and inadequacy in contemporary commemorations (e.g., the TikTok ones) and a fear of future loss when Holocaust memory might cease to be commemorated. Furthermore, widely held perceptions of TikTok as a negative form of social media (as exemplified by Schellewald, 2021, and Southerton, 2021), along with the general belief that social media is a harmful realm of memory (as discussed by Murphy et al., Chapter 8, this volume) may have further contributed to these concerns.

However, this is clearly a partial perspective. According to Wang's insights (Chapter 2, this volume), our actions on social media are intricately influenced by the complex interactions among users, the platforms we utilize, and the cyber communities in which we participate. Wang (Chapter 2, this volume) asserts that these actions have a profound impact on our sense of self and overall well-being. This is also true with the TikTok example in our case. Following a more complex understanding of social media mnemonic practices, Ebbrecht-Hartmann and Divon (2020) claimed that the Holocaust challenge represents a noble practice of involved youth that use the tools they know and like when engaging with a sensitive topic such as the Holocaust. As such, it is worth exploring these two projects using Hoskins's perspective of the memory of the multitude in order to better understand the logic behind Holocaust commemorations in the digital era.

Changing Parameters of Memory in the Eva Stories and the TikTok Challenge

The first feature of the memory of the multitude is the "softening" of history, a process that changes the parameters of who is remembering, what is being remembered, when we engage in the remembering process, and why we do so (Hoskins, 2017). Indeed, both the Eva Stories and the #HolocaustPOVchallenge vividly demonstrate how the answers to such questions in our digital era differ from those regarding traditional memory projects. In the TikTok challenge case, those who remember are just regular users. They are "TikTokers" who both watched videos and produced them. They are clearly not institutional producers of media or official and established actors of Holocaust memory institutions. They are not even memory activists operating outside state channels to promote counterhegemonic narratives about the past (Gutman, 2017).

The Eva Stories present a different situation. Instagram users are indeed the targeted audience of the project's creators. However, these creators, while not being part of the traditional Holocaust memory industry, cannot be considered regular users. The Eva Stories project was led by Mati and Maya Kochavi, private entrepreneurs who, according to them, invested several million dollars in the project (Kershner, 2019). Indeed, without such a heavy investment, the project would not have obtained public attention and could not even be produced since it is a cinematic adaptation of a written diary disseminated over Instagram to a wide and highly dispersed audience.

Both projects answer the question of what is remembered in two words: Holocaust victims. In the TikTok case, however, the actual victims cannot be identified. They have no names and no concrete stories. They are merely avatar victims using social media as a last attempt to speak out and to be heard by a contemporary audience. The Eva Stories case is decidedly different. The story focuses on a specific and identifiable Holocaust victim, Éva Heyman, whose story was somewhat known to a relatively limited audience due to her family's efforts to publish her diary after her death (Yad Vashem, n.d.). The creators of the Eva Stories deliberately selected Éva as a protagonist as, they said, there was "something very modern and relatable about [her]" (Kershner, 2019, n.p.). Maya Kochavi explained that Eva is a figure that "a modern kid in 2019 could connect to with an unrequited middle school crush, family drama and grand ambitions to become a news photographer" (Scharf & Horowitz 2019). Last, there is a resemblance between Éva Heyman and Anne Frank (Van Es, 2019), and users were in fact invited to think about Éva as "Anne Frank 2.0" (Wenkert, 2019). As such, while the TikTok challenge represents a multiplicity of figures being "remembered," the Eva Stories maintained the traditional logic of memory making in which a single identifiable person is being highlighted and remembered, serving as a representative of all Holocaust victims and an illustration of a central narrative.

The TikTok challenge comprises thousands of videos, uploaded at different times and from various locations, most of which are no longer available on TikTok. It is almost impossible to explore or understand the motives of those users participating in the challenge. In anonymous interviews to established media following the outcry that the challenge created, some of the TikTokers claimed that their goal was to educate people. "I have always been interested in the history of the Holocaust," said one of the creators, "and just wanted to make a creative video informing people about it" (quoted in Ebbrecht-Hartmann & Divon, 2020, n.p.). Clearly, to better understand why people created such videos, there is a need for further research that will locate these users and ask them directly to explain their motivation and intent. In the Eva Stories case, this task is easier. According to Mati Kochavi, the aim of @Eva.stories was to engage new audiences with the memory of the Holocaust. "In the digital age," he explained, "when the attention span is low but the thrill span is high, and given the dwindling number of survivors, it is imperative to find new models of testimony and memory" (Kaplan-Sommer, 2020, n.p.). And, indeed, the project was described by established media as "an innovative, if provocative, effort to engage screen-hooked post Millennials in Holocaust education and remembrance as the last generation of survivors is dying out" (Kershner, 2019, n.p.).

After winning the Webby award in 2020, the people behind the project explained that they enabled young audiences "to relate to very complicated historical moments." Once the story is internalized, young audiences are "empowered to become the newest storytellers of history" (Webby Awards, 2020).

Last, it appears that both projects completely alter the answers to the question of when we remember. The two projects were produced in social media and thus change the temporality of remembering in a fundamental way. We can remember whenever we want to from wherever we are. Holocaust-related narratives are within our reach, using the Instagram app or the TikTok app available on the smartphone resting inside our own pocket. We are not obliged to remember in an official, "sacred," time frame (e.g., an official day of remembrance). When engaging with both the Eva Stories and the TikTok challenge, we secularize the commemorative process. We do not have to visit the "universal temples" of Holocaust remembrance (Goldberg, 2012) to contemplate their messages. Yet, in the case of the Eva Stories, the timing of airing the project was not in the least accidental. The project was launched on Israel's official Holocaust Remembrance Day. The producers of the Eva Stories took advantage of the public attention paid to Holocaust-related stories on the official day of remembrance to promote their project. Subsequently, on January 27, 2020, the International Holocaust Remembrance Day, the Eva Stories was launched on Snapchat. While the story remained the same, the specific platform differed. As such, it seems that while the TikTok challenge was indeed an ephemeral yet ubiquitous phenomenon, the Eva Stories remained closely tethered to national and global "memory calendars."

The Crisis of Moral Holocaust Remembrance

According to Hoskins (2017), we struggle with a declining capacity to remember in face of multiple (digital) distractions. As we lack the ability to select, sift, and discern among the pieces of information about the past that are now available to us, Hoskins (2017) notes that we experience a decline in normative remembering and forgetting. We don't know exactly what we should remember. This is an ethical crisis of memory (Margalit, 2002; Thompson, 2009). When it comes to Holocaust memory in our digital age, one aspect of this crisis stems from the abundance of new interactive platforms of Holocaust denialism. The digital affordances so readily capitalized created greater opportunities for Holocaust deniers to thrive and spread their messages. Indeed, the fear of Holocaust denialism and trivialization fueled some of the harsher critics against both examples used in this study. In response to this criticism, TikTok eventually blocked their users' ability to search the term: #Holocaustchallenge in an attempt to curtail the challenge's virality ("TikTok Holocaust trend 'hurtful and offensive,'" 2020). Moreover, according to the creators of the Eva Stories, one of the main reasons to initiate the project was to confront and tackle Holocaust denial.

However, questions regarding the ethics of memory go much deeper than the resistance to Holocaust denialism. The morality of memory is connected to questions regarding what people ought to remember, are obliged to remember, and the nature of such obligations (Margalit, 2002; Thompson, 2009). Indeed, a commonly held perspective is that "a collective failure of remembrance is . . . an invitation to moral or political disaster" (Rieff, 2016, p. 55). Traditionally, the answers to such moral questions and obligations within the context of the Holocaust have been clear. We are entreated to remember the horrors of the Holocaust and its victims—to remember and never forget in order to prevent yet another Holocaust from happening (see David, 2020). Performative aspects accompanied this cautionary moral remembrance. Lest we forget, we need to learn about what happened and to participate in commemoration ceremonies. We silently mediate and reflect on Holocaust monuments and are invited to watch Holocaust-related content during the dedicated time frames, "acting appropriately" while we watch.

This ritualistic behavior does not take place when we watch the Eva Stories on Instagram or when we engage with TikTok videos of Holocaust victims. The venue of the "public realm" has changed. While the creators of such POV videos were criticized for being one step away from Holocaust denial, it seems that the moral perplexity of other TikTokers engaging with such content on their social media feed (what in TikTok jargon is termed the "For You Page") is the main issue we need to explore. Questions such as, "Is it really OK to remember the Holocaust while in bed, scrolling around my social media?" are new questions for audiences experiencing Holocaust-related content.

The case of the Eva Stories is also intriguing. When the Eva Stories was "live" on Instagram, users' comments were enabled and appeared right beside the stories. Some of the comments were cynical and even offensive, occasionally promoting Holocaust denial. Indeed, Holocaust deniers used the opportunity to spread their agenda while the stories were live and only mildly refereed, if at all. Moreover, we know that the comments quickly turned into a bitter political contest between rival Israeli and Palestinian supporters. As such, while trying to tackle the ethical crisis of Holocaust remembrance in the era of the memory of the multitude, the Eva Stories turned into a digital arena that illustrates this very crisis. Indeed, there seems to be a zero-sum game between the contested memories of both Israelis and Palestinians; however, one cannot imagine that these memories would have had the opportunity to butt heads while visiting Yad Vashem or the US Holocaust Museum in Washington, D.C.

Narratives of Digital Holocaust Memory

The third important aspect of the memory of the multitude focuses on the changing role of the audience in the digital memory environment and its effect on memory narrativization. In the memory of the multitude, memory is devoid of a coherent single narrative since the narrative is in a perpetual state of becoming (Hoskins, 2017). The fluid nature of the memory of the multitude leads us to wonder if narratives are in fact provided to digital audiences, and if so, what they are and how they differ from established Holocaust narratives.

In both the Eva Stories and the #HolocaustPOVchallenge, users are encouraged to engage with and even actively participate in the content made available to them. The users are those who choose when, where, and how to engage with both the stories and the TikTok POV videos. They are encouraged to disseminate the content to their friends and followers, and they can comment on and share their thoughts over various social networks in real time. However, while in the TikTok challenge users can upload videos of themselves as part of an unfolding trend, the Eva Stories offers preset content, which can be discussed but not altered through audience engagement. Therefore, it prompts us to question the extent to which user participation in the case of Eva Stories has the power to significantly reshape the narratives proposed by the memory actors responsible for producing the project.

The protagonist of the story is clearly Éva Heyman, and Éva's deportation to Auschwitz marks the end of the story. In the final episode of the "story," the producers dedicate the project to the "memory of the 6 million Jews who perished in the Holocaust." If memory in the era of the multitude defies narrativity, the Eva Stories, it seems, is not a "pure" example of it. While users can comment on and share the stories, the project itself is a narrativized story delivered over digital media, offered to users (active as they may be) who engage with the touching story of a young Jewish Hungarian girl, whom the producers of the content sought to commemorate. In the final episode, a fictional scene is added, in which Eva asks her friend Annie whether she believes people will remember them. "Yes Eva," Annie answers. "Your journal. . . . Everyone will remember us." As such, the narrative is as follows: Jews were persecuted in Europe prior to and during WWII, and they suffered from a murderous attempt to annihilate them. As evident by the last episode, the project is infused with a moral purpose—to remember and never forget—and users realize the importance of watching the Eva Stories.

The TikTok example is indeed very different. Users uploaded their videos based on fictional stories and characters. While the common theme focused on victims and victimhood, the videos contained various characters and lacked any apparent binding narrative. The messages conveyed in those videos lacked a clear beginning, middle, and end and did not convey any explicit moral imperative. While one video can depict a girl supposedly examined by Nazi officers before being taken away to what seems like her final moment on Earth, another video can show a 19-year-old girl that describes being taken with her mother to the gas chamber.[3] No names are used to identify the characters in the videos, beyond the usernames of the TikTokers uploading them. As such, it seems that the #HolocaustPOVchallenge is a good exemplar of a digital memory project in the era of the multitude as user participation and involvement create an ongoing memory that defies crystallization into a coherent historical narrative. Indeed, these videos represent an ongoing commitment to Holocaust memory, including its victims, the "final solution" to the "Jewish problem," and the particularities of the annihilation, topics that are considered an integral part of the Holocaust "master narrative" (Bauer, 2020). However, neither this narrative nor any other singular focus is presented in the TikTok project in the form of a predetermined story containing both a beginning and a morally infused ending.

Conclusions

The memory of the multitude (Hoskins, 2017) is the form of social and political memory that "is for the many, seen as being many," using Paulo Virno's (2004, p. 22) terminology. In this chapter, I used Hoskins's (2017) framework to analyze the Instagram project of Eva Stories and the TikTok #HolocaustPOVchallenge. Understanding the underlying logic behind recent mnemonic projects helps uncover new elements of memory in our Instagram and TikTok Era.

Interestingly, the two projects operate under different modes of commemoration logic. While the TikTok challenge is a representative of memory in the era of the multitude, the Eva Stories perpetuates the logic of "collective memory." TikTokers taking part in the challenge escaped the institutional gaze of official Holocaust memory institutions and offered a new commemorative language that was not understood by disapproving official gatekeepers. However, while the Eva Stories encouraged users' participation through engagement with the story content, the memory actors behind the project did not allow users to actively contribute to the story itself. The narrative the Eva Stories employed was fixed and dictated by the project creators. As shown, it was infused with moral imperatives to remember and take part in active remembrance rituals.

According to Kansteiner (2014), digitalization of Holocaust memory is used primarily to reproduce established Holocaust narratives. The audience, he claims, "have generally no power over the conceptual framing, narrative employment, and visual display of the violent pasts which they are urged to remember" (Kansteiner, 2014, pp. 404–405). In their recent systematic literature review, Tirosh and Mikel-Arieli (2023) similarly found that scholarship on digital Holocaust memory focuses on case studies that emphasize established Holocaust narratives and not on projects that commemorate more marginalized Holocaust narratives. In a way, this can describe the situation with Eva Stories as well.

The memory of the multitude enables the presentation of multiple memories and fragmentation of moral imperatives in a process that defies the narrativization of the past and rejects the crystallization of a shared collective memory. This is clearly the case of the TikTok challenge, but not Eva Stories. The TikTokers involved in the challenge commemorated the Holocaust through engaging with issues that are integral to the Holocaust's master narrative (Bauer, 2020), but without offering a coherent narrative. They did so without making demands on the viewers to obey a set of predetermined ethical considerations.

As we ponder the future of Holocaust memory, an important question arises: What will happen if the multitude replaces the collective in shaping social memory? In the era of digital media, where monolithic collective memory is giving way to a decentralized and eclectic memory (Hoskins, 2017), we must consider the social and political implications of such a transformation. Can we envision a Holocaust memory culture in which narratives and predetermined lessons for the future are absent, as exemplified by the TikTok example highlighted in this chapter?

It appears that there exists an inherent contradiction between the aspirations of established Holocaust memory institutions like Yad Vashem, which seek to promote a coherent and hegemonic Holocaust narrative, and the nature of memory, remembrance, and forgetting in the age of a memory multitude. In this memory landscape that is "softening" history, promoting audience participation, and challenges normative imperatives of remembrance, Holocaust memory will undergo profound changes. These changes might be so significant that Holocaust memory could no longer be described as the foundational past of the Western world (Confino, 2011). Maybe, we will no longer have a foundational past. Walt Whitman claimed that we are big enough to contain multitudes. Only the future will tell if Holocaust memory culture can contain them as well.

Notes

1. As part of the: "Song of Myself" (1892), Whitman writes:
   Do I contradict myself?
   Very well then I contradict myself,
   (I am large, I contain multitudes.)
   https://www.poetryfoundation.org/poems/45477/song-of-myself-1892-version
2. The video is available online: https://twitter.com/i/status/1295784314550931458
3. Both videos are available online: https://twitter.com/i/status/1295783195682562049, https://twitter.com/i/status/1295783436083290113

References

Ankel, S. (2020, August 23). TikTok creators are pretending to be Holocaust victims in heaven in a new trend dubbed "trauma porn." *Insider*. https://www.insider.com/tiktok-trend-shows-people-pretending-to-be-holocaust-victims-heaven-2020-8

Assman, J., & Czaplicka, J.)1995(. Collective memory and cultural identity. *New German Critique*, *65*, 125–133.

Auschwitz museum calls TikTok Holocaust Trend "hurtful and offensive." (2020, August 26). The Guardian. https://www.theguardian.com/technology/2020/aug/26/auschwitz-museum-calls-tiktok-holocaust-trend-hurtful-and-offensive

Bauer, Y. (2020, May 5). *The distortion of Holocaust memory* [Keynote lecture]. Holocaust Research in Challenging Times: An Online Conference of Holocaust Researchers. https://youtu.be/drO-jqE6k98

Boulianne, S., & Larsson, A. O. (2023). Engagement with candidate posts on Twitter, Instagram, and Facebook during the 2019 election. *New Media & Society*, *25*(1), 119–140.

Commane, G., & Potton, R., 2019. Instagram and Auschwitz: A critical assessment of the impact social media has on Holocaust representation. *Holocaust Studies*, *25*(1–2), 158–181.

Confino, A. (2011). *Foundational pasts: The Holocaust as historical understanding*. Cambridge University Press.

DataRePortal. (2023, May 11). *TikTok users, stats, data & trends*. https://datareportal.com/essential-tiktok-stats

David, L. (2020). *The past can't heal us*. Cambridge University Press.

Ebbrecht-Hartmann, T. (2021). Commemorating from a distance: The digital transformation of Holocaust memory in times of COVID-19. *Media, Culture & Society*, *43*(6), 1095–1112. https://doi.org/10.1177/0163443720983276

Ebbrecht-Hartmann, T., & Divon, T. (2020). Let TikTok creators pretend to be victims of the Nazis. It strengthens Holocaust memory. *Haaretz.com*. https://www.haaretz.com/us-news/.premium let tiktok-users-pretend-to-be-victims-of-the-nazis-it-strengthens-holocaust-memory-1.9141182

Eldridge, A. (2023, May 14). Instagram. *Encyclopedia Britannica*. https://www.britannica.com/topic/Instagram

Erll, A. (2011). Travelling memory. *Parallax*, *17*(4), 4–18.

Erll, A. (2018). Media and the dynamics of memory—From cultural paradigms to transcultural premeditation. In B. Wagoner (Ed.), *The handbook of culture and memory* (pp. 304–324). Oxford University Press.

Filimonov, K., Russmann, U., & Svensson, J. (2016). Picturing the party: Instagram and party campaigning in the 2014 Swedish elections. *Social Media + Society*, *2*(3), 1–11. https://doi.org/10.1177/2056305116662179

Frosh, P. (2018). The mouse, the screen and the Holocaust witness: Interface aesthetics and moral response. *New Media & Society*, *20*(1), 351–368.

Goldberg, A. (2012). The "Jewish narrative" in the Yad Vashem Global Holocaust Museum. *Journal of Genocide Research*, *14*(2), 187–213.

Gutman, Y. (2017). *Memory activism: Reimagining the past for the future in Israel-Palestine*. Vanderbilt University Press.

Hautea, S., Parks, P., Takahashi, B., & Zeng, J. (2021). Showing they care (or don't): Affective publics and ambivalent climate activism on TikTok. *Social Media + Society*, 7(2), 1–14. https://doi.org/10.1177/20563051211012344

Henig, L., & Ebbrecht-Hartmann, T. (2022). Witnessing Eva Stories: Media witnessing and self-inscription in social media memory. *New Media & Society*, *22*(1), 202–226. https://doi.org/10.1177/1461444820963805

Holmes, O. (2019, May 8). Instagram Holocaust diary Eva.Stories sparks debate in Israel. *The Guardian*. https://www.theguardian.com/world/2019/may/08/instagram-holocaust-diary-evastories-sparks-debate-in-israel

Hoskins, A. (2009). Digital network memory. In: A. Erll & A. Rigney (Eds.), *Mediation, remediation and the dynamics of cultural memory* (pp. 91–106). De Gruyter.

Hoskins, A. (2011). Media, memory, metaphor: Remembering and the connective turn. *Parallax, 17*(4), 19–31.

Hoskins, A. (2017). Memory of the multitude—The end of collective memory. In: A. Hoskins (Ed.), *Digital memory studies—Media pasts in transition* (pp. 85–109). Routledge.

Kansteiner, W. (2014). Genocide memory, digital cultures, and the aesthetization of violence. *Memory Studies, 7*(4), 403–408.

Kansteiner, W. (2017). Transnational Holocaust memory, digital culture and the end of reception studies. In T. Sindbæk Andersen & B. Törnquist-Plewa (Eds.), *The twentieth century in European memory: Transcultural mediation and reception* (pp. 305–343). Brill.

Kaplan-Sommer, A. (2020, January 22). Tweeting the Holocaust? The perils of using social media to discuss the Holocaust. *Haaretz.* https://www.haaretz.com/israel-news/.premium-the-perils-and-perks-of-social-media-to-remember-the-holocaust-1.8434463

Kaye, D. B. V., Zeng, J., & Wikström, P. (2022). *TikTok: Creativity and culture in short video.* Polity.

Kershner, I. (2019, April 30). A Holocaust story for the social media generation. *New York Times.* https://www.nytimes.com/2019/04/30/world/middleeast/eva-heyman-instagram-holocaust.html

Margalit, A. 2002. *The ethics of memory.* Harvard University Press.

Meyers, O., Zandberg, E., & Neiger, M. (2014). *Communicating awe: Media memory and Holocaust commemoration.* Palgrave Macmillan

Neiger, M., Meyers, O., & Zandberg, E. (2011). *On media memory: Collective memory in a new media age.* Palgrave Macmillan.

Reading, A. (2009). The globytal: Towards an understanding of globalized memories in the digital age. In A. Maj & D. Riha (Eds.), *Digital memories: Exploring critical issues* (pp. 31–41). Inter-Disciplinary Press.

Rieff, D. (2016). *In praise of forgetting: Historical memory and its ironies.* Yale University Press.

Rothberg, M. 2009. *Multidirectional memory: Remembering the Holocaust in the age of decolonization.* Stanford University Press.

Scharf, I., & Horowitz, A. (2019, April 30). Instagram story of young Holocaust victim Eva aims at new generation. *Times of Israel.* https://www.timesofisrael.com/instagram-story-of-young-holocaust-victim-aims-at-new-generation/

Schellewald, A. (2021). Communicative forms on TikTok: Perspectives from digital ethnography. *International Journal of Communication, 15*, 1437–1457.

Southerton, C. (2021). Lip-syncing and saving lives: Healthcare workers on TikTok. *International Journal of Communication, 15*(2021), 3248–3268.

Thompson, J. (2009). Apology, historical obligations and the ethics of memory. *Memory Studies, 2*(2), 195–210.

TikTok Holocaust trend "hurtful and offensive." (2020, August 27). BBC. https://www.bbc.com/news/newsbeat-53934500

Tirosh, N., & Mikel-Arieli, R. (2023). What we talk about when we talk about digital Holocaust memory: A systematic analysis of research published in academic journals, 2010–2022. *Communication Review, 26*(2), 151–170.

Trezise, B. (2012). Touching virtual trauma: Performative empathics in second life. *Memory Studies, 5*(4), 392–409. https://doi.org/10.1177/1750698011426355

Turnbull-Dugarte, S. J. (2019). Selfies, policies, or votes? Political party use of Instagram in the 2015 and 2016 Spanish general elections. *Social Media + Society, 5*(4), 392–409.

Van Es, B. (2019, May 25). Anne Frank: The real story of the girl behind the diary. *The Guardian.* https://www.theguardian.com/books/2019/may/25/anne-frank-full-story-bart-van-es

Virno, P. (2004). *A grammar of the multitude—For an analysis of contemporary forms of life.* Columbia University.

Wang, W., & Wu, J. (2021). Research perspectives on TikTok & its legacy apps. Short video platforms and local community building in China. *International Journal of Communication, 15*, 3269–3291.

Walden, V. G. (2022). What is "virtual Holocaust memory"? *Memory Studies, 15*(4), 621–633. https://doi.org/10.1177/1750698019888712

Webby Awards. (2020). Eva.Stories. https://www.webbyawards.com/collaborate-monday/eva-stories/

Wenkert, W. (2019, May 1). Instagram account telling the story of a Jewish girl during the Holocaust ignites debate. *Calcalist.* https://www.calcalistech.com/ctech/articles/0,7340,L-3761362,00.html

Yad Vashem. (n.d.). *The diary of Éva Heyman.* https://www.yadvashem.org/he/education/educational-materials/books/eva-heyman-diary.html

Zeng, J., Crystal, A., & Schäfer, S. M. (2021). Research perspectives on TikTok and its legacy apps—Introduction. *International Journal of Communication, 15*(2021), 3161–3172.

Zeng, Z., Schäfer, S. M., & Allgaier, J. (2021). Reposting "till Albert Einstein is TikTok famous": The memetic construction of science on TikTok. *International Journal of Communication, 15*(2021), 3216–3247.

18

Remembering in Pandemic Time

A Digital Museum's "Slow Memory" Work

Karen Worcman and Joanne Garde-Hansen

When the Museu da Pessoa (Museum of the Person) began its own experience on the Internet in 1996 it was pioneering a convergence of storytelling, oral history, and archiving memories from Brazilian people from all parts of the country through digital media. It did not foresee the fast memory culture (dates, events, likes, connections, access, retrieval, anniversaries, *your year in photos*, etc.) that has become the socially mediated memory of the twenty-first century. Rather it sought to create space and time for reflection, inclusion, and diversity wrought through collaborative storytelling and methodical digital memory work. It was storing, story-ing, and circulating memories and life stories online long before Facebook's commercial socialization of memories or the digital solutionism of the multiplatform museum with curators as social media champions (Proctor, 2010). The Museu da Pessoa has a liminal positionality offering not so much an "extension of autobiographical memory" by/through the Internet (as highlighted by Wang, Chapter 2, this volume) of already well-recorded citizens or a space for the "unremembered self" (defined by Hoskins, Chapter 3, this volume) to be redeemed or destroyed by the Internet's unforgetting. Rather, it became a virtual museum whose priority was to foster the caring, careful, and collaborative recording of personal memories, where life story was worked through and worked on between those called to remember and those doing the memory work.

It was a period during which abstract concepts, such as the idea that everyone can make a museum collection and exhibitions (even those in the collection or being collected), present since the foundation of the Museu da Pessoa in 1991, could be applied. The idea of an open network-built museum that would allow, as widely as possible, the public to participate as creators and curators of their collections and exhibitions. This idea was not fast or efficient, but it was accessible, spreadable, and inclusive. It made it possible to rethink the traditional concepts of space, collection, and preservation, as well as create space for the transformation of the museum production chain itself insofar as the public could become a potential producer of memory (Worcman, 2002). This differentiates

Karen Worcman and Joanne Garde-Hansen, *Remembering in Pandemic Time* In: *The Remaking of Memory in the Age of the Internet and Social Media*. Edited by: Qi Wang and Andrew Hoskins, Oxford University Press.
 DOI: 10.1093/oso/9780197661260.003.0018

the Museu da Pessoa from a community museum, whose process not only is essentially bottom-up, but also differentiates it from a traditional museum, whose process is characteristically top-down. In short, even though it was initially conceptualized as an initiative inspired by the oral history movement, the Museu da Pessoa evolved toward new concepts of collection, space, and dissemination that made it explore, through its collaborative platforms, the possibilities of expansion of public participation to become a virtual museum. In some ways, it grew into a museum faster than most because it was "born digital," but in other ways that we explore in this chapter, the Museu da Pessoa produced slow memory for an Internet Age. While the 1990s saw the beginning of an accelerated time of faster connectivity and cheaper digital tools and services, the 2020s has revealed the unevenness of that transformation, the prospect of "de-growth and aesthetic limitation" and the ecological concerns/limits around policies that drive innovation in cultural economies (Banks, 2020). In fact, during COVID-19, the Museu da Pessoa was operating under a right-wing government that was delegitimizing science around the pandemic and favored deforestation in favor of economic growth. The museum was and is still working hard with Indigenous communities, combining memory and technology for preserving intangible heritage among Indigenous communities. One of the results is a "forest of stories," which means that for each elder that is interviewed a tree is planted, another instance of slow memory.

The museum's mission was renewed during *pandemic time* (recently defined as a "'Corona time' of 'new social rhythms'"; Erll, 2020) where "slow violence" (Nixon, 2011), "slow memory" (Wüstenberg, 2023),[1] and slow methods emerged as ways of knowing and feeling and working. In 2020, the Museu da Pessoa, like other organizations in many parts of the world, created open calls for individuals to share their daily lives, work challenges, dreams, memories, and hopes online. It was a reversion to the traditional private diaries of sharing stories on open platforms but recognized (as does Pogačar, Chapter 16, this volume) that retreat of the state in times of emergency also reveals the "mnemonic distress" of a civil society expected to be always already *resilient* (shoulder the weight and duration of the event and bounce back in the aftermath). What the Museu da Pessoa's project did was reveal that distress as a cascade of stories and memories speaking to the preexisting and overlapping vulnerabilities that have made accelerating transformations so unevenly experienced. In the context of Brazil, "the state" and "citizenship" are also not foregone conclusions, so the idea was to create quotidian and intimate memories of pandemic time for future generations, recognizing that previous outbreaks had failed to be collectively remembered and shared. Therefore, in a time of slowing down, rapid response collecting (and research and writing) emerged all over the world as a way of ensuring the pandemic was remembered with care (see Debono, 2021).

Reflections on the Museu da Pessoa's project and on the wider context of producing collective memories have recognized that the labor, administration, and power relations often work against remembering well, and that "immobility" (Reading, 2021) and slowing down are spatial-temporal requirements for memory work. Memory—personal, collective, social, digital—is a real effort, and if it is to be transmitted, it must be accessible, affordable, and collaboratively administrated (see M. Allen, 2015; Garde-Hansen et al., 2009). From museums to family albums, to register and to share memories needs resources, time, and work if the effort is to be sustained over time, and for a digital museum this is even more apparent. Power and resources are crucial elements in the production, circulation, and preservation of collective memory in Internet-enabled societies. Cultural memory economies rely on the heft of computing and technology industries, and even in oral societies the social preservation and transmission of memories (as intangible cultural heritage requires powerful policy advocates) are performed by people with special skills and training. How to find an approach that is lower in its resource demands and higher in its participatory potential in the context of a twenty-first-century modernity that Rosa describes in *The Uncontrollability of the World* as a "will to escalation" generated by individuals and collectives, driven not by "the promise of improvement in our quality of life but by the unbridled threat that we will lose what we have already attained" (2020, p. 9). Memory loss is one such twenty-first-century threat when speed and managing data have defined the growth imperative.

While the digital revolution has brought these possibilities to a new level in that many persons have the power to produce, select, and share content and memory, their digital memories are stored and shareable through platforms owned by a handful of global private corporations (Facebook, Instagram, WhatsApp are now all Meta). While private and everyday life have been brought to the center of the stage, we have not yet fully developed the capacity for more deeply expressing and experiencing digital personhood, and digital feelings with online solidarity, communities, and cultural/social values. Spaces and places of digital memory, the online spaces available to most people, offer the managerialist approach to organizing, retrieving, storing, and recirculating memories, and it is questionable how far these have supported community and personal well-being. The Museu da Pessoa, as an organization has always addressed the pursuit of digital and online cultural capital (the labor and success of creating value from the past) with a variegated approach that privileges subjectivity, emotion, and bodily feelings (see Cutcher et al., 2016). One way in which the Museu da Pessoa has addressed a "poverty of memory" (M. J. Allen, 2016) has been to include the impact of the economy, work, labor, use of natural resources, anthropology, and ecology in the production of personal memories as connected to Brazil's history and natural resources. Thus, connecting the fast memory of rapid post-1950s human development in Brazil (and countries like it) to the slow memory of environmental change, degradation, deforestation, and climate risks.

The "social memory technology" (Worcman & Garde-Hansen, 2016) of the Museu da Pessoa is the principal methodology that has been created to help individuals, communities, and organizations produce, preserve, and share their own memories. It creates "connective memory" (Hoskins, 2011), but the essential points are *conscience* and *consciousness* of a scarcity of connectedness in parts of the world where institutions are not connecting with individuals at all. It starts from the individual creating a consciousness about their own life narrative, and it goes on to create a collaborative group discussion about those memories and narratives. By providing the individual and the community with possibilities to become curators of a museum's collections and to become legitimate authors of social memory narratives, such methods provide greater opportunities for the collective—and collaborative—construction of new memories, along with new spaces that challenge society's established perceptions and structures. A social technology approach to memory, we have argued, is a "theory, practice, action" (Worcman & Garde-Hansen, 2016, p. 4) with four underlying principles:

> **Principle 1** The idea that any individual can and should be considered a key actor in a global and a local (mediated) heritage through the narration of his or her life story,
>
> **Principle 2** The right of every group to produce their own memory (emerging as a very strong policy—implicit and explicit—in Brazil and many developing countries in the twenty-first century, which parallels the focus on the people's memory in developed regions),
>
> **Principle 3** The practice and outcomes of communities and individuals producing their memories, life stories, and heritage should be open, transparent, and inclusive,
>
> **Principle 4** The potential for change—social, cultural, and theoretical—should be a key outcome of (re)constructing and (re)performing the past in the present as personal memory.

It was created after the systematization of various territorial and community processes led by the Museu da Pessoa. The entire systematized methodology was guided by a tripartite process that should always be simple, low cost, and participatory and have the possibility of contributing, through memory, to social change. The proposal was based on the concept that every life story is valuable and is part of the social memory of a person and the objective of creating methodological instruments through which every person, group, organization, and community could record and share their memory narratives with their communities and integrate them into the set of narratives of memories of society. The objective of creating these methodological instruments was to establish, based on the principles of social technology, the principles, parameters, and guidelines of what could become a *social memory technology* (Lopez, 2009).

The systematization of the methodology represented a major milestone in the trajectory of the Museu da Pessoa as a digital museum. The first aspect was its ability to foster a practice of recording, preserving, and socializing life stories as a way of facing cultural and social challenges of different groups. It was a leap in scale and scope that made it possible to expand the Museu da Pessoa's objective of making life stories a way to connect different people and social groups to contribute to social justice and to combat prejudice and intolerance. The second aspect was to combine awareness and meaning with the process of recording, preserving, and socializing stories. This aspect is increasingly relevant as memory records have become, with many digital technologies, ever faster forms of alienation of the subject, thus any careful digital practice that reconnects person to life story should be a slower, more deliberative solution.

Memory and the Slower Narratives of the Self

Every memory narrative is a translation of an experience lived and preserved in memory. Not every memory narrative is a life story. A narrative can simply be the evocation of a single memory, such as a description of a smell, a taste, an image. A life story narrative is a creative act from which the individual is constituted. When we talk about life story narratives, we assume that they refer to a single object, the self of the individual narrator. When narrating his/her own life, every individual narrator necessarily institutes a self to historicize. Sometimes, throughout the narrative, the individual produces reflections about himself/herself, and, at others, the person only tells events. When narrating, the individual investigates emotionally, affectively, and rationally the set of personal experiences. As Wang et al. (2017) have thematized, memory in terms of narrative and self-narrating is culturally constructive, dynamic in process and timescale, and developed early in life (intra- and interpersonally).

Behind the construction of a life story narrative, there is always a set of choices that result from selections, articulations, organizations, and justifications that the individual makes about himself/herself and others. As the person explores his/her memory, the individual positions himself/herself as an object and sees a narrated self that appears before him/her. The first hearing of a life narrative is that of the narrator. The subjective aspects that are revealed in a life narrative stem from the impact the event had on memory at the time it was recorded or, if it was a recent event, not only the interest the event arouses at the moment the memory reveals itself, the connections that the fact in question awakens, but also the sensations favorable or unfavorable that are generated by a particular psychic fact, which blocks against the reproduction of something likely to generate a feeling of displeasure or that leads to the release of a feeling of displeasure (Freud, 2010, p. 35).

These same subjective aspects are also affected by historical, cultural, and social contexts that delimit the cultural models from which possible memory narratives are established (Bruner, 1987, and more recently, Wang et al., 2017). They are also present in disputes over memories—whether these are within the scope of individual memories or those resulting from the individual's cultural and social conflicts with respect to the group. Life narratives are created from mental models available in the current sociocultural context; but mental models also follow from the narratives. In this overlap between the particular of each one and its context, a narrative dialectic is established that reflects the possible lives of one's culture:

> In the end, we become our autobiographical narratives through which we "tell" our lives. And, due to the cultural formats from which I refer, we also become variants of the canonical narrative forms that our culture establishes. (Bruner, 1987, p. 694)

The context that delimits the life story narratives produced in the Museu da Pessoa is a specific context that makes the memory narratives, and more specifically the life story narratives, have very particular characteristics that differentiate them from the narratives produced, for example, in therapies and in diverse social interactions such as conversations, job interviews, journalistic interviews whose main objective is the production of thematic information. The Museu da Pessoa encourages the production of individual narratives with the aim of recording, preserving, and disseminating life stories to a wider community. Still, the act of narrating one's life is more than organizing and telling one's story. It is a creative and conscious exercise that results in a transformation of the self. Retelling life is an interpretive action that can sometimes have a therapeutic aspect: "Remembering our own life is crucial for our being . . . working on this memory can strengthen, or recapture, self-confidence" (Thompson, 2017, p. 260). As Wang et al. have argued: "Narrative can be simultaneously used to examine the processes of remembering and meaning-making" and "culture plays a central role in shaping memory and self-identity through the act of narration" (2017, p. 200). What happens, though, when one's life story experiences a dramatic shock, such as during a pandemic?

During *pandemic time*, digital technologies were used in many ways. While this meant connection and quick information, it also meant fake news and disinformation for both the "enclaved rich" and the "outcast poor" for whom the eventful violence of the pandemic made strong claims on everyone's time, and no one was remote enough from its lethality (Nixon, 2011, p. 8). In this context, the case we are presenting exemplifies an initiative of the Museu da Pessoa as a pandemic-ready form of transnational slow memory work, in which everyone was invited to share their daily experience so it could become a collective and collaborative memory for the future. The initiative *Diário para o Futuro*[2] (*Diary of the Future*) campaign was a collaboration between the Museu da Pessoa and the School of Fine and Performing Art of Fontys University (Netherlands). While it was restricted to two countries and, very possibly, did not cover all sectors of society, it was an attempt to shed light on human experiences and bring conscience and care to the production of memories throughout this period.

The Experience of *Diário para o Futuro*

In 2020 the new coronavirus took the world by surprise. In Brazil, cultural institutions and social organizations, which had already been suffering as a result of the policies of the extremist right-wing Bolsonaro government, were keenly affected. Museums, theaters, exhibitions, and cinemas all saw their doors closing. Even more dramatically, civil society organizations and collectives located in and serving the peripheries of society were forced to face new challenges, such as a drop-in work opportunities and income, and a rise in disease and hunger.

During this period, *Diário para o Futuro* initiative focused on recording everyday memories for the construction of a collaborative history of pandemic time. The pandemic had created even more challenges for the global social, cultural, and environmental crisis. The United Nations Report on the goals of the millennium pointed out how the pandemic made visible on a very explicit level the social inequality of our contemporary world.

> The COVID-19 pandemic serves as a mirror for the world. It reflects deeply rooted problems in our societies: insufficient social protection, weak public health systems and inadequate health coverage, structural inequalities, environmental degradation and climate change.[3]

In Brazil, some researchers of memory and environmental disasters switched from collecting community memories to delivering food and care packages (Calvillo et al., 2022). Research had to be responsive and responsible and the Museu da Pessoa collected memories in the moment as the 'the collective forced deceleration' became 'an opportunity to experience a new "resonance" with our immediate surroundings (Erll, 2020, p. 863). Pandemic time created an opportunity for human beings to think, as individuals or as part of societies, and this thinking was not only about time (much needed) but was about time itself (slowing down in times of speed and change). *What are the legacies we have inherited and what are the legacies we, as a society, want to create?* Even though collective memory and historical narratives (of events) change over time, the global pandemic had the specific characteristics of a digital era. It had created a common global time for "digital media and methods make it possible to track the global spread of a virus with unprecedented precision" (Erll, 2020, p. 863). Through the use of an online tool, the Museu da Pessoa invited the public to talk about their personal experiences during this pandemic time. The experience of collecting memories relating to the pandemic allowed the museum to not only question the historical importance of the moment (eventness) we were all living through, but also investigate the way in which those participating were communicating their feelings and thoughts during the pandemic situation as slow memory work. What choices would they be making in relation to sharing experiences specifically relating to this moment in time? To what extent could the act of sharing memories of suffering contribute to the collective signifying or resignifying of the pandemic period?

Out of the *Diário para o Futuro*, in searching for greater engagement and an even more effective sharing of experiences, another development arose: the *Jornada Diário para o Futuro* (*Journey of the Diary for the Future*), in which the participants signed up to take part in a kind of journey of memories. The aim of the questions (Table 18.1) was to allow the participants to travel through their memories and, through references to remembered spaces and objects, to recognize and share their fears, dreams, and lives.

Between June and October 2020, the Museu da Pessoa received stories from all over Brazil and from a wide range of age groups, ranging from children aged 13 to an 89-year-old woman. A total of 582 memories/stories were recorded, received from 247 people located in 17 Brazilian states. As part of the reporting process, the participants in the journey were invited to use tags that assisted in the indexing of their memories, while also providing their stories with titles and providing some personal data (sex, age, profession; see Table 18.2). Through the mapping and analysis of these and other data offered by the users, and through statistical analysis, Lira (2021, p. 5) sought to outline the various possibilities in relation to the anxiety residing in a future collective memory generated during pandemic time. To do so, the researcher selected a sample of fifteen participants from the *Jornada Diário para o Futuro*. Her criterion was to study the participation of those who had contributed to all the stages of the process or, in other words: fifteen people, sending in seven histories each, thus totaling 105 reports. In addition to the reports, Lira also analyzed the 1,147 tags that these participants used.

Table 18.1 Subject of Each Stage

Day	Stage	Proposition
1	First memories	The first moment of life that you remember;
2	Object	Memories and feelings related to an object of great emotional and personal value;
3	Home	Significant stories related to your residence or emotional spaces;
4	People	Stories and the character of the relationships with the people who most affected the personal path through life;
5	Moments	A significant moment experienced on the same day as the statement is made;
6	Future	Confabulations, fears and unease when catching a glimpse of yourself and society in the future;
7	Dreams	Desire and dreams for yourself and those around you in the medium and long term.

Table 18.2 Professions of Participants

Professions	Number of Participants
Journalist	2
Teacher	2
Environmentalist	1
Architect	1
Artist	1
Librarian	1
General coordinator	1
Trainee	1
Student	1
Commercial manager	1
Nutritionist	1

Source: Lira (2021, pp. 44–45).

Despite the relatively small size of the sample, it did reflect those of the other participants in the campaign: There was much greater participation by women, with a broad sweep across all ages and areas of activity (Figure 18.1).

Lira noted that, in general, despite the term pandemic having been most frequently used for indexing purposes, it was possible to recognize nuances in the

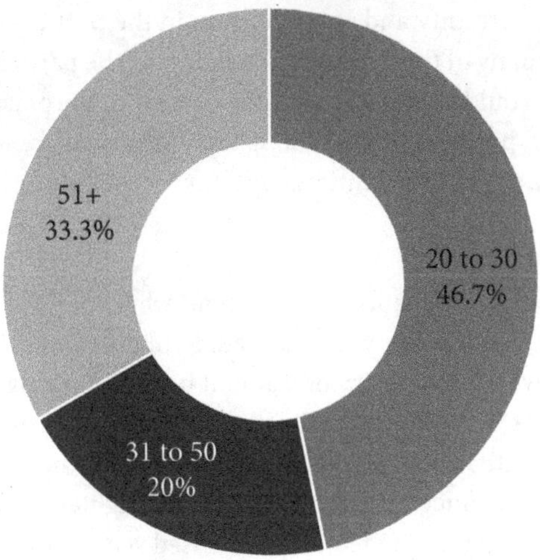

Figure 18.1 Age group of participants selected in the *Jornada Diário para o Futuro.*

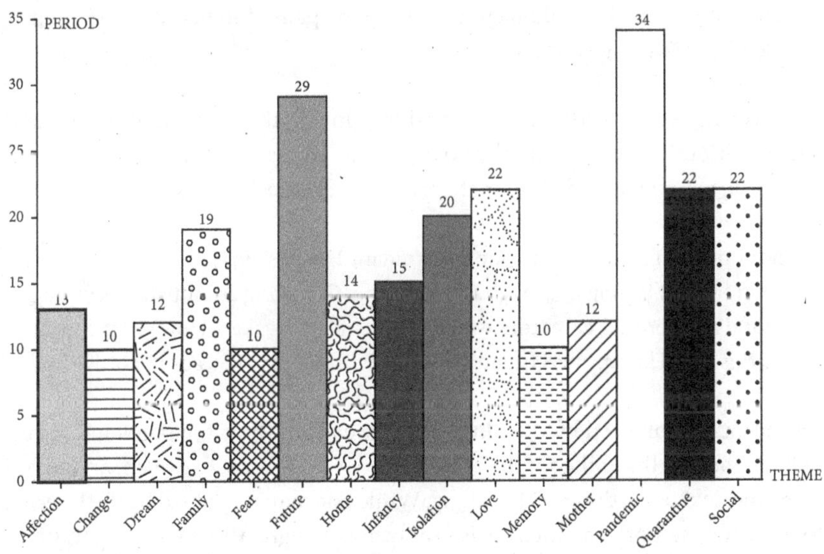

Figure 18.2 Frequency of use per tag (Lira, 2021, p. 49).

distribution of terms related to understanding how COVID-19 was being folded into daily life in line with the issues suggested in the journey (Figure 18.2).

In those stages in which the participants were invited to talk about the present and the future, the use of more contextual terms, relating to the pandemic, and more emotional terms, relating to spiritual states, reinforced the importance of the scenario of uncertainty and apprehension in the participants' development of discourses. In many of the accounts, for example, the participants highlighted the fact that they would be starting with the context of the pandemic before then moving on to an expression of their thoughts. Within this context, the pandemic thus appears to be a type of conditioning factor for the future:

> March 31, 2021
>
> It's not just about the pandemic. It's about what comes as well, what was brought to the surface, the way that people like you and I are treated in our everyday lives. It's a history of fear and hope, balancing the two for the majority. And it's not just me, in the place that I live. It's about how others feel as well—in other places and in other contexts. And what comes next seems strange and uncertain. The bedroom is tighter, and seems empty. The walls are closing in. I'm fed up with closed spaces. I want open rooms. Without ceilings. Without walls. Without doors. To breathe. To feel. To dream. . . . There are no hugs, kisses, people to turn to, just the damned Internet. And memories. . . . It's not the pandemic itself, but I'm in so much pain—more than I could imagine. Bearing the pain of so many others—not just mine. (Man, age not provided)

However, it was noted that relationships, in all their different forms and configurations, were the main theme of the chosen tags—even when the subject of the journey concerned other matters (objects, spaces). For example:

> She hopes that I will miss her more. (Woman, 23 years old)
>
> I'm tired of feeling as though I were falling. Of feeling as though everything around me were a dream from which I could never awaken. How much longer will this last? I lost my best friend. Who else will I lose? (Man, age not provided)

The accounts collected by the Museu da Pessoa show how the pandemic seems to have affected the ability of the subjects to develop plans, to dream, and to imagine the next paths they will be taking. While one man is enabled by the Internet to share the memory, the Internet is simply not enough. And it is during this moment that the sharing of experiences with "the other" (in this case the Museu da Pessoa as bridge to the other), with all those who read or hear these experiences through the museum's platform, acts as an escape valve. The platform has become a space for escape and in which to breathe, and it has provided a sense of belonging and memory (you will be listened to as your memory is read). In the reading of the experiences of suffering that are unrelated at the same time that they are shared and have re-signified what is experienced, it also became a place for sharing mourning and grief.

May 6, 2020
The emptiness sets the dimensions on our uncertainties. We are adapting ourselves, managing the difficulties. We will certainly never be the same again! (Woman, age not provided)

August 22, 2021
I think that people will understand that it's time to start taking stock because of such painful events. Now is the time for us to make plans for the future together. (Woman, 56 years old)

September 4, 2020
I'm learning a lot dealing with this anxiety, but I want to record this moment because I'm sure that in the future people will laugh at it. (Woman, 50 years old)

The *Diário para o Futuro* and the memory journey were social memory actions of the museum that operated along two strands: The first involved using memory as a means of building the individual's connection with themselves and with the other during the period of isolation; the second strand involved inviting the individuals to collaboratively build a private memory of a period that had an impact on global society both temporally and spatially. This was born out of a reflection on what we could have learned from and reflected on in relation to the effects of past pandemics if we had had access to the personal accounts of those who experienced large scale pandemics, such as the Spanish flu or cholera, for example. Though the Spanish flu can be considered the greatest disaster of the twentieth century, it does not have the same representation on collective narratives like the great world wars, for example. Maybe biological or natural disasters are less interesting to become historical traumas like wars or genocides. But it brings lots of opportunities for understanding how societies dealt with and deals with diseases, death, social privileges, vulnerabilities, and exclusions and how all this is remembered afterward. As Erll argues: "What the Spanish flu lacked (a consciously created archive in the first place) is exactly what Corona is characterised by: it is the first worldwide digitally witnessed pandemic, a test case for making a global memory in the new media ecology" (Erll, 2020, p. 867).

Conclusion

In looking back at the memories shared in the brief snapshots that were the thoughtful expressions of Brazilians in the online spaces afforded by *Diário para o Futuro* and the memory journey, we can begin to analyze how public healthcare policies came to attach value to life and assess how death was handled in different contexts. However, in the context of this chapter on slow memory work, what we learned from the Museu da Pessoa's intervention was that those who took the time to share their memories were indeed entangled with slower processes of personal, social, and environmental risk. Yes, the Internet affords a multitude of possibilities for extending the self (and memory), but where are the safe spaces for slow memory to work its way to the surface? Pain, anxiety, uncertainty, and grief were brought to the surface during pandemic time, as rediscovery and re-evaluation of the self and what matters to human beings was revealed. As Garde-Hansen argues in *Media and Water* (2021) "daylighting" and "deculverting" from river engineering (Wild et al., 2010) are a useful way of thinking about memory work: that it is the bringing of channeled and culverted waterways back to the meandering surface means more than making room for water in a changing climate. It challenges the late nineteenth-century techno-solutionism to human and natural environment interactions and by extension the techno-solutionism of Internet-enabled platforms for managing human story worlds:

> There are many fronts of change: new roles for the citizen (from modern to ecological), the backlash to nostalgic nationhood and colonialist attitudes to the environment, the rise of digital participation, the empowering of young people through social networks and movements, the bringing of less heard voices to the water governance table (addressing flows of power and privilege) and the daylighting of hidden waterways in cities. All of these involve narrative, storytelling and media, and individuals and communities are demanding inclusion. (Garde-Hansen, 2021, p. 34)

In daylighting the ordinary memories, feeling, and stories during pandemic time, the Museu da Pessoa engaged in a form of listening that it is well practiced in, valuing what has been forgotten and the voices that are easily ignored. This action is complemented by the suggestion that listening to someone else, or more precisely to someone else's suffering, could be a means of providing empathy, solidarity, and understanding between different people, groups, and social classes. The work of constructing a cultural and digital memory should be seen as a task that produces awareness and, therefore, visibility, insofar as it is a heritage and a legacy. This process is a transformative process (Worcman & Garde-Hansen, 2021). By assuming the responsibility for promoting actions of this type, the Museu da Pessoa has, during pandemic time, sought, in practical terms, to restate, exercise, and promote what it understands to be the slow memory work of "connected listening": a "micro mode" that promotes belonging and memory through caring for others' stories: how they are told, shared, curated, and sensed (see Gardner, 2023). In doing so, it has not rejected speed and fast access/retrieval but rather through rapid response collecting and a ready sense of responsibility, it has normalized how memory work can in fact create a digital museum able to speak about stress, anxiety, fear, uncertainty, confusion, and grief: All states that slow down remembering in an Internet Age, perhaps necessarily so.

Notes

1. See the *EU COST Action 2021–2025 Slow Memory*, which covers work, welfare, politics, conflict and the environment: https://www.slowmemory.eu/about/
2. The online exhibition is at the museum's platform: https://www2.museudapessoa.org/exposicoes/diarios-da-pandemia/?lang=en
3. The Sustainable Development Goals Report, 2021. United Nations. P.3.

References

Allen, M. (2015). *The labour of memory: Memorial culture and 7/7.* Palgrave Macmillan. https://doi.org/10.1057/9781137341648

Allen, M. J. (2016). The poverty of memory: For political economy in memory studies. *Memory Studies, 9*(4), 371–375. https://doi.org/10.1177/1750698016661131

Banks, M. (2020). Creative economy, degrowth and aesthetic limitation. In K. Oakley & M. Banks (Eds.), *Cultural industries and the environmental crisis: New approaches for policy* (pp. 11–23). Springer. https://doi.org/10.1007/978-3-030-49384-4_2

Bruner, J. (1987). *Actual minds, possible worlds.* Harvard University Press. https://doi.org/10.4159/9780674029019

Calvillo, G.-H., Lima-Silva, T. & de Albuquerque, J. P. (2022). From extreme weather events to cascading vulnerabilities: Participatory flood research methodologies in Brazil during COVID-19. *Journal of Extreme Events, 9*(2), 2241002. https://doi.org/10.1142/S2345737622410020

Cutcher, L., Dale, K., Hancock, P., & Tyler, M. (2016). Spaces and places of remembering and commemoration. *Organization, 23*(1), 3–9. https://doi.org/10.1177/1350508415605111

Debono, S. (2021). Collecting pandemic phenomena: Reflections on rapid response collecting and the art museum. *Collections, 17*(2), 179–185. https://doi.org/10.1177/1550190620980844

Erll, A. (2020). Afterword: Memory worlds in times of Corona. *Memory Studies, 13*(5), 861–874. https://doi.org/10.1177/1750698020943014

Freud, S. (2010). *Huit Études sur la Memóire et ses Troubles.* Editions Gallimard.

Garde-Hansen, J. (2021). *Media and water: Communication, culture and perception.* IB Tauris. https://doi.org/10.5040/9781788317788

Garde-Hansen, J., Hoskins, A., & Reading, A. (Eds.). (2009). *Save as . . . Digital memories.* Palgrave Macmillan. https://doi.org/10.1057/9780230239418

Gardner, A. (2023). *Listening, belonging and memory.* Bloomsbury Academic.

Hoskins, A. (2011). 7/7 and connective memory: Interactional trajectories of remembering in post-scarcity culture. *Memory Studies, 4*(3), 269–280. https://doi.org/10.1177/1750698011402570

Lira, A. (2021). *Memórias Comunicadas em Pandemia: Uma análise quanti-qualitativa das tags utilizadas na Jornada Diário para o Futuro.* Belo Horizonte.

Lopez. I. (2009). *Tecnologia Social da Memória.* Fundação Banco do Brasil.

Nixon, R. (2011). *Slow violence and the environmentalism of the poor.* Harvard University Press.

Proctor, N. (2010). Digital: Museum as platform, curator as champion, in the age of social media. *Curator: The Museum Journal, 53*(1), 35–43. https://doi.org/10.1111/j.2151-6952.2009.00006.x

Reading, A. (2021). "I can't breathe": Metabolising (im)mobile antisocialities. In A. Hill, M. Hartmann, & M. Andersson (Eds.), *The Routledge handbook of mobile socialities* (pp. 256–270). Routledge. https://doi.org/10.4324/9781003089872-25

Rosa, H. (2020). *Uncontrollability of the world* (J. C. Wagner, Trans.). Polity.

Thompson, P. (2017). *The voice of the past* (4th ed.). Oxford University Press.

United Nations Report. (2021). *The sustainable development goals report 2021.* United Nations Statistics Division.

Wang, Q., Song, Q., & Koh, J. B. K. (2017). Culture, memory, and narrative self-making. *Imagination, Cognition, Psychology, 37*(2), 2. https://doi.org/10.1177/0276236617733827

Wild, T. C., et al. (2010) Deculverting: Reviewing the evidence on the "daylighting" and restoration of culverted rivers. *Water and Environment, 25*(3), 412–421. https://doi.org/10.1111/j.1747-6593.2010.00236.x

Worcman, K. (2002). Digital Division is Cultural Exclusion. *But Is Digital Inclusion Cultural Inclusion? D-Lib Magazine, 8*(3). https://www.dlib.org/dlib/march02/worcman/03worcman.html

Worcman, K., & Garde-Hansen, J. (2016). *Social memory technology: Theory, practice, action.* Routledge. https://doi.org/10.4324/9781315774732

Worcman, K., & Garde-Hansen, J. (2021). The right to produce memory: Social memory technology as cultural work. In A. Reading & N. Tirosh (Eds.), *The right to memory* (pp. 132–148). Berghahn Books. https://doi.org/10.3167/9781800738577

Wüstenberg, J. (2023). Towards slow memory studies. In Brett Ashley Kaplan (Ed.), *Critical memory studies: New approaches* (pp. 59–68). Bloomsbury Academic. 10.5040/9781350233164.ch-4

PART VII
CONCLUDING REMARKS

19

"Don't Panic"

Navigating the New World of Memory's Remaking

Louis Klein and Amanda J. Barnier

In the concluding chapter of this volume, we consider whether the challenge of the Internet and social media to human memory has reached an unprecedented point. Although previous generations of scholars have asked questions about harmful effects of new technologies, in our 'infodemic' age we are subject to rivers of information unmatched in their scale, speed, and ubiquity. Reflecting on the arguments, concerns, and advice of our colleagues in this collection, we propose a taxonomy to characterize the locus and nature of memory's remaking as well as to direct future research. We especially recommend that scholars consider how different forms or processes of memory 'in the head' versus 'in the wild' might be changing, compare the influence on cognition of different online platforms, and measure the different abilities of 'first-generation' versus 'natural-born' digital citizens to adapt successfully to an online world. Finally, we counsel optimism and interdisciplinarity in mapping memory's new, extended cognitive and collective frontiers.

Asking Questions about Memory

> Worries about information overload are as old as information itself, with each generation reimagining the dangerous impacts of technology on mind and brain. From a historical perspective, what strikes home is not the evolution of these social concerns, but their similarity from one century to the next, to the point where they arrive anew with little having changed except the label.
>
> Vaughn Bell, *A History of Media and Technology Scares from the Printing Press to Facebook*, 2010

This book asks whether the Internet and the social media platforms it has enabled over the past quarter century have fundamentally transformed individual and collective human memory, from the input of encoding, organizing, and storing

Louis Klein and Amanda J. Barnier, *"Don't Panic"* In: *The Remaking of Memory in the Age of the Internet and Social Media.* Edited by: Qi Wang and Andrew Hoskins, Oxford University Press. © Oxford University Press 2024.
DOI: 10.1093/oso/9780197661260.003.0019

to the output of recalling, sharing, and acting on our experiences of the past. In some ways this question is not new. Vaughan Bell (2010), and many others, remind us that similar concerns about the harmful effects to individual minds of new technologies and their rivers of information have focused over decades if not centuries on the printing press, radio, television, personal computers, and other innovations. While recognizing that adaptation to innovation always has been a part of our cognitive blueprint, this book considers whether the challenge of technology to our ancient human memory systems has reached an especially novel, profound, and/or unprecedented point (see Chapter 1).

The editors and authors of this book acknowledge, appropriately, that human cognition, including mental activities, memory, and remembrances, do not fit neatly in a box inside the head but rather are, and have always been, extended or distributed beyond the mind and across our physical and social worlds (see Chapters 4, 5, 7). According to influential theories of distributed cognition, extended mind, and transactive memory (e.g., Clark, 2008; Sutton, 2008; Wegner, 1987), as well as the empirical findings that support them (e.g., Barnier et al., 2008; Sutton et al., 2010; see also Chapters 4, 12), human cognitive processes are tightly interconnected with the external world. Although different versions of different theories see memories as individual recollections triggered by the environment, as predominantly personal recollections manifested in social settings or as a true collective product (Barnier et al., 2008), memory has evolved in not only the head but also the wild and in tandem with people, places, and things around us (Barnier & Hoskins, 2023; Clark, 2008; see also Chapter 5).

And memory continues to evolve. Take, the smartphone, for example, since most of us can recall our lives before and after their advent. In 2010, one of us (Amanda) described receiving an iPhone as a birthday gift and wrote:

> I too have come to think of my iPhone as part of me, especially with respect to memory. But it goes further. I believe the iPhone is compensating for impairments in my current capacity to "process and use information" . . . I now rely on—and have altered my memory practices to best integrate with—a range of iPhone applications ("apps") that: keep track of my appointments; collect, organize and remind me of tasks at work and home; warn me of family and friends' birthdays or to pay bills; remember my menu plan for the week and the groceries I need to buy; record events that happen each day; and even tell me what I should be doing at any moment of the day. (p. 293)

I concluded that, as a memory system: "Together, my iPhone and I currently are more successful than just me alone" (Barnier, 2010, p. 294).

In relying on smartphones to store and retrieve information and experiences, engage with diverse knowledge sources, access and analyze data, and support our decision-making, it seems reasonable to assume that if human cognition was not distributed by default, we could not have integrated (past or) modern technology so effectively into our lives. And while there is little doubt that smartphones, powered by the Internet and gushing torrents of online data, shape how individuals and collectives encode, store, retrieve, and use the past (see Chapters 2, 3, 4, 5, 6, 7, 8, 9, 12), perhaps these modern technologies are no different from the printing press, radio, television, and other information innovations after all? However, this book makes a more strident claim: That memory as we know it is being *remade* by the scale, speed, ubiquity, and algorithms of the Internet and social media platforms (see Chapter 1).

We are not alone in noting, worrying, and exploring these new cognitive frontiers. In 2020, the World Health Organization adopted the term *infodemic* (which was coined during the 2002–2004 severe acute respiratory syndrome [SARS] outbreak) to describe "excess information, including false or misleading information, that spreads in digital and physical environments during a public health emergency" (Wilhelm et al., 2023, p. 2). Wilhelm et al. argued that "the COVID-19 pandemic has been accompanied by an unprecedented global infodemic that has led to confusion about the benefits of medical and public health interventions, with substantial impact on risk-taking and health-seeking behaviours, eroding trust in health authorities and compromising the effectiveness of public health responses and policies" (p. 2; see also Chapter 16).

Infodemic research seeks to map how and why, in a significantly more crowded and complex information-processing environment, people struggle to locate and evaluate trustworthy sources and instead fall back on cognitive heuristics not adapted to this new digital 'savannah.' For instance, we may be more likely to accept information that confirms preexisting beliefs (confirmation bias), rely on information from a single source without cross-checking (source dependence), base judgments of the likelihood of an event on how easily its features come to mind (availability heuristic), or trust information merely because it comes from someone we—as a nonexpert—view as an expert (authority heuristic). Broader social effects, from sharing information via social media platforms, may exacerbate individual-level biases such as believing something because we observe others endorsing it (bandwagon effect) or forming and participating in online social media communities whose restricted set of talking points become dominant and dogmatic to the exclusion of reasonable alternative points of view (echo chambers) (e.g., Balakrishnan et al., 2022; Cinelli et al., 2020; Ecker et al., 2022; Wilhelm et al., 2023; see also Chapters 8, 9).

Likewise, amid our radically connected technological and social lives, this book seeks to map individual and collective impacts of and on remembering. Asking questions about the impacts of technology on memory and cognition may not be new, but the generation of questions asked in these chapters, in the shadow of a global pandemic (see Chapters 16, 18) and in the face of a still rampart infodemic (see Chapters 8, 9, 10, 11) and the rise of artificial intelligence (see Chapters 13, 17), is entirely new for the social sciences and humanities. In this final chapter, we reflect on the locus and nature of memory's remaking, as discussed across the chapters, and methods for measuring and grounding our conceptual and practical concerns.

The Locus and Nature of Memory's Remaking

> I suppose earlier generations had to sit through all this huffing and puffing with the invention of television, the phone, cinema, radio, the car, the bicycle, printing, the wheel, and so on, but you would think we would learn the way these things work, which is this:
>
> 1) everything that's already in the world when you're born is just normal;
> 2) anything that gets invented between then and before you turn thirty is incredibly exciting and creative and with any luck you can make a career out of it; and
> 3) anything that gets invented after you're thirty is against the natural order of things and the beginning of the end of civilisation as we know it until it's been around for about ten years when it gradually turns out to be alright really.
>
> Apply this list to movies, rock music, word processors and mobile phones to work out how old you are.
>
> Douglas Adams, *How to Stop Worrying and Learn to Love the Internet*, 1999

Nearly 25 years ago, not long after the birth of the Internet age, English author and futurist Douglas Adams (1952–2001) reflected on the magnitude and kinds of change promised by this technology and, of most relevance to us, on generational differences in people's views or stance toward this "new-fangled stuff."[1] Noting that earlier inventions such as television, phones, cinema, radio, cars, and printing likely elicited similar reactions (echoing Bell's comments discussed in the beginning of the section "Asking Questions about Memory"), Adams suggested that as the Internet and social media evolve rapidly if not exponentially, some of us are 'first-generation' users of this technology, with the assumptions and worries of a receding world. Some of us are trying to map, match, or marry ways and means of the older and newer. And some of us—our children especially—are 'natural-born citizens', where online living in digital worlds via a multiplex of avatars is pervasive and unremarkable.

There's an inference of optimism versus pessimism in Adams' parsing of generations. A casual search on Google, for instance, of "mobile phones in schools" gives a quick sense of such generational divides, or at least one (pessimistic) side of just one argument. But our children are awake to the contradiction of being told to put away their phones while being required to complete tests, assignments, and other educational obligations on devices or online.[2] Why, they ask us, is technology or the Internet bad in one instance but not in the other? What cases or classes of relevant phenomena fall where? And along what dimensions?

It is likewise interesting to note more optimistic versus pessimistic stances in the chapters of this book. For instance, in Chapter 2, Wang opens the book by arguing that "as a unique cultural tool of our time, the Internet and social media have drastically empowered memory sharing" (p. 15). Although she recognizes potential negative consequences for the self of sharing online, influenced in turn by individual psychological characteristics as well as social and cultural norms, she highlights the value of digitally mediated lives to our sense of self and well-being. In Wang's telling, Internet and social media users are active agents in their online sharing and co-creation. This optimistic view contrasts with Hoskins' more pessimistic view in Chapter 3 of this volume. He characterizes human rememberers as at the mercy of machines, as "information accidents waiting to happen" (p. 43), and whose overabundant yet scattered memory data, produced, curated, and shared via apps on digital devices, add up to nothing; a self that is "unknown, unrecognized and unremembered" (p. 44). In his telling, memory agents have become memory zombies.

Whereas Adams' somewhat glib generational taxonomy implies a gut reaction to technology—it's goodish, it's badish—by younger versus older people, the stances adopted by authors of the chapters in this book do not reflect generational or even obvious disciplinary differences. They are deliberative and nuanced and instead reflect views on the locus and nature of memory's remaking. To assist in mapping (not moralizing about) these impacts of the Internet and social media on human communities, lives, and cognition, we offer a conceptual taxonomy in place of Adams' (for influential examples of other taxonomies of memory phenomena, see Connerton, 2008; Roediger et al., 2002; Schacter, 2022).

We propose a 2 × 2 matrix defined by two dimensions. The first dimension captures where memory phenomena are conceptualized as located: Predominantly 'in the head' (enshrined in studies of individual cognition) or predominantly 'in the wild' (enshrined in studies of social and cultural domains) (Barnier & Hoskins, 2018, 2023). The second dimension captures how memory phenomena are changed by the Internet, social media, and other technologies: Whether the information environment of existing memory processes is changing or the memory processes themselves are changing. Combining these dimensions, we derive four quadrants, which we believe capture a number of the arguments, phenomena, and concerns across the chapters of this book, although perhaps unequally:

1. Memories are fundamentally in the head and, while memory processes are not themselves changing, they are operating in a different information environment and are therefore producing different memory outcomes or products;
2. Memories are, again, fundamentally in the head but due to the different information environment and operating demands, memory processes are adapting, changing, and being transformed;
3. Memories are not in the head but are in the wild, where memories are fundamentally distributed across agents and external sources. Nonetheless, memory processes are not themselves changing and are instead responding to a different information environment and operating demands; and
4. Memories are fundamentally in the wild, and memory processes are being changed and transformed by the different information environment and concomitant operating demands.

How do the various contributions collected in this book fit (or evade) this framework? Perhaps because social media itself is fundamentally distributed and participatory, many contributions appear to fall into our first quadrant. For instance, in Chapter 2, Wang views the Internet as a new platform for autobiographical memory and highlights psycho-cultural impacts on individual's self-perception and well-being. In Chapter 4, Stone, Dockery, and Vasquez explore the motives and mnemonic consequences of sharing personal memories on social media, delineating psychological and memory effects for both "producers" and "consumers." In Chapter 8, Murphy, Egan, and Greene delve into the influence on memory of online misinformation for public events, while, in Chapter 9 Tay and Ecker analyze the continued influence of misinformation even after correction. Common across these accounts is the view that memory agents exist in, and respond to, their environments; large shifts in these environments produce dramatic changes in—and place cognitive burdens on—remembering and forgetting at the level of the individual.

Falling into our second quadrant, where memory processes in the head are transforming due to differences in the information environment, Rajaram in Chapter 12 stands out in her exploration of the role of adaptive efficiency in memory. She examines how the Internet's characteristics appear to be fundamentally reshaping memory structure and operation. This chapter and others suggest how memory processes can be transformed in response to digital demands and meaning-making in highly social, online spaces.

Falling into our third quadrant, which focuses on memory that is not in the head but fundamentally 'in the wild' as well as responsive to the new information environment, are chapters that explore how memory is distributed across agents and external sources. In Chapter 5, Risko, Kelly, Lu, and Pereira offer a framework for understanding external aids for memory (more on this later in this section), while in Chapter 14, Tirosh analyzes Holocaust memories on platforms like Instagram and TikTok. She shows that these digital environments shape engagement with historical narratives. Contributions situated within this quadrant share a focus on memory phenomena at the level of the collective rather than the individual, despite the fact that memory processes themselves are not presumed to be transformed. Rather, they worry that our existing understanding of memory inadequately captures the dynamics of memory at the group level.

Falling into our fourth quadrant, where memory processes are fundamentally in the wild as well as changed by the digital environment, contributions share a (subdued) sense of panic that everything is changing, everywhere, all at once. In Chapter 6, Storm, Bittner, and Yamashiro review how Internet usage alters the dynamics of shared memory retrieval, discussing both potential enhancements and disruptions to memory processes and the methodologies that make them tractable. In Chapter 13, Smit investigates how digital platforms transform memories into data and underscores a growing dependence on these platforms for memory storage and retrieval; we take up this issue in more detail at the end of this section. Finally, in Chapter 15, Merrill emphasizes the need for hybrid methodologies to study memory in the post-digital age. Unsurprisingly, contributions in this fourth quadrant also share a concern that our conceptual, statistical, and laboratory methods need to be adapted and extended to capture the dynamics of memory in the age of the Internet and social media.

Of course, some contributions (e.g., Wang's in Chapter 2 and Stone et al.'s in Chapter 4) fit more neatly into this framework—at least by our reckoning—whereas others (such as Smit's in Chapter 13 and Tirosh's in Chapter 14) blur the boundaries of our matrix, suggesting a more complex intersection of the dimensions at play. This framework also might be used to drill deeper. We have focused so far on the locus and nature of memory's remaking at a general level (i.e., all kinds of memories, all kinds of information environments), but it is possible that different kinds of memory products and/or processes respond differently to certain features of specific online platforms or environments.

Consider, for example, autobiographical memory, a form of episodic memory that plays a crucial role in personal, social, and cultural identity (Harris et al., 2014). As Wang in Chapter 2 and Tirosh in Chapter 14 explore for individuals and collectives, online platforms shape how personal or social narratives as well as identity are constructed, remembered, and commemorated, sometimes in unexpected or controversial ways. Wang's triangular theory of self adds to previous theorizing a new role for the social media audience in digital and transactive "extensions." It is not yet clear whether similar (or different) extensions are needed for other classic forms of memory such as procedural or semantic memory (Roediger et al., 2002).

As these cases and many others offered by our colleagues make clear, it no longer is sufficient to conceptualize or study how memory is changing in isolation from the specific platforms that people engage with. Being chronically online now means having a Facebook account, Instagram, Twitter (now called X) handle, supplemented with a YouTube account, Reddit, Snapchat, LinkedIn, Discord, Twitch, Tumblr, or TikTok—not to mention an array of utility apps that serve other elements of our digital lives, such as WhatsApp, Telegram, Signal, WeChat, LINE, and Baidu. Remembering, revising, and/or forgetting on each of these platforms are heavily dependent on their distinct operating demands. This "platformization of memory," as Smit explains in Chapter 13, highlights how tightly integrated some or all of these apps have become with our daily lives, and how memory and cognition are deliberately or incidentally shaped, facilitated, co-constructed, and censored by the machinations of, typically proprietary, algorithms (see also Lewandowsky & Pomerantsev, 2022). This platformization presents significant methodological challenges for scholars, which we return to in this section, below.

Another challenge is capturing potential trade-offs in new manifestations of memory. In Chapter 5, Risko et al. explore the role of the Internet as a "near-limitless . . . external memory store" (p. 69) and propose a framework for organizing instances of cognitive offloading that differentiate: (a) External storage in addition to internal storage versus external only storage and (b) whether cognitive capacity freed up by offloading is conserved or redeployed. This account offers a modern update on classic information-processing approaches: Where and how mental processes happen and how much they cost. This account also raises interesting questions about source memory or monitoring.

According to Risko et al., when people offload to the world they conserve cognitive capacity by recalling where, not what (see also Sparrow et al., 2011). But as we live our multiplatform lives online, are the cognitive savings of offloading offset by greater cognitive costs of source monitoring; of tracking where exactly we uploaded, updated, saved or deleted? And as the infodemic rages on, and we offload to a broader and broader array of external sources, surely the trustworthiness of these sources will become crucial to our confidence in the content we later retrieve? Our burgeoning information sources need to be evaluated more critically than ever or how can we trust what we are recovering from the world? Do we need some form of embedded remembering (or forgetting) "metadata," and what might this look like? And will these additional trust requirements burden internal memory systems in the absence of formal authentication practices common in the online world? While some colleagues have begun this work of integrating memory and belief concepts, processes, and practices (see Chapters 8, 9, 10, 11), a greater understanding is needed regarding when and how we trust cognitive contents that flow between people and the world.

Counting What Counts

In his 1963 book *Informal Sociology: A Casual Introduction to Sociological Thinking*, sociologist William Bruce Cameron offered the following advice, which has proven so useful that it is now often incorrectly attributed to Albert Einstein: "Not everything that counts can be counted, and not everything that can be counted counts" (Cameron, 1963, p. 13). One consistent and important theme throughout this book is the need for methodological and measurement innovation to capture the complexities of memory's remaking (see especially suggestions by Stone et al. in Chapter 4, Fawns in Chapter 7, and Merrill in Chapter 15 but see also Chapters 2, 8, 16, 17). At its heart, this is an issue of ecological validity.

As discussed in the field of cognitive psychology (Barnier, 2012), ecological validity demands that research methodologies not only mimic the complexity of everyday life but also resonate with the actual experiences and environments of individuals. This involves constructing research projects, designs, questions, and settings that reflect or capture real-life contexts so that findings can be generalized beyond the confines of the laboratory. Achieving this level of realism and relevance requires a careful balance between our need for experimental control and the messiness of the world. Human behavior and cognition are influenced by myriad constantly changing, temporal, and situational variables. And as Stone et al. convey well in Chapter 4, when we attempt to count the outcomes of groups (not individuals) interacting online (not face to face in front of us), complexity compounds:

> Perhaps the crux of the problem is not each factor individually, as they can be isolated and examined "in the lab" to a certain degree. Rather, the critical question is how they may interact and lead to varying degrees of mnemonic consequences. (p. 59)

So, in this closing section, we briefly suggest four ways to ensure we count what counts for the digitally enabled memories of individuals and groups, in the head and in the wild.

First, we should consider whether our methods match our views of the locus and nature of memory's remaking as laid out in our four quadrants above. If we believe that underlying memory processes are merely adapting to a different information environment (Quadrants 1 and 3), then our existing methods of inquiry might be appropriately redeployed in this new context. However, if we believe that memory processes themselves are changing (Quadrants 2 and 4), then our existing methods of inquiry, developed and validated with memory processes relevant to a previous generation of questions and paradigms, might not capture and quantify the new nature of memory. Similarly, if we locate memory fundamentally as in the head (Quadrants 1 and 2), aligning with a long tradition of individual rememberers in laboratory settings, we might redeploy or extend these individualistic approaches but finesse them to capture new forms of memory products, processes, or places. However, when we investigate memories that extend into the world via other agents or artifacts (Quadrants 3 and 4), we must update our methods to handle multiagent multinomial inputs, range over time longitudinally or with lag, and address challenges associated with searching for statistical signals in a fundamentally noisier environment. The important point is that our methods are able to validly and sensitively test our claims.

Second, and returning to our discussion of the platformization of memory in the previous section (Chapter 13), our methods also must be sensitive to both general kinds of new information environments and to specific instances of them. Each upgrade in user interface implementation, each enterprise-designed content algorithm, each variation in button layout potentially confounds our desire to generalize statistically and conceptually about what and how we remember, a knot that only becomes harder to unravel with each new version release of an app or iPhone. Indeed, it is commonplace when we perform online experiments to collect data about the browsers in which participants participate, but do we always examine the impact of different browsers on our dependent variables as part of our preliminary analyses? New protocols and standards in scientific practice need to be developed and adopted to address this set of fast-paced technological challenges, which also can undermine ecological validity.

Third, ecological validity extends to a consideration of participant diversity, ensuring that our study populations reflect the broad spectrum of relevant human experiences across different ages, genders, cultures, and socioeconomic backgrounds. In recent years, researchers in psychology especially have acknowledged the limitations of their "WEIRD" samples, that is, participants from Western, Educated, Industrial, Rich, and Democratic populations (Henrich et al., 2010). In their transformative article, Henrich et al. (2010) argued:

> Researchers—often implicitly—assume that either there is little variation across human populations, or that these "standard subjects" are as representative of

> the species as any other population. Are these assumptions justified? Here, our review of the comparative database from across the behavioral sciences suggests both that there is substantial variability in experimental results across populations and that WEIRD subjects are particularly unusual compared with the rest of the species—frequent outliers. (p. 1)

Importantly, they recommended that to address these concerns, researchers "can either acknowledge that their findings in many domains cannot be generalized beyond this unusual subpopulation (and leave it at that), or they can begin to take the difficult steps to building a broader, richer, and better-grounded understanding of our species" (Henrich et al., 2010, p. 23).

In much the same way, scholars interested in exploring the impacts of the Internet and social media on human memory and cognition, whether individual or collective, must move not only beyond WEIRD samples but also routinely to 'WIRED' samples; that is, to people who differ in known ways in their exposure to and use of various technologies and platforms. This brings us back to Douglas Adams' taxonomy of first-generation users versus natural-born citizens of our digital age. There is not enough developmental or longitudinal memory research covering the online worlds of different generations, especially children and adolescents. Gen Zs and Alphas are living quite different digital lives from those of Gen X, Millennials, and the Boomer generation before them, and must also be represented in the story of memory's remaking.

Fourth and finally, ecological validity in memory research is challenging solely within the siloes of single disciplines. We have highlighted elsewhere the value of integrating theories, methods, and insights from various fields (e.g., Barnier & Hoskins, 2023; Barnier et al., 2018), but we particularly recommend interdisciplinary collaborations among memory scholars and technologists who can help to ground our claims of concern. As several authors in this book point out, online environments and platforms are highly technical and constantly evolving; casual use or understanding of Facebook, Instagram, Twitter/X, and other online spaces cannot replace an expert appreciation of the mechanics and subsequent consequences of these technologies for individual and collective memory. We also can look for inspiration to memory colleagues in the social sciences and humanities, such as Catherine Loveday, Martin Conway, and Andy Clark, who have developed transformative collaborations with technologists in the service of their new theories and findings on human memory in the head and in the wild (see Loveday & Conway, 2011; MacFarquhar, 2018).

With the ideas, frameworks, tools, and tactics outlined across the chapters of this book, together we can and will map the cognitive frontier of our online memories, identities, and lives. We need not panic; there is reason for optimism, especially in the ability of the Internet and social media to build community and collectives at a scale and pace almost unprecedented in human history. But we must remain alert and alive to the challenges of technology and ensure that it enriches and not rewrites our essential human nature.

Notes

1. Of course, Douglas Adams also is famous for his wildly popular 1979 science fiction novel, *The Hitchhiker's Guide to the Galaxy*, which follows the adventures of earthman, Arthur Dent, and his alien friend, Ford Prefect, after they hitch a ride on a passing spaceship just as Earth is destroyed. In the story, *The Hitchhiker's Guide to the Galaxy* is a digital travel book (pre-dating Kindles and other book readers by decades) that Ford loans to Arthur as they navigate the wonders and terrors of intergalatic travel; Arthur appreciates its reassuring message on the cover, "DON'T PANIC."
2. For an example of a recent ban, see https://education.nsw.gov.au/news/latest-news/mobile-phones-now-banned-in-all-nsw-public-schools, and for a broader discussion of the logic of banning phones in schools, see https://theconversation.com/why-a-ban-on-cellphones-in-schools-might-be-more-of-a-distraction-than-the-problem-its-trying-to-fix-211494.

References

Adams, D. (1999, August,). How to stop worrying and learn to love the Internet. *The Sunday Times*, 4. https://douglasadams.com/dna/19990901-00-a.html

Balakrishnan, V., Ng, W. Z., Soo, M. C., Han, G. J., & Lee, C. J. (2022). Infodemic and fake news—A comprehensive overview of its global magnitude during the COVID-19 pandemic in 2021: A scoping review. *International Journal of Disaster Risk Reduction*, *78*, 103144. https://doi.org/10.1016/j.ijdrr.2022.103144

Barnier, A. J. (2010). Memories, memory studies and my iPhone: Editorial. *Memory Studies*, *3*(4), 293–297. https://doi.org/10.1177/1750698010376027

Barnier, A. J. (2012). Memory, ecological validity and a barking dog. *Memory Studies*, *5*(4), 351–359. https://doi.org/10.1177/1750698012461243

Barnier, A. J., & Hoskins, A. (2018). Is there memory in the head, in the wild? *Memory Studies*, *11*(4), 386–390. https://doi.org/10.1177/1750698018806440

Barnier, A. J., & Hoskins, A. (2023). Editorial II: Meeting at the crossroads of *Memory*, Mind & Media. Memory, *Mind & Media*, *2*, e3. https://doi.org/10.1017/mem.2023.3

Barnier, A. J., Klein, L., & Harris, C. B. (2018). Transactive memory in small, intimate groups: More than the sum of their parts. *Small Group Research*, *49*(1), 62–97. https://doi.org/10.1177/1046496417712439

Barnier, A. J., Sutton, J., Harris, C. B., & Wilson, R. A. (2008). A conceptual and empirical framework for the social distribution of cognition: The case of memory. *Cognitive Systems Research*, *9*(1–2), 33–51. https://doi.org/10.1016/j.cogsys.2007.07.002

Bell, V. (2010, February). Don't touch that dial! A history of media technology scares, from the printing press to Facebook. https://slate.com/technology/2010/02/a-history-of-media-technology-scares-from-the-printing-press-to-facebook.html

Cameron, W. B. (1963). *Informal sociology, a casual introduction to sociological thinking*. Random House.

Cinelli, M., Quattrociocchi, W., Galeazzi, A., Valensise, C. M., Brugnoli, E., Schmidt, A. L., Zola, P., Zollo, F., & Scala, A. (2020). The COVID-19 social media infodemic. *Scientific Reports*, *10*(1), 16598. https://doi.org/10.1038/s41598-020-73510-5

Clark, A. (2008). *Supersizing the mind: Embodiment, action, and cognitive extension*. Oxford University Press.

Connerton, P. (2008). Seven types of forgetting. *Memory Studies, 1*(1), 59–71. https://doi.org/10.1177/1750698007083889

Ecker, U. K. H., Lewandowsky, S., Cook, J., Schmid, P., Fazio, L. K., Brashier, N., Kendeou, P., Vraga, E. K., & Amazeen, M. A. (2022). The psychological drivers of misinformation belief and its resistance to correction. *Nature Reviews Psychology, 1*(1), 13–29. https://doi.org/10.1038/s44159-021-00006-y

Gaerlan, E. (2023, August). Why a ban on cellphones in schools might be more of a distraction than the problem it's trying to fix. *The Conversation*. https://theconversation.com/why-a-ban-on-cellphones-in-schools-might-be-more-of-a-distraction-than-the-problem-its-trying-to-fix-211494

Harris, C. B., Rasmussen, A. S., & Berntsen, D. (2014). The functions of autobiographical memory: An integrative approach. *Memory, 22*(5), 559–581. https://doi.org/10.1080/09658211.2013.806555

Henrich, J., Heine, S. J., & Norenzayan, A. (2010). The weirdest people in the world? *Behavioral and Brain Sciences, 33*(2–3), 61–83. https://doi.org/10.1017/S0140525X0999152X

Lewandowsky, S., & Pomerantsev, P. (2022). Technology and democracy: A paradox wrapped in a contradiction inside an irony. *Memory, Mind & Media, 1*, e5. https://doi.org/10.1017/mem.2021.7

Loveday, C., & Conway, M. A. (Eds.). (2011). SenseCam: The future of everyday memory research? [Special issue]. *Memory, 19*(7), 1–124.

MacFarquhar, L. (2018, March). The mind-expanding ideas of Andy Clark. https://www.newyorker.com/magazine/2018/04/02/the-mind-expanding-ideas-of-andy-clark

NSW Department of Education. (2023, October). Mobile phones now banned in all NSW public schools. https://education.nsw.gov.au/news/latest-news/mobile-phones-now-banned-in-all-nsw-public-schools

Roediger, H. L., III, Marsh, E. J., & Lee, S. C. (2002). Kinds of memory. In H. Pashler & D. Medin (Eds.), In *Steven's handbook of experimental psychology: Memory and cognitive processes* (pp. 1–41). John Wiley & Sons.

Schacter, D. L. (2022). Media, technology, and the sins of memory. *Memory, Mind & Media, 1*, e1. https://doi.org/10.1017/mem.2021.3

Sparrow, B., Liu, J., & Wegner, D. M. (2011). Google effects on memory: Cognitive consequences of having information at our fingertips. *Science, 333*(6043), 476–478. https://doi.org/10.1126/science.1207745

Sutton, J. (2008). Between individual and collective memory: Coordination, interaction, distribution. *Social Research, 75*(1), 23–48. http://www.jstor.org/stable/40972051

Sutton, J., Harris, C. B., Keil, P. G., & Barnier, A. J. (2010). The psychology of memory, extended cognition, and socially distributed remembering. *Phenomenology and the Cognitive Sciences, 9*(4), 521–560. https://doi.org/10.1007/s11097-010-9182-y

Wegner, D. M. (1987). Transactive memory: A contemporary analysis of the group mind. In B. Mullen and G. R. Goethals (Eds.). In *Theories of Group Behaviour* (pp. 185–208). Springer-Verlag.

Wilhelm, E., Ballalai, I., Belanger, M.-E., Benjamin, P., Bertrand-Ferrandis, C., Bezbaruah, S., Briand, S., Brooks, I., Bruns, R., Bucci, L. M., Calleja, N., Chiou, H., Devaria, A., Dini, L., D'Souza, H., Dunn, A. G., Eichstaedt, J. C., Evers, S. M. A. A., Gobat, N., . . . Purnat, T. D. (2023). Measuring the burden of infodemics: Summary of the methods and results of the Fifth WHO Infodemic Management Conference. *JMIR Infodemiology, 3*, e44207. https://doi.org/10.2196/44207

Index

For the benefit of digital users, indexed terms that span two pages (e.g., 52–53) may, on occasion, appear on only one of those pages.

Tables and figures are indicated by an italic *t* and *f* following the paragraph number.